"[Watts] has gifted us a thought-provoking study that combines able curation and analysis with a passionate advocacy for an under-utilized framework in the study of Late Antiquity. . . . The volume stands as a highly welcome addition to the historical literature for its sympathetic and illuminating approach to how actual historical personages experienced some of the major transformations of Late Antiquity."
—*The Classical Review*

"Watts's . . . latest work provides great insight into the everyday practices of the devout in the fourth century as well as the turbulent and often cruelly violent transition from traditional pagan worship to Christianity in the Roman Empire. . . . It is truly a comprehensive picture and because of the prodigious notes and sources, a great jumping-off point for deeper research into the era."
—*Library Journal*

"[This] book is well written, carefully structured, and clearly argued. . . . accessible and engaging for students and general readers . . . "
—*Bryn Mawr Classical Review*

"Watts builds his case through literary evidence such as letters, orations, poems, and contemporary historical accounts. What emerges is a vivid account of the final pagan generation and a detailed view of their social and professional environment."
—*Journal of Late Antiquity*

". . . an original and thought-provoking narrative of the history of the fourth century A.D. . . . [Watts] has many interesting new things to say about almost every topic he discusses. His greatest contribution, however, is the weaving together of different strands of imperial history, illuminating their impact on the life of actual people, whose feelings, expectations, and ambitions acquire a concrete dimension that is rarely seen in traditional narratives of this period."
—*The Journal of Roman Studies*

"Watts's book is a confrontation of what is perhaps the key question in the long history of the West: how was it that a polytheistic world . . . succumbed within the span of a century between 300 and 400 A.D. to a wholesale religious transformation? . . . Watts's model enables him to offer an engaging, learned, and vivid presentation of lives lived and experienced from cradle to grave . . . "
—*Journal of Religion*

The Final Pagan Generation

TRANSFORMATION OF THE CLASSICAL HERITAGE
Peter Brown, General Editor

I. *Art and Ceremony in Late Antiquity,* by Sabine G. MacCormack

II. *Synesius of Cyrene: Philosopher-Bishop,* by Jay Alan Bregman

III. *Theodosian Empresses: Women and Imperial Dominion in Late Antiquity,* by Kenneth G. Holum

IV. *John Chrysostom and the Jews: Rhetoric and Reality in the Late Fourth Century,* by Robert L. Wilken

V. *Biography in Late Antiquity: The Quest for the Holy Man,* by Patricia Cox

VI. *Pachomius: The Making of a Community in Fourth-Century Egypt,* by Philip Rousseau

VII. *Change in Byzantine Culture in the Eleventh and Twelfth Centuries,* by A.P. Kazhdan and Ann Wharton Epstein

VIII. *Leadership and Community in Late Antique Gaul,* by Raymond Van Dam

IX. *Homer the Theologian: Neoplatonist Allegorical Reading and the Growth of the Epic Tradition,* by Robert Lamberton

X. *Procopius and the Sixth Century,* by Averil Cameron

XI. *Guardians of Language: The Grammarian and Society in Late Antiquity,* by Robert A. Kaster

XII. *Civic Coins and Civic Politics in the Roman East,* A.D. *180–275,* by Kenneth Harl

XIII. *Holy Women of the Syrian Orient,* introduced and translated by Sebastian P. Brock and Susan Ashbrook Harvey

XIV. *Gregory the Great: Perfection in Imperfection,* by Carole Straw

XV. *"Apex Omnium": Religion in the "Res gestae" of Ammianus,* by R.L. Rike

XVI. *Dioscorus of Aphrodito: His Work and His World,* by Leslie S.B. MacCoull

XVII. *On Roman Time: The Codex-Calendar of 354 and the Rhythms of Urban Life in Late Antiquity,* by Michele Renee Salzman

XVIII. *Asceticism and Society in Crisis: John of Ephesus and "The Lives of the Eastern Saints,"* by Susan Ashbrook Harvey

XIX. *Barbarians and Politics at the Court of Arcadius,* by Alan Cameron and Jacqueline Long, with a contribution by Lee Sherry

XX. *Basil of Caesarea,* by Philip Rousseau

XXI. *In Praise of Later Roman Emperors: The Panegyrici Latini,* introduction, translation, and historical commentary by C.E.V. Nixon and Barbara Saylor Rodgers

XXII. *Ambrose of Milan: Church and Court in a Christian Capital,* by Neil B. McLynn

XXIII. *Public Disputation, Power, and Social Order in Late Antiquity,* by Richard Lim

XXIV. *The Making of a Heretic: Gender, Authority, and the Priscillianist Controversy,* by Virginia Burrus

XXV. *Symeon the Holy Fool: Leontius's "Life" and the Late Antique City*, by Derek Krueger

XXVI. *The Shadows of Poetry: Vergil in the Mind of Augustine*, by Sabine MacCormack

XXVII. *Paulinus of Nola: Life, Letters, and Poems*, by Dennis E. Trout

XXVIII. *The Barbarian Plain: Saint Sergius between Rome and Iran*, by Elizabeth Key Fowden

XXIX. *The Private Orations of Themistius*, translated, annotated, and introduced by Robert J. Penella

XXX. *The Memory of the Eyes: Pilgrims to Living Saints in Christian Late Antiquity*, by Georgia Frank

XXXI. *Greek Biography and Panegyric in Late Antiquity*, edited by Tomas Hägg and Philip Rousseau

XXXII. *Subtle Bodies: Representing Angels in Byzantium*, by Glenn Peers

XXXIII. *Wandering, Begging Monks: Spiritual Authority and the Promotion of Monasticism in Late Antiquity*, by Daniel Caner

XXXIV. *Failure of Empire: Valens and the Roman State in the Fourth Century* A.D., by Noel Lenski

XXXV. *Merovingian Mortuary Archaeology and the Making of the Early Middle Ages*, by Bonnie Effros

XXXVI. *Quṣayr 'Amra: Art and the Umayyad Elite in Late Antique Syria*, by Garth Fowden

XXXVII. *Holy Bishops in Late Antiquity: The Nature of Christian Leadership in an Age of Transition*, by Claudia Rapp

XXXVIII. *Encountering the Sacred: The Debate on Christian Pilgrimage in Late Antiquity*, by Brouria Bitton-Ashkelony

XXXIX. *There Is No Crime for Those Who Have Christ: Religious Violence in the Christian Roman Empire*, by Michael Gaddis

XL. *The Legend of Mar Qardagh: Narrative and Christian Heroism in Late Antique Iraq*, by Joel Thomas Walker

XLI. *City and School in Late Antique Athens and Alexandria*, by Edward J. Watts

XLII. *Scenting Salvation: Ancient Christianity and the Olfactory Imagination*, by Susan Ashbrook Harvey

XLIII. *Man and the Word: The Orations of* Himerius, edited by Robert J. Penella

XLIV. *The Matter of the Gods*, by Clifford Ando

XLV. *The Two Eyes of the Earth: Art and Ritual of Kingship between Rome and Sasanian Iran*, by Matthew P. Canepa

XLVI. *Riot in Alexandria: Tradition and Group Dynamics in Late Antique Pagan and Christian Communities*, by Edward J. Watts

XLVII. *Peasant and Empire in Christian North Africa*, by Leslie Dossey

XLVIII. *Theodoret's People: Social Networks and Religious Conflict in Late Roman Syria*, by Adam M. Schor

XLIX. *Sons of Hellenism, Fathers of the Church: Emperor Julian, Gregory of Nazianzus, and the Vision of Rome*, by Susanna Elm

L. *Shenoute of Atripe and the Uses of Poverty: Rural Patronage, Religious Conflict, and Monasticism in Late Antique Egypt,* by Ariel G. López

LI. *Doctrine and Power: Theological Controversy and Christian Leadership in the Later Roman Empire,* by Carlos R. Galvão-Sobrinho

LII. *Crisis of Empire: Doctrine and Dissent at the End of Late Antiquity,* by Phil Booth

LIII. *The Final Pagan Generation,* by Edward J. Watts

LIV. *The Mirage of the Saracen: Christians and Nomads in the Sinai Peninsula in Late Antiquity,* by Walter D. Ward

The Final Pagan Generation

Edward J. Watts

UNIVERSITY OF CALIFORNIA PRESS

University of California Press, one of the most
distinguished university presses in the United States,
enriches lives around the world by advancing scholarship
in the humanities, social sciences, and natural sciences. Its
activities are supported by the UC Press Foundation and
by philanthropic contributions from individuals and
institutions. For more information, visit www.ucpress.edu.

University of California Press
Oakland, California

First Paperback Printing 2020

Library of Congress Cataloging-in-Publication Data

Watts, Edward Jay.
    The final pagan generation / Edward J. Watts.
        p.   cm. — (Transformation of the classical
        heritage ; LIII)
    Includes bibliographical references and index.
    ISBN 978-0-520-28370-1 (cloth, alk. paper);
    978-0-520-37922-0 (pbk. : alk. paper);
    978-0-520-95949-1 (electronic)
        1. Paganism—Rome.   2. Christianity and other
religions—Rome.   3. Rome—Religion.   I. Title.   II.
Series: Transformation of the classical heritage ; 53.
BL432.W38   2015
292.07—dc23   2014014003

Manufactured in the United States of America

23   22   21   20
10   9   8   7   6   5   4   3   2   1

To my parents, Dan and Karen Watts

Contents

List of Illustrations   *xi*

Acknowledgments   *xiii*

Introduction   *1*

1. Growing Up in the Cities of the Gods   *17*
2. Education in an Age of Imagination   *37*
3. The System   *59*
4. Moving Up in an Age of Uncertainty   *81*
5. The Apogee   *105*
6. The New Pannonian Order   *127*
7. Christian Youth Culture in the 360s and 370s   *149*
8. Bishops, Bureaucrats, and Aristocrats under Gratian, Valentinian II, and Theodosius   *167*
9. Old Age in a Young Man's Empire   *191*
10. A Generation's Legacy   *213*

Notes   *221*

Bibliography   *305*

Index   *321*

Illustrations

1. The Serapeum site / 2
2. Coin image of Serapis enthroned in temple / 3
3. Coin images of different Roman temples, 2nd–4th century AD / 20
4. Temple of Hanuman, Mathura, India / 21
5. The Birla Mandir, Jaipur, India / 21
6. Rural temple, Jaipur, India / 22
7. Coin images of sacrificial scenes, 1st century BC–4th century AD / 27
8. Evolution of Constantinian portraiture on coins, 310–26 / 41
9. Sol Invictus on Constantinian coinage / 45
10. Coins of Valentinian and Valens / 131
11. Coin of Procopius / 134
12. Coins of Theodosius I and Gratian from Concordia series (379–83) / 177
13. Coin of Arcadius crowned by God / 178
14. Theophilus standing atop bust of Serapis / 214

Acknowledgments

I have accumulated many debts over the three years I have worked on this project, and I owe far more thanks than I can ever possibly give. I have long wanted to write a book that examines a generation whose voice has been drowned out by the louder or more interesting ones that came before and after it. This is perhaps a preoccupation of every member of Generation X, a generation that was named after a baby boomer rock band by a baby boomer author and now has seen its voice somewhat eclipsed by the much larger cohort of millennials. This is that book—but it would never have taken shape without a great deal of help.

I must first thank two institutions that have supported this work. The project began when I was working at Indiana University, and it was supported there by a fellowship from the College Arts and Humanities Institute in 2011 and by the History Department's Roman History fund. In 2012, I moved to the University of California, San Diego. At UCSD, I have received teaching releases and financial support from the Department of History, the office of the Dean of Arts and Humanities, and UCSD's new Hellenic Studies Center. I have also benefited greatly from conversations with my new colleagues in the Department of History and the members of the San Diego Hellenic Cultural Society. I am especially thankful to Carol Vassiliadis for her remarkable support of Byzantine studies in San Diego.

I have benefited greatly from the undergraduate and graduate students who participated in the seminars on which this book is based and where some of its ideas were first vetted. I always learn a great deal from every member of these classes, but Richard Barrett, David Jamison, David Maldonado, and Tola Rodrick in Indiana and Chad Macdonald, Gary Mikaelian, Ruthann Mowry, Ken Hedrick, and Ryan Ward in San Diego made teaching this material particularly rewarding. Audiences in Bloomington, San Diego, Austin, Columbus, Riverside, Berkeley, Davis, New Orleans, Ann Arbor, Princeton, Rome, Göttingen, Lund, and Zurich have both indulged some of the wilder ideas once in this book and helped me to refine its arguments considerably.

My friends and colleagues have made this book possible in numerous ways. Bart Wright prepared the map in the book. Katharine Calandra is responsible for the best author photo ever taken of me. Shane Bjornlie, Glen Bowersock, David Brakke, Alan Cameron, Filippo Carlà, Catherine Chin, Rafaella Cribiore, Beth DePalma Digeser, Susanna Elm, Tom Gallant, Fritz Graf, Geoffrey Greatrex, Veronika Grimm, Sarah Iles Johnston, Anthony Kaldellis, Derek Krueger, Michael Kulikowski, Lilian Larsen, Seth Lerer, John Matthews, Heinz-Günther Nesselrath, David Potter, Eric Robinson, and Samuel Rubenson have all offered advice and suggestions at key points in the writing process. Their input has collectively greatly improved the manuscript. I owe special thanks to Scott McGill, who was willing to take the time to explain to me the joy and artfulness of Ausonius's poetry (though he is by no means responsible for my subsequent comparison of Ausonius to Eminem). Charles Aull, Noel Lenski, Michele Salzman, and Brad Storin all have taken the time to read and comment on various chapters of this book—for which I am most grateful. Michele, Brad, and Charles as well as Peter Gemeinhardt, Dayna Kalleres, Alberto Quiroga Puertas, Peter Van Nuffelen, and John Watt have all generously shared forthcoming book and article manuscripts with me. Lieve Van Hoof has been a great conversation partner on all things Libanian and has shared with me much of her excellent forthcoming work on Libanius. These are projects for which we will all be much richer, and I am thankful to her for giving me an advanced look.

Cristiana Sogno has been an immense help throughout the writing and revising process. Not only did she willingly read (and reread) individual chapters, but she helped me *get* the later Roman senatorial world and its unspoken assumptions, prejudices, and rivalries. In the course of this, she made it possible for an avowed Hellenist like me to develop a fascination with and genuine like for men like Symmachus—no small feat.

It took a series of conversations with Peter Brown to really help me to understand what, in particular, framed the imaginations and worldviews of the final pagan generation. I had the great privilege of reading various versions of the typescript of Peter's breathtaking *Through the Eye of a Needle*. The conversations that grew out of those chapters were, I suspect, far more rewarding for me than they were for him, and inspired some of the core ideas of this book. I owe him a great deal of thanks as well for his suggestions about my own manuscript once I had a manuscript to share with him.

As the project moved from manuscript to book, Eric Schmidt at the UC Press has been a wonderful champion. He has provided great input throughout the process and taught me how to have a simultaneous conversation with scholars and nonscholars. Every author should have the privilege of working with so energetic, dedicated, and generous an editor and friend as Eric. I am also very appreciative of everything. Cindy Fulton, Maeve Cornell-Taylor, Aimee Goggins, and Marian Rogers have done to make this work a finished product.

Final thanks go to my family. Their involvement with this project has extended across three years and four continents. My in-laws Sunanda and Brij Ballabh Bhargava have been vital to this project in many ways, serving as everything from teachers to tour guides to babysitters. The trip to India that played a crucial role in allowing me to think in new ways about religious space would not have been possible without Punita Bhargava, who helped a suburbanite from New Jersey appreciate how alive a city can become during a religious festival. In India, Brij Bhushan and Sudha Bhargava and Brij Pal and Madhu Bhargava were generous hosts and encyclopedic guides who patiently shared their homes, experiences, and wisdom with me as I struggled to think about religious and social life in new ways. Brij Narain and Nancy Bhargava have also helped open my eyes to these things in the course of many conversations in the United States. Ashwin Bhargava and Daphne Siefert-Herron kept us sane whenever the combination of travel and general chaos threatened to overwhelm our Indian adventure.

My children, Zoe and Nathaniel, have been eager participants in this project. Each served as a staff photographer, taking pictures of the coins this book features and the sites we visited in India and Italy. Zoe has a keen eye for lighting and details, while Nathaniel is the only one in the family able to dodge trucks on major Indian highways and take pictures of temples in the countryside. My wife, Manasi, has patiently endured the growth of this project, the long hours of travel it entailed, the young children it induced to run across roads, and the myriad other disruptions it has caused. She has also regularly stepped in to make sure that the ideas in it remain grounded and accessible. That last skill is priceless.

This book is dedicated to my parents, Dan and Karen Watts. They afforded me the leisure to search for something about which I was passionate. They gave me the freedom to develop that passion. And they instilled in me the confidence to believe that I could achieve any possible task while also recognizing those tasks that were impossible. I hope that my children will be as lucky as I have been.

Carlsbad, California
October 7, 2013

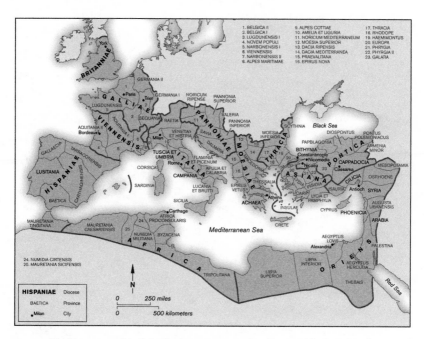

1. BELGICA II
2. BELGICA I
3. LUGDUNENSIS I
4. NOVEM POPULI
5. NARBONENSIS I
6. VIENNENSIS
7. NARBONENSIS II
8. ALPES MARITIMAE
9. ALPES COTTIAE
10. AMELIA ET LIGURIA
11. NORICUM MEDITERRANEUM
12. MOESIA SUPERIOR
13. DACIA RIPENSIS
14. DACIA MEDITERRANEA
15. PRAEVALITANA
16. EPIRUS NOVA
17. THRACIA
18. RHODOPE
19. HAEMIMONTUS
20. EUROPA
21. PHRYGIA
22. PHYRGIA II
23. GALATIA

24. NUMIDIA CIRTENSIS
25. MAURETANIA SICIFENSIS

HISPANIAE | Diocese
BAETICA | Province
• Milan | City

0 — 250 miles
0 — 500 kilometers

MAP I. The Roman world of the final pagan generation. Prepared by Bart Wright.

Introduction

In 392, Theophilus, the bishop of Alexandria, requested and received imperial permission to convert into a church an old imperial basilica that had been abandoned and left to decay for most of the past quarter century. When the renovation began, workmen found a network of man-made underground caverns, and religious artifacts hidden within them.[1] Theophilus took possession of the objects, organized a procession of them through the city, and mocked them publicly. This provocative act caused pagans to riot.[2] Enraged, they marched into the streets and began brawling with Christians. At first there were small skirmishes, but the conflicts soon degenerated into what a contemporary called "open warfare."[3] After these initial street battles, the pagan crowd retreated to the Serapeum, a large temple of the god Serapis well fortified on a hill high above Alexandria (see fig. 1). Under the leadership of the philosopher Olympus and other teachers, like the grammarians Helladius and Ammonius, the pagans launched multiple attacks on the city's Christians. Their actions belied the stereotype of intellectual restraint. According to Christian sources, the people captured by these men and their students were "forced to sacrifice at burning altars."[4] If they refused, the Serapeum garrison tortured them by breaking their shins, attaching them to pitchforks, and throwing them into caves once used to store the blood that dripped from the temple's altars.[5] The Serapeum site proved too difficult for either Alexandria's Christian leadership or its civilian and military authorities to storm. It took a letter from

FIGURE 1. The site of the Serapeum, Alexandria. Photo by Manasi Watts.

the emperor offering a full pardon to the pagan garrison to clear the temple of its defenders.

After the pagan fighters left their stronghold, a crowd of Christian Alexandrians and soldiers swarmed the hill. One of them took an axe and with all his strength struck the jaw of the monumental statue of Serapis (see fig. 2).[6] The crowd then hacked the rest of the statue into pieces and dragged the fragments off to each of the city's regions to be burned. They took the torso (presumably the largest fragment) down the hill and burned it in the amphitheater. This spectacle set off a further round of destruction. Within Alexandria, "the busts of Serapis, which were on the walls, in the entryways, on the doorposts, and even in the windows of every single house, were completely torn down and scraped away" so that there no longer remained any trace of the god.[7]

The destruction of the Serapeum was a momentous event, second perhaps only to the Gothic sack of Rome in 410 for the amount of attention it received from contemporary sources.[8] In the same way that the sack of Rome shocked an empire unaccustomed to questioning its military superiority, the disappearance of Serapis's temple in Alexandria highlighted the vulnerability of large centers of traditional religion that had once seemed a permanent fixture of Roman life. However, like the sack of Rome, the destruction of the Serapeum was both a singular

FIGURE 2. Coin of
Antoninus Pius (A.D. 148/9)
showing Serapis enthroned
in temple (Emmett 1668).
Courtesy of the author.
Photo by Zoe Watts.

event and the culmination of a longer process. In retrospect, many events clearly prefigured the Goths' capture of Rome under their king Alaric: the Gothic migration across the Danube, the Roman defeat at Adrianople, the emperor Theodosius's peace treaty with the Goths, Gothic anger following the battle at the Frigidus, and Alaric's years of aggression in Greece and Dalmatia. Alaric's attack emerged from a set of historical trends that had been developing for nearly forty years. Romans knew that these things were happening, but no one imagined that they could actually result in the capture of the city of Rome. In fact, before Alaric, few imagined that Rome could ever again be sacked. When Alaric actually breached the city's walls, however, he fundamentally altered assumptions about what was possible in the Roman world.[9] He revealed to all the existence of a new world in which barbarians truly threatened the very existence of Roman imperial power.

The destruction of the Serapeum similarly capped a period of increasingly severe threats to the temples and synagogues of the Roman Empire's traditional religious communities. In the 380s, emperors cut funding for traditional cults in Italy and denied an appeal to restore the Altar of Victory in the Roman senate house; administrators in the East attempted to cut the sacred grove at Daphne outside of Antioch and led a sustained campaign against rural shrines in Mesopotamia, Syria, and Egypt.[10] The same social and religious trends that propelled these anti-pagan actions also led to the events at the Serapeum. This Alexandrian event, however, seems to have fundamentally changed many people's awareness of the threat to traditional religious institutions. For the first time, pagans understood that Christian attacks could reach the most permanent and impressive elements of the urban religious infrastructure. Christians now saw temple destructions, both within and outside of cities, as a realistic way to remake the religious topography of the empire.

Everyone appreciated the significance of these actions against traditional religion, but people reacted to them differently depending on their age. Younger individuals saw the potential for these events to reshape the world and responded vigorously to them. Older men, however, were less alarmed and more measured both in their assessment of these developments and in their response to them. These differences in imagination grew out of a profound generation gap.

Though it has not before been acknowledged, the pagan and Christian perpetrators of the violence of the 380s and early 390s, the imperial officials in charge of controlling it, and the emperor who presided during it were almost exclusively young and middle-aged men. The attitudes and actions of these men, most of whom belonged to the generation born following the death of the first Christian emperor, Constantine, sometimes contrast markedly with those of the pagan and Christian elites born in the 310s and early 320s. These younger pagan and Christian religious warriors were born into a world in which Christianity was clearly ascendant. They anticipated its destructive and transformative power, and as they matured, they came increasingly to understand that the dawning new religious order threatened the very existence of traditional Roman cults. Men like Rufinus and Olympus saw the conflict between a rising Christianity and traditional religion as the defining struggle of the fourth century, and they fought hard to advance the interests of the religious community with which they identified.

Older men did not see the world in this way. They generally shared neither their juniors' interest in creating sharply defined religious identities nor their tendency toward violent religious confrontation. The temple destructions and Christian provocations of the 380s and early 390s dismayed these older men, but, unlike some younger men of similar social and economic station, they did not violently resist these acts. They reacted instead as if they could not imagine a world in which traditional religious practices did not have a part. They had good reason to think this way. This generation was born during or immediately following a time of Christian persecution when the old gods had ruled, without interruption, for thousands of years. They were raised in the politically functional and economically prosperous environment created following the third-century stabilization of the Roman Empire by the tetrarchy. The empire of the fourth century depended on an administrative system in which locally prominent men could play important administrative roles. It nurtured a social system based on shared cultural values that bound elites across the empire. It created an economy in which the introduction of a stable new gold coinage greatly increased the wealth of the upper class.[11] The great wealth and opportunities that the Roman system provided to those who were willing to play by its rules steadily shaped these men into loyal and cooperative superintendents of imperial stability. Romans born in the first quarter of the fourth century consequently showed little inclination to challenge this prosperous imperial order. And yet it was this generation's faith in the foundations of the imperial system and their craving for political stability that enabled Christian emperors to mount increasingly powerful challenges to established religious life in the later fourth century.

At first glance, it is puzzling that this generation proved unable to anticipate the degree to which the Roman world would change as imperially sponsored Christianity took hold. Their stories are, after all, usually told alongside those of younger contemporaries who were very much aware that the world was changing around them. These were men like Ambrose, Gregory Nazianzen, Basil of Caesarea, and John Chrysostom, who abandoned legal, administrative, and teaching positions in the system their fathers perpetuated so that they could instead pursue careers in the church or lives as ascetics. Others, like the emperor Julian and the pagan sophist Eunapius, threatened the system's cohesion by aggressively asserting what they understood to be traditional religious identities. These younger men made these choices while occupying the same positions of authority that once restrained their elders. The Alexandrian events that culminated in the Serapeum's destruction reflect the confessional interests and confrontational tendencies of this younger generation.

The first children of the Christian Roman Empire drove the events with which this study concludes, but this book focuses on their parents, the "final pagan generation." By that phrase, I do not mean the last Roman pagans. Pagan communities continued to thrive in the Roman world into the seventh century and beyond.[12] Indeed, there is a good argument to be made that, in many parts of the fourth-century Roman Empire, some form of paganism long outlasted Roman political control.[13] In using the phrase "final pagan generation," I also do not mean men and women who were exclusively pagans. In fact, a number of the figures on whom this discussion will focus were Christians.

The "final pagan generation" I will speak about is made up of the last group of elite Romans, both pagan and Christian, who were born into a world in which most people believed that the pagan public religious order of the past few millennia would continue indefinitely. They were the last Romans to grow up in a world that simply could not imagine a Roman world dominated by a Christian majority.[14] This critical failure of imagination is completely understandable. At the beginning of the second decade of the fourth century there had never been a Christian emperor, and the childhood and early adolescence of members of this generation living in the East coincided with moments when the resources of the Roman state were devoted to the suppression of Christianity.[15] The longest-lived of this group died in an empire that would never again see a non-Christian sovereign, and that no longer financially supported the public sacrifices, temples, and festivals that had dominated Roman life in their youth. They lived through a time of dramatic change that they could neither anticipate nor fully understand as it was unfolding.[16] This generation represents the last cohort of Roman children to grow up believing that religious practice would continue in the way that it always had. They also represent the first generation of adults forced to respond to the significant political and demographic changes that Christianity's rise had produced.

Both ancient and modern accounts of the fourth century see as inevitable an ending that no one could possibly have anticipated when the final pagan generation was born. With the exception of two short treatments of fourth-century events, no history written by a member of the final pagan generation survives intact.[17] The major accounts of this period were written by members of the generations to which either the parents or the children of the final pagan generation belonged.[18] These are valuable texts, but they reflect the distinct concerns of older and younger men. The Christian members of the final pagan generation were too young to share Eusebius's thrill when Constantine's victories removed the looming threat of religious persecution. And its non-Christian members were mostly too old to experience the steady tightening of restrictions on traditional religious practice in the early fifth century. All of them died too soon to appreciate that these fifth-century policies grew out of fourth-century trends. Their fourth century was instead a time when a relatively stable imperial system provided elite men and women across the empire with unprecedented opportunities for wealth and power. These men expressed concerns to friends about the empire's evolving religious environment throughout their lives, but this was only one concern among a great many that shifted as these men aged. Indeed, most members of this generation pursued their personal and professional interests and advocated for those of their friends much more frequently and with much greater vigor than they fought for their God or gods.

This history of the final pagan generation attempts to restore to them the unique generational perspective that we have long overlooked. The work of scholars such as Glen Elder has shown that, in the modern world, social and economic conditions experienced during childhood shape people's behaviors for the rest of their lives.[19] People who grew up at different times and under different conditions often do not understand the same event in the same way because their life experiences have conditioned them to react to certain stimuli and ignore others. Their different worldviews are not shaped by any one dramatic day. They instead reflect the slow process of learning to live in the world in which they were born. We know intuitively that older and younger people now share neither the same concerns nor the same reactions to events, but we often forget that this generation gap existed in antiquity as well. Obscuring or ignoring generational differences, then, prevents us from seeing the full implication of historical events.

One can see the importance of recovering this picture by looking at how another revolutionary period is sometimes remembered. When young people today think of the 1960s in the United States, their minds turn to a set of iconic images now recycled endlessly by the media. On one side are happy images like Burk Uzzle's couple embracing at Woodstock. On the other are more troubling photos like Eddie Adams's photo of Nguyen Van Lem's execution or Charles Moore's pictures of Birmingham civil rights marchers being sprayed by fire hoses. These images greatly simplify the chaotic and sometimes frightening experience of living through the 1960s in the United States, but they fit neatly into the narratives that now comfortably sanitize the 1960s for nostalgic baby boomers, Generation Xers, and millennials. These images capture moments that really happened, but the media story into which they have been placed is a later creation that relates only somewhat to the actual decade it purports to describe.

There are different, more mundane stories of everyday life that make for much less powerful photography but that better capture the concerns and experiences of most people alive in the 1960s. To take just one example, Uzzle's iconic 1969 Woodstock photo of the unmarried couple Nick Ercoline and Bobbi Kelly embracing as Jefferson Airplane serenaded the morning sun seems a poignant symbol of the dramatic loosening of societal conventions in the late 1960s.[20] And yet, as always, the reality is much more complicated. The poor sound quality on Max Yasgur's farm meant that many of the five hundred thousand people assembled could not even hear Grace Slick sing that morning. An uncropped version of Uzzle's photograph also reveals that the three people nearest to the embracing couple were asleep, as was at least half of the crowd in the background. The cropped image may have brilliantly captured the Aquarian spirit that younger people now associate with Woodstock, but it failed to capture the actual damp and sometimes dreary experience of most of those attending.

In the same way that Uzzle's photograph of Woodstock does not capture the experiences of many of those who attended the festival, the festival itself poorly reflected the life of most Americans in August 1969. The five hundred thousand people at Woodstock represented less than one-quarter of 1 percent of the US population. Though Woodstock has become emblematic of the baby-boomer generation, at most six-tenths of 1 percent of baby boomers attended. Far more boomers likely spent that weekend washing their cars than straining to hear music in upstate New York. Indeed, four weeks later the number of boomers attending the opening games of the college football season dwarfed that Woodstock crowd.[21] And while artists like Jefferson Airplane, Janis Joplin, and Jimi Hendrix have come to define the music scene of late 1969, only one act that played Woodstock topped the *Billboard* chart that year.[22] Acts like Elvis and Henry Mancini as well as semiforgotten ones like the Archies all sold more records than the icons of Woodstock that year.[23] Even Jefferson Airplane's "Somebody to Love," the soundtrack to Uzzle's photo, was only the twenty-second best-selling single of 1967, finishing below such artists as The Box Tops, Frankie Valli, and The Monkees.[24] Listening to Grace Slick's "morning maniac music" on August 17, 1969, may have later become symbolic of the baby boomer experience, but it was in fact shared by relatively few members of that generation. Whatever Woodstock's nostalgic resonance forty-five years later, it neither defined the nation nor reflected the interests that many Americans had on that day. Most of the baby boom generation (and the vast majority of the rest of the country) had different things on their minds that morning. That mundane reality is important for historians to remember even if twenty-first-century popular culture has decided to forget it.

Rufinus's portrait of the Serapeum destruction, like Uzzle's Woodstock photograph, is cropped so as to preserve his own evocative artistic representation of a specific historical moment that mattered greatly to people his age. It fit into a prepackaged narrative that idealized an event but made no attempt to describe the experiences or attitudes of most Romans alive in 392. And while everyone remotely familiar with the history of the United States knows that Uzzle's photograph tells nothing about the experiences and attitudes of the parents of the baby boomers in August 1969, we seldom recognize that Rufinus's account similarly fails to capture the perspective of an older generation. It says nothing about how his elders imagined the future when they were younger, or how their (ultimately inaccurate) imagination of this future influenced their reactions to events throughout their lives. A teenaged member of the final pagan generation was as likely to imagine the destruction of the Serapeum in the 320s as a young Laura Ingalls Wilder was to imagine Woodstock, but, despite their failure of imagination, these generations of older people created the conditions that permitted the youth-driven events of 392 and 1969.[25] This book is, in a sense, the history of the people who spent the fourth century doing the equivalent of going to work, washing their cars, and mowing the lawn while their children participated in the unfolding of a revolutionary age. These men and women were the mid-fourth century's silent majority. Their story deserves to be recognized as both distinct from that of their children and worthy of reconstruction on its own terms.

It is easy for a historian to distill the events of a man's entire lifetime into a short lecture, but it is often hard for us to remember that this person about whom we speak lived in real time. A year lasted just as long in the fourth century as it does now. This fact demands that we slow our narrative of the period down to account for the steady rhythms of life as it was lived. In order to do so, this book proceeds chronologically. Each chapter balances a discussion of the issues that concerned members of the final pagan generation at each stage of their lives with a discussion of the imperial political and religious dynamics that prevailed at that moment in time. This will give a contemporary perspective to these imperial developments while permitting us to understand how this generation's priorities shifted as they aged.

It is important to clarify at the outset which members of this generation will be the focus of this book. The vast majority of the perhaps twenty million Romans born in the 310s have disappeared completely from the historical record. This is particularly true of peasants, farmers, and much of the urban underclass of the empire, but it is also the case for many members of the Roman elite. A smaller (but still substantial) number of people are known only through funerary inscriptions or brief mentions in literary and legal texts. Nevertheless, four extremely prominent and productive figures born in this period made such a lasting and sustained impact that we can closely follow the evolution of their careers and concerns through to the last decade of the fourth century. These are Libanius, Themistius, Ausonius, and Praetextatus. All of them belonged to the Roman elite for their entire lives, and, as such, they enjoyed wealth, interesting career opportunities, and prominent social positions. Their experiences are exceptional and not representative of those of the vast majority of Romans living through the fourth century. At the same time, these men were involved in the decision-making processes in their cities and very much interested in the state of the empire in which they lived. Their experiences were not the same, but, together, they give us a sense of the way in which men of a similar age and background behaved during the period of time on which we are focused.

It is to our great advantage that these men wrote a lot of material that still survives. Libanius, a prominent teacher of rhetoric in Constantinople, Nicaea, Nicomedia, and Antioch from the 340s until the 390s, left us with 1,544 letters, 64 orations, 51 declamations, a set of *progymnasmata* (or school exercises), and even an epigram. This extensive record offers personal accounts of most major events in his life. Themistius carved out for himself a unique political position, serving as the philosophical counselor to emperors and as the main recruiter for the senate in Constantinople. Still extant are a chronologically diverse collection of 34 of his orations, a number of philosophical commentaries, and one letter (that evidently came from a larger published collection that has since been lost). The earliest of these works come from the mid-340s, and the last dates to the 380s. Although Themistius's material offers fewer personal reflections than that of Libanius, it provides greater insight into the ways that members of this generation could influence events.

Whereas Libanius and Themistius figured prominently in the Eastern half of the Roman Empire, two other important and extremely well-documented figures allow us to understand the experiences of men of this generation living in the West. The first of these, the Christian Ausonius, began his career as an advocate before becoming a teacher of rhetoric. A native of Burgidala (modern Bordeaux), Ausonius taught there until he was summoned to court by the emperor Valentinian to serve as tutor to his son Gratian (who was later to become emperor). This position led to a series of high imperial offices. He served as consul (the office that capped only the most accomplished senatorial careers) and held the praetorian prefectures of Gaul, Italy, and Africa, each of which represented that region's highest administrative office. Ausonius's surviving works include letters, poems, and an oration all written between the 360s and the 390s.

The final central figure, Vettius Agorius Praetextatus, differs from the others because of the very prominent social position that he occupied.[26] The other three men were members of the local elite who became important people in the empire. Praetextatus, however, occupied a social rung well above even these elites. He belonged to a family in which the consulship was not an achievement to be overly celebrated but an honor to be expected.[27] He held many of the empire's most important offices, including an urban prefecture of Rome (the figure who served as the effective governor of the city) and a praetorian prefecture, as well as a number of prominent public and private priesthoods in and around the city of Rome. One other feature distinguishes Praetextatus. Unlike the three other figures mentioned, no literary works by Praetextatus survive (though we know of at least one lost work written by him).[28] He is otherwise well attested, however. Praetextatus is honored by at least ten different surviving inscriptions, he is the addressee of nearly a dozen extant laws, he received twelve letters from the senator Symmachus,[29] and he appears as a character in a range of literary texts.[30] He is also the subject of a laudatory poem written by his wife, the second-longest poem authored by a woman to survive from late antiquity,[31] and the object of attack in the anonymous *Poem against the Pagans*.[32] The lack of surviving writings means that Praetextatus's motivations are often opaque to us, but his extensive and well-documented public activities make up for this. While Libanius, Themistius, and Ausonius allow us to know about the concerns that percolated through the minds and conversations of members of this generation, Praetextatus gives us a sense of the range of actions that his peers would have deemed possible and prudent.

These four men will be the characters around whom this discussion is built, but they will not be its sole focus. Instead, their histories will be folded into a narrative that speaks about the experience of living amid the fourth century's dramatic changes. The information these figures provide will also be supplemented at times with that deriving from other men and women born in the 310s. The concern throughout will be to understand what each stage of life was like for these people and the degree to which larger political, social, and religious developments affected them. Each chapter will concentrate on the specific question of what it was like to be, for example, a twenty-something member of the elite in the 330s. This focus means that each chapter will have its own balance. Libanius, for example, will figure much more prominently in discussions of life under Constantius and Theodosius (the periods from which most of his letters date) than he will in discussion of the 370s. The development of imperial policies and religious attitudes will be discussed throughout, but the most weight will always be given to how these developments were seen by and affected people born in the 310s.

This book has nine chapters and a short conclusion. Chapter 1 describes the Roman world into which the final pagan generation was born. The empire of the first decades of the fourth century contained millions of religious structures, artifacts, and materials that cities and individuals had fashioned over the past millennia to honor the traditional gods. Festivals honoring the gods crowded the calendar, and fragrant smells connected to their worship filled the air of cities. The gods were everywhere in the early fourth century. Indeed, they were so pervasive that a person could (and probably often did) ignore their presence as he went about his daily routine. For thousands of years the most significant threat to these gods had been neglect as wooden statues decayed and temples fell into disrepair. It was simply inconceivable that the material basis for traditional religious practice would ever be threatened. Chapter 1 then considers how the young men born in the 310s were raised and how their families, attendants, and teachers taught them to function in this world pervaded by traditional religion.

Chapter 2 treats the events of the final pagan generation's childhood. It discusses the rise of Constantine and the general religious and political trends he set in motion. Despite Constantine's conversion in 312 and a series of initiatives designed to privilege Christianity while disadvantaging traditional religion, the emperor and his Christian advisers struggled to imagine what a Christian empire might look like and how it might be created. This and the general resistance to radical change that the Roman administration presented meant that the overwhelming presence of traditional gods remained unthreatened. This was especially true of the Eastern half of the empire, territory that Constantine conquered in 324. The youth of the 310s, however, likely failed to notice the significance of much of what Constantine did to openly promote Christianity. They spent most of the later reign of Constantine learning grammar and rhetoric in a relatively closed social and intellectual world. They occupied themselves with studying, partying, socializing, and making mischief with fellow students, who, it was hoped, would eventually form part of their network of friends. This education trained them to be productive members of the imperial elite, but it also gave them little time or inclination to pay attention to the new religious initiatives coming out of the imperial court.

Chapter 3 concerns the period when most members of this generation took on their first significant public roles. They finished their schooling in the 330s and early 340s and then took their first tentative steps into professional life. The political reform of the Roman Empire undertaken by the emperor Diocletian and continued by Constantine had brought a degree of stability to the empire that had not been seen since the 230s. It dramatically increased the size of the Roman government as well as the number of employment opportunities and honors it could provide. As the final pagan generation came of age, an economic expansion had also begun that would greatly enhance the fortunes of the empire's elite. This was, as Peter Brown has called it, a "New Age of Gold" whose opportunities the privileged and ambitious young men of the 330s readily embraced.[33] While these men focused on their families and careers, this was also the period when Constantine's sons first began implementing their vision for a new empire governed by Christian sovereigns. The members of the final pagan generation, however, paid little attention to these developments as they competed for positions of influence in the imperial educational and administrative infrastructure.

Chapter 4 describes the period between 350 and 361. This was the moment when the children of the 310s began to work their way up the professional ladder. Libanius set up a school in his home city of Antioch after stints spent teaching abroad. Themistius perfected his public persona as a politically astute philosopher who advised emperors. Praetextatus held a sequence of governorships that put him on a track for an eventual urban prefecture. Ausonius continued to work as a well-placed provincial teacher. At the same time, the demographic realities of late Roman life added an element of uncertainty to their personal lives. Ausonius suffered the loss of his wife, and Themistius lost both his wife and his only son in the span of a few months. These personal concerns unfolded against the background of increasingly significant religious developments. Following the defeat of the usurper Magnentius, the emperor Constantius began tightening legislation against traditional sacrifice and restricting access to temples. These changes were certainly noticed by members of this generation, but their personal concerns and those of their family again took precedence. Despite their misgivings about policies pursued by Constantius, they again elected largely to play along with an imperial system from which they derived great benefit.

Chapter 5 considers the experiences of these men during the reigns of the emperors Julian and Jovian. The death of Constantius and the accession of Julian brought a series of significant changes to the professional lives of our four protagonists and men like them. Figures like Themistius who had thrived under Constantius found themselves marginalized by Julian, who was attempting to revitalize the worship of the old gods. Others, like Libanius, capitalized on the fall of Constantius's associates and ingratiated themselves with the new emperor. This shift, combined with Julian's sometimes disruptive religious policies, forced men like Libanius to balance their support for certain policies they favored with advocacy for friends who were adversely affected by Julian's initiatives. Just as they had under Constantius, the final pagan generation sought a way to use the imperial system to buffer the effects of an emperor's personal and policy shifts.

Chapter 6 examines the period when the brothers Valentinian and Valens controlled the empire. They shared an interest in administrative stability and a general faith in the imperial system's ability to maintain the prosperity and the tranquility of the empire. This led to a period of relative religious tolerance that, with slight exceptions, extended through the 360s and 370s. While imperial attitudes toward traditional religious activity remained more stable than they had been since the conversion of Constantine, other social dynamics shifted greatly as Valentinian and Valens replaced with new men the elites who had served Julian. While some, like Themistius, Praetextatus, and Ausonius, benefited almost immediately from the new regime, Libanius saw his fortunes and influence sink. These shifts in social life and influence again occupied far more time and attention than did concerns about the religious life of the empire.

Chapter 7 discusses the elite Romans who came of age in the 360s and early 370s. Many of these young men shared their parents' faith in the post-Constantinian imperial system's ability to provide them with opportunities, wealth, and honors. By the 360s, however, texts like Athanasius's *Life of Antony* catalyzed a movement through which some elite Christians turned against the careers for which they had prepared. Some became bishops, while others joined ascetic circles organized by their peers. Intriguingly, the networks of friends they developed as youths helped make their rejection of elite social norms and aspirations possible. This led young aristocrats like the former governor Ambrose, the former teacher Gregory Nazianzen, and the former lawyer John Chrysostom to exchange the careers for which they had trained for ecclesiastical or ascetic pursuits. Networks of like-minded friends also helped these young dropouts weather the disapproval of parents, friends, and family members. The rise of this Christian youth culture gave large numbers of young elites an alternative model of aristocratic success that existed outside of the mainstream imperial system.

Chapter 8 focuses on the years between 375 and 384 and the process through which the generation of the 310s began to hand control of the empire over to their children. These years represented a sort of valedictory moment for many of the surviving elite of the final pagan generation. Ausonius, Themistius, and Praetextatus all held the highest offices of their careers during this period, and each played a major role in imperial administrations for much of the decade. Ausonius in particular used his influence at the court of Gratian to bring young Gallic aristocrats into some of the empire's most influential governorships and prefectures. He aimed to recruit a new generation of administrators that shared his faith in the post-Constantinian order. At the same time, men like Ambrose, the bishop of Milan, who had abandoned the pursuit of high office for careers in the church, began to claim a different type of authority that grew not from imperial service but from their positions in the clergy. The early years of the reign of Theodosius I and the first months of the regime of Valentinian II both show moments when imperial legitimacy depended on a sovereign's ability to draw support from both the old elite and these new, Christian leaders. By 384, however, a controversy over the Altar of Victory once housed in the senate house in Rome brought Ambrose and the traditional Roman senatorial order in direct conflict. The issue was resolved in Ambrose's favor, its outcome showing the potency of nontraditional models of authority.

Chapter 9 looks at the years between 384 and 394, the decade during which all of this study's protagonists died. As these men entered their eighth decade, their health began to fail, many of their friends passed away, and their careers reached their final stages. Contrary to ancient expectations, however, these elites did not always step away from the public careers they had once enjoyed. Libanius in particular remained extremely active until right before his death. At times, Libanius worked to advance the same goals as Christian dropouts like John

Chrysostom, but by the late 380s, Libanius often felt compelled to speak out against the anti-pagan attacks that Christian bishops and ascetics encouraged. This religious violence clearly displeased him, but Libanius reacted to it in the way that men of his generation had been taught. He penned orations critical of the officials who permitted these rogue attacks, and he complained to friendly administrators about overzealous Christians. Sometimes, but not always, his appeals worked. At the same time, so much religious infrastructure remained untouched within the empire that Libanius's concerns about traditional religion formed only one part of a larger set of interests that he spent his time protecting. He fought for the temples, but not with the all-consuming urgency that fueled the Christian attackers or the younger defenders of the Serapeum in Alexandria.

This book concludes by returning to the Serapeum to consider how the legacy of the final pagan generation differed from that of their children. While the attack on the Serapeum helped to define the lives of many of the remarkable men and women who imagined a radically different Roman social and religious order in the 390s, it plays no role in the historical legacy of the men born in the 310s. These figures are instead remembered as exemplars of a wealthy, stable, and cultured social and political order. Subsequent centuries saw Libanius, Ausonius, Themistius, and Praetextatus not as confessional warriors but as cultural connoisseurs whose eloquence and good taste represented the elite experience of the fourth-century age of gold.

Thus the final pagan generation offers an unconventional, though no less dynamic, history of the fourth century in which personal goals largely overshadowed confessional concerns, and honors trumped dogma. Its members allow us to see a Roman world shaped not by massive, irresistible, and impersonal historical forces but by the small and regular choices made every day by fallible people who lived life in real time. This book will, I hope, recover some of the forgotten human dimensions of a century in which world-changing events sometimes seem to overshadow the seemingly mundane concerns of the men and women whose actions made them possible.

CHAPTER I

Growing Up in the Cities of the Gods

The Roman Empire was full of gods in 310. Their temples, statues, and images filled its cities, towns, farms, and wildernesses. Whether they willed it or not, people living within the empire regularly experienced the sight, sound, smell, and taste of the gods' celebration. Traditional divinities also dominated the spiritual space of the empire as figures whose presence could not be sensed but whose actions many felt they could discern.[1] Although such a situation seems quite foreign to the modern Western mind, people of the time saw this as an unremarkable reality that had existed for millennia. Later Romans could draw on a long history of living in a world like this, and they had developed ever more sophisticated technologies and techniques for interacting with the gods around them. The gods belonged to the empire's natural environment, and Romans had spent centuries learning how to make use of this vital resource.

The religious infrastructure of the Roman Empire cannot be equated to the aqueducts, pipes, and fountains that enabled Romans to redirect the water of rivers and streams into their cities and homes, but both systems attempted to channel in productive ways forces that could either sustain life or unleash immense destruction. Indeed, while a water system dependent on aqueducts and pipes differed dramatically from a spiritual system dependent on temples and rituals, both also produced a sort of passive and unconscious acceptance of their necessity. Temples, statues, and festivals were so omnipresent that they mostly faded into the sensory background as a sort of white noise or ambient odor that lurked without much acknowledgment within the empire's physical space.

RELIGIOUS INFRASTRUCTURE

A short fourth-century catalog of the types of buildings found in the city of Alexandria offers a window into this environment. It lists almost 2,500 temples in the city, nearly one for every twenty houses.[2] Some of these were massive structures, like the Serapeum described in the introduction. The Serapeum sat on the highest spot in the city, an augmented limestone ridge at the southwestern edge of Alexandria's walls. Alexandria was a densely populated city of perhaps five hundred thousand filled with multistory houses and apartment buildings, but the Serapeum mount was visible in much of the city, and the tall temple perched atop it would have been a landmark. The senses of those who visited the site would have been altogether overwhelmed by the abundant and extravagant decorations of Serapis's temple and the other buildings around it. The site was crowded with statues and adorned with fine marbles, precious metals, rare woods, and (probably) jeweled objects.[3] On most days, the indiscriminate rumblings of activity from worshippers and priests milling around the temple, scholars and students consulting the library, patrons and merchants doing business at the neighboring shops, and (on race days) the crowd of people filing into and out of the adjacent Hippodrome provided a wall of white noise that blocked out the regular cacophony of the city.[4] The pleasant odors of incense and other offerings further set the complex apart from the filthy, smelly city that seethed below it.

The sense of physical and sensory separation that an urban monumental temple complex created for its visitors was, however, a luxury that few Romans enjoyed on a regular basis. This was not for lack of piety. Instead, it reflected a far more mundane reality. Massive temples like the Alexandrian Serapeum, the Roman Capitoline temple, or those on the Athenian Acropolis dominated the city's skyline, but their heights, locations, and many stairs made it inconvenient to access them regularly. The Serapeum, for example, was perhaps a thirty-minute walk from the center of the city, a walk that would force one to dodge traffic while enduring dust, smoke, and the stench of all sorts of dung and rot. Once one reached the temple, a climb up nearly a hundred stairs still remained. This could not be a regular part of most people's daily routine.

Fortunately, Alexandrians did not have to go far to encounter a temple. Neighborhood temples filled the city. They likely took many forms and ranged from imposing structures like the Serapeum to structures so modest that a distracted passerby would not notice their presence (see fig. 3). The diversity of Hindu temples one sees in cities in modern India can perhaps help one to imagine this type of environment. If one takes the city of Mathura in Uttar Pradesh as an example, a driver along the main highway to the west of the town will see massive temples like the Jai Gurudev mixed in with temples like the small one dedicated to Hanuman just four-tenths of a mile to its southeast (fig. 4) and another of similar size two miles to its north. Within the cities, one sees even greater diversity. The area around the center of Jaipur, for example, houses major temples like the Birla Mandir (fig. 5) and much smaller ones that are barely larger than a full-grown man (fig. 6). The bigger temples in India tend to have more visitors and dedicated attendants, while smaller temples attract less traffic and are not regularly staffed, but temples of all sizes play an active role in the larger religious life of Hindu communities.

One can see evidence that temples in the later Roman world functioned similarly. Rufinus's description of the Alexandrian Serapeum indicates the presence of a more or less permanent staff of priests and devotees of the god. In the neighboring city of Canopus, one hears about a philosopher who took up residence on the site of the large Serapis temple there and answered questions posed by visitors.[5] Smaller temples, by contrast, were likely not staffed regularly. Priests and priestesses were summoned when their expertise was needed or a sacrifice required.[6] Even without the constant presence of priests, however, these smaller temples could be used regularly. They often made cultic images visible to passers-by and permitted visitors to leave offerings in front of the building.[7] This provided a more flexible way to approach and honor the divine that enabled devotees to worship when and where it was most convenient.

The Roman countryside housed an even greater array of sacred sites. These included large temple complexes,[8] grottoes and other rustic sacred locations,[9] and a large category of rural structures that served, in effect, as temples run by the household that controlled the land. Here too a focus on the size of the temple buildings can obscure their ubiquity. Houses across the empire had their own household shrines that ranged from wall niches to entire rooms that served as the focal point of domestic rituals.[10] On estates, privately administered cult locations

FIGURE 3. Temples depicted on
Roman coins. From top, hexastyle
temple (*RIC* VI.258, A.D. 310–11),
temple and sacred grove at Zeugma
(SNG Copenhagen 35, A.D.
247–49), and temple in Rome (*RIC*
III.290a, A.D. 159). All coins
courtesy of the author.

FIGURE 4. Temple of Hanuman, Mathura, India. Photo by author.

FIGURE 5. The Birla Mandir, Jaipur, India. Photo by Zoe Watts.

would be even larger and possibly designed to visually resemble temple-market complexes. Religion played an intimate role in defining the rhythms of agricultural life, and, for this reason, landowners often erected freestanding temples on their estates that could serve as cultic centers for their laborers.[11] Many of these temples were placed where access points joined the estate to larger roads, a feature that made it

FIGURE 6. Rural temple, Jaipur, India. Photo by Nathaniel Watts.

possible for both travelers and workers to use them.[12] Although the temples were open to the public, the priesthoods associated with them tended to remain firmly within the family of the estate's owner.[13] The temples also could serve as the center for the family's funerary cult and the rituals associated with it.[14]

The many thousands of temples scattered across the Roman world collectively held millions of images. The Alexandrian Tychaion, one of the 2,500 shrines in that city, occupied most of a city block and was "completely adorned from floor to ceiling" with statues and images of the gods and quasi-divine historical figures like Alexander the Great and Ptolemy Soter.[15] The Tychaion was located across the street from a major bath complex and at a crossroads where two porticoed streets met. If one adds the statues found in the bathhouse and those likely housed in the niches of the porticoes to those housed in the Tychaion, there were probably upward of a hundred different images of gods in and around this one intersection. In the fourth century, the Tychaion was a medium-sized and middle-aged temple. Older and larger sacred precincts would have contained even more images of the gods. In Athens, for example, recent reconstructions of the statuary decorating the late antique Athenian Acropolis show it absolutely packed with nearly one thousand years of dedicatory statues honoring both men and gods.[16] We even see in inventories from the island of Delos that temple precincts housed statues, vases, and other dedicated vessels in all conditions—including some that were broken but could not be discarded because of their cultic association.[17] This undoubtedly would have been the case in the precincts of most major cultic centers by the turn of the fourth century.

Even more numerous were statues of divine figures located elsewhere in the city. Images of the gods decorated later Roman streets in much the same way that they now adorn modern Indian cities. When Rufinus spoke about the destruction of the Serapeum, he mentioned that it was followed by Christian mobs tearing images of Serapis from every street corner in the city.[18] Despite this, an Alexandrian mob ninety-five years later was still able to find so many wooden statues of gods in and around the city that they could fuel a bonfire with them for an entire day.[19] Halfway across the empire, in Rome, each crossroad in the city contained shrines at which honey cakes were offered to the Lares Compitales and, after 12 BC, images representing the Genius of the emperor.[20]

Even more images were found in private homes. Every home in which a devotee of traditional religion lived likely housed representations of the gods. These took many forms. In the West, household shrines to guardian spirits (the *lararia*) contained representations of gods, either as statues or paintings.[21] In some homes (like the House of Menander in Pompeii) these seem to have been confined to the servants quarters, but shrines like these could be located in any room of a house, including the public reception areas of elite homes.[22] In the House of the Vettii in Pompeii, there were two *lararia,* one of which was hidden from view and the other of which was located amid a series of wall paintings.[23] Some of these images of the gods were devotional, but many others were simply decorative. Collections of small mythological statuettes found in a range of Gallic villas reveal that representations of the gods and their associates were an unremarkable part of home decor.[24] More intriguing is the case of Theophanes of Hermopolis, a traveler whose expense account has been preserved for us. In his ledger, he lists a tacky souvenir wine jug in the shape of Silenus among the purchases he made as he passed through Phoenicia in the 310s.[25] No one would mistake that particular object for something connected to religious practice, but even that piece of kitsch contributed to the sense that one shared domestic space with the divine.[26]

While temples convey the overwhelming architectural presence of the divine in later Roman cities, and images show their physical ubiquity, festivals offered some of the most powerful ways to interact with the divine. These festivals literally dominated the Roman year. An illustrated calendar listing the holidays and festivals celebrated in Rome in the year 354 gives a sense of how frequently the gods and their servants appeared publicly.[27] The calendar classifies fully 177 days of the year as holidays or festivals.[28] Not all of these were given the same weight. Those that lasted for multiple days and involved circus races mandated, among other things, a day of rest and the closure of the law courts.[29] Less important were days whose festivals involved games or spectacles but no required closures. Days devoted to cultic ritual that involved neither races nor spectacles ranked the lowest.[30] Overall the calendar marks the public celebrations of the cults of thirty-three different gods and goddesses—and this does not account for the various commemorations of imperial birthdays and divinized emperors.[31] Some gods and goddesses had multiple days in their honor. So, for example, the calendar contains eleven festival days that involved the cult of the Egyptian god Isis.[32] Isis was neither native to the city of Rome nor among the most prominent goddesses in the Roman pantheon. This was a specialty cult from the provinces, but it still stood among the many, many others that claimed multiple spaces on the city's very full festal calendar.[33]

The large number of festivals and holidays did not mean, of course, that Romans spent half of the year on vacation or attending games. Many of these festivals were publicly funded, but participation in them was optional, and most people would have been too busy or disinterested to take part.[34] Festivals honoring gods and goddesses frequently filled all of one or more days. By the fourth century, some celebrations had even blended together to form long, multiday events with activities taking place both in the home and in public spaces.[35] Even those who attended part of the festivities need not have participated in all of them.[36] In traditional Roman religion, there was usually no problem with people using their time for something other than a religious festival.

The individuals who opted not to participate in a given festival could not expect to remain unaffected by it. The novelist Achilles Tatius, for example, describes what it was like to arrive in Alexandria during the celebration of a festival for the god Serapis. "It was," he writes, "the single greatest spectacle I have ever beheld. For it was late evening and the sun had gone down, but there was no sign of night—it was as though another sun had arisen, but one distributed into small parts in every direction."[37] This spectacle left the narrator so awestruck that he followed the procession until its end. For Alexandrians who chose not to participate, however, the Serapis parade represented a source of unwelcome but unavoidable traffic, noise, and light pollution. They could not escape it even if they wanted to do so.[38]

Smaller festivals also intruded on the peace and quiet of those who did not participate. In the second century, Apuleius provided an extensive account of an Isaic procession. As one would expect, the procession was heard long before it was seen.[39] When the parade came into view, costumed figures dressed as soldiers, huntsmen, philosophers, and magistrates led a motley crew of tamed bears, apes, shepherds, and women scattering flowers.[40] Apuleius then describes women who combed the hair of the goddess's statue while sprinkling the street with scented unguents. They were followed by a parade of people carrying lanterns and torches, musicians playing pipes and flutes, and a choir of young boys singing a song that explained the origins of the festival.[41] Linen-clad initiates followed the musicians, the priests who presided over the ceremony came next, and the procession concluded with people holding images of other gods. When the group reached the temple, the priests and initiates returned the divine images to their proper places. The priest said a prayer on behalf of the emperor, the senate, and Roman seamen, and then dismissed the congregation.

As Apuleius explains, Isaic celebrations were visually impressive, extremely loud, and very fragrant affairs. While only the devotees of the gods or goddesses being celebrated could take part in everything, many people throughout the city were involved in some aspects of the event—even if only to watch, march in one of the processions, or attend a related spectacle.[42] In the same way that temples and sacred images helped form the early fourth-century visual background of Roman life, these festivals provided some of the noise common to all Roman cities in the period.

Less well recognized is the degree to which traditional religion also provided some of the olfactory backdrop to Roman life. Apuleius mentions two different moments in the Isaic procession when the devotees spread pleasant smelling things in front of the crowd.[43] The significance of this can be lost on a modern audience, but such actions had a practical effect in antiquity. Between the smells of animal waste, trash, sewage, and general rot, the streets of an ancient city reeked unbearably.[44] Unguents, flowers, burning incense, and roasting meat formed important components of a traditional religious festival precisely because they stood out from the foul odors common to public spaces. When combined with the bright lights and cacophonous sounds of a procession, these fragrances helped to create a distinctive environment that indicated the special status of the god. But they were neither enclosed nor self-contained. The sights, sounds, and smells of traditional religion spilled freely out into cities and towns to be enjoyed or endured by devotees and nondevotees alike.[45]

While sacred processions tried to control the olfactory environment through which gods and their worshippers passed, they could have only modest success against a city's stench. People had far greater control over the smell of their homes. Romans felt that odors exercised incredible power. Foul air was thought to be a cause of disease, and odorous substances that masked it were used for pest control, fumigation, cleaning, and medicine.[46] Households took a range of steps to control bad smells and to replace them with more healthful and pleasant ones. Romans perfumed their baths and the walls of their homes, they wore fragrances on their bodies, they decorated the home with pleasant-smelling flowers and wreaths, and they burned incense to clean the air.[47] Most Roman households likely tried all of these remedies, but the ability to effectively control foul odors in the home came to be recognized as an indication of elite social status.[48] The large number of ingredients and the range of concoctions one could create from them made a full complement of aromatics quite expensive.[49]

The practical steps that later Romans took to control smells and cleanse the air of a house often mirrored those taken when they wished to honor the gods. While blood sacrifice occurred in the early fourth century, it was by no means the most popular way that people showed their devotion to traditional gods.[50] Furthermore, it would almost never have been part of a household routine.[51] Offerings of incense or fragrant cakes at temples would have been much more numerous than blood sacrifices (fig. 7), and they would have been far and away the most common way of showing reverence for the divine in a domestic setting.[52] Fragrant offerings in the home included incense burned before statues of gods, laurel wreaths and scented lamps placed at doorways, and altar tables that glowed with offerings during dinner parties.[53]

The "offering of incense" to the gods actually covers a wide range of substances and practices. In the second century, for example, worshippers of Isis and Osiris offered different types of aromatics to the gods depending on the time of day and air conditions. In the morning, "they burn resin on their altars, revivifying and purifying the air by its dissemination, and fanning into fresh life the languished spirit in the

FIGURE 7. Sacrificial scenes depicted on coins. From top, incense sacrifice (*RIC* IV.263, A.D. 218–20), sacrifice of an ox (Sear *RCV* 2000 #296, a *denarius* of 81 B.C.), and libation offering (*RIC* VI.35, A.D. 307–8). Courtesy of the author.

body."[54] In the middle of the day, "they burn myrrh on the altars; for the heat dissolves and scatters the murky and turgid elements in the surrounding atmosphere."[55] At night, they offered cyphi, which doubled as a sleep aid, because some of its ingredients "thrive in cold winds and shadows and dews and dampness."[56]

The home of a member of the Roman elite would contain a mix of smells. Many of these were simply pleasant or healthful, but some were connected to the worship of the gods. A visitor who smelled these things would not be able to decipher their source. For most Romans this would not have mattered very much. Beginning in the third century, however, some Christian authors started to express concern about how Christians should situate themselves in such an environment. Clement of Alexandria expressed a general suspicion about the soul being carried away by pleasant odors. He called for Christians to smell "not of perfume but of perfection," while acknowledging that aromatic products could still be used because they were essential for health and hygiene.[57] The North African Tertullian took a stronger view, criticizing the prevalence of wreaths and flowers that could lead Christians astray.[58] He even argued against mixed marriages involving pagans and Christians because they would subject the spouse to the smell of burning offerings given to the gods.[59] Those odors were a part of life, and avoidance, while ideal, was often impractical. For most Christians, this avoidance was not even desirable.[60] They lived in a world where the structures, sights, sounds, and smells of the gods were everywhere—just as they had been for millennia.

THE CHILDHOOD OF THE FINAL PAGAN GENERATION

Members of the final pagan generation spent their childhoods learning to navigate this world. Their childhoods differed from those of people in the modern West in very significant ways. Bearing and raising children were dangerous, difficult, and emotionally fraught activities in antiquity. The Roman world saw ghastly rates of death in childbirth; current estimates suggest that a Roman woman had a 17/1000 chance of dying each time she gave birth.[61] Despite this, women were expected to have many children. A woman who lived until age fifty would likely give birth to six children in her life, two or three of whom might live into adulthood.[62] Childbirth presented a major danger, but the simple reality of life in a major urban center posed even more significant health risks. Most of the Roman elite spent at least some of their time in cities. Roman cities, like all premodern urban areas, were death centers that never came close to sustaining their populations. Some estimates suggest that the average Roman city may have lost nearly 3 percent of its people each year and required constant immigration from the countryside just to keep its population stable.[63] Overcrowding and terrible sanitation created a perfect storm in which contagious diseases (like cholera and tuberculosis) that thrive in highly concentrated populations competed as killers with water and food-borne pathogens.[64] The elite generally could flee the cities for rural estates during the times of year when regular disease outbreaks could be expected or when unexpected pandemics broke out, but they remained susceptible to random (sometimes fatal) illnesses that could arise at any time.[65] To this one must also add the very real risk of accidents that could be immediately fatal or could lead to death if the injuries they caused became infected.[66]

These high rates of mortality meant that the modern ideal of a nuclear family did not reflect the realities of Roman domestic life.[67] Composite families were instead the norm. First marriages typically joined a woman in her teens to a man in his late twenties and lasted for about fourteen years.[68] Many widowers remarried, and it was assumed that children of both marriages would live together in the father's home and be brought up as part of one family unit with him at its head.[69] Even so, child rearing remained extremely difficult. When a baby was born in antiquity, there was a strong chance that it would not live a week. Babies were not usually given names until they reached that milestone.[70] Once a baby was named, it then had to be registered with the Roman state within thirty days.[71] Even if a baby passed this second milestone, there remained a real likelihood that he or she would not make it to adulthood.

Ausonius's *Parentalia* shows that these demographic realities were not mere abstractions. The *Parentalia* provides short, individualized poems that celebrate the lives of thirty-one deceased relations.[72] A number of these highly stylized poems describe the unexpected or premature deaths of Ausonius's family members that occurred when he was young. Two in particular commemorate siblings who died prematurely. The twenty-ninth poem of the group commemorated his sister Aemilia Melania with whom he "shared one cradle when we were infants of almost one age" before she died in infancy.[73] His younger brother Avitianus also died young, in his case "without enjoying the pleasurable flower of youth or passing the bounds which mark the end of boyhood."[74]

We can perhaps identify with the emotions that Ausonius evokes in these poems, but the attachments family members had to one another developed in ways that often differed significantly from what one sees in the modern West. In most elite households (and possibly most Roman households generally), the care of new children was outsourced to wet nurses.[75] In some ways, the selection of a wet nurse resembled the process today of selecting a nanny. The ideal wet nurse was supposed to be a young, chaste, abstemious, and healthy mother who had given birth a number of times.[76] Since she would be the one speaking the most to the child, she should be relatively eloquent, and, in the West, able to converse in both Greek and Latin.[77] She also needed to be patient. The child spent most of the first months of its life tightly swaddled, sometimes in a dark room.[78] The wet nurse often lived with the family and nursed the child until age two or three.[79] As the child grew, the wet nurse became responsible for more than just the child's feeding. There were no bedrooms for children and no specified play areas; they seem to have slept in the servants quarters alongside their wet nurses.[80] Wet nurses were expected to comfort the children, cradle them, and play with them. They also were the main disciplinarians, though they were expected to balance stern punishments with calming techniques. Whippings for misbehavior were sometimes followed by a comforting story or song.[81]

As one can imagine, wet nurses and their charges often developed very close bonds. The special relationship between them was legally recognized. The wet nurse was the only nonfamily member legally permitted to file charges of untrustworthiness against the guardian of a minor. Wet nurses were also the only slaves that a slave owner who had not yet reached the age of twenty was legally permitted to manumit.[82] Babies fed by wet nurses could be quite generous to them later in life. The Roman senator Pliny gave his wet nurse a farm, and there are many examples of epitaphs written for wet nurses by the grown-up infants for whom they once cared.[83] The wet nurses often seem to have reciprocated. So great was the devotion shown to the emperors Nero and Domitian by their wet nurses that it was only through their intervention that the disgraced emperors received proper funerals.[84]

Once a male child reached the age of six or seven, he transitioned from the wet nurse to another surrogate caretaker, the pedagogue. The pedagogue was a male attendant (often but not always a slave) who initially tutored the child in language and moral conduct. As the student got older and moved from rudimentary instruction in letters to grammar and rhetoric, the pedagogue also played a role in choosing which teachers the student would patronize.[85] Once the child began school, the pedagogue walked him to class, pushed him to focus on his studies, and tried to discourage misbehavior.[86] Libanius describes pedagogues as the ones who gave young men "the compulsion required by study and, far more important, the habit of self-control."[87] They also served as "the guardians of youth in its flower, its protections, and its defense; they repel unsavory admirers, send them packing, and keep them at a distance."[88] In times of illness, Libanius continues, "they either vie with the mothers or outdo them . . . for the attendants (pedagogues) sit at the bedside (and) give the patients what they need."[89]

The pedagogue's main job, however, was to ensure that the boy under his care did well academically. To this end, "the attendant brings himself and the lad to the light of the lamp, and first of all, wakes himself up, and then goes to the boy and outdoes the crowing roosters, for he rouses him with his hand."[90] He also took it on himself to make sure that the student remembered what was taught in class that day. The method, Libanius says, "is for the attendant to apply pressure, shout at them, produce the cane and wield the strap, and drive the lesson into their memories."[91] As Libanius indicates, the discipline a pedagogue meted out could range from verbal commands all the way up to beatings.[92]

Most of the time, the relationship between pedagogues and their charges was a good one. Libanius mentions a case where a father died and the pedagogue "became the rightful guardian to the boy," and other cases where the pedagogue regularly visited the tombs of charges who had died.[93] These feelings were often reciprocated. The emperor Augustus honored his pedagogue with a public funeral, Nero awarded public positions to his pedagogue, and the *Digest* of Roman law compiled under the emperor Justinian mentions a case where a pedagogue received a substantial inheritance.[94]

This was not always the case, however. The pedagogue tended to have a less nurturing personality than a wet nurse, and when this was combined with the fact that he handled adolescents instead of infants, his charges occasionally rebelled in ways that younger children could not. Sometimes this took the form of passive resistance to the pedagogue's calls to study. Augustine mentions a pedagogue who shouted for his charge to stop playing in the mud and start studying only to see the young man turn his head and ignore him.[95] Sometimes the resistance could take a more serious turn. Libanius, in a speech written in 390, writes about a pedagogue being "carpeted" by his students. This involved taking the man, placing him in a carpet, and using it to throw him up in the air repeatedly. Not surprisingly, the pedagogue eventually fell off the carpet and sustained serious injuries.[96] Libanius's reaction to the situation suggests that it was not unprecedented, but it was certainly not representative of the way that most pedagogues were treated either.

While pedagogues and wet nurses had specific roles to play at particular moments in a child's life, extended family played active roles in the acculturation and education of elite children throughout their lives. Ausonius makes plain in his *Parentalia* that his maternal uncle and grandmother played extremely influential roles in his upbringing. Ausonius saw his uncle Aemilius Magnus Arborius as a second father.[97] He writes that Arborius was "as my father and mother, who in my infancy, boyhood, youth, and manhood instructed me in the arts which it is a delight to have learned."[98] Ausonius felt a different sort of affection for his grandmother, Aemilia Corinthia Maura. She was called Maura because of her dark complexion and was a stern woman "not ready to overlook shameful indulgences."[99] While Ausonius certainly did not enjoy his interaction with Aemilia Maura in quite the same way as his experiences with Arborius, he definitely saw his relationship with his grandmother as a meaningful and important part of his life.

At the same time, the affection for Arborius and Maura that Ausonius expresses in *Parentalia* 3 contrasts strongly with the dry and unemotional profiles of Ausonius's parents in *Parentalia* 1 and 2. He comments about the medical skill and the long life of his father and describes his mother, Aemilia Aeonia, as chaste, sober, and with "hands busy spinning wool."[100] Combined, these two poems take up less space than that devoted to Arborius alone. This does not suggest that Ausonius did not love or respect his parents. It is quite clear that he felt the dutiful respect a son was expected to show toward his parents—and he may have felt far more genuine affection for them than these texts imply.[101] While parents exercised important influences on children, the extended family would often have been at least as important in framing children's understanding of the world around them.

LEARNING TO LIVE IN THE CITIES OF THE GODS

Young children began to learn how to interact with the divine almost immediately. Families held a naming ceremony on either the eighth or ninth day after a child's birth.[102] The ceremony included sacrifices, a procession around the home, two different moments in which family members used a broom to clear the home of evil spirits, and a sequence of other rituals that culminated in a banquet.[103] This was such a crucial rite of passage that even touchy Christians like Tertullian saw it as essential.[104]

Tertullian was less forgiving of Christian participation in annual holidays that celebrated domestic and family relationships. Here he was in a distinct minority, probably even among Christians.[105] Children would have grown up observing these important and regular commemorations of family life.[106] The Roman Parentalia, for example, spanned nine days and involved a public sacrifice by the Vestal Virgins as well as family activities that showed *pietas* (like traveling to a necropolis to offer dead ancestors tiles covered in wreaths and corn sprinkled with salt).[107] Almost immediately following the conclusion of the Parentalia in the festival calendar was the Caristia, another festival that involved the family honoring its gods collectively. Ovid makes clear that the Caristia shifted activities from the tombs back to the homes and involved giving the family gods incense and plates of food.[108] A family banquet would then follow, to which all family members (and even some nonfamily members) were invited.[109]

These festivals and family celebrations linked a young Roman's regular veneration of the gods to the rhythms of the year. They signified membership in the family, loyalty to its particular hierarchy, and the evolution of a child's role within it. In these contexts children would learn what to do by observing how others behaved. Young children likely did not think very much about why a ritual was done in a specific way or what particular meaning was attached to it. These were simply regular adult behaviors that members of their family exhibited. Pagans and Christians who grew up in these households would have seen participation in the meals, processions, and rituals associated with a holiday as perfectly normal behavior. The Christian Ausonius, for example, prefaces his *Parentalia* by linking it to the "solemn day so called in ancient times that was appointed as long ago as the time of Numa for offerings to departed relatives."[110] He knew the holiday and seems to have understood it as a celebration that had familial but not confessional meaning.

The stories told by wet nurses and the early instruction that children received under the supervision of pedagogues similarly helped children learn about the gods. As we saw above, wet nurses were known for the stories that they told to calm children and control their behavior. Some authors thought that these tales caused children to become infatuated with undesirable things like chariot racing,[111] but the geographer Strabo writes that these stories could create a living awareness of the gods that could regulate children's behavior.[112] The pedagogue further expanded this knowledge. The beginning stages of literary education explained how honors for the gods fit into one's daily routine and helped to determine the rhythms of the year. One of the most common exercises that students saw in school encouraged them to practice their writing by going through an account of daily activities. These colloquia often formed part of larger collections of *hermeneumata,* schoolbooks that could also contain dictionaries (organized both alphabetically and topically) as well as short texts.[113] The works are, in the words of a modern editor, "thoroughly pagan," with the gods, sacred buildings (*de aedibus sacris*), sacrifices (*de sacrificiis*), festival days (*de diebus festis*), and pagan priesthoods (under the heading *de magistribus*) all featured.[114]

An exercise contained in one of the most extensive such manuscripts can give a sense of how such texts worked. After a short preface explaining that the text will describe things essential for the appropriate behavior of boys and girls, the exercise outlines an elite child's typical day. It begins with a summons for the nurse to wake the child up before daybreak, call the slave to get his clothes, and help him dress.[115] He was then to be washed so that he could "go out in public to school."[116] The next step was for "us to worship all the gods and ask them to grant a good path through and success during the entire day."[117] The young man left the house for school with his pedagogue and greeted his parents, relatives, and the household staff as he passed them on his way out the door. The student then went to school, greeted his teacher and friends, and did classwork.[118] He came home for lunch, observed the preparations for dinner, headed to the baths, and then got ready for bed.[119]

These exercises outline the daily life of young people in the later Roman Empire, but for our purposes it is important to recognize how casually the *Hermeneumata* present the young person's interaction with the divine. The prayers to "all the gods" are just one mundane aspect of a typical day. It was expected that a boy would offer them routinely in much the same way that he gave regular orders to his nurse, spoke with his pedagogue, or socialized with his friends. By the 370s, however, Ausonius felt strongly enough about the subtle effects of these aspects of the *Hermeneumata* that he penned the *Ephemeris,* his own, Christian adaptation of these colloquia.[120] The *Ephemeris* follows the same basic pattern as the *Hermeneumata* described above except that it "does not call for incense to be burnt nor for any slice of honey-cake." Instead, Ausonius forcefully says, "I must pray to God and the son of God most high, co-equal."[121] The *Ephemeris,* however, is a later work written after the emperor Julian's attempt to make education serve as a tool to promote traditional religious identification.[122] While it does show that Ausonius later appreciated the potential implications of including elements of traditional religion in school exercises designed for young children, there is no evidence that he or his peers thought much about these things as children in the 310s and early 320s.

Children had a similar attitude toward teaching about the festival calendar. Students were required to memorize the calendar, but some later Romans thought that any educated person needed a fuller knowledge of festivals and their origins than a simple list would provide. In the early fifth century, the Christian Macrobius composed the *Saturnalia,* a fictional dialogue set in the home of Praetextatus that discussed traditional religion, its festivals and holidays, and their characteristics.[123] Macrobius aimed for the text to serve as a repository of knowledge that could teach and guide his son. It would be, he felt, "a pleasure to read, an education to have read, and of use to remember" because "everything in it is calculated to quicken your understanding, strengthen your memory, to give more dexterity to your discourse, and make your speech more correct."[124] Macrobius was not alone in thinking that knowledge of traditional religion and its festivals helped mark one as cultured. The pagan senator Symmachus, writing in 395, impatiently informs his brother that he should stop reminding him of religious obligations because, as his brother surely knew, Symmachus is "knowledgeable concerning the ceremonies of the gods and festivities of the divinity that have been commanded."[125] Symmachus could respond in this way because, as the Christian Macrobius suggests, the education of elite men and women ensured that they would know about the dates, origins, and customs of festivals and holidays. If they did not, this reflected their lack of cultivation more than their lack of piety.

. . .

The final pagan generation was born into a world that contained a vast sacred infrastructure that had been built up over the past three millennia. The size, age, and pervasiveness of this infrastructure likely would have made it difficult for anyone to appreciate fully all of the ways in which traditional religious practice influenced the rhythms of public, domestic, and family life. Children needed to learn how this world functioned and what parts of it merited their attention. The authoritative figures with whom they interacted early in life helped provide that instruction. These figures modeled religious behaviors by performing rituals and attending festivals. They told stories that informed a child's understanding of the sacred world, and they encouraged children to regularly honor the divine. Many of these behaviors involved religious activities, but their meaning was often much more complicated. The Parentalia, for example, honored the family dead at a time of the year when many people were sick and dying.[126] The sacrifices and prayers were part of an activity that celebrated the living family and its obligation to its deceased members. In cases like this, the lines between "idolatry" and normal participation in family and community life could be difficult for even adults to see.

Writing nearly a lifetime before the final pagan generation was born, the Christian author Tertullian acknowledged this difficulty. His *On Idolatry* (*De idolatria*) tried to show Christians how to recognize the traditional religious elements in daily life and separate them from normal social, commercial, and familial activities. Idolatry, he claims, is "a crime so widespread, . . . [that] it subverts the servants of God."[127] While most people simply "regard idolatry as interpreted by the senses alone, as for example, if one burns incense," Tertullian warns that Christians must be "fore-fortified against the abundance of idolatry" and not just its obvious manifestations.[128] He then walks the readers through all of the unnoticed places where idolatry exists. He points to those who make and sell idols, the astrologers and teachers who practice in the presence of idols, and the other trades that tainted Christians by bringing them into contact with idols.[129] Tertullian then considers the various aspects of daily life that one must avoid in order not to be tainted by "idolatry." This comprehensive list includes festivals and holidays, military service, the swearing of oaths, the acceptance of blessings in the name of the gods, and even certain types of clothing.[130]

At the center of the work, however, Tertullian pauses to try to answer an interesting rhetorical question. If all of this is prohibited, he asks, "How is one to live?"[131] Tertullian evidently struggled to find an answer. He initially ducks the question and returns to it only in his conclusion. Then he states, "Nothing can be easier than caution against idolatry, if the fear of it be our leading fear; any necessity whatever is too trifling compared to such a peril."[132] He is, of course, exaggerating. In truth, Tertullian's text shows just how daunting a prospect it was to try to disentangle one's daily activities from the gods and their presence. He wrote in order to point out all the places where the gods lurked because most people, both pagan and Christian, likely did not notice them. Their children and grandchildren would not either. This was simply a natural consequence of growing up in a world that was full of gods, had always been full of gods, and always would be full of gods, at least as far as anyone could tell in 310.

CHAPTER 2

Education in an Age
of Imagination

By the mid-320s, all but the youngest members of the final pagan generation had begun their formal education outside of the home. The biggest step involved the transition from the elementary instruction provided by a pedagogue and a teacher of letters to the training offered by grammarians and rhetoricians. While elementary education taught basic skills like reading and writing, the move to study under a grammarian began in earnest the process of teaching young men how members of the Roman elite talked and behaved. Although fundamentally literary in character, later Roman education did as much to socialize students as it did to familiarize them with the works of a classical canon. Students learned about, commented on, and practiced the behaviors that marked one as a member of polite society.[1] Their teachers went to great pains to outline for them how they should treat other men and what role they ought to play in their home cities.[2] The nature of this teaching changed slowly because it created and sustained the reciprocal relationships essential to the functioning of an elite social system that had existed for centuries.

When students attended schools, they immersed themselves in a world of young people governed by a unique, seemingly timeless, set of ideals and codes of conduct that differed in significant ways from those of the wider world. The intense social experience of learning in a late antique school also kept students somewhat insulated from the changes gripping the society around them. This is particularly important because the time that Libanius, Themistius, Ausonius, and Praetextatus spent studying grammar and rhetoric overlapped exactly with one of the most important periods of transition in the history of the empire. In 324, the emperor Constantine, who had converted to Christianity in 312, defeated the Eastern emperor Licinius in a naval battle near the city of Byzantium and in a land battle at Chrysopolis in Asia Minor. He then took sole control of the entire Roman Empire. For the next thirteen years, he worked to increase the prominence and influence of Christianity in the empire. There was no plan for how this would be done and, aside from the promotion of Christianity, no clearly defined objective. While some Christians clearly appreciated what Constantine was trying to do, those Christians and pagans who paid less attention to the nuances of his policies would not have been overly concerned. Enveloped in their scholarly bubbles, the final pagan generation surely fit into this second category of Romans.

This chapter will do two things. First it will examine the process by which Constantine and those around him imagined and began to build a Christian empire. Second, it will consider the experience of being a student in the mid-320s and early 330s and the degree to which members of the final pagan generation seem to have been paying attention to the pro-Christian policies and actions of Constantine. In the end, it will become apparent that many of these young men were so preoccupied with their own lives that they seem not to have thought about Constantine's religious policies very much.

IMAGINING A CHRISTIAN EMPIRE

In the twenty-first century it is deceptively easy to think that Rome's move from a pagan empire to a state in which Christianity played the dominant role followed a clear and well-defined path.[3] In truth, in the early fourth century it was as easy to conceive of a Christian Roman Empire as it was to imagine a Roman imperial rail network. Both of these things are, after all, the products of innovative technologies imagined by bright thinkers and implemented over time by a determined, capable, and sophisticated political and social system. Though Christianity's eventual dominance of the Roman state is often seen as a natural outcome of the religion's steady growth, its triumph over traditional religion represents an extremely difficult intellectual, political, and social achievement that was by no means inevitable.

Two related tendencies among Christians who had become accustomed to living for three centuries in a hostile Roman world made the triumph of Christianity particularly challenging. During that time, selected Christians faced prosecution and death because of their failure to participate in traditional Roman sacrifices. More would be caught in 250 when the emperor Decius issued an edict requiring every person in the empire to offer a public sacrifice to the gods. Even this produced relatively few victims.[4] As Éric Rebillard has recently shown, most Christians would likely have obeyed the emperor's order without seeing a particular conflict between compliance and their Christian identity.[5] The minority of Christians who refused to perform the one sacrifice required of all residents of the empire would now be recognized, but their continued absence from all other traditional religious activities would remain unremarkable.

Persecution was by no means the average Christian experience, however. As the previous chapter showed, the cities of the Roman world were diverse religious marketplaces and the absence of an individual or individual family from civic religious activity was seldom noticed. Some Christians took advantage of this by quietly absenting themselves from the processions and sacrifices that conflicted with their beliefs. Many more of them continued to regularly participate. But the sporadic participation of Christians in traditional religious activities did not make them particularly conspicuous. Many people, both Christian and pagan, skipped the religious festivals and public sacrifices that crowded the calendar, for a range of reasons. Libanius, for example, once required his students to skip a festival for Artemis because their declamations needed work.[6] Christianity then represented but one of an infinite number of possible explanations for one's absence.

When Roman persecution of Christians ended in the 310s, these long-standing Christian patterns of silent disengagement from traditional religious life did not immediately disappear. Some of this was likely force of habit, but this Christian reticence also had a deeper cause. The centuries of intermittent persecution and de facto toleration had enabled Christians to imagine a world that tolerated Christianity and chose not to persecute it.[7] But they never saw this as anything more than a midpoint in the process through which a Christian future would emerge. Roman Christians instead imagined themselves waiting patiently for the moment when the tangible reality of Roman rule would one day be superseded by a "heavenly and angelic empire" governed by Christ.[8] This focus on a process of development through which the earthly empire of Rome would ultimately give way to a heavenly empire of Christ made it extremely difficult for Roman Christians to imagine a

Roman world dominated by Christianity. It also made them hesitant to venture confidently out into the licit religious marketplace with a plan to enhance Christianity's visible presence and social standing. It is not surprising, then, that no such plan existed when Christianity found an imperial champion in the emperor Constantine.[9]

Neither Constantine's triumph nor his embrace of Christianity would have been thought likely in the first years of the fourth century. Constantine had taken power in somewhat dubious fashion following the death of his father in York in 306.[10] The empire at that time was still administered according to the emperor Diocletian's tetrarchic system. Its leadership consisted of two junior Caesars and two more senior Augusti, all governing the empire collaboratively. When Constantius died, however, his army proclaimed Constantine Augustus without consulting any of the three other members of the imperial college.[11] Constantine quickly traveled from Britain to his father's old capital at Trier, and, from this position of strength, he came to an agreement with his father's colleagues that secured their recognition of his authority in exchange for his acceptance of the junior rank of Caesar.[12]

Constantine's promotion prompted a reaction from Maxentius, a son of the retired tetrarch Maximian, who had also once been advanced as a possible future member of the imperial college.[13] Capitalizing on the close relationships he enjoyed with the army once commanded by his father, Maxentius had himself proclaimed emperor in October 306.[14] In 307, he secured his position by defeating two separate invasions led by the Augusti Severus and Galerius. Each victory followed a similar script. Maxentius fortified the city of Rome and blunted the numerical advantage each opponent held by causing the defections of significant numbers of their troops. By the end of 307, he had captured, imprisoned, and ultimately killed Severus and forced the ignoble retreat of Galerius.[15] While his position was never entirely secure, his victories enabled him to establish firm control over Italy and gave him space to fortify it against further invasion.[16]

Maxentius's victories over Severus and Galerius revealed to Constantine that the tetrarchic system was teetering. By the early 310s, Constantine began to sense that his future success lay in expansion into the territory controlled by Maxentius.[17] While his early coins and propaganda displayed Constantine's place in the tetrarchic college and his physical similarity to his colleagues, those from the mid-310s instead emphasized his individual qualities, often to an absurd degree (see fig. 8).[18] A panegyric delivered in Gaul in 310 even presented to its audience a ficti-

FIGURE 8. Evolution of Constantinian portraiture. From top, coin of 313 (*RIC* VII.5 Siscia), 317 (*RIC* VII.132 Trier), and 325–26 (*RIC* VII.34 Cyzicus). Courtesy of the author.

tious genealogy that tied Constantine to the popular later third-century emperor Claudius Gothicus, a laughable idea that Constantine's court seems nevertheless to have encouraged.[19] Even though Constantine was clearly developing a unique personal profile that could serve to define him in a post-tetrarchic world, he still refrained from breaking openly with his tetrarchic colleagues.

In the spring of 312, Constantine shrewdly made his play by leading an army of approximately forty thousand men into Italy to attack Maxentius.[20] This reflected Constantine's particular political genius. The attack on Maxentius, who had not received official recognition by the remaining tetrarchs, allowed Constantine to seize additional territory while still maintaining the pretense that he remained a loyal member of the imperial college. But Constantine was not the only member of the college who eyed Maxentius's territories. Constantine's move came while Licinius, the recently appointed Augustus of the East, was planning his own invasion of Italy, an invasion that would have confined Constantine to the empire's far western corner had it succeeded.[21] The Christian historian Eusebius would later describe Constantine's invasion as one designed to avenge the defeats Maxentius had inflicted on other legitimate emperors.[22] Revenge served as a convenient pretense, but the desire for the particular security that greater territory could provide in future civil wars certainly motivated Constantine far more.

Constantine's attack represented a calculated gamble. He knew that Maxentius had managed to turn back two invasions by larger, better supplied imperial armies in 307, and that Maxentius had further strengthened his defenses over the past five years.[23] Maxentius was less popular in 312 than he had been in 307, but he remained a formidable foe.[24] Constantine was further disadvantaged by the fact that, unlike Severus and Galerius, he would be leading a numerically inferior force against Maxentius.[25] Additionally, Constantine had to advance on Maxentius through cities of northern Italy in which Maxentius had a substantial troop presence.[26] The bishop Eusebius's narrative of the campaign dramatizes the perfectly plausible scene in which the emperor reflected on the numerical and tactical challenges he faced. This convinced the emperor that "he needed some more powerful aid than his military forces could afford him . . . he sought divine assistance . . . believing that the co-operating power of an invincible Deity could not be shaken."[27] Constantine famously then came to the conclusion that he would prevail if his troops fought under a Christian sign, possibly because of a vision that caused him to find new meaning in a glimpse of a solar halo that he once had seen.[28] He followed this suggestion and "made a likeness of that sign which he had seen . . . to use it as a safeguard in all engagements with his enemies."[29]

It is impossible to say when Constantine's armies first marched under this sign, but it probably occurred during the Italian campaign or even before he crossed the Alps.[30] With the confidence of this divine protection, Constantine advanced efficiently into northern Italy. His forces seized the garrison city of Segusio, secured the surrender of Turin, and ultimately defeated Maxentius's main army outside the city of Verona.[31] He then moved slowly and deliberately toward Rome, the seat of Maxentius's power. Hoping to repeat the successes he had against Severus and Galerius, Maxentius cut the bridges to the city and filled it with supplies in case the capital was again besieged.[32]

On October 28, however, Maxentius made a strange decision. He ordered his forces to march out of Rome and meet those of Constantine on a field north of the city. They were put to flight, retreated to the Tiber, and, in the chaos, Maxentius fell into the river and drowned.[33] Maxentius's attack across the Tiber clearly baffled his contemporaries, some of whom tried to explain it as the result of divine action or misguided soothsaying.[34] For Constantine, though, Maxentius's bizarre behavior capped a campaign against a well-entrenched usurper that succeeded because of his prayers to the Christian God. From this point forward, if Eusebius is to be believed, Constantine was a Christian.[35]

If one reads a Christian narration of Constantine's reign, pro-Christian policies become apparent almost immediately after his victory over Maxentius. After arranging the marriage of his sister to Licinius, the member of the imperial college whose invasion of Italy Constantine's victory has forestalled, Constantine and his new brother-in-law reached an agreement to "grant to the Christians and others full authority to observe that religion which each preferred."[36] They also mandated the return of Christian communal property that had been seized by imperial authorities over the past decade. This was a law that, at least initially, both Constantine and Licinius supported so strongly that, in Eusebius's telling, it became part of the rationale for the war the two waged against Maximinus Daia, the third remaining member of the imperial college.[37]

For Christians who had lived through the horrors of the great persecution, this state of affairs was almost unbelievable. They had long hoped for this sort of explicit imperial support for Christianity—but they had not really ever expected it. The emperors' actions left Eusebius feeling so exuberant that he updated his *Ecclesiastical History* with a ninth book discussing the war fought by Constantine and Licinius against Maximinus.[38] He concluded the book with the following statement: "The impious ones having been thus removed, the government was preserved firm and undisputed for Constantine and Licinius, to whom it fittingly belonged. They, having first of all cleansed the world of hostility to the Divine Being ... showed their love of virtue and of God and their piety and gratitude to the Deity, by their ordinance on behalf of the Christians."[39]

While Christians saw the imperial support lent by Constantine (and Licinius who, in Eusebius's words, "had not yet become insane") as the end point of a long narrative of imperial persecution, Romans unfamiliar with this Christian view of the world would have seen nothing particularly revolutionary about this type of imperial action. Licinius and Constantine's so-called Edict of Milan in some ways just expanded on an edict of toleration issued in 311 by Galerius.[40] While Constantine was a Christian, Licinius remained devoted to the traditional gods, and Galerius had such suspicions toward Christianity that he had pushed hard for the initiation of the persecution in 303. Toleration was a policy that could be endorsed regardless of one's confession, and, for most Romans, the suspension of the persecution would be understood as the conclusion of a failed imperial initiative. Only certain Christians likely viewed it as the beginning a new religious order.[41]

The later 310s and early 320s saw Constantine continue to occupy a unique position where Christians understood him to be a transformative religious figure, while most non-Christians saw nothing threatening in his behavior. Constantine deftly mixed policies and propaganda in order to appeal to both groups.[42] Christians could see unprecedented concern for their community in his deployment of imperial resources to try to resolve an episcopal succession issue in the North African church.[43] Non-Christians, however, could look at Constantinian coinage from the period and see Sol Invictus, the sun god who had once graced the coins of Maximinus, still depicted on the reverse (see fig. 9).[44] Constantine had good reason to behave this way. His alliance with Licinius had quickly frayed after the defeat of Maximinus and the dozen years between 312 and 324 saw the two emperors engage in on-again, off-again warfare. As long as Constantine had a non-Christian rival, he had to be careful not to antagonize the large majority of non-Christians over whom he ruled. This changed, however, when he defeated and executed Licinius in September 324.[45] From that point forward, Constantine ruled without a pagan rival.[46]

FIGURE 9. Sol Invictus on a coin of Constantine from 317 (left, *RIC* VII.132 Trier) and a similar portrait on a coin of Maximinus Daia from 312 (right, *RIC* VI.167b Antioch). Courtesy of the author.

Eusebius's *Ecclesiastical History* shows that the years bracketing Constantine's victory over Licinius saw Christians begin to imagine a Roman world that not only tolerated Christianity but even welcomed its widespread physical and social presence.[47] Constantine himself apparently endorsed this goal and tried to further it through a series of legislative and administrative measures.[48] Some of these explicitly favored Christianity. Constantine exempted Christian clergy from financial obligations to city councils,[49] he supplied Christian bishops with large amounts of money and goods that they could use to support their congregations,[50] he paid for the construction of new churches, and he gave bishops a form of judicial power that they could use to manumit slaves and resolve legal disputes within their communities.[51]

Offering privileges to Christians and support for the church represented only part of the struggle, however. The emperor and his advisers also began to think that the de-paganization of the empire formed an essential part of its Christianization. A Roman state in which Christianity assumed a legitimate visibility while one waited on the emergence of a divine empire was no longer enough. Instead, the empire of this world could become more Christian—but only if it simultaneously became less pagan. This was no easy task. Even if one ignored the political challenges associated with directing anti-pagan activity in an empire that was perhaps 80 or 85 percent pagan, the suppression of the non-Christian elements of Roman society was extremely difficult, energy intensive, time consuming, and expensive.[52] Christians then faced practical limits on how much de-paganization could really be done. They not only had to imagine what a new religious order could be like, but they had to decide what pagan elements of the Roman world could, if necessary, be allowed to remain. They then needed to come up with policies that might further these goals.

Eusebius's *Life of Constantine,* a work written soon after Constantine's death, provides a rough sketch of what some Christians seem to have decided.[53] In it, Eusebius discusses a *nomos* (literally, a law) issued immediately after Constantine took control of the Eastern half of the empire in 324. This *nomos* forbade provincial governors and their superiors from offering sacrifice.[54] Eusebius then continues by stating, "Soon after this, two laws were promulgated about the same time; one of which was intended to restrain the idolatrous abominations which in time past had been practiced in every city and country." Eusebius explains that it also required that "no one should erect images, or practice divination and other false and foolish arts, or offer sacrifice in any way."[55] A second law was connected to this and ordered officials to build churches according to specified dimensions, "as though it were expected that, now that the madness of polytheism was wholly removed, pretty nearly all mankind would henceforth attach themselves to the service of God."[56]

The model of de-paganization that Eusebius here describes is rather roughly sketched, but it did have an underlying rationale. Eusebius drew on two strands of thought. The first was the long-standing Christian abhorrence of sacrifice, a view laid out in depth by numerous second- and third-century Christian authors.[57] The second strand was far older and evoked the only case Eusebius knew about in which a religious group claimed to have successfully suppressed an established traditional religion. This was the account of the Israelite conquest of Canaan in Deuteronomy, a story in which God commanded his people to "demolish completely all the places where the nations whom you are about to dispossess served their gods."[58] Eusebius imagined that Roman paganism would die away in the same way that traditional Canaanite religion did if sacrifice was restricted, temples torn down, and the emperor readied churches for the new Christians his policies would create. A Christian empire filled with churches and believing congregations would naturally emerge, but only as a result of Roman de-paganization.

This policy proved far easier to articulate than it was to implement. The Roman legal system in the imperial period depended on a dialogue between ruler and ruled in which the sovereign and his advisers primarily offered legal remedies to local challenges and conditions.[59] Legal initiatives either originated with the emperor's own inspiration (*spontaneus motus*) or, much more frequently, as a response to some situation that a prefect or a bishop had brought to the emperor's attention.[60] The situation and proposed remedy were then discussed within the imperial consistory, a body of advisers that included praetorian prefects, the master of the offices (the *magister officiorum),* the head of the palace administration, the two counts of the treasuries, the person responsible for drafting the texts of laws (the imperial *quaestor*), and a number of counts of the consistory.[61] The consistory first considered the matters brought to its attention. If it agreed that a legal remedy was necessary, it asked the imperial *quaestor* to draft a law. The consistory then discussed the text of the law before passing it along to the emperor for his signature. Once the law was issued, it was passed along to praetorian prefects and, eventually, to provincial governors so that they could disseminate it and implement it in ways appropriate to local conditions.[62]

The system, of course, offered ample scope for policy initiatives undertaken by emperors, but these were implemented across the empire only to the degree that elite opinions and local conditions permitted. Emperors needed to move slowly and consider carefully how many significant changes in their daily lives their subjects could tolerate. There were considerable checks built in to control this process. The consistory was designed to produce frank discussions of these laws that guarded against imperial caprice and prevented the implementation of policies that would prove too disruptive. This usually worked, and when it did not, elites in the consistory or senate could often convince the emperor to moderate laws.[63] Prefects and local governors could also selectively implement laws either by silently ignoring them (an all-too common aspect of Roman administration) or by providing locally tailored implementation instructions.[64] The most effective emperors charted new social directions not by using coercion but by communicating their preferences and creating legal mechanisms that could advance their goals without prompting resistance. The laws that emperors issued and the way in which they communicated their preferences then reveal both what policy objectives emperors desired and the degree to which they thought society was prepared to accept those policies.

Constantine's policies related to traditional religion show that the emperor understood this dynamic. The *Life of Constantine*, which here treads a careful line between a retrospective description of Constantine's actions and a prescriptive treatise laying out the actions expected of an ideal Christian sovereign, speaks about "successive laws (*nomoi*) and ordinances (*diataxeis*)" that forbade everyone "to sacrifice to idols, dabble in divination, have cult statues erected, conduct secret rites, or to pollute cities with gladiatorial games."[65] Eusebius records that Constantine removed "the venerable statues of brass" from pagan temples so that they could be "exposed to view in all of the public places of the imperial city [Constantinople]."[66] He describes the confiscation of some temple doors, roofs, and statues made of precious metal to help fund the construction of the capital.[67] Eusebius also notes that he ordered the destruction of four temples, three devoted to the goddess Aphrodite and one to Asclepius. One of the temples of Aphrodite was located on the supposed site of Christ's resurrection. It was replaced by a church. Two others dedicated to Aphrodite were centers of ritualized prostitution, a practice that the emperor deemed "unlawful commerce of women and adulterous intercourse."[68] Only the fourth of these, a temple of Asclepius in the city of Aegeae, was closed without obvious reason.[69]

Eusebius claims that the removal of statues, the destruction of temples, and restrictions on sacrifice were all legally sanctioned by the emperor. This, then, seems to be the ultimate plan Eusebius endorsed for how imperial power could eliminate paganism. And yet, even imperial power had its limits. Aside from the gladiatorial games ban that Eusebius mentions in passing, nothing shows up in surviving legislation to indicate that Constantine issued laws ordering any of these things. They are known only from Eusebius's text—and Eusebius's account does not agree with other literary evidence. Libanius, for example, wrote in the late 380s that "Constantine made absolutely no changes in the traditional forms of worship," and elsewhere blames Constantine's son Constantius for first prohibiting sacrifice and closing temples.[70] Even the *Letter to the Eastern Provincials* that Eusebius includes later in the *Life* shows Constantine condemning non-Christian belief while simultaneously refusing to force people to become Christians.[71]

Scott Bradbury has proposed an interesting way to resolve the apparent contradictions between the Constantine profiled by Eusebius, the emperor who appears in the laws of the *Theodosian Code,* and the figure mentioned in Libanius's oration. Bradbury argues that Constantine's prohibition of sacrifice appeared in an imperial letter.[72] Imperial letters did have the force of law, but they usually served only to state the basic principles guiding imperial policy. They did not often specify steps to implement these policies nor did they specify penalties for disobedience. If one examines Eusebius's discussion of the *nomoi* against sacrifice issued by Constantine, one is struck by the absence both of any specified penalties and of any people actually punished for violating these laws. These were statements of legal principle, but they were deliberately left without enforcement mechanisms. This makes it possible for both Eusebius and Libanius to be right. Constantine could issue the laws Eusebius describes while also "making no changes in traditional forms of worship." This is because, while Constantine opposed much of traditional worship on principle, he apparently did nothing more to deter its practice than to suggest that he found it distasteful.

Similarly, his actions against statues and temples can have much more nuance than Eusebius allows. While Eusebius sees religious meaning in Constantine's importation of statues of gods to his new capital of Constantinople, it is just as likely (as Sarah Bassett has suggested) that these represent artistic adornments for the city chosen for their beauty.[73] A sense of context and proportion is also useful when considering the temple destructions. The Roman Empire was packed full of temples, and, as late antique sources admit, a well-maintained temple was extremely difficult to destroy. In a world without dynamite, proper destruction of a temple was an expensive and time-consuming process that required demolition experts and a significant number of workers.[74] Destruction of temples also potentially threatened neighboring buildings and left gaping open spaces in cities. Even if an emperor had the will to attack many such temples, the state would be hard pressed to meet the tremendous logistical challenges of such an effort.

At the same time, many temples were not well maintained. Temples, even large and impressive ones, regularly fell into disrepair and were either abandoned or torn down. The Alexandrian Serapeum, described as the second greatest temple in the world by a fourth-century author, was actually a second century AD reconstruction executed after the Ptolemaic Serapeum had essentially been condemned.[75] Traditional religion had been practiced in the Mediterranean region for millennia, and paganism's sacred buildings often showed their age. It is not surprising (and not unprecedented) that an emperor would sanction the destruction of an existing temple.[76] What was new, of course, was Constantine's decision to replace an existing temple with a church devoted to the Christian God, though again this was a reasonable way to fill the urban space left empty by the temple's destruction. These destructions also had different impacts. While the three temples of Aphrodite seem not to have been missed, well into the 360s the destruction of the temple of Asclepius at Aegeae elicited speeches of mourning and other impassioned reactions from devotees of traditional religion.[77] Aegeae may, then, have been a case where Constantinian religious initiatives went farther than the public was willing to tolerate.

While Eusebius's *Life of Constantine* portrays the emperor as a Christian champion poised to redefine the Roman religious landscape, non-Christians could still convince themselves that Constantine fit the religious profile of previous Roman emperors.[78] Indeed, on some level, he could hardly have done otherwise. Just as there was no model for what a Christian empire would look like, there was also no template for what a Christian emperor should and should not do. So, for example, Constantine remained *pontifex maximus* until his death,[79] he issued laws reiterating well-established religious practices,[80] and, in the 330s, he agreed to the request of the city of Hispellum to construct a temple honoring him and his family.[81] These actions remain difficult to understand. They may have reflected Constantine's political prudence, but they may also be understood as the actions of an emperor who was trying as best he could to perform the functions expected of him.[82]

Whatever Constantine's motivation, some devotees of traditional religion insisted on treating him as they would any previous emperor. In 326, not long after Constantine's letter disapproving of sacrifice, the Athenian sophist Nicagoras honored the emperor with a graffito written on the wall of the tomb of Ramses VI in the Valley of the Kings. This short text identified its author as "the torch bearer of the most holy mysteries at Eleusis" and "gave thanks to the gods and to the most pious emperor Constantine" for making the trip possible.[83] If Nicagoras was aware of Constantine's religious missives, he shows no sign of it here. Similarly, around 330, the Athenian pagan Praxagoras composed a thoroughly conventional history of Constantine's reign that celebrated his virtues and made no mention of either his Christianity or his religious policies.[84] Both Athenians thought it perfectly appropriate to honor Constantine in the same way that they would any pagan imperial predecessor.

STUDENT LIFE

If Praxagoras, Nicagoras, and the elders of Hispellum did not acknowledge the monumental intellectual and religious developments of the age of Constantine, one could hardly expect the members of the final pagan generation to do so. Libanius, for example, seems to have been vaguely aware that Constantine did something regarding traditional religion, but he is not entirely clear about the specific details.[85] His confusion is not surprising. These things occurred while Libanius and his peers were studying grammar, rhetoric, and philosophy. Because the temples remained open, sacrifices continued, divine images remained in place, and festivals still regularly filled the cities with noisy crowds, most students would have noticed little appreciable difference between the age of Constantine and that which preceded it. In addition, the nature of student life meant that they had much more than current events on their minds. They would have had little time to read all of the imperial letters and other *nomoi* posted in the public squares and little inclination to parse the meaning of the imperial communications they did read. Instead, they devoted most of their waking hours to the study of language and to their friendships with fellow students.

The education they received was designed around these twin aims.[86] The majority of people in the Roman world were effectively illiterate, and most young people probably received little formal education at all,[87] but Libanius, Praetextatus, Ausonius, and Themistius all undertook the expensive and time-consuming training of the elite. This provided specialized education that emphasized grammatical rules, eloquent composition, and the mastery of a canon of authors. Late antique students followed a variety of paths to develop these skills, but the most conventional one began at the school of a grammarian.[88] Students generally spent their preteen and early teenage years with grammarians and got from them a flexible education that responded to their individual needs.[89] Grammarians taught everything from basic reading and writing skills to the rudiments of rhetorical composition.[90] When students were sufficiently advanced, the grammarian began a series of exercises called the *progymnasmata* that taught students how to elaborate on stories or themes using the grammatical skills they had developed earlier.[91]

Probably around the age of thirteen or fourteen these students moved on to schools of rhetoric.[92] They could continue this study until sometime around the age of twenty, though many students either completed or abandoned their training before that age.[93] Sometimes the move to rhetoric represented an abrupt jump from one teacher to another, but it seems to have been common for a student to take a bit of time to adjust to the new environment. Libanius, for example, spent his fourteenth year taking classes in both grammar and rhetoric.[94] Even when a student enrolled exclusively under a rhetorician, he often continued with the *progymnasmata* under the tutelage of one of the rhetorician's assistants.[95]

Rhetorical schools geared their training toward the production of complete student orations, but this was done in a systematic fashion. The path began with relatively simple exercises designed to teach students to interpret short memorable sayings. As they progressed through their training, students developed this modest base into a detailed knowledge of the texts and tendencies of a range of esteemed authors. They read and commented on the work of orators and historians, they composed rhetorical exercises based on literary and mythological situations, and they developed anthologies by copying favorite passages.[96] Eventually, students progressed to the point where they were ready to write, memorize, and deliver their own rhetorical compositions.

This process, Ausonius claimed, "led toward good living, sound learning, and forceful speaking" while giving one the cultural credentials to function among the Roman elite.[97] It often proved physically and emotionally draining. The memorization of texts consumed immense amounts of time and energy. Libanius claimed to have "applied myself to study day in and day out, save for those days reserved for official holidays, and they were not many."[98] He felt a perverse pride when rhetorical training made him sick, and criticized the laziness of poor students who had become "fat with plenty of flesh."[99] Ausonius also suggests that he found this training all-consuming. Writing to his grandson, Ausonius reminds him to take the occasional break if he wants to thrive in school.[100] This was no idle concern. Ausonius later describes the schools as "resounding with the sound of lashes" as the schoolmaster who "brandishes the cane" and "has a full outfit of birches" sows "scared confusion" among the ill-prepared students.[101] While Ausonius probably overstates the amount of physical punishment that teachers actually inflicted, the threat of occasional beatings and regular verbal chastisements certainly kept students on edge.[102]

The social adjustment to studying in schools of grammar and rhetoric could be just as jarring. Though pedagogues continued to monitor most boys, the physical and social environment both within and beyond a school greatly influenced their behavior. When a student enrolled at a school he entered into a new social world. The majority of late antique students probably continued to live at home and attend the classes of a local teacher, but many young men also traveled to teachers based in Athens, Alexandria, Rome, Antioch, Bordeaux, and any number of less famous centers of teaching. Both Libanius and the fourth-century rhetorician Himerius (who was himself a child of the 310s) make it clear that teachers worked hard to court students from abroad through a process that mixed recruitment with admissions. Himerius, for example, delivered two orations, one in person and one in print, to Arcadius, the father of a student whom he particularly wanted to admit.[103] Libanius simultaneously courted and vetted new students through a series of letters that advertised his teaching and attempted to measure the quality of the prospective student's skills.[104]

This type of personalized recruitment mattered because both teachers and students understood that enrollment in an intellectual circle symbolized the beginning of a new life. Teachers and students alike commonly described the members of their school as a second family. Ausonius, Libanius, and their peers called their teachers "father" or "mother" and their peers "brothers."[105] Teachers saw the boys they taught as their children.[106] This was not empty rhetoric; the correspondence of Libanius and Ausonius offers many examples of students depending on their professors for protection and assistance.[107] Himerius gave orations that recounted students' achievements on their birthdays and celebrated their recovery from serious illnesses.[108] Students reciprocated by cheering if their professors gave a public performance,[109] avoiding the lectures of other professors,[110] and even fighting the students of rival schools.[111] In the years that they remained at school, students were expected to function as a part of this scholastic family.

Most students arrived fully prepared to participate in this new world. Libanius, for example, grew up hearing "from older men about Athens and the affairs there."[112] Sometimes these accounts highlighted great rhetorical triumphs, but many of the stories involved "tales of the fighting between the schools . . . and all of the deeds of daring that students perform to raise the prestige of their teachers."[113] Later in his life, Libanius even speaks fondly about the fathers who used to take pride when they saw "on their sons' bodies the evidence of the battles they fight on their teacher's behalf, the scars on the head, face, hands, and on every limb."[114] Among the other activities Libanius had heard about and longed to take part in were "the kidnapping of arriving students, being taken to Corinth for trial on kidnapping charges, giving many feasts, blowing all [his] money, and looking for someone to give him a loan."[115]

Libanius's words show that students, teachers, and even magistrates understood that schools operated under a different set of rules than the rest of late Roman society. Students were encouraged to develop new loyalties to their scholastic families and permitted to demonstrate those loyalties through actions (like brawling or kidnapping) that would normally be considered criminal. Indeed, in a justly famous passage, Augustine comments that students "often commit outrages that ought to be punished by law, were it not that custom protects them."[116] One's student status legitimized normally unacceptable behaviors and, in some cases, even marked them as positive contributions to the fabric of an intellectual community.

Rituals of inclusion particular to intellectual communities helped to reinforce the sense that students lived in a social world with its own particular set of rules. The best-attested such rituals come from the Athenian rhetorical schools of the mid-to late fourth century. When students arrived at an Athenian school, they swore an oath to study under a specific teacher.[117] Himerius treated his newly enrolled students to a welcoming oration in which he greeted them individually by noting the regions from which they came.[118] The welcoming address concluded with a call for the students to be initiated. They were then divided into senior and junior initiates before they processed past their fellow students on the way to the baths.[119] This procession was intended to be a frightening thing and included screamed threats and some physical violence.[120] Once the initiates reached the bathhouse, they were "washed, dressed, and received the right to wear the scholarly robe."[121] When this was completed, Gregory Nazianzen says, the students received the newcomer "as an equal."[122]

The initiation ceremony represented a liminal phase in a student's academic life. He had now become a part of the school and, if a student of rhetoric, he also now wore a robe to distinguish himself from the wider public.[123] He was a scholar not a civilian, but he occupied the lowest rung of a scholastic hierarchy that defined his interaction with other students and professors. Professors, the heads of these intellectual families, rested atop a steep pyramid. Below them were the assistant teachers and senior students who, in larger circles, served as intermediaries between the professor and his youngest and least advanced charges.[124] The average students represented the broad base of this pyramid. Their ranks too were organized according to a well-defined hierarchy. They were led by a designated student leader and ranked based on their time in the school.[125] Not surprisingly, hazing of the youngest and newest students occurred, evidently with some regularity.[126]

The experience of studying under the same teacher helped many students forge strong friendships. Gregory Nazianzen's description of the bond he developed with Basil of Caesarea in Athens is perhaps the best-known portrait of a scholastic friendship, but others offer equally interesting (and often more reliable) snapshots.[127] The sophist Eunapius, for example, tells how the students Prohaeresius and Hephaestion both arrived in Athens at the turn of the fourth century so impoverished that they shared a room and the same scholarly robe.[128] The philosopher and bishop Synesius, whose wealth never forced him into such a situation, still could reminisce about the intimacy that he enjoyed with fellow students.[129] Indeed, late antique graduates looked back on their student days with the same fondness as their modern counterparts. Many of them maintained the social networks that they first built while studying, and even reunited with each other after they all moved on from school.[130]

Fourth-century schools succeeded in creating this type of cohesive, hierarchical scholastic environment in part because they physically and emotionally insulated students from the larger world. Teaching occurred in a variety of locations in the fourth century. Some instruction occurred in dedicated classrooms, but the majority of late antique professors gave their lessons in less formal spaces like homes, temples, tombs, and the open air.[131] During his teaching career, Libanius taught in his home, beside a pool in a bathhouse, alongside a temple, and in a room within Antioch's *bouleuterion* (the city council building).[132] This last space included a "covered lecture room and four colonnades with a courtyard that had been turned into a garden with vines, figs, and other trees."[133] No remains of Libanius's various teaching spaces have been found, but a number of "classrooms" have been uncovered in other cities throughout the eastern Mediterranean. The most impressive are found in a late antique university quarter unearthed at Kom el-Dikka in Alexandria. In the late fifth and early sixth centuries, perhaps as many as twenty-five lecture halls were constructed in the center of the city, abutting a late Roman bath.[134] These seem to have been part of a larger scholastic quarter that included a public theater, a colonnaded portico, and a large open space in which people could congregate. Intriguingly, all of the lecture halls were entered from the portico, all contained two or three rows of stone benches built to line three walls, and all had a raised central seat from which (presumably) the professor conducted class.[135] Their capacity varied, but, aside from the much larger theater in the south of the complex, twenty to thirty people could sit in each room.[136]

Whatever its physical layout, a late antique classroom helped to separate a teacher and his students from the rest of the world by defining the space in which teaching occurred. Thematically appropriate artwork could help. One Athenian classroom featured statues of former students along its walls, while the person who taught in the Atrium house of Aphrodisias decorated its apsidal room with the portraits of Greek philosophers and rhetoricians.[137] Each classroom was designed to help the students sitting in a group to focus their attention on school. In addition, teachers used these spaces to communicate the undeniable hierarchy of a school. Although this hierarchy is most apparent in the raised seats reserved for professors at the center of the Alexandrian classrooms, ancient depictions of teachers usually show them seated in an imposing chair before a student or a class of students.[138]

Two other features of later Roman educational life made it difficult for the final pagan generation to appreciate the new world emerging under Constantine. First, devotees of traditional religion dominated the Roman schools in the 320s and 330s. With the possible exception of Ausonius's teacher Arborius (whose religious identity is difficult to discern), all of the teachers and teaching assistants under whom Libanius, Ausonius, Themistius, and Praetextatus are known to have studied were devotees of traditional religion.[139] Irrespective of their family background or whatever they perceived the religious identification of the emperor to be, the extremely hierarchical scholastic setting strongly encouraged students to identify with an intellectual family that was overwhelmingly pagan. This type of environment did little to prompt young men to think too much about the religious policies of the emperor and his advisers.

The curriculum that these young men studied also had an important role in creating a view of the unchanging religious rhythms of the world. The grammatical and rhetorical curricula focused extensively on classical mythology and pagan theology,[140] and offered direct instruction in "how a man must bear himself in his relationships with the gods."[141] It occurred in a space that, like most public spaces in the Roman world at that time, was saturated with things connected to traditional religious practice. Tertullian characteristically points this out in his *De idolatria*. Schoolmasters, he says, are completely complicit in the promotion and functioning of the traditional religious system. Not only do they "preach about the gods, express their names, genealogies, and honorable distinctions," but they also observe the gods' sacred days and festivals.[142] Even the most resolutely Christian students could find it "hard not to be carried along and led away" by the devotees of traditional religion.[143] For most students in the 320s, however, this seems not to have been troubling. Ausonius, for example, speaks fondly about his time studying grammar and rhetoric under his uncle in Bordeaux, his Christian faith in no way adversely affected by the environment.[144] In the 320s, the traditional religious elements that infused the curriculum and surrounded the classrooms would have seemed neither exceptional nor endangered. They simply formed natural elements of an educational environment designed to train young men how to meet the same social, religious, and civic obligations that their ancestors had fulfilled for centuries. There was no reason to suspect that anything would change.

. . .

Libanius, Ausonius, Themistius, and Himerius all speak about the experience of studying in fourth century, but each does so as an older man reconstructing his younger self from memory. This is a particularly important point because the older men who describe these experiences remain immersed in the intellectual worlds they are describing. Libanius particularly "remembers" a younger self whose conduct and attitudes embodied ideals that he hoped his students would absorb. Ausonius too embellished his youthful educational experiences in such a way that they mirrored the literary and social virtues on which he would later base his career. From Libanius's description of kidnappings and violence in Athens to Ausonius's claims about the regular beatings that students in his day received, the frailty of memory and the thematic aims of individual authors have likely combined to distort some of details contained in these autobiographical portraits of scholastic life.[145] These accounts do, however, accurately capture the flavor of student life and the types of concerns that students had. While the authors may exaggerate some of the events they describe, these undoubtedly were the sorts of things that they did and talked about when they were students.

This makes it particularly notable that Libanius, Ausonius, Themistius, and Himerius all make no mention of the political and religious developments of the 320s and early 330s when they write about this time in their lives. While Constantine and his advisers imagined ways to change the imperial religious landscape, Libanius and his peers were immersed in classical literature, fixated on the rivalries between schools, and entranced by their older colleagues' "tales of daring." With their minds and attentions focused elsewhere for most of Constantine's reign, it is unlikely that they realized that they were living through what later historians would see as a transformative age.

The generation's insularity began to change in the mid-330s. For some members of this generation (most notably Praetextatus) the early 330s saw their initial foray into public life, a step that certainly increased their awareness of the age's political developments. Others, like Ausonius, would have seen their awareness increase when they began studying law or pleading cases. As members of the final pagan generation moved into their midtwenties, their focus shifted from the classrooms and parties of intellectual centers like Athens and Bordeaux to the social and political life of members of the imperial elite. These young men began assuming the duties and responsibilities of mature citizens. As the next chapter will show, they did so with a mixture of seriousness and conservatism that would become characteristic of their approach to public life.

CHAPTER 3

The System

The death of the emperor Constantine in 337 roughly coincided with the moment when the members of the final pagan generation finished their schooling and entered the adult world. They were very much the children of the world he had created. Ausonius and Praetextatus had never lived under another emperor, while Libanius and Themistius were children when Constantine took the East from Licinius. For all of their mature life, the final pagan generation knew only the regime of Constantine. And, with the exception of the regime of Magnentius, endured by Ausonius and Praetextatus, all of them would live under one of Constantine's sons for almost the next quarter century.[1]

This meant that the men of this generation were born, raised, and came of age in an empire whose basic rules changed little during the first fifty years of their lives. One must dwell for a minute on how important this is. Their grandfathers had spent most of their life in a radically different Roman state characterized by political and economic instability. Nearly sixty emperors and imperial pretenders had paraded through in the five decades between the death of Alexander Severus in 235 and the accession of Diocletian in 284. In their wake, they had left political and economic instability. Surviving sources show evidence of villages being abandoned as plague, insecurity, and excessive taxation made life in them unbearable.[2] These political and economic uncertainties were met by repeated currency debasements as emperors reduced the amount of precious metal in gold and silver coinage in order to cover expenses.

Throughout much of the third century, the relative value of gold and silver coinage remained pegged in such a way that smaller denomination coins retained their relative value. By the early 270s, however, the market's faith in the basic worth of Roman silver and bronze coins had been shattered.[3] The market responded quickly by adjusting prices upward, an inflation that created further economic instability, especially for those who were unable to keep their savings in gold.[4]

Under the leadership of Diocletian and his imperial colleagues, the empire refashioned itself to deal with these internal inefficiencies and to counter its external threats.[5] The often impossibly large provinces governed lightly by members of a narrow senatorial elite were transformed into smaller, more easily governed units.[6] In those provinces with a military presence, the emperors of the 280s and 290s stripped military command from the governors and gave it instead to new, purely military officers called *duces*.[7] They created a superstructure of twelve imperial dioceses, each of which had a *vicarius* (vicar) superintend civilian activities and a higher-level *duces* manage military affairs.[8] They multiplied the number of imperial courts, increased their size, and redefined the offices held by the officials around them.

The reign of Constantine saw further refinement as the functions and duties of officials were divided between multiple new offices with more circumscribed and well-defined functions. So, for example, the praetorian prefect, who, under Diocletian, "wielded a wide authority in almost every sphere of government, military, judicial, financial and general administration,"[9] became a purely civilian officer who took charge of the administration of a defined group of provinces. The numbers of prefects grew from two to five, and, by the 340s, each prefecture came to have its own financial and judicial staffs.[10] The military responsibilities once given to a prefect ultimately passed to purely military officials, each of whom again had his own staff and geographic responsibility. The number of new positions created is staggering. By the year 400, it has been estimated that there were 6,000 senior administration positions available per generation and another 17,500 bureaucrats on the staff of the prefects, vicars, and governors at any one time.[11] Similar growth may be assumed in the staff sizes of military officials as well.[12]

Government efficiency increased along with its size. Because they now had responsibility for fewer tasks and smaller areas, governors and military commanders could be more responsive to the needs of citizens. This helped make tax collecting more efficient and fair. Diocletian and his colleagues introduced a process that regularly assessed the tax obligations of landholders based on a formula that took into account both the quality of their land and the number of people working it.[13] High-quality land worked by many hands was taxed at a higher rate than less productive land. The emperor also scheduled regular reassessments in order to ensure that the tax valuation reflected the land's current condition.[14] Collection itself was left to the town councils, a move in keeping with imperial precedent. This ensured that those collecting the taxes both knew the area and could be held directly accountable if the required taxes were not paid.[15]

Imperial efforts to stabilize the economy went beyond comprehensive tax reform. In the mid-290s, the emperor Diocletian and his colleagues instituted a sweeping reform of the Roman currency.[16] The new system centered on a gold coin that contained 1/60 of a pound of gold, a silver coin containing 1/96 of a pound of silver, a silver-clad bronze coin called the *nummus,* and two smaller bronze denominations.[17] This reform had two purposes. First, the emperors hoped to create new high-, medium-, and low-value coins of a predictable precious metal content whose relative value would remain constant. In doing so, they hoped to break the inflationary fever that the mid-third-century debasements and retariffing of the coinage had caused. Second, and perhaps more importantly, this reform also allowed the emperors to communicate an implicit message of political stability.

As the fourth century progressed, the monetary system developed in a way that Diocletian and his colleagues could not have envisioned. The gold *solidus* coin held its value exceptionally well. Its gold content was reduced once, from 1/60 of a pound to 1/72 of a pound in the reign of Constantine, but it would retain this purity for centuries. The emperors had then succeeded in creating a stable, high-value coin. Unfortunately, they had less success creating intermediate-value coins. The pure silver coinage never became more than a secondary part of the new monetary system. It ceased to be minted regularly or in large quantities after 305.[18] The beautiful silver-plated *nummus* coin intended to serve as the centerpiece of the reform utterly failed. Its silver content plummeted over the next half century from 4 percent until, by the 340s, it was only 0.4 percent silver.[19] As its silver content decreased, the coin's value relative to the gold coinage collapsed as well.[20] This meant that fourth-century Romans had access to a remarkably stable, high-value coin (the *solidus*), a set of bronze and silver-clad bronze coins whose value decreased regularly, and very few intermediate-value coins that could bridge the gap between them.

Not surprisingly, the revolutionized imperial system crafted by Diocletian and improved by Constantine brought a great many tangible benefits to the wealthy, the capable, and the ambitious who had access to the *solidus*. The empire now needed more governors, vicars, and prefects as well as many more people to staff their offices. These offices provided jobs that ranged from entry-level clerks to senior officials like notaries, assessors, and tribunes. The highest-level positions offered both a generous salary paid in *solidi* and (crucially) an exemption from the obligation to pay for public services in one's home city.[21] The fourth century provides many examples of men who made fortunes through the expanded (and well-compensated) positions in the military and civilian bureaucracy that these emperors created.

The careers of two very different contemporaries who came of age as this system was taking shape show the opportunities it opened. Gratian, the father of the future emperors Valentinian and Valens, was born in a Pannonian town to a humble family. He enlisted in the army as a common soldier. After his great physical strength attracted attention, he rose through the ranks, "serving successively as a staff-officer and tribune" before being appointed as the military official in charge of Africa in the 320s.[22] In the 340s, he again served as an imperial official in Britain, at which time he may even have hosted the emperor Constans.[23] At the end of this lucrative career, he retired to an estate in Pannonia to enjoy the wealth and security his service had provided for him.

About ten years before Gratian's birth, the future rhetorician Prohaeresius was born in Armenia. His family lost its property when he was a youth and Prohaeresius spent his early life in relative poverty. He showed promise as a rhetorician and was sent to Athens to study, but he had so little money that he could attend classes only every other day because he and his roommate shared a school uniform.[24] When he finished his studies, Prohaeresius stayed on as an assistant teacher in Athens before eventually setting up his own school. By the 340s, he enjoyed an imperially funded chair at Athens, audiences with the emperor Constans, and extensive direct imperial financial support.[25]

Men like Gratian and Prohaeresius were helped immensely by the ways in which they were compensated. Salaries for jobs ranging from higher-level imperial administrators to municipal teaching positions were often paid in gold or in goods that could be readily converted to gold.[26] Payment in gold was important because of the particular sort of economic order the *solidus* produced. As Peter Brown has recently remarked, the fourth century witnessed a stark demarcation between "those areas of society where the mighty *solidus* circulated and a bleak social hinterland where the *solidus* was absent or difficult to obtain."[27] The limited circles in which the gold coinage circulated in quantity allowed great wealth to concentrate in the hands of those officials and landholders who had ready access to the *solidus*. While the rich held their fortunes in stable gold coins, poorer Romans were forced to pay for smaller items with sealed leather purses sometimes containing thousands of bronze coins.[28] The anonymous author of a fourth-century military treatise spoke of the consequences of this: "It was in the age of Constantine that extravagant grants assigned gold instead of bronze . . . there ensued an even more extravagant passion for spending gold . . . which meant that the houses of the rich were crammed full and their splendor increased to the detriment of the poor."[29]

Other sources confirm this concentration of wealth around the fourth-century elite. Olympiodorus, a visitor to the city of Rome in the early fifth century, spoke of the wealthiest households receiving an income of "four thousand pounds of gold per year [$60,960,000 at current gold prices] from their properties."[30] At roughly the same time, the estates of the Roman noblewoman Melania were reckoned to have produced nearly 120,000 *solidi* a year.[31] This much money simply could not be spent as fast as it came in. As a result, masses of *solidi* and hundred-pound gold ingots simply sat in an inner chamber of her home.[32] The homes themselves were as massive as the fortunes that supported them. Olympiodorus remarked that "each of the great houses in Rome contained within itself everything that a medium-sized city could hold, a hippodrome, fora, temples, fountains, and different kinds of baths."[33] It seems that the later fourth century even produced a sort of building boom (complete with massive new mansions and teardowns of older, smaller homes) like the one that swept the East and West Coasts of the United States in the first decade of the 2000s.[34]

The elite of the fourth century immensely enjoyed the pleasures that this wealth made possible. Late in his life, Ausonius's grandson Paulinus of Pella reminisced about the fourth century of his youth. He had "a fine horse decorated with special trappings, a tall groom, a swift hound, and a shapely hawk" when he would go out hunting.[35] He thrilled in wearing the latest fashions from Rome and spent his days racing his horses as fast as they would go. While Paulinus seems a bit like a modern college student who drives a Maserati, Ausonius preferred a less frenetic sort of elite decadence. He had no interest in racing horses, but Ausonius seems to have been something of a foodie. Ausonius once wrote forty-one lines of poetry devoted to a snarky description of all of the different types of oysters he had sampled. "These are known to me," he claimed, "not from common company nor from taverns . . . but because I myself have often celebrated festivals . . . or gone to banquets as an invited guest when a friend observed a birthday or a marriage feast or a drinking party."[36]

Oysters aside, these parties and banquets were not the sedate affairs one might imagine. Once the food and alcohol began flowing, so too did the jokes and bawdy poems. Ausonius acknowledges writing one poem while drunk at a party, and he penned many others that would go over quite well with a drunken audience.[37] One of them, an epigram entitled "An outlandish medley to a marble statue of *liber pater* in my country house, having the attributes of various gods," hardly seems like the product of a sober poet.[38] However, any audience who heard Ausonius's verse description of Eunus the lecherous pedagogue's performance of a sexual act could not help but break out in laughter. This epigram used Greek letters to enable the audience to picture various stages of sexual intercourse before it concluded with a θ to symbolize Eunus's head being put in a noose after his indiscretions became known.[39] This epigram and a host of others like it were the works of a talented artist, but we should not work too hard to find high culture lurking in these melodious poems. Ausonius here works almost like a fourth-century Eminem, whose lyrics titillate and entertain the sort of men who spent their leisure time drinking fine wine, sampling different kinds of oysters, and ogling servants.[40] Such works served not to edify the rich but to amuse them.

The age of gold opened up the pleasures of wealth to two groups that would not usually have enjoyed this type of life in centuries past. Capable men like Gratian and Prohaeresius who collected imperial salaries in gold could rise from the middling ranks of the city councillors to great riches.[41] But those who were already rich made equally good use of this new economic and political order. While we typically think of the rich of the later empire as a group of Italian senators, the regionalization of the Roman world meant that every part of the empire had its own local elite based in the cities and towns of each province.[42] These men owned large granaries or wine-making facilities that could hold and process the produce that they collected in rent from tenants and purchased from neighbors. These elites alone could bring to market enough agricultural production that they would be paid for it in large quantities of *solidi*. The *solidus* economy may have made the fourth century an age of opportunity for the capable, but it did nothing to diminish the economic position of those already on top.

The system did, however, change the horizons of these traditional local elites. Since the advent of Roman imperial rule, the empire had largely allowed councillors the freedom to run their cities as they wished. They were responsible for tax collection and the provision of many municipal services, but they were also allowed to enjoy local honors and special, legally defined privileges such as freedom from disfiguring physical punishment and torture.[43] Fourth-century emperors encouraged people of curial rank to look beyond these provincial horizons by drawing them into imperial service and, by the middle of the century, extending senatorial status to imperial officials and thousands of the most prominent local elite.[44] A roster of the Thamugadi council erected inside the Numidian city's council building ranks its nearly two hundred members in order of social standing. Atop the list were ten senators, all of whom occupied the highest rung of the local social ladder.[45] Many remained engaged with their home cities, but their new status often exempted them from the onerous financial obligations the council could impose. In this way, many of the old local aristocratic families joined capable and ambitious men like Gratian and Prohaeresius as members of the fourth century's gilded imperial elite. They formed an aristocracy that retained ties to their home or adopted cities, but one that enjoyed the luxury of choosing how and whether they would be financially involved in their administration. Ultimately many of them looked to the court not the curia.

JOINING THE SYSTEM

Gratian and Prohaeresius were born in the last years before Diocletian began the process of stabilizing and recreating the later Roman state. They belonged to the first generation of men who came of age in the new empire of Diocletian and Constantine and were among the first to test both its vast potential and its many limitations. This was not always an easy process. Tying one's star to a system that so closely connected the imperial court with the generation of tremendous wealth and privilege had its dangers. Imperial favor could be incredibly fickle, as both Gratian and Prohaeresius learned.[46] Gratian, whose rise from obscurity was directly tied to his service to the state, fell afoul of the emperor Constantius when the usurper Magnentius visited while passing by Gratian's estate during a civil war. When the war concluded, Gratian was stripped of his lands and compelled to move.[47] Prohaeresius too angered an emperor when he turned down the emperor Julian's offer of an exemption from a law prohibiting Christians from teaching.[48] He was forced out of his public teaching position and lost the salary it provided.

Since the time of Augustus, the emperor's subjects had worked to reap the advantages of imperial attention while avoiding the pitfalls of imperial anger. But never before the fourth century had so many people tied their fortunes so directly to the whims of imperial favor. This meant that the fourth-century expansion of economic and career opportunities brought with it an accompanying expansion of the risk peculiar to autocracies. While cases like those of Gratian and Prohaeresius did happen, the most remarkable thing about this new system was the relative infrequency of such mistakes. By and large, the teachers, imperial bureaucrats, military officials, and landed elites enriched and empowered by this system managed to preserve their gains even as the tides of imperial favor shifted. Indeed, it is surprising how much continuity there was within the military and civilian administrations of different emperors and how few senators and other notables were affected when an emperor died. For every Gratian who was punished for giving hospitality to a usurper, there were countless men like Symmachus, who was allowed to gracefully apologize for publicly lending support to an imperial challenger.[49] There seems to have existed an unspoken understanding between the governing and the governed that this administrative and social system was indispensable even if the occasional miscalculating individual proved disposable.

Some of the stability of this system came from its reliance on elite social networks to identify and incorporate talent. When young men completed their education, many of them attempted to translate their skills into positions in imperial service. The reasons for this varied and often overlapped. Imperial service could be lucrative, it brought exemptions from mandatory councillor financial obligations, it could open the door to higher office and honors, and it gave men whose fathers still controlled the family lands a source of income.[50] Many people wanted these jobs, but the state did not have a centralized mechanism for identifying new talent. There was no civil service examination nor an *École nationale d'administration*. Young men seeking these positions depended on family members, friends, and friends of friends to bring their particular combination of skills to the attention of the right imperial administrators. All of these people would be asked to write letters introducing a young man to people who might be able to help him get established in a new city.[51] He would present these letters to their various addressees. They were then expected to host the letter bearer in their homes and introduce him to others who might be helpful.[52] If all went well, this initial introduction could serve to establish a relationship between the young man and his host that resembled in many ways that of a patron and client.[53]

A set of five letters that Libanius wrote in 360 shows how this process worked in practice. The first group of these concerned Miccalus, the son of a family friend, who traveled from Antioch to Constantinople in the summer of 360 in the hope of securing a position in the imperial service.[54] He carried with him three surviving letters from Libanius (and probably letters from other writers as well). The first was sent to Libanius's cousin Spectatus, a notary in imperial service who had recently served as an envoy to Persia.[55] The second went to Florentius, an Antiochene who served as the master of offices at the time.[56] The third, which was carried by Miccalus and delivered to Themistius, was not a formal letter of introduction but still served as a way to put the two men in contact.[57]

The letter to Themistius reveals why Libanius made such effort on Miccalus's behalf. It asks that Themistius intervene to resolve an unpaid debt that had wrongly been attributed to Miccalus's brother Olympius when he had been transferred from the Roman senate to its Constantinopolitan counterpart in 358 or 359.[58] The letter mentions Miccalus in passing only to say that he can provide more details about the situation. By sending this letter with Miccalus, Libanius offers him the opportunity to meet Themistius. If Miccalus made a good impression on his host, Libanius hoped that he might convince Themistius to solve Olympius's legal problem and help Miccalus find an administrative position. As the subject of this letter makes clear, Libanius extended Miccalus this favor only because of his relationship with Olympius.[59]

The other two letters from Libanius that Miccalus carried to Constantinople show a similar dynamic. Libanius requests assistance by deftly blending allusions to his personal relationship with the addressee, mentions of Miccalus's connection to Olympius, and intimations that any favors offered Miccalus will be returned by Olympius. Libanius's letter to Florentius begins by saying that Libanius sometimes writes letters of introduction for people out of obligation. This letter for Miccalus, however, conveys genuine enthusiasm for the task. This is because Miccalus's brother Olympius "has labored long on my behalf and it would be wrong of me not to make some contribution to help [Miccalus] on his way."[60]

Libanius then continues by commending Florentius for the speed with which he has responded to similar requests in the past and emphasizing that Miccalus needs to quickly secure "some honor suitable to people like him."[61] He needs to get married soon, Libanius explains, and, without a job, this is unlikely to happen.[62] This marriage will be good for Miccalus, but also a blessing for Olympius, who "prays that his brother will be called by the name father."[63] Libanius concludes by emphasizing that any good done for Miccalus will consequently be recognized and remembered by both Libanius and Olympius.

Libanius's letter to Spectatus asks the same favor, but takes a very different approach. It begins by upbraiding Spectatus for the many times he has ignored Libanius's requests for help. Libanius insists that he has told Miccalus about this but that Miccalus pressed him to write nonetheless. Libanius agreed because, even if Spectatus does not help Miccalus for Libanius's sake, he knows that Olympius is "formidable in speech, formidable in action, and he both knows how to return a favor and exact justice. I know that you'll fear his thunder. In order to keep the air clear for yourself, you'll decide to help Miccalus."[64]

Each of these letters hardly mentions Miccalus's own qualities and capabilities.[65] Instead, they focus on Libanius's relationships with Spectatus and Florentius and the power of Miccalus's brother Olympius. Spectatus and Florentius were not to consider helping Miccalus secure a position because he was a bright, capable, and ambitious young man (in fact, Libanius does not suggest that Miccalus was any of these things). They were instead to help Miccalus because he was the brother of a senator and an acquaintance of Libanius, and both Libanius and Olympius could reliably return a favor. This seems to have been good enough. By 362, Miccalus, now married, had risen high enough to be appointed governor of Thrace.[66]

Two other letters from 360 show more of this dynamic. In the winter of 360, Libanius wrote to Modestus, the *comes Orientis* (the Count of the East) whose office was based in Antioch, and asked that he grant the privilege of arguing cases in his court to all of Libanius's students rather than just the select few who already had such standing. This is important, Libanius argues, because it will allow the wealthy to get some honor, and the poor some income.[67] Advocates were not necessarily well paid, and their status was not generally high enough to merit a curial exemption, but these positions were points of entry into the imperial system. They provided young men still under their father's control with an independent source of income, and these positions could eventually develop into something more significant. Here again we see young men depending on a well-connected patron to get their careers started.

Bassus, a poor but gifted student of Libanius who hoped to establish himself as a sophist, carried the most interesting of this set of letters. It was addressed to Andronicus, the governor of Phoenicia, and explains that Bassus worked hard to develop his oratory. Bassus carried with him a panegyric of Andronicus. Libanius urges the governor to listen to the speech and give Bassus some payment for it so that he might both "assist him and encourage others toward eloquence."[68] The unspoken hope is that, on meeting Bassus and seeing him perform, Andronicus will help the young man get a teaching position somewhere in his province. This seems to have worked. A later letter, addressed to a Chromatius based in Palestine, suggests that Bassus now held the title of sophist in Phoenicia.[69]

All five of these letters use Libanius's relationships with prominent figures to provide young men with points of entry into the Roman administrative system. These points of entry differed depending on the type of figure Libanius was recommending. Miccalus obviously expected some sort of high office that would immediately confer a good salary and a curial exemption. Not everyone who initially aimed so high was as fortunate as he, but a man with his family background could hardly settle for anything less.[70] The young students who sought standing to plead cases before the *comes* had more modest expectations, at least at first. They aimed to join the system at a low level, earn an income, and (if all went well) advance from that starting point. Bassus, who came from neither wealth nor influence, evidently sought only the opportunity to audition for a spot in the elite. Each man, however, hoped that Libanius and his network of correspondents could help him.

This personal dependency had a moderating effect on the activities of men like Miccalus, Bassus, and others who entered the later Roman system. Their status and wealth grew out of the efforts of their friends and families. Once established, they were expected to repay those who had helped them. Depending on their position, the favor requested could be as small as making sure that an appeal quickly reached higher officials or hosting another young person seeking to establish himself in a new city. But the favor needed to be repaid, with interest if possible. Young elites were pushed to be ambitious so that the initial social capital invested in them would pay ever-larger dividends as their careers advanced.[71]

All of these things required that young men do their jobs, expand their network of connections, and, above all, remain politically relevant.

Successful people were rewarded socially with greater prestige and ever-widening circles of friends. Incompetence in office, indifference to friends, and political miscalculation had the opposite effect. Such people failed to attract new friends, shrank existing networks, and risked angering the people who once helped them. Occasionally the sponsors of particularly flawed candidates even faced public ridicule.[72] This meant that few bureaucrats and military officials directly challenged the policies they were charged with implementing. There was simply too much risk of something going wrong, especially when the social and personal consequences of a misstep could be quite severe. This was the inadvertent genius of the later Roman system. By offering material and social rewards for competent imperial service, Diocletian and Constantine created a moderately capable, reliably ambitious, and generally obedient class of administrators, teachers, and soldiers.

THE FINAL PAGAN GENERATION COMES OF AGE

The final pagan generation knew no empire other than the one governed by this system, and all four of the men at the center of this study built their public careers within it. By 350, each of them had held or was holding an imperially funded post. Each had made it, at least in fourth-century terms, but they found success in different ways. Praetextatus came from the ranks of the old Roman senatorial aristocracy and advanced in the same basic way as many of his ancestors. Ausonius was from a family of elite provincial intellectuals and joined the family business. Themistius too was from a family of prominent teachers, but they were less well-positioned and less helpful to him. Libanius came from an Antiochene family not unlike that of Praetextatus, but he ended up as a teacher not a senator. Because each of these paths was so different, it is worth pausing to consider how each man began his career and the way in which this reflects his understanding of the age's possibilities.

Praetextatus was the youngest of the four, but he had the earliest start to his official career. As a child, Praetextatus took part in the ceremonies inaugurating Constantinople in 330,[73] an occasion that provides the one firm date around which one can construct his early activities.[74] His participation in this event prefigured a string of offices that he held from roughly the time of Constantine's death until the late 350s. These included a quaestorship, a praetorship, a stint as *corrector* of Tuscany and Umbria (a provincial governorship in Italy), and a term as *consularis Lusitaniae* (governor in Spain).[75] He also held an augurate and possibly some other priesthoods (he would eventually hold ten) in this period.

While these offices are known, the dating of them is not; the first office that Praetextatus held for which we have a firm date is his service as proconsul of the province of Achaea from 362 to 364. At the same time, we can get an approximate idea of when he held each of these positions. A Roman of aristocratic background usually held a quaestorship around age sixteen and a praetorship in his early twenties.[76] It was not atypical for such men to also hold one or more priesthoods by the time that they turned twenty-five.[77] It is likely, then, that Praetextatus's quaestorship and possibly his selection as augur followed not long after his trip to Constantinople. His praetorship would have happened in the early 340s, and his service as *corrector* perhaps came not long after that.[78] His governorship of Lusitania, the next item on his list of offices, probably dates to the mid- to late 350s.[79]

The particular circumstances surrounding Praetextatus's appointments are unknown, but the experiences of contemporaries show how these appointments would have worked in general terms. Praetextatus's participation in the inauguration of Constantinople represented a symbolic duty for which the young Praetextatus was chosen not because of any attributes of his own but because of the particular pull of his family and their friends.[80] The quaestorship, augurate, and priesthood were similar situations. All of these were honors that young aristocrats were expected to accrue regardless of their individual talents or characteristics. Praetextatus received them when he did because he was the right age and from the right sort of family.[81] The praetorship was something different. While Praetextatus received the office as a symbolic passage into an adult senatorial career, praetors had some real duties as trial judges and very significant symbolic responsibilities.[82]

Praetextatus's tenures as quaestor and praetor also represented the moments that first defined his public profile. Quaestors and praetors (or, more accurately, their parents) sponsored lavish public celebrations in an effort to make a favorable impression on the people of Rome.[83] Surviving sources say nothing about the games Praetextatus's family organized, but, in the later fourth century, families spent anywhere from 1,200 to 4,000 pounds of gold (between $35 and $115 million at current prices) on their son's *praetura* (a quaestor's *quaestura* was only somewhat more modest).[84] The games consisted of a weeklong celebration featuring tightrope walkers, dancers, mock naval battles, musical performances, gladiatorial combats, and fights between skilled huntsmen and exotic animals like crocodiles, bears, and lions drawn from all corners of the empire.[85] They required a huge outlay of money (though, given the income earned by elite families, it was far from crippling). Successful games also demanded that families make use of the social network that bound the Roman elite together. The actors, exotic animals, freshly captured prisoners of war, and ivory for the souvenir diptychs all had to be secured from suppliers, often in the face of competition from sponsors of spectacles elsewhere in the empire.[86] Successful games required a sponsor who could ask favors from members of a large social network that spread across the empire's entire expanse, and, if necessary, jump ahead of others also asking for the same limited resources. This meant that young men like Praetextatus matured into social debts that they would be expected to repay.

At the same time, Praetextatus entered public life primed to succeed. Organizing the *quaestura* and *praetura* games required his family to mobilize their friends and associates across the empire on his behalf. This gave Praetextatus an opportunity to build his own relationships with these well-placed family friends and a chance to make an impression on senators, imperial officials, and the emperor himself. Symmachus, for example, gave silver baskets and ivory tablets to senatorial friends who had helped or who had attended the games of his son Memmius. He also sent a gold-framed tablet commemorating the occasion to the emperor.[87] The games and related gestures symbolized the maturation of a young man and gave momentum to his new career.

We can date one other event in Praetextatus's early adulthood. In 344, he married Fabia Aconia Paulina, the daughter of the former prefect and consul Aco Catullinus.[88] She was thrilled, later writing, "My parents' distinction did nothing greater for me than to make me seem worthy of my husband."[89] Though this evidently became a loving marriage that lasted for forty years,[90] Paulina's and Praetextatus's initial feelings about one another mattered very little. This union joined two important aristocratic families and was likely the product of a long and intense process of negotiation that involved both their families and, in all likelihood, their friends too.[91] It also represented another tie that bound Praetextatus to the fourth-century political and economic system. Praetextatus's promise placed him in the position to marry Paulina, but it now became his obligation to live up to his potential.

Praetextatus was a well-educated man who had such an interest in philosophy that he translated a paraphrase of Aristotle's *Prior and Posterior Analytics* originally done by Themistius, but intellectual pursuits remained a leisure activity for him.[92] He was primarily concerned with managing his estates and fulfilling his sacred and political obligations. The opposite was true of Themistius and Ausonius. Both would have significant political careers, but these developed out of their successes as teachers of philosophy and rhetoric. Between 337 and 350, both Themistius and Ausonius established teaching circles, positioned themselves for imperial or civic chairs that would pay a salary in gold, and secured exemptions that would make their civic duties optional once they inherited or purchased land. Political life for each man came later.

Both men were the heirs to intellectual dynasties, but Ausonius came from the far more impressive line. He was the son of a doctor and the nephew of Arborius, the rhetorician who tutored Constantine's nephew Dalmatius.[93] When he completed his schooling, Ausonius first began work as an advocate in the courts, but he soon came to realize that he wanted to teach.[94] Although Ausonius does not say much about how he secured a professorial appointment, it seems that he was teaching in Bordeaux, the Oxford of Gaul, when he was barely twenty-four.[95] The age at which he secured a public position and the speed with which he apparently advanced from grammarian to rhetorician suggest that his success resulted from more than natural talent. Ausonius was helped by the prominence of his family and the close relationship his uncle enjoyed with the imperial court. A number of his less well-connected contemporaries and fellow students found academic employment much harder to secure. His fellow student Acilius Glabrio, for example, had to continue studying essentially as an advanced graduate student under Ausonius's direction until Ausonius's promotion to teacher of rhetoric opened up the grammarian position in Bordeaux.[96] Luciolus, another of Ausonius's classmates, took even longer to establish himself.[97] And Marcellus and Sedatus, both contemporaries of Ausonius from Bordeaux, had to move to Toulouse and Narbonne in order to secure positions.[98] Their experiences would have been much like those of Libanius's friend Bassus, the young Phoenician rhetorician who traveled from governor to governor armed with letters of introduction and prepared speeches in the hope that he would impress someone enough to win a funded teaching position.

Ausonius likely experienced very little of this. His connections reached much higher and ensured that a teaching position could be had more or less when he wanted it. This also meant that, unlike Libanius's friend Miccalus (who needed to establish himself professionally before marrying), Ausonius could begin a family earlier in life. At roughly the same time that he began teaching in Bordeaux, Ausonius married

Sabina, the eighteen-year-old daughter of a local senator.[99] Here again one sees Ausonius accruing rewards suspiciously early. He had only just stopped pleading cases and begun teaching. This suggests that, like the marriage of Praetextatus, Ausonsius's wedding reflected the prestige he had inherited from his family more than his own achievements.[100]

Themistius followed a somewhat harder route. He came from a family of Paphlagonian intellectuals who moved to Constantinople soon after its founding in 330.[101] The family was not rich, but it was one with a distinguished intellectual history.[102] Themistius's grandfather had been honored by Diocletian for his accomplishments as a philosopher, and his father, Eugenius, had quickly established a great reputation for himself in the new capital.[103] After completing his initial grammatical studies in Paphlagonia, Themistius was sent by his father to a school of rhetoric in Neocaesarea in the province of Pontus.[104] Around 337, Themistius moved to Constantinople and began studying philosophy under his father.[105] Then, sometime in the mid-340s, he set out to find a teaching position. While well respected, his father had neither the resources nor the influence to get Themistius put into a position in Constantinople right away. So Themistius instead began interviewing for positions in cities in western Asia Minor.

His first surviving oration comes from this period and shows him trying to set up a school in Diocletian's former capital of Nicomedia, probably sometime around the year 344.[106] It reads like the job talk of a nervous academic, with Themistius's descriptions of "the extreme tact and charm of my rivals that will carry you away,"[107] and his promise to organize a corps of students that has "its moderate share of pleasures."[108] The first part of the speech lays out the distinctive type of training that Themistius claimed to provide. This teaching mixed the best virtues of philosophy and rhetoric and nurtured a unique ability to command and channel "these two mothers of learning."[109] After describing the qualities that he would bring to a cohort of students, Themistius then switched to a panegyric of the city of Nicomedia itself in order to better appeal to his audience of potential employers.

The context for Themistius's oration resembled the job search of Bassus much more than it did the process through which Ausonius ensconced himself in the schools of Bordeaux. Although Themistius mentions competitors in the oration, it is not clear whether he came to Nicomedia to compete for a funded chair or if these competitors were simply other teachers active in the city.[110] If he did seek an imperially funded chair, the competition could be fierce, especially given Nicomedia's beauty and prominence. One needed strong recommendations and unambiguous support from recognized teachers to even be considered. If chosen as a finalist, he could expect interviews, hostile questions from those running the search, and heavily scrutinized public performances.[111] Even if this oration merely represents an attempt by Themistius to position himself uniquely among the teachers active in Nicomedia, it betrays a level of professional insecurity that one does not see in his later orations. This was the speech of a man trying to climb a professional mountain, not one looking down from its summit.

By 348, it seems that Themistius had moved on from Nicomedia and was teaching philosophy in Constantinople, quite possibly as the holder of an imperially funded chair.[112] The circumstances surrounding his move are unclear, but two things are certain. First, his ambitions apparently always extended beyond Nicomedia, perhaps in part because the city proved more receptive to rhetorical teaching than to philosophy.[113] Second, Themistius required powerful connections to make this move. His father was still alive, which may have helped, but Themistius had certainly been developing his own network of friends as well. In 347, the influence of these friends enabled him to secure an opportunity to speak before the emperor Constantius while he was stopped in Ancyra.[114] Themistius gave the speech of his life. In return, the impressed emperor apparently invited Themistius to Constantinople and recognized him as a leading intellectual in the capital.

Themistius's professional successes in the 340s paralleled those in his personal life. He married the daughter of another Constantinopolitan philosopher in the early part of the decade, possibly while he was teaching in Nicomedia.[115] In the later 340s, they had a son, also named Themistius, and at least one other child.[116] The details surrounding this marriage are lost but, like Praetextatus's marriage to Paulina, one must again imagine this as a union arranged by parents with the goal of strengthening ties between two families.[117] Themistius was a rising star, and it is conceivable that, like many other promising teachers in late antiquity, he was marrying into a wealthier and more socially prominent family of intellectuals.[118]

Themistius's family was not as important as that of Ausonius, but, like his Gallic contemporary, Themistius belonged to an intellectual dynasty. He was the third generation of his own family to teach philosophy, and he married into a family of philosophers as well. This undoubtedly helped him, his complaints about his father and father-in-law not being able to imprint their teachings on him notwithstanding.[119] Themistius was also helped by the fact that Constantinople required all kinds of new resources and new people as it exploded out of the shell of old Byzantium. This meant that there were new jobs for skilled teachers in the city. These new teachers also did not have to compete against an old, entrenched scholastic establishment. While one could question how much of Ausonius's initial success derived from his talent and how much was inherited, Themistius undoubtedly built his career by capitalizing on the opportunities presented by these advantages of birth and family.

Libanius faced a different sort of challenge. His father's family had once been among the most wealthy and influential in Antioch, but, in 303, his grandfather's role in organizing the city's opposition to a rebellious general led to his execution and the confiscation of his property.[120] The family of Libanius's mother apparently came through this trauma unscathed and remained among the leading families in Antioch throughout most of Libanius's life.[121] They did for Antioch what the family of Praetextatus did for Rome. His mother's brothers Panolbius and Phasganius each independently sponsored the Antiochene Olympic games, Panolbius in 328 and Phasganius in 336.[122] One of their sons sponsored an Olympics and also served for four years as syriarch. As syriarch, he presided over the provincial assembly of Syria and was responsible for the extravagant games that marked the beginning of the assembly meeting.[123] Antioch was not Rome, but the games its notables put on looked quite a bit like their Roman contemporaries. They too featured collections of acrobats, exotic animals, and other performers that demanded a significant outlay of personal and financial capital.

Libanius's parents raised him with the expectation that he might someday join this world, but the death of his father before Libanius turned eleven seems to have derailed this plan.[124] Had his father lived, Libanius would later write, "I would now be engaged upon . . . a career in local politics or law or even, by God, imperial administration."[125] After his father's death, however, Libanius stepped back from the festivals and other activities sponsored by the Antiochene aristocracy. He even failed to turn up for the races, performances, and staged combats organized by his own uncle Panolbius for the Antiochene Olympics of 328.[126] His passions turned instead to rhetoric.

The study of rhetoric by no means precluded the sort of civic or imperial career that Libanius's family members undertook. Many of Libanius's contemporaries followed the example of Praetextatus and moved seamlessly from the schools into conventional aristocratic careers. One of Libanius's students, in fact, even took a turn as Syriarch in 364.[127]

Libanius, however, wanted to jump from the path of Praetextatus to the one that Themistius would pursue. As his interests shifted away from a civic career, Libanius also decided to turn down the multiple marriage offers from leading Antiochene families with eligible daughters.[128] By the time he was twenty, Libanius had memorized the works of the great Greek authors of the past and decided to leave Antioch for Athens, the site of the most prestigious schools in the Eastern empire.[129]

He arrived in the winter of 336 as an older student with little patience for the antics that his younger colleagues so relished.[130] He claims to have instead devoted himself entirely to his studies and, by his account, quickly become known as a dedicated scholar and gifted speaker.[131] In 339, the reputation that Libanius seems to have diligently cultivated put him in a position to claim a rare honor. That year a massive student riot caused the governor of Achaea to strip imperial support from all of the men who held Athenian chairs.[132] Libanius had not participated in this riot, and, as a result, he was one of three sophists selected by the governor to replace the deposed teachers. He was then only twenty-five and the youngest of the three new appointees by ten years. Unfortunately for Libanius, the governor ultimately relented, took away his position, and reinstalled the deposed teachers.[133]

Libanius had narrowly missed securing one of the most desirable teaching positions in the entire empire, but the aftermath of this incident became extremely unpleasant for him. The teachers who had returned to their jobs did not hide their hostility toward the three men who had briefly been tapped as their replacements. Libanius feared both their vengeance and, more importantly, the possibility of violent treatment by their students.[134] Despite the risks, the tantalizing prospect of being tapped again for an Athenian chair made him want to stay in Athens for at least another four years.[135]

This plan changed when, in the summer of 340, he agreed to accompany a friend to the city of Heraclea in Asia Minor. The two men went by land, and though Libanius does not say so explicitly, they must have carried with them a significant number of letters from Athens to potential hosts in the towns through which they passed. They stopped many times to meet friends and friends of friends in these towns, and, Libanius says, "in every town through which we passed, we had praises and blessings showered on us."[136] The highlight, though, came in Constantinople. There "many men of letters who had come from all over the world to reside there . . . welcomed us and gave and received their mead of praise."[137] Though this praise would not have come had Libanius lacked talent, his access to these men would have been impossible had he not carried with him letters of introduction like those he would eventually write for other young travelers to the capital.

The networking that Libanius did in Constantinople paid off. When he returned to the capital on his way back from Heraclea later that summer, Nicocles of Sparta, a teacher whom Libanius likely met on his first pass through Constantinople, approached him. Nicocles implored him not to return to Athens but to stay in Constantinople. As an inducement, he indicated that he could secure a teaching position and forty pupils for Libanius immediately.[138] Libanius accepted, sailed to Athens to settle his affairs there, and then returned to Constantinople by road only to learn that the offer had expired (if it had ever been a serious offer at all), and another man was sitting in the imperial chair Libanius had been promised.[139]

Libanius then asked advice from Flavius Dionysius, an old family friend and former governor of Syria who was now living in the capital.[140] Dionysius encouraged Libanius to participate in public rhetorical competitions and promised to use his influence to help him in any way that he could. Libanius then set to work. His success in competitions and the influence of friends like Dionysius caused his cohort of students to quickly grow to eighty. Some of these were new students who came to Constantinople particularly to study with Libanius, but much of the growth came at the expense of his rivals.[141]

Unlike the successes of Themistius, Ausonius, and Praetextatus, that of Libanius would prove short-lived. By 342, a combination of opposition from his professional rivals and accusations of pederasty drove him from Constantinople.[142] He would teach for two years in Nicaea and five years in Nicomedia before an imperial summons ordered him back to Constantinople in 349 to resume his career as the holder of an imperial chair. Libanius had grown to loathe the capital to which he returned, but even he could not deny that the position that drew him to it represented a major achievement, especially for a rhetorician who was only thirty-five at the time.

Libanius's *Autobiography* presents each of these triumphs as a reward that grew naturally out of his prodigious talent and his great skill in rhetorical competition.[143] They actually were products of a network of friends he had carefully cultivated. His move to Nicaea in 342 came after envoys from the city "persuaded" him to settle there after learning of his expulsion from Constantinople.[144] His move to Nicomedia also came following a summons, this time from the governor of the province of Bithynia.[145] And the return to Constantinople came because of an imperial decree that conferred on him a chair of rhetoric.[146] None of these summonses were spontaneous. In the first two cases, Libanius had likely indicated that he would accept the invitation were it to be offered. And, in the case of the imperial summons, this was a reward extended to him in gratitude for a panegyric on the reigning emperors that Libanius delivered in 349.[147] As Themistius's career shows, the opportunity to speak before an emperor was highly sought after, and Libanius needed to secure an invitation. Libanius's skills made it possible for him to take full advantage of the opportunities his friends and associates presented, but these triumphs were not self-generated. Countless letters, visits, conversations, and dinner parties had gone into making them possible. The relationships built and sustained in these ways now bound Libanius to the fourth-century Roman social, political, and economic systems that had made his success possible.

. . .

The new imperial system fashioned by Diocletian and Constantine succeeded for much the same reason as the earlier system constructed by Augustus. It managed to simultaneously administer the empire efficiently, preserve aristocratic privileges, and open lucrative opportunities for new groups of people whose talents had not previously been fully utilized. Both systems also generated impressive amounts of new wealth by calming a generation of political turbulence. The currency reforms of Diocletian and the introduction of the gold *solidus* further amplified the wealth that those fortunate to possess large estates or those chosen for government positions could accumulate.

These riches never went exclusively to the most deserving or the most capable. Diocletian, Constantine, their co-emperors, and successors all understood that they had neither the capacity to identify such people nor the power to sideline the entrenched elites that a true meritocracy would exclude. They instead bestowed positions of influence on men whose names were pushed forward from the vast web of family and social connections that bound together the later Roman elite. Although some of the brightest men in the empire likely lost positions to more influential (and less capable) men, this system proved an effective way to populate a larger imperial and military administration. It also enabled the emperors to better draw on the provincial elite, who, in the past, would have turned their attention toward civic service rather than imperial administration.

The cronyism inherent in this selection process also made the fourth-century imperial system self-perpetuating. Once you were a part of this system, it was hard to get out again. The money and privileges that came along with imperial positions could prove difficult to give up, but honors and social payoffs like invitations to great parties and marriages to the well-endowed daughters of prominent families were even more addictive. Even if one could stomach giving up the perks of this life, tremendous costs accompanied any decision to opt out. The men who secured positions as publicly funded teachers or imperial administrators accumulated substantial debts of social capital to those who wrote letters on their behalf, hosted them as they traveled, and recommended that they be hired. Everyone involved in this process expected these debts to be repaid, with interest. The man who returned these favors could fashion himself into a peddler of influence and, ultimately, a patron of the next generation of rising young men. The man who ignored them could expect verbal abuse and social isolation. Once a person decided to play this game, he had great incentives to continue to do so. Tremendous costs prevented him from quitting it.

The late 330s and early 340s saw the elite of the final pagan generation work hard to find their place in this world. By 350, the best and best-connected had done so. Praetextatus, Ausonius, Themistius, and Libanius were all successes. They held prestigious positions that gave them access to many influential people. They owed these positions to the help of others, but they were now in a position to repay these debts—and all of them felt bound to do so. The late 330s and the 340s had been the time to establish themselves and their position in the empire. The 350s would be the time to build on these initial successes. The final pagan generation had come of age. It was now time for them to take their place at the highest levels of the empire.

CHAPTER 4

Moving Up in an Age
of Uncertainty

Men like Praetextatus, Ausonius, Themistius, and Libanius spent the
330s and 340s climbing from schools to teaching positions and imperial
offices. By 350, these men had started their careers and, in many cases,
begun their families. The next decade would provide the opportunity to
build on these initial successes, but it also presented a series of political
and personal challenges. Success in the later Roman world was not a
steady state. If all went well, a man could improve his status, increase
his wealth, and expand his network of friends. If fortune did not cooperate, however, positions could be lost, friendships forgotten, and marriages ended.

As these men entered middle age, their professional ascents and personal lives became more complicated. The honors and offices to which
they now aspired were the highest in the empire, and the quality of their
competitors increased. At the same time, the Roman political and
religious climate was changing. Although the emperor Constantius II
ruled all of the empire for much of the 350s, the decade was far from
stable politically. It began with the usurpation of Magnentius, saw its
middle years shadowed by the difficult tenure of the Caesar Gallus in
the East, and ended just before the future emperor Julian took up arms
against Constantius. These shifting political conditions required the
ambitious to make careful calculations so that they could take advantage of legitimately good opportunities while they avoided association
with figures whose political aspirations were likely to fail. They also

needed to do this in a way that gave them cover in the event that they miscalculated.

Imperial religious policy also proved challenging to elites participating in public life. After an effective pause in the 340s, the 350s saw a resumption of imperial efforts to reshape the empire's religious dynamics. These included bans on sacrifices, the closure of some temples, the transfer of others to Christian authorities, and a tacit agreement to allow materials taken from abandoned temples to be reused for other purposes. In principle, these policies represented an escalation of the initiatives undertaken in the 330s by Constantine. In practice, most of them were largely symbolic. They clearly displeased some people, but the measured reaction to them consisted mainly of public support for the emperor mixed with private expressions of dissatisfaction.

These delicate political calculations occurred at the same time that demographic realities began to have an impact on the family life of many members of the final pagan generation. Ausonius lost his wife and some of his children in the late 340s. Themistius lost his father, his wife, and his son in the mid-350s. And Libanius suffered the loss of his uncle, mother, and dearest friend within a span of a few months in 359. These losses had material as well as emotional consequences. The deaths of fathers and uncles transformed many members of the final pagan generation from young men supporting themselves with salaries drawn from imperial positions into heads of households responsible for family lands and fortunes. This transformation in status brought with it new responsibilities for family members and fellow citizens. If members of this generation could not obtain high-enough imperial positions to earn exemptions, they were now responsible for the curial financial obligations attached to family lands. They were also now the figures responsible for supporting younger members of the family.[1] Contested inheritances and the lawsuits that could result from them further added to these burdens.

This chapter examines the ways in which the final pagan generation navigated the challenges that came along with early middle age. It begins by discussing political and religious developments in the 350s. These set the boundaries within which elite men and women operated and established the limitations against which they pushed. It then considers how Themistius and Libanius, the two members of the final pagan generation whose activities in the 350s are best known to us, balanced their career ambitions, personal concerns, and feelings about imperial policy. It concludes by examining the changing personal and familial responsibilities that men in their late thirties and early forties often encountered.

As they reached middle age, elites like Themistius and Libanius still aggressively pursued honors and advancement, but personal obligations frequently diverted their attention from their careers. These obligations also bound them ever more tightly to a social and political system that expected public quiescence even while it tolerated private disagreement.

POLITICAL AND RELIGIOUS DEVELOPMENTS IN THE 350S

The contours of political life in the 350s developed out of the events immediately following the death of the emperor Constantine in 337. Constantine had apparently envisioned that, upon his death, the empire would revert back to a system like that set up by Diocletian, in which his three sons Constantine II, Constantius II, and Constans as well as a cousin named Dalmatius would each bear responsibility for the administration of one-quarter of the imperial territories.[2] All four characters were made junior emperors in the 320s and 330s. They were each given their own praetorian prefects to serve as chief administrators and their own support staff.

When Constantine died, however, his vision for imperial power-sharing died with him. The troops stationed around Constantinople refused to serve under anyone but a son of Constantine, and they assassinated Dalmatius along with most other male members of Constantine's family when they learned of the emperor's death.[3] The imperial bureaucracy seems to have been equally unsettled. The death of Constantine also brought with it the fall of the domineering Christian prefect Ablabius, an action sanctioned by the twenty-year-old Constantius following some significant intrigues.[4] It took three months for the military and political situation to settle down, and when it did, Constans and Constantius had divided Dalmatius's territory among themselves, leaving Constantine II with only the provinces along Europe's Atlantic coast. By 340, this imbalance caused Constantine II to invade Italy, igniting a civil war that ended when he was killed outside of Aquileia in 340.

Constantius and Constans shared power from the 340s through January of 350. This seems to have had a moderating effect on both emperors. Constantius in particular seemed to recognize the folly of battling with a brother who administered twice the territory he did. Constantius became much more assertive after the usurper Magnentius overthrew Constans in January 350. Magnentius took immediate control of Constans's western and northern territories, but figures loyal to Constantius took control of Illyricum in March and Rome in June.[5] In March 351, Constantius appointed his cousin Gallus as Caesar with responsibility for governing the East and assembled a force to march against Magnentius.[6] Magnentius and Constantius circled around each other for most of early 351 before meeting in battle in Pannonia in September. Constantius prevailed, and Magnentius was forced to retreat west, first to Italy and then into Gaul, before his final defeat in 353.[7]

The two years following the defeat of Magnentius were only slightly more settled. Gallus proved to be an arrogant and unpopular administrator whom Constantius felt compelled to recall and execute in 354.[8] In August 355, Silvanus, a Frankish commander who had been energetically defending Gaul, rebelled against Constantius after the emperor had moved his main army to Italy. Silvanus seems to have fallen victim to a whisper campaign and turned against the emperor in a desperate (and ultimately futile) effort to save himself from execution.[9] At the same time, his usurpation and the circumstances that provoked it seem to have highlighted for Constantius the need to have a strong imperial hand present in Gaul. In November of that year, Constantius named Julian, his last living male cousin, as Caesar and sent him to the Rhine frontier to keep an eye on both the Alamanni and the restless Roman commanders tasked with fighting them.

This instability forced everyone in the empire to act carefully. The example of Athanasius, the Nicene Christian bishop of Alexandria, is instructive. Athanasius had been at the center of religious controversies since the 320s. He had been charged with assault, theft, and murder in the 330s, and, by 335, the charges expanded to include possible threats to block the shipment of grain from Egypt to Rome.[10] This last charge led to his exile in 335. Athanasius returned in 337, only to find himself again exiled by Constantius in 339. He returned to Egypt in 346 after Constans had threatened to invade unless his brother agreed to the bishop's restoration.[11] Because Athanasius's conflict with Constantius had nearly caused a civil war in the 340s, it was natural that Magnentius would ask for Athanasius's support against Constantius.[12] Constantius too wrote to Athanasius and promised that he would continue to treat the bishop as he had when Constans was alive to protect him.[13] Athanasius would subsequently deny ever communicating with Magnentius, but this is almost certainly untrue.[14] Instead, Athanasius tried to maintain good relations with both parties in this civil conflict until he had a reasonable sense of who was likely to prevail. It would have been a fatal mistake to back one side too soon. Once he determined that Constantius had the upper hand, Athanasius rushed to embrace him and was allowed to pretend that the communication with Magnentius had never occurred.

In the same way that Athanasius hedged his bets in early 350, Constantius moderated his policies during this time of uncertainty. He knew that Magnentius's rebellion had shown his subjects an alternative to his rule. To prevent them from imagining that Magnentius offered a preferable and viable rival, Constantius needed simultaneously to convey a degree of administrative moderation and to project enough strength that Magnentius seemed doomed to fail. Here again his interactions with Athanasius are instructive. A church council had condemned Athanasius in 349, and, in response, Constantius had sent the praetorian prefect to Egypt with orders to replace Athanasius. When he learned of Constans's death in 350, however, Constantius quickly dispatched the *comes* Asterius and another senior official to Egypt to prevent the order from being implemented.[15] He realized that the deposition of Athanasius would be unnecessarily divisive. At the same time, the fact that the *comes,* a military official, carried this message communicated the emperor's continued control of Egypt and emphasized the usurper's utter absence from it.

Both Constantius and Athanasius skillfully managed this situation, but Egypt was far from the front lines of the conflict, and its distance afforded one the freedom to deliberate and avoid rash decisions. Others who were closer to the zones of combat had less wiggle room. One such figure, whom we met in the previous chapter, was Gratian, the father of the future emperors Valentinian and Valens. Around the time of the first major battle that Magnentius fought with Constantius, Gratian hosted Magnentius when he and his army passed near Gratian's estate.[16] There is no way to know how strongly Gratian supported Magnentius before this visit, but if Gratian had any reservations about the usurper, the circumstances left him with no choice. Magnentius was present, and Constantius was not. This meant that Gratian had neither the time nor the space to elegantly flit between the two imperial contenders. He had to offer Magnentius hospitality, and this unfortunate circumstance cost him his estate.

After the spate of civil conflicts ended in 355, Constantius's moderation dissipated. Without Constans to balance him and usurpers to challenge him, Constantius could govern the empire in a way that reflected his priorities. He rewarded those who had been dependable, punished those he suspected, and pursued objectives that would have been impractical if government was shared with another sovereign. Like all emperors, Constantius still vetted his initiatives through advisers and battled bureaucratic inertia, but he was now unquestionably setting the tone for imperial policy. And the tone was unforgiving. Ammianus writes of the period that "any military officer or civil dignitary or person of standing who was even faintly suspected of having favored the opposing side was loaded with chains and dragged away like an animal."[17] This dramatically overstates things, but Constantius and his associates did show little restraint in punishing some of those who openly cooperated with the usurpers of the early 350s. Old feuds suspended by the outbreak of hostilities were also joined again now that the emperor lacked colleagues and rivals. So Athanasius, who had remained in Alexandria for as long as imperial political affairs were unsettled, was forced from the city by the emperor in early 356.[18] With no alternative power to which he could appeal, Athanasius remained in exile until after Constantius's death.

The increasing freedom of action that Constantius enjoyed after 355 influenced his policies toward traditional religion as well. Constantius attempted to set legal limits on traditional religious practices while simultaneously shielding administrators from the reactions that the full implementation of those policies would provoke. The *Theodosian Code* preserves a set of laws issued by Constantius that lay out a series of anti-pagan principles. The first law dates to the period when the presence of Constans still moderated Constantius's religious initiatives. In 341, the two emperors issued a simple prohibition of sacrifice that commands:

> Superstition shall cease; the madness of sacrifices shall be abolished. For if any man, in violation of the law of the sainted Emperor (Constantine), Our Father, and in violation of the command of Our Clemency, should dare to perform sacrifices, he shall suffer the infliction of a suitable punishment and the effect of an immediate sentence.[19]

This law restates Constantine's *nomos* from the 320s and differs from it only by adding an unspecified penalty that was so ill defined that it rendered the law effectively unenforceable. This was more a symbolic act designed to reaffirm the brothers' continued commitment to their father's anti-pagan principles than an actual attempt to eliminate sacrifice.

Christians understood this. Some even criticized the emperors for not moving aggressively enough. In the 340s, Firmicus Maternus repeatedly urged Constantius and his brother Constans to truly ban sacrifice and overthrow pagan temples.[20] In *De errore* 16.3, for example, Maternus describes temples as tombs that keep the "ashes of the dead, so that the daily blood of victims may commemorate their bitter end." He appeals to the emperors to utterly eradicate and destroy these practices through "the severest laws so that the deadly error of this delusion no longer stains the Roman world."[21] Later he informs the emperors that "the benevolent Godhead of Christ has reserved the extermination of idolatry and the overthrow of the pagan temples for your hands . . . rejoice in the destruction of paganism."[22] Maternus even anticipated the objection that such a legislative remedy might be too politically painful, and preemptively responded by saying that "sick people like what is not good for them, and, when ill health takes control, the sufferers make perverse demands."[23]

Maternus's comments show that, in the 340s, temple closings and a ban on sacrifices remained at the center of Christian ideas about how a world free from paganism might be created. This suggests that a consensus had begun to develop among radical Christians about what steps needed to be taken to extinguish traditional religion. Because these steps had been identified, Maternus expressed a growing impatience with the emperors who were unwilling to take them. His impatience, though, reflected positively on the political strategy adopted by the emperors and their advisers. Constantius and Constans had carved out a position between the extreme calls of Christians for temple closings and the idea that traditional practices should continue without disruption. Because they appeared to be positioned between two extreme positions, their policies could make it through the imperial consistory and levels of imperial bureaucracy without great resistance. This enabled the emperors to claim to militant Christians that they were pushing for change while also allowing them to make the case to everyone else that they were not beholden to Christian extremists.

By the time that the political challenges of the early 350s had been sorted out, the moderating figure of Constans was gone. Constantius then felt free to break with the precedents set by Constantine. Instead of just stating imperial disapproval of sacrifice, Constantius elected to give his anti-pagan policies some teeth. In 356, he took the important legislative step of prescribing actual penalties for sacrifices. *Theodosian Code* 16.10.6, a law of February 20, 356, proclaimed, "If any persons should be proven to devote their attention to sacrifices or to the worship of images, We command that they be subjected to capital punishment." A further expansion came on December 1 of the same year, likely in response to the imperfect (or incomplete) implementation of *CTh* 16.10.6. This additional law, *Theodosian Code* 16.10.4 (misdated in the manuscripts to 346),[24] ordered that "all temples should be immediately closed in all cities and access to them forbidden so as to deny to all abandoned men the opportunity to commit sin." The law then continued by restating the ban on sacrifice and the imposition of capital punishment on violators. It concluded with an interesting new provision: "The governors of the provinces shall be similarly punished if they should neglect to punish such crimes." This last provision suggests that Constantius learned that some of his governors had decided not to implement the law. Indeed, disregard for the law seems to have been widespread. Not only did public festivals involving sacrifice continue throughout the empire, but there is also no record of anyone being charged under this law.[25]

Although the law mandated the closure of temples, it apparently aimed primarily to prevent temples from serving as locations in which sacrifices could be conducted.[26] In fact, Constantius's policies on temples were much more nuanced. A law of 342, which remained in effect for the rest of the fourth century, instructed that rural temples should be protected because they often served as centers that sponsored theatrical performances, races, festivals, and other popular amusements.[27] This shows that Constantius understood that widespread temple destructions might so seriously disrupt life in the Roman world that they could provoke a violent reaction. At the same time, he did take other, less dramatic, actions against temples. He transferred to the Christian church some temples belonging to the emperor, including the large Caesareum (a temple honoring the divinity of the emperors) in the city of Alexandria.[28] He sanctioned a small number of temple destructions,[29] and he permitted people to take materials and statuary from temples for use in the construction or decoration of their homes. No surviving Constantian legislation encourages this sort of activity, but private possession of temple property was retroactively criminalized and punished by Constantius's successor, the pagan emperor Julian. Oddly enough, the frenzied appeals from people, both pagan and Christian, who were penalized by Julian's law suggest that Julian not Constantius may have been the one who forced people to adjust their behavior in uncomfortable ways.[30]

ADVANCING ONE'S CAREER AMID THE CHAOS

Members of the final pagan generation reacted to Constantius's religious and political initiatives in a measured way. In public, most of them supported the emperor and served under him when called.[31] They took

care to steer a safe path through the various rebellions of the early 350s
and led no violent reactions to the emperor's religious policies. In private, their later writings suggest that they were less enthusiastic. Themistius later criticized Constantius for the massacres he sponsored and
his paranoid inability to share power.[32] He also endorsed a policy of
religious toleration at odds with the anti-pagan religious initiatives that
Constantius introduced.[33] Libanius, for his part, later observed that
Constantius, "ruling under orders from others, was persuaded to follow
other bad policies so that sacrifices no longer were permitted."[34] In 358,
after Gallus's death, he penned an oration attacking Gallus for his bru-
tality (though he refused to allow a critical portion of it to be read
publicly).[35] Libanius also effusively praised a monody written by the
father of one of his students that mourned the temple of Asclepius at
Aegeae, a structure that he says Constantius shuttered.[36]

With the exception of Libanius's oration on Gallus, these complaints
appeared publicly only after the death of Constantius. While the
emperor lived, such sentiments resided only in the hearts and homes of
the elite. There was little direct criticism and no violent protests led by
men like Libanius or Themistius. They had too much to lose and little
sense that resistance was necessary. Constantius's political retribution
touched only a few unlucky or stupid members of the elite, and his religious policies were largely ineffectual. Sacrifice continued despite Constantius's ban, temples remained open despite his injunction to the contrary, and the emperor himself even toured the (still open) temples in the
city of Rome when he visited in 357.[37] The gods remained present everywhere in forms that could be seen, heard, smelled, and touched in
every city across the empire. Constantius's policies may have been disa-
greeable, but they hardly seemed to be a pressing or universal threat.

There was no legal penalty per se for speech critical of the emperor
or his policies, but possible social and professional consequences made
such criticism inadvisable.[38] The elite of the final pagan generation had
better things to worry about. There was money to be made, honors to
be gained, and fun to be had by those who could cooperate openly with
the regime, even if they chose to criticize it privately. At the same time,
there were different strategies that one could follow to not just survive
but thrive in such an environment. Themistius and Libanius show two
different ways in which ambitious, rising elites could do this. It is to
their experiences in the 350s that we will now turn.

Themistius followed the steadier path of the two. He lived under the
authority of Constantius for the entire period that the emperor ruled, he

owed his advancement to his close cooperation with the emperor, and he never faced the sort of difficult choices encountered by men caught between imperial contenders. Themistius had established himself as a publicly funded teacher by the late 340s, but the event that propelled him to the top of imperial political life was a panegyric that he delivered before Constantius in 347.[39] The speech deftly mixed personal biography, flattery, and a pitch-perfect sense for what the emperor wanted to hear about himself. In it, Themistius first defined himself as a politically impartial philosopher who, because of his commitment to philosophical truth, would speak only as reason dictated.[40] He then proceeded to praise Constantius as an ideal ruler who embodied philosophical virtues and whose policies reflected the principles of Plato and Aristotle. It was a masterful performance that immediately seems to have earned Themistius the gratitude and trust of the emperor.

This oration redefined Themistius. He was no longer just a skilled interpreter of philosophical texts who could speak well. His unique combination of philosophical accomplishment, rhetorical skill, and willingness to speak openly in defense of imperial policies made him immensely useful as an imperial propagandist. Constantius recognized this, and Themistius managed to transform the positive reaction to his panegyric into a sustained relationship with the emperor. In 355, Constantius bestowed a unique award on Themistius. Although he had never served in any office that qualified him for membership, Themistius was added to the membership of the Constantinopolitan senate.[41] The letter in which the emperor recommends Themistius for his honor makes clear that Constantius's relationship with Themistius had continued to develop in the years since their initial meeting. Constantius speaks of his desire as both a king and an individual to "repay Themistius' virtue with an honor appropriate to it, by enrolling him in the assembly of the most illustrious fathers."[42] This virtue, the emperor claims, truly marked an illustrious man, and Themistius both taught and embodied it.[43] "For in the matter of how one should treat the people and honor the senate," Constantius continues, "he is quite simply the tried and true yardstick for the whole state."[44] Themistius's honor, Constantius concludes, is a gift that the emperor has given to the entire city, because it "augments the senate with an addition that improves the souls of those who dwell in her."[45]

One can easily probe beneath the emperor's flattery to see why Themistius received this attention. He was indeed recognized as a philosopher who shaped the minds of the people of the city, but Themistius also claimed the role of a philosopher who provided wise counsel to political leaders.[46] Constantius could claim that the Constantinopolitan senate would now consistently benefit from Themistius's philosophically inspired input, but the contents of his counsel could often seem quite close to pro-regime propaganda. Themistius was now to share with the senate the sort of obsequious, pseudophilosophical descriptions of imperial character and explanations of imperial policy that he unveiled in Ancyra in 347. Constantius needed this sort of rhetorical support. His treason investigations and religious laws of the mid-350s had begun to create the perception that he was vindictive and overly influenced by the attitudes of his advisers.[47] Themistius's willingness to publicly characterize Constantius as a philosopher provided a useful rhetorical counter to this perception.

Themistius apparently was enlisted in this effort as early as January 357, when he gave an oration celebrating the joint consulships of Constantius and Julian,[48] but his most important such performance took place in May of that year in Rome before the Roman senate.[49] This speech shows Themistius's great utility to Constantius. Constantius had come to Rome in April 357 in order to build relationships with members of the senatorial elite.[50] During this visit, Constantius toured the city, spoke to the senate, and sponsored elaborate games.[51] He also performed one of the essential duties of *pontifex maximus* by appointing pagan priests to a number of vacancies in the traditional Roman priestly colleges.[52]

The highlight of the visit, though, was Constantius's triumphal procession through the city, which communicated in vivid terms the unchallenged power he now enjoyed. Constantius famously stood immobile throughout it, unmoved by the cheers of the crowd but bowing his head slightly whenever he passed under a high gate.[53] The symbolism of this spectacle would have been clear to all who witnessed it. The emperor had become like a living imperial statue whose strength and permanence seemed superhuman.[54]

Themistius's speech to the Roman senate capped this performance. He had ostensibly come to Rome as an envoy selected by the Constantinopolitan senate to present Constantius with a gold crown that honored his triumphs in the recent civil wars.[55] In reality, he was also serving as a propagandist who could explain Constantius's victory and legitimize his rule for a Western audience. The speech was perfectly designed to appeal to audiences in both the Roman and the Constantinopolitan senates. In it, Themistius speaks as much about Constantius's great care for

Constantinople, his capital for twenty years, as he does about Constantius's victory. He begins by characterizing the speech as one "freed from suspicion" because it is delivered by a philosopher "who must speak the truth."[56] He then turns to "those feats of prowess and triumphs" of Constantius for which Constantinople "sent support and mobilized."[57]

These victories, Themistius continues, were won using the great resources of Constantinople, but they grew out of the virtue of the emperor. This allowed him to wisely manage the campaign against Magnentius and enabled him to persuade Vetranio, the imperial pretender who briefly held Illyricum and Macedonia, to give up his empire without a fight.[58] "You are," Themistius tells Constantius, "lenient in victory, you lead your life with more self-control than the most moderate of private citizens, you set the highest value on education," and you embody all the attributes that Plato claimed a philosopher-king possessed.[59] Most importantly, Themistius continued, "you accept these words from a philosopher while philosophy accepts the truth from you and your thanks for her praises because she does not lie."[60]

While philosophy may not lie, its spokesman here stretched the truth considerably. Constantius came to Rome having been neither particularly lenient in victory nor notable for the moderation he showed to those who opposed him. Part of the purpose of Constantius's trip was to reassure senators who may have been close to Constans or who had supported Magnentius that the emperor respected the Roman senate, its members, and their traditional prerogatives. The speech also tried to mend fences with a senate that felt abandoned by Constantius after it threw its support behind him in the recent civil war.[61] Some of this Constantius had tried to accomplish through earlier measures like the appointment of a prominent pagan senator to the urban prefecture in January,[62] but Constantius needed a messenger to explain the significance of all of his actions. Themstius, the pagan philosopher and Constantinopolitan senator, represented the perfect figure to frame this imperial message for his Western senatorial colleagues.

Themistius may have been uncomfortable with some of Constantius's actions, but, in 357, he swallowed these feelings in exchange for rich rewards. These flowed from a set of imperial initiatives that Themistius previewed in the published version of his speech at Rome, a document that differed in some important ways from what Themistius had actually said to the Roman senate.[63] Much of the oration argues that Constantinople was not quite Rome's equal in honor, but Constantius had made it Rome's peer by building similar urban amenities. Themistius also makes it plain that Constantinople had contributed more resources to Constantius's campaigns than the old capital had. This was all likely said to the Roman senate, but, in the published speech, Themistius goes further. He there unveils Constantius's plans to make Constantinople the administrative equal of Rome.

The emperor quickly implemented these plans. The city saw its governor elevated from a proconsul to an urban prefect in 359, an honor it shared only with Rome itself.[64] In addition, the size of Constantinople's senate increased, the honorific title of its senators became identical to that held by Roman senators, and members of both senates now enjoyed the same legal privileges.[65] By 360, the Constantinopolitan senate was in every way the equal of Rome.[66] And, as a reward for the rhetorical cover he provided, Constantius put Themistius in charge of Constantinople's senatorial expansion.

The year after his trip to Rome, Themistius again traveled on senatorial business, this time spending much of 358 and 359 traversing the Eastern empire to recruit new senators for the expanded Constantinopolitan senate.[67] That winter, Libanius recognized Themistius's new status as the leading figure in the senate by "rejoicing with you for guiding the City, but no more than I do with the City for turning her reins over to you."[68] By May 361, Themistius had come to be seen as so vital to the functioning of the senate that a law was issued requiring the attendance of "Themistius, the philosopher, whose learning enhances his rank," in addition to at least ten former consuls or prefects, before the senate could appoint new praetors.[69]

There can be little doubt that Themistius attained this position because of his willingness to defend Constantius and his policies after 355. One can see how Themistius's status changes by observing the letters he received from Libanius between 355 and 360.[70] The earliest letter to Themistius that Libanius included in his collection dates to November 355, congratulates Themistius on his admission to the senate, and frames this as a triumph for him as a philosopher. In the spring of 356, another surviving letter offers a last, fleeting glimpse of a Themistius whose primary pursuit remained intellectual life. It chastises Themistius for permitting the public reading and copying of a letter that Libanius had sent that was not meant for general consumption.[71]

Following Themistius's star turn in Rome and his elevation to the highest position of influence in the senate, the nature of Libanius's letters changes. The number of published letters increases, but they no longer center on relatively petty quarrels like the unexpected publication of private letters. Instead, they mainly concern Themistius's selection of new senators and the consequent financial and political implications of those choices.[72] Libanius apparently only exaggerated slightly when he said that Themistius ruled the city in 358. Themistius had grown from a fellow intellectual who enjoyed prominence because of his teaching into a political power-broker.

Libanius's career could have followed a similar path, but he had different goals. In 349, Libanius delivered a panegyric of Constans and Constantius that so pleased the emperors that Constantius summoned him to Constantinople to take a publicly funded teaching post in the city.[73] Libanius was thrilled with the emperor's positive reaction, but unexcited about the reward. He loathed the capital and had no interest in leaving his current position in Nicomedia, especially since his previous stint in Constantinople had ended with him being forced from the city, possibly under a cloud of scandal.[74] He obeyed the imperial summons because he had to, but he immediately began looking for ways to leave the capital again. He spent the first two summers of his new appointment in Nicomedia, "though no one let me go and many threatened me."[75] Libanius was clearly using these visits to prepare for the possibility of a return to Nicomedia, but each time circumstances forced him to return to Constantinople.[76] Then, in 352, Libanius considered accepting a chair appointment in Athens before ultimately deciding to stay in the capital when the emperor gave him an additional salary funded by imperial estates.[77]

In 353, Libanius explored the possibility of a new destination. That summer he asked for and was granted imperial permission to travel home to Antioch, with the stipulation that he return when the summer ended.[78] He did, but the pull of his home city and "his grey-haired mother, her brother who had not yet lost the name of father, his elder brother already a grandfather, all his schoolfriends . . . and his father's friends" proved too great.[79] He began laying the groundwork for a permanent return. He arranged to give a series of panegyrics praising prominent officials (including one before Caesar Gallus). Friends in Antioch then attempted to get Gallus's support for a transfer and "promised to give [Libanius] other, greater things if he could arrange things so that he could live among them."[80] Libanius also spoke with his uncle Phasganius and made arrangements to marry Phasganius's daughter the following year.[81]

Libanius came back again the following summer, this time armed with a doctor's note prescribing the healthful Antiochene climate as a cure for his various ailments.[82] When he arrived, however, he found a different situation than he expected. The cousin to whom he was engaged had just died, and the financial support promised by the city did not materialize.[83] Gallus also proved a less effective patron than Libanius had hoped. While Gallus rode out to greet Libanius on his return to the city and responded favorably to the panegyric that Libanius offered in return, he granted Libanius permission to stay in Antioch only temporarily.[84] Despite the legal requirement that he eventually return to the capital, Libanius was determined not to do so. Instead, he began teaching in Antioch. His first school was based in his house and enrolled only the fifteen students that he had brought with him from Constantinople. Once local demand picked up, Libanius and his students moved to a spot next to the marketplace.[85] In 355, he took over the city's sophistic chair (which gave him access to public classrooms) before finally winning imperial permission to stay in Antioch permanently in 357.[86]

Libanius shared Themistius's ability to anticipate what imperial leaders wanted to hear about themselves and his skill at framing praise so that it matched their expectations. But Libanius used these considerable talents to pursue a different goal. Themistius sought the highest honors that the capital could offer a philosopher and turned his talents entirely over to Constantius, the one man in the 350s who could give Themistius what he wanted. Libanius too craved imperial recognition, but he also wanted nothing to do with the capital. Once he found himself there, he used his talents as best he could to get permission to leave.

Libanius gave up a great deal to return to Antioch. Not only did his departure from Constantinople cut him off from the possibility of a career like that of Themistius, it also forced him to walk away from the prestigious imperially sponsored teaching position that he already possessed. Libanius did not give up everything to return home, however. He refused to relinquish the allowance backed by imperial estates that Constantius had awarded to him as part of the retention package assembled to try to keep him in Constantinople.[87] He also diligently maintained his personal and professional relationships with friends and family members who still worked in the capital. Though Libanius had lived in four different cities in the 340s, friends and associates from his times in Athens, Nicomedia, and Constantinople pop up as both facilitators and beneficiaries of his patronage for the rest of his life. Libanius made considerable sacrifices to return to Antioch, but they were not made arbitrarily. Libanius knew that he could withstand the loss of his Constantinopolitan teaching position, but he also knew that he would not recover if he turned his back on his Constantinopolitan friends.

FAMILY LIFE

Libanius's decision to forgo honors in Constantinople and return to his friends and family in Antioch shows that personal factors could trump the pursuit of the highest imperial rewards. As the final pagan generation passed into middle age, family concerns and personal obligations demanded as much attention as career ambitions. Much of this had to do with the particular demographic realities of later Roman life. While Roman men in their later thirties and early forties tended to be relatively healthy, they faced an unfortunate confluence of threats to the family members most dear to them. This would have been prime child-bearing age for their wives, many of whom would not survive giving birth or would succumb to other illnesses.[88] Their children also were living through the most dangerous period of their lives. Probably at least half of the children born in the 350s did not live to see the 360s. Added to this was the fact that the fathers and uncles who had headed the families in which these middle-aged men grew up were also reaching the end of their lives.[89] The death of the head of a household often led to serious legal hassles as the details of his estate were sorted out and his heir(s) became responsible for any civic duties attached to his property.

Themistius and Libanius again provide good, well-documented examples of the sort of personal and familial considerations men of their social position faced in the 350s. Because we lack his letters, the personal challenges that Themistius faced in the period are more obscure than those that confronted Libanius. They were not insignificant, however, and they all seem to have hit him between the time of his admission to the senate in 355 and the first part of 359.[90] When Constantius recommended Themistius to the senate, Themistius was married, had a son, and was fortunate enough to have his father attend the ceremony.[91] By 359, all of these family members were gone, and Themistius was forced to confront a host of new, sometimes unanticipated responsibilities.

The death of Themistius's father was probably not a complete surprise, but it did leave Themistius genuinely distraught.[92] Themistius was called on to deliver his father's funeral oration not long after the event. In it he claimed to have been occasionally "overwhelmed by grief and brought to tears."[93] The oration honored Eugenius by emphasizing his achievements as a philosopher and the ways in which he embodied this teaching in life.

Themistius considered the philosophical training that his father gave him to be an inheritance greater than "land and fields and flocks,"[94] but he also makes clear that he received property from his father. The oration describes how his father lovingly worked the land of his estates "planting or cleaning things up or moving something from one place to another or feeding water into conduits so that his plants would be irrigated."[95] It was beautiful, but also productive. Eugenius thought it foolish to have land that was decorated with pretty trees but produced no nourishment.[96]

Whether or not Themistius believed his father that "in agriculture one could find the only kind of rest that is suitable for a philosopher,"[97] he did not follow his father's example by working the land personally. The estate was in Paphlagonia,[98] hundreds of miles from Constantinople, and Themistius needed to find a caretaker for it.[99] But things could have been worse. The inheritance appears not to have been contested, and Themistius enjoyed exemptions from curial service that freed him from financial obligations to the council of the Paphlagonian city to which his father's property was attached. Many of his peers were not so lucky and inherited debts and local financial obligations along with their family property.[100]

The death of Eugenius was emotionally difficult and thrust on Themistius a set of new responsibilities, but its effect paled in comparison to that of the passing of his wife and son, both of which presumably had happened by 357.[101] None of his orations mention his wife or her death, but a surviving letter of Libanius alludes to the death of his son. The letter has a somewhat eerie feel. Years before his son's death, Themistius had written an oration that worked from the principle that "a philosopher is not ashamed of loving his children any more than he is ashamed of loving wisdom."[102] The oration was, in some ways, quite prescient. It contrasted philosophy, the offspring of the soul, with the offspring of the body and emphasized that the properly trained soul could "endure very courageously any misfortunes" that afflicted children.[103] This is by no means a novel idea,[104] but it was one that Libanius felt compelled to remind Themistius of in a short letter written after his son had passed. When he felt grief begin to rise, Libanius urged Themistius to let philosophy support him.[105]

If philosophy could help Themistius manage the emotional aftermath of these deaths, it was of limited use when he confronted the tangible implications of them. The death of his wife severed the marriage bond that joined Themistius to the family of his father-in-law, ending the possibility of a philosophical dynasty that combined the resources and reputations of the two clans. The death of his only son was even more significant because the young man was the only heir to Themistius's property. Themistius was still a relatively young man when his son died, and the lack of an heir pushed him to marry again. By 359, he had married a woman from Phrygia with the goal of starting a new family.

A letter that Libanius wrote to Themistius in 359 shows that the new marriage had caused a shift in Themistius's priorities. The letter begins somewhat awkwardly with a statement that Libanius hopes that "this womb will bear you heirs, both for your goods and your wisdom."[106] Libanius then congratulates Themistius on his new marriage, requests that Themistius help the letter bearer with his affairs in Constantinople, and asks him to honor the visitor with the performance of an oration.[107] Libanius had misjudged the situation, however. A marginal note in one manuscript of Libanius's letters preserves a part of Themistius's reply. Themistius wrote back: "Now is not the time for me to produce orations, but children from my wife. I have recently married her and hope soon to be the father of children."[108]

Themistius had only just returned from his senatorial recruitment trip in 359, but his slightly tongue-in-cheek response to Libanius shows that he had already shifted some of his attention away from the senate. He was, to borrow a cliché, stepping back from public life to spend more time with his family. This does not mean that Themistius suddenly became inactive. Libanius sent him seven more letters in 359 and early 360, all of them asking Themistius to use his connections and influence to help friends. Most of them apparently got the desired response. Themistius did not and could not opt out of the system of asking and granting favors, but he does seem to have decided to scale back some of the activities that fueled his meteoric rise through it.

Libanius's experiences did not exactly mirror those of Themistius, but they do show why deaths and other family concerns could take up so much time. The year 358 was as hard for Libanius as the period between 355 and 359 had been for Themistius. That year, he writes, "[I saw] my mother, who was all in all to me, and my uncle . . . who was a tower of strength to me, snatched away from me by Fortune . . . and there had also occurred the earthquake at Nicomedia and the death of Aristaenetus, buried in the ruins of the city, a shocking event that caused me such extreme grief that my hair went white."[109] Libanius was undoubtedly emotionally affected by all of this, but he carefully structured this section of his *Autobiography* and rearranged the order of the deaths so that their rhetorical effect is greatly amplified.[110]

The events were clearly traumatic for Libanius, but each in a different way. The Nicomedian earthquake visited a horror unlike anything a modern mind can imagine. On August 24, 358, when the massive earthquake hit the city, the elegant houses lining the terraced streets and colonnades snaking up the hillside from the sea collapsed on one another, creating an avalanche of masonry that cascaded down from hill to harbor.[111] Soon afterward, the city was hit by a tsunami and then by a fire that burned for five full days.[112] While the majority of victims seem to have died at once, some people "whose skulls had been broken or who lost arms or legs hovered between life and death, and were abandoned in spite of their loud cries for help."[113] Nicomedia's spectacular natural location made this event exponentially more horrible. In antiquity, as today, the main road passing through the city runs close by the shore and follows an extremely narrow path on the bits of flat land that separate the mountains from the sea on the west and south sides of the city. The earthquake not only destroyed Nicomedia's harbor (cutting off aid from the sea), but also would have blocked this road, probably in multiple places leading to the city.[114] This difficulty of access, the lack of modern heavy equipment, and the five days of fire meant that many, including Libanius's friend Aristaenetus, "were imprisoned unhurt by the sloping roofs of their houses to await an agonizing death from starvation."[115]

Libanius claims to have been paralyzed by grief after learning of the earthquake, but he actually began working quite hard in its aftermath. He penned two monodies, one celebrating Aristaenetus (which, unfortunately, has been lost) and another lamenting the destruction of the city itself. The Nicomedian monody uses Libanius's grief at the city's destruction as a device that simultaneously emphasizes the horrible devastation of the city and offers a way to cope with its emotional aftermath.[116] Once composed, Libanius then began the process of publicizing these rhetorical masterpieces. Both orations went out as texts accompanying letters to well-placed friends who could give them a good public reading.

A short letter from that winter shows his approach. It is addressed to Strategius, the recently retired praetorian prefect who was also a friend of Aristaenetus.[117] Libanius begins by describing his physical maladies that summer. Upon learning of Nicomedia's destruction, Libanius continues, a second blow "took hold of me and it filled my soul with gloom and caused many of my friends to sit by me for a long time trying by incantations of every kind to save my reason."[118] After learning this, he "took no thought for meals, tossed my oratory aside, refused to sleep, and lay for the most part in silence" until he was convinced to compose "an oration of mourning for the city and for him who, God knows, deserved no such death."[119] He concludes by saying that he would beg some further consolation from Strategius if they were not both suffering from the same blow.[120] The implication seems to be that the orations cured Libanius of his grief, and they could do the same thing for others.

The earthquake's aftermath brought with it a new set of responsibilities for Libanius. Because of his ties to Nicomedia, Libanius seems to have taken it upon himself to serve as a defender of the refugees who fled the smoldering city after its destruction. In 361, for example, Libanius wrote to Anatolius, the governor of Phoenicia, asking him to defend a displaced Nicomedian woman who had been raped by the low-level government official who lived next to her.[121] The fact that Libanius was approached by the victim's husband "because he knew that I loved Nicomedia when it existed and weep for it when it has fallen" suggests that Libanius did other, more mundane favors for the displaced Nicomedians as well.

The death of Libanius's uncle Phasganius in 358 offered less material for rhetorical spectacle (though Libanius did deliver an oration in his honor) and more real-world complications.[122] Since Libanius's return to Antioch, Phasganius had served as his main patron and protector. His influence had helped keep rival sophists from encroaching on Libanius's privileged position in the city and, apparently, also made it possible for Libanius to keep drawing the imperial salary that Constantius had originally offered him to stay in Constantinople.[123] When Phasganius died, however, Libanius's rivals in Antioch began to stir. His letters begin to complain about Eubulus, a sophist who worked against Libanius and felt that "he must win in everything."[124] More important, though, was the decision by Helpidius, the praetorian prefect of the East, to cut the payments of produce that Libanius continued to draw from imperial estates.[125] Libanius dispatched his friend Olympius to deal with this but thought that "Olympius will stir everything up but will accomplish nothing."[126] One suspects that Phasganius would have been a more effective patron, especially since Helpidius's daughter ultimately married into Phasganius's family in 363.[127]

The fight over Phasganius's estate proved equally difficult for Libanius. Because his daughter had died in 354, Phasganius had no living direct descendants. He willed his estate to Libanius and Libanius's cousin Spectatus. Libanius was to inherit Phasganius's lands, and Spectatus was slotted to take possession of his town house once Phasganius's wife died.[128] Because both Libanius and Spectatus had exemptions from curial service, the Antiochene council contested Phasganius's will so that it would not lose the revenue that it had become accustomed to receiving from this property.[129] Other lawsuits followed that forced Libanius to defend himself against claimants who charged that Phasganius owed them money.[130] One claimant apparently hoped to approach Spectatus in order to settle with him separately. This would have ensured that one of Phasganius's heirs acknowledged the debts, and then would have given the creditor a better chance of collecting money from Libanius.[131] When this did not work, the creditor sent messengers to the estate threatening the peasants who worked on it with punishments for "crimes against the imperial house" if they remained in place and continued to pay rent to Libanius.[132]

These problems proved to be manageable, but their management took the greater part of two years and a considerable amount of political capital. Libanius had to fend off the council, he needed to convince Spectatus to hold out against a compromise that would have made his life considerably easier, and he worked to enlist the support of a *comes rei privatae* (an official who managed the imperial properties) in order to prevent the further harassment of his tenants.[133] He owed this success in large part to the network of friends and family members with which he had been exchanging letters and favors for years. Other heirs with less robust networks had more trouble. Sebon, a Cretan friend of Libanius, had been willed an estate by a man who had visited him. The dead man's brothers contested the will, and the slow, expensive fight went on for more than four years.[134] Libanius was fortunate that he was able to wrap up his lawsuits in a little less than half that time.

. . .

The later years of the reign of Constantius began a new era in imperial religious politics. The emperor had overcome a series of political challenges in the first half of the 350s that, by the end of 355, left him free of serious political opposition. This enabled him to act against traditional religion more forcefully than any emperor had before. By the time of his death in 361, Constantius had mandated the death penalty for those who sacrificed, and tried to cut off access to pagan temples. This was what Christian thinkers like Eusebius and Firmicus Maternus had hoped to see since the initial euphoric moments after Constantine's unification of the empire. To them, the Christian Empire was at hand.

Their enthusiasm would likely have confused members of the final pagan generation like Libanius or Themistius. They certainly did not approve of the sort of policies that Christian extremists like Maternus had been pushing, but they also saw little that could be gained by actively opposing them. Most temples remained open despite the laws, statues and images of the gods stared down from every corner of cities, public sacrifices continued to be offered in many parts of the empire (including in Rome itself), and the traditional religious routines of households throughout the empire could continue unaffected. At the same time, there were careers to advance, honors to be earned, positions to be gained, transfers to better jobs to be secured, deaths to mourn, issues of inheritance to resolve, new marriages to arrange, and fun to be had. This was not a good time to raise concerns about ineffectual religious policies or to wage foolish crusades against a powerful emperor. It made much more sense to swallow one's discomfort with a set of largely symbolic policies and work with the emperor and his administration. While great rewards awaited those who could succeed in doing so, principled opposition to the regime promised nothing and posed significant risks. On balance, these seemed like foolish risks to run.

Themistius and Libanius embody the spirit of the times. Both men had serious reservations about aspects of Constantius's reign, but each of them put those reservations aside and delivered glowing panegyrics of the emperor that greatly pleased him. And both were richly rewarded for this. Themistius first became a senator, then served as a trusted emissary of the emperor, and ultimately rose to become the most important figure in the senate of Constantinople. Libanius received an imperial chair of rhetoric in Constantinople and an additional grant of income from imperial estates to induce him to stay in the capital. He even nurtured strong enough relationships with influential people that he was able to keep this income when he eventually moved home to Antioch. Other members of this generation obviously did less well. Ausonius seems to have had a quiet decade, and Praetextatus likely did too, aside from a governorship of Lusitania.[135] All of them, however, chose cooperation with the emperor over resistance to him.

In retrospect, one could certainly fault men like Themistius and Libanius for pursuing their own personal objectives instead of actively opposing the religious and political initiatives of Constantius. But they can also be forgiven for failing to imagine that the religious policies of Constantius pointed the way toward a future in which traditional religion was marginalized. The final pagan generation clearly took the easier path in the 350s, but their decision to do so was understandable. And, as the 360s dawned, their prudence would seem to have been rewarded. The new decade soon brought with it a new regime that swept away all of the anti-pagan policies of the past forty years, a development that would seem to validate the measured way that the final pagan generation responded to Constantius's legislative overreach.

CHAPTER 5

The Apogee

The reign of Julian is one of the most fascinating and intensely documented periods in all of Roman history, but it was also short.[1] Julian reigned as sole emperor for about two and a half times as long as Vitellius, a historical footnote of an emperor known mostly for his girth and his appetite for exotic foods.[2] But Julian was a busy emperor who worked hard to undo what he saw as the most distasteful aspects of Constantius's reign. He punished many of the highest officials responsible for Constantius's later cruelties, he marginalized those who supported his predecessor in less noxious ways, and he undertook a series of initiatives that he hoped would restore the prominence of traditional religion. The results were mixed. Julian cleansed from the state some of the toxic figures and aggressive policies Constantius had backed, but he failed to reverse all of Christianity's advances. He did, however, churn the waters of the Roman Empire with such speed and ferocity that his subjects sometimes felt that basic elements of their world were changing faster than they ever imagined or could adapt to. Julian obviously had a great impact on the imaginations of the people who lived under and after him, but their lives neither slowed down while Julian lived nor sped up once he died. The ambitions, concerns, and challenges that animated their lives persisted even as the klieg lights of history dimmed.

This chapter will balance a narration of the political events and religious reforms that changed the empire between 360 and 364 with a discussion of the particular experiences of the men at the center of this study. Their experiences varied greatly. Ausonius continued teaching in Bordeaux, but his career was not yet particularly distinctive, and, perhaps because of this, few writings by him survive from the period. Praetextatus steadily gained stature across this four-year span. In 362, Julian awarded him the proconsulate of Achaea, an administratively unique and symbolically influential governorship, but the peak of his career still lay ahead. Themistius began the 360s as a leading voice in the Constantinopolitan senate who had used his standing as a philosopher to defend and support the regime of Constantius. After Julian took control of Constantinople, Themistius saw his fortunes decline. Julian had training as a philosopher and understood the insincerity of many of the "philosophical" pronouncements that Themistius had made. He sent Themistius back to the philosophy classrooms, from which he would fully reemerge only after Julian's death. Libanius had the most uneven experience of any of these men. He had known Julian when the emperor was a student in Nicomedia and became one of Julian's most dependable associates during the difficult winter of 362/3, which the emperor spent in Antioch. After Julian's death, however, Libanius saw his influence evaporate. In the span of two short years, Libanius rose up from the schools of Antioch to become a friend of the emperor before falling back again after Julian died.

The chapter begins with a discussion of the larger political, social, and religious developments of the early 360s. It then considers the individual experiences of Themistius and Libanius, two men whose activities between 360 and 364 are particularly well documented. Their own experiences are, of course, important to understand, but equally vital are the ways that they responded to the challenges faced by friends and relatives who found themselves adversely affected by new administrators or policies. Whatever enthusiasm the final pagan generation had for the last pagan emperor was tempered by their obligation to help associates adversely affected by the many disruptions his regime caused.

THE FIRST PAGAN EMPIRE

In 360, the emperor Constantius had good reason to feel secure in his position. He shared power with his younger cousin Julian, who, despite a series of unexpectedly decisive victories along the Rhine frontier, was universally acknowledged as Constantius's junior colleague. Julian, however, had begun to think himself worthy of an equal share of power. Following a major victory outside of Strasbourg in 357, for example,

Julian wrote a panegyric for his cousin that described Constantius as Agamemnon to Julian's heroic Achilles.[3] Not long after the battle, Constantius sent an envoy to Julian requesting the transfer of "his Herulian and Batavian auxiliaries together with the Celts and Petulantes and 300 picked men from each of the other divisions of his army."[4] These troops were needed as Constantius sought to reverse the Persian capture of the city of Amida, but the way in which they were selected seems designed to demoralize Julian's army.[5] The auxiliaries Constantius summoned were Germans from across the Rhine who would now be pulled far from home, an order quite clearly against both their preferences and promises that had been made to them previously that they would never serve south of the Alps.[6] The three hundred men who would be removed from each of Julian's other divisions were "the strongest and most active," the soldiers whose absence in battle would be felt most acutely by the less able who were left behind.

It seems that Julian had anticipated Constantius taking an action like this. Constantius had communicated his suspicions that Julian was growing restless in 359 when he sent the notorious investigator Paul the Chain and a group of imperial monitors to Gaul to shadow the Caesar. Julian, for his part, had set his winter quarters in Paris, an out-of-the-way city far from the prying eyes and increased scrutiny one found in Trier, the usual regional base used by fourth-century emperors.[7] Julian's response to Constantius's order also reflected careful advanced planning that allowed him to explore the loyalties of his troops while he contemplated rebellion. Julian had allowed the picked men drawn from his regular divisions to depart with Constantius's messenger while he tried to feel out the loyalties of his German auxiliaries. His main advisers had absented themselves from what they viewed to be a politically perilous situation, and Julian was left to decide on a response more or less by himself.[8] He ultimately summoned the auxiliaries from their winter quarters to Paris. When they arrived, Julian greeted them personally and hosted their officers at a dinner party. "At nightfall, they broke out into open revolt . . . and saluted Julian as Augustus with terrifying shouts, urgently demanding that he should come out to them."[9] Julian accepted the acclamation that he had hoped would come. He then began making overtures to Constantius for a power-sharing arrangement while also preparing for war.[10]

In some important ways, the situation that Julian confronted in February 360 resembled that faced by Constantine when he confronted Maxentius nearly fifty years earlier. Like Constantine, Julian faced a strong opponent who would use the same techniques that had won a series of previous civil wars for him.[11] Also like Constantine, Julian proceeded against that opponent with what he felt was the backing of a supreme power. The reports of this vary, but Ammianus said that the Genius of Rome appeared to Julian the night before he was proclaimed Augustus and told him that it "desired to place him in a higher position."[12] Julian himself claimed, "I prayed to Zeus . . . I entreated the god to give me a sign; and thereupon he showed me a sign that told me to yield and not oppose myself to the will of the army."[13]

Accounts of Julian's divine blessing spread as part of a delicately crafted propaganda campaign designed to make him seem both magnanimous and favored by the gods. In March 360 he offered to share power with Constantius, but when the offer was turned down, he formally broke with his cousin.[14] Julian sent letters to Athens, Rome, Corinth, and Constantinople in which he drew stark contrasts between his administration and the regime of Constantius. Julian attacked the sitting emperor as a murderer who was unfit for office,[15] and emphasized that he had been saved by the gods in order to restore just and balanced rule to the Roman world.[16] The letters seem to have been unpersuasive, at least initially. The Roman senate, for example, sent a delegation to Antioch to tell Constantius that it still backed him.[17] But Julian combined these epistolary appeals with an audacious military strategy. Despite being outnumbered by Constantius, Julian elected to split his forces and send small detachments out to take control of cities in Italy and along the Danube before engaging with Constantius's main army.[18] Constantius, by contrast, spent much of 361 systematically securing North Africa and the eastern frontier before marshaling a great army with which to confront Julian.[19]

Had the armies met, Constantius would almost certainly have won.[20] His army was larger, his reputation for victories in civil wars was formidable, and his strategic position was better. Julian's control over Italy remained tenuous as long as Constantius held North Africa, the source of much of the grain that fed the province.[21] Despite Julian's advance down the Danube, Constantius still held the passes that led out of the mountains to the plains of Thrace. Julian had neither numbers nor time on his side. He had perhaps hoped that Constantius would make a mistake by rushing to confront him prematurely. But Constantius did not made this mistake. Instead he seemed to be following the same strategy that had worked convincingly when he confronted the usurper Magnentius ten years earlier.

Despite Constantius's careful planning, the armies never met in battle. Constantius died on October 5, 361, while on the road to engage Julian's army. His death was sudden, evidently the result of a fever. While he was still lucid, Constantius named Julian as his successor. In this way Julian won one of the most unlikely victories in a civil war. His march to a near-certain defeat suddenly was transformed into a triumphant procession to the capital. The paths into Thrace now lay open, and Julian "seemed almost to fly through the air" as he traveled on to Constantinople.[22]

JULIAN THE EMPEROR

Julian had been raised as a Christian, but he "had nursed an inclination towards the worship of pagan gods, which gradually grew into an ardent passion as he grew older."[23] While Constantius lived, "fear of the consequences had kept him from practicing its rites, except in the greatest possible secrecy." When Constantius died, "this fear was removed," and Julian ordered "that the temples should be opened, sacrifices brought to their altars, and the worship of the old gods restored."[24] A pagan emperor again ruled the Roman world.

Julian's turn away from Christianity had been more gradual than Constantine's conversion to it, but the circumstances of his life made Julian embrace his new religion just as tightly. Julian's entire public career from 355 to 361 had been a sequence of improbable successes. He won military victories along the Rhine despite a lack of command experience and actions in battle that put him at great personal risk.[25] He had survived as a Caesar for six years despite Constantius's suspicions of those with whom he shared power. And, most miraculously of all, he had emerged victorious following a rebellion against an emperor known for systematically and cruelly destroying usurpers. Julian could not help but believe that the gods had chosen and supported him throughout his most unlikely rise.[26]

Julian arrived at Constantinople with a few immediate objectives, the most pressing of which involved cleaning up the excesses of Constantius's later reign. This involved limiting the ostentatiousness of the court, punishing those of Constantius's advisers who had participated in the investigations of regime opponents, and walking back the emperor's religious policies. In December, Julian convened a tribunal of five men in Chalcedon and charged it with investigating high officials who may have abused power in the later years of Constantius's reign.[27] According to Ammianus, eleven men were charged at Chalcedon. One was acquitted. Six other men were sent into exile, and four (including the notorious Paul the Chain) were executed.[28]

While Ammianus makes much of the tribunal at Chalcedon, complaints about these types of investigations are so common in Roman historiography as to be almost formulaic. The Chalcedon trials actually involved a relatively small number of people, most of whom were singled out primarily because of their role in the execution of Julian's brother Gallus.[29] In reality, the tribunals targeted only a small number of officials who had served under Constantius, a number that increases only slightly if one includes figures like the former prefect of Gaul Florentius who decided to go into hiding rather than face the possibility of investigation.[30]

This did not mean that the change of regime had no consequences for others who had enjoyed high positions under Constantius. Julian had very different ideas about the nature of his court than his predecessor had held. Ammianus says that Julian immediately dismissed all of those who staffed Constantius's imperial palace when he learned how much money the imperial barber made each day.[31] Others close to Constantius could not be fired in quite so abrupt a fashion, but they did see their influence evaporate as they were pushed out of public life. Julian dismissed a host of imperial secretaries and turned over many of the higher offices in the state.[32] Because Julian hoped to create a court befitting a philosopher, he replaced these courtiers with some of the intellectuals who had taught him.[33] Among the most prominent of these was the philosopher Maximus of Ephesus, who, Susanna Elm has argued, was to be to Julian what Themistius had been to Constantius.[34]

Julian is best known, however, for his recalibration of imperial religious policies. His own paganism drove this shift, but some of his initiatives were defensible on practical as well as confessional grounds. Between Constantine's conversion and Constantius's victory over the usurper Silvanus in 355, imperial policy had carefully worked to create a reality in which traditional religion slowly melted away.[35] It was only after 356 that Constantius began to reach aggressively for this goal by proposing specific penalties for sacrifices, closing some temples, transferring others to the Christian church, and allowing materials taken from temple sites to be reused in new construction.[36] This was an extreme policy, especially when paired with the actions that Constantius took against Nicene Christians like Athanasius of Alexandria, but it was consistent with the other autocratic excesses of his later court.

After Constantius died, Julian reset this dynamic. Sacrifices were reinstituted, temples were reopened, and Nicene bishops were recalled to their sees. Because Julian forcefully advocated his pagan beliefs, these actions have been seen as somehow revolutionary. They were not. The empire had nominally prohibited sacrifices since at least 324, but the first law against sacrifices with enforceable penalties appeared only five years before Julian's accession.[37] And, while the law was technically enforceable, not only do we know of no person ever prosecuted under that law, but we have a great deal of evidence that public sacrifices continued to be performed between 356 and 361.[38] *Theodosian Code* 16.10.4, which forbids access to temples, similarly seems not to have been widely enforced even if it was technically enforceable.[39] In these cases, Julian simply reversed an ineffective policy that had been in place for only a relatively short time.

Some of the other initiatives that Julian undertook in late 361 and early 362 had more profound effects. His order to reopen and restore the temples given to Christian bishops or otherwise despoiled in the reign of Constantius would seem at first glance to be another simple reversal of previous policy. In practice, it proved far more complicated to implement. The laws against sacrifice regulated future conduct and, if removed, the conduct they restricted could resume immediately. Temples and their property were physical objects that could be destroyed, altered, or scattered. And all of these things happened to temple properties in the later years of Constantius's reign. In Alexandria, for example, the bishop George had "seized the most sacred shrine of the god [Serapis] and stripped it of its statues and offerings and all the ornaments in the temples."[40] Constantius had also turned over to George a number of temples in Alexandria, including a basilica with a Mithraeum in the basement.[41] Outside of Antioch, the shrine of Apollo at Daphne had seen the installation of a martyr cult of Saint Babylas (ironically by Julian's brother Gallus).[42] And, according to Libanius, the shrine to Asclepius at Aegeae was destroyed, and its pieces came into the possession of many different people.[43] Julian seems genuinely to have wanted to remedy all of this damage, but the measures he needed to take were different in each place and had to be calibrated to each specific circumstance. While he began the process in 362, it was one that he could not quickly complete.

Julian's program involved more than simply undoing the policies that Constantine and (especially) Constantius had put in place to limit traditional religion. It reflected the ideas of a child of the 330s who had been born in Constantine's empire, was educated under the careful supervision of Constantius and his Christian associates, and entered adolescence just as his cousin started to implement his vision of a Christian empire. Julian understood intimately both Constantius's goals and the institutions that he used to further them in ways that average members of the final pagan generation could not. Unlike those older men, Julian understood that Constantius's initiatives pointed toward a world in which traditional religious practices were suppressed and temples replaced by churches. That frightening thought prompted Julian to build new institutions that would strengthen non-Christian cults and return a more traditional religious balance to the Roman world.[44]

Julian thus decided to revitalize traditional religion in ways that had not previously been tried. As a part of his response, Julian created a pagan priesthood modeled on the system of imperial administration in which worthy figures were appointed governors (*achieros*) of all of the temples in a defined region.[45] While their fundamental duty was to encourage men not to violate the laws of the gods,[46] their conduct was in every way to be guided by the principles of philanthropy. Julian broadly defined philanthropy to include sharing "money with all men" even with the wicked and the Christian, because all humanity fundamentally derives from a common origin.[47] His priests were to care for others by providing them with instruction and by sharing clothes and food with them because such generosity is inherent in the proper worship of the gods.[48]

In practice, service as one of Julian's regional priestly governors was more an administrative post than a spiritual one. The high priests "appointed priests in every city" in their region, "assigned to each whatever is appropriate," and disciplined the priests in their areas.[49] They were put in charge of the recovery of temple property, they organized festivals and sacrifices, and they ensured the good order of shrines.[50] They were to be the generals in Julian's new religious campaign.

These officials struggled to get cities to cooperate with the emperor's plans. Alexander, the governor of Syria in 363, was compelled to threaten punishment when the city councillors of Apamea claimed to be unable to pay for the costs of proper sacrifices.[51] The emperor himself encountered this problem when he turned up for a festival of Apollo at Daphne to find only an old priest and a goose waiting to celebrate with him.[52] These incidents are perfectly explicable, however. The young, excitable emperor demanded that devotees of traditional religion think about their obligations to the gods in a new way. In the past, pagans could follow their own spiritual paths without specific requirements that they attend or sponsor any particular festival or event. Julian now required that his subjects become systematically and regularly involved in cultic activity, but he left it to his overwhelmed priests to figure out how to make this happen without compelling obedience.

Perhaps the most innovative and potentially disruptive part of Julian's religious program involved the regulation of belief, a feature of Roman religious life that had not previously been touched by law. Prior to Julian, Roman law had regulated religious conduct. Both pagan and Christian emperors issued laws regarding the offering of sacrifices, access to sacred spaces, and the proper treatment of sacred objects.[53] None had ever tied particular privileges or rights to what one believed. If one acted appropriately, belief did not matter. In mid-362, Julian changed this. He issued two related laws directed against Christian teachers.[54] The first law seemed innocuous enough. It simply mandated that all "masters of studies and teachers ought to first excel in personal character, then in eloquence."[55] To make sure that they did, the emperor required that "if anyone wishes to teach,[56] . . . he shall be approved by the judgment of the municipal senate and shall obtain the decree of the decurions with the consent and agreement of the best citizens."[57] The local approval would then be forwarded to the emperor so that he could sign off on the teacher's moral qualifications. While the Roman Empire was not exactly calling out for greater regulation of teachers, no one would question that teachers of bad character should be kept from students.[58]

The way in which Julian enforced this vague standard proved truly innovative. Moral uprightness in the late ancient world generally was thought to manifest itself in one's conduct, not in the ideas that one claimed to believe. So, for example, the philosopher Ammonius Hermeiou was called by a contemporary "the best commentator [on philosophical texts] who ever lived" but was seen as a terrible philosopher because his cowardly behavior conflicted with philosophical ideals.[59] A person reading this law in 362 could reasonably assume that Julian was targeting pederasts, mentally unstable teachers, or other people whose predilections should reasonably keep them out of the classroom.

A second law, issued sometime between July 18 and mid-September 362,[60] clarified the character standards that the emperor wished to apply. Its text is lost, but a surviving letter of Julian reveals that this law defined personal virtue in a new and unexpected way. By Julian's reasoning, the virtuous teacher taught only ideas that he believed to be true. This meant that a teacher who taught the traditional school curriculum would have to believe the truth of the pagan religious ideas inherent in this curriculum. Christian teachers then had to choose: "Either do not teach the things which [you] do not think honorable or, if [you] wish to teach, first persuade [your] students that neither Homer nor Hesiod nor any one of these, the authors about whom [you] lecture and explain, is guilty of any impiety."[61]

With this law, Julian came perilously close to explicitly legislating belief. It could be argued that Julian here was prohibiting dishonesty in teaching—and lying could be an indication of poor character. But the letter makes clear that Julian's real goal for this law was to eliminate Christian teachers. All ambitious students, both Christian and pagan, would now need to study with pagan teachers whose convictions might be expected to guide students to a belief in the truth of the ideas and stories that underpinned traditional religion.[62] The emperor was not proscribing a set of beliefs, but he was very clearly establishing a legally preferred category to which only those who believed in the pagan gods could belong.

Julian's initiative created three significant problems. First, it was not exactly clear what it meant for one to think Homer and Hesiod "honorable" and not guilty of impiety. There was no unanimity about this even within pagan philosophical traditions. There was certainly no general consensus among non-Christians about how one should properly interpret Homer and Hesiod; even some pagan teachers may not have approached the texts as Julian expected.[63] Second, and more problematic, this law created a division in the empire that had not previously existed. Julian's new legal categories neither reflected two existing groups whose identities were clear nor grew out of differences that both groups could easily recognize.[64] Finally, this law was actually enforceable. Unlike Constantius's bans on sacrifice that depended on governors for their enforcement, Julian could use the central registry of teachers in the empire he had earlier created to enforce his teaching ban from the imperial center. While anti-sacrifice laws yielded no known prosecutions in the 350s, a number of prominent Christian teachers are known to have lost their positions because of Julian's law.[65] This meant that Julian's opponents could point to actual victims of his legislative program.

Julian's teaching law also had larger, more disconcerting consequences. The people who lost positions under it were the gatekeepers of the later Roman social and economic system. By inserting his own ideas about appropriate religious identities into that system, Julian threatened the cultural and social bonds that joined members of the later Roman elite. He also threatened the basic premises on which the post-Diocletianic system rested. The ability of Christian elites to hold office, collect imperial salaries, and return favors was now endangered simply because they fell on the wrong side of a religious standard set by the emperor. But social networks and personal obligations were not determined by one's confession. Pagans and Christians were locked together in the mutual exchange of favors. If the standards applied to teachers' participation in the imperial system were extended more widely, Julian risked tearing the social fabric of the empire apart by disrupting the economy of favors that bound elites together.

JOVIAN

Julian did not live long enough to apply these new legal standards to any other parts of Roman life. He spent the winter of 362/3 in Antioch busily preparing for a Persian campaign, writing prolifically, and dealing with the messiness that came along with imposing religious initiatives on an unready empire. Julian wanted the Persian campaign to prove both the certainty of his divine calling and his superiority over Constantine and Constantius, the two Christian emperors who had been unable to defeat the Persians decisively.[66] He had planned for it to proceed with the same combination of speed and tactical riskiness that had proved so successful when fighting the Alamanni and attacking cities loyal to Constantius in the Balkans. The Persian war instead ended with Julian's death on June 26 and the Romans' retreat through Mesopotamia.[67] On June 27, the commanders in his army met to choose a replacement.[68] After a first compromise candidate turned the position down,[69] the commanders settled on Jovian, an officer with experience serving in the imperial bodyguard under both Constantius and Julian.[70] Jovian quickly signed a disastrous peace treaty that secured safe passage for the Roman army out of Persian territory, and then set off with his army for Constantinople.[71]

Jovian would never make it all the way to the capital. He died en route on February 17, 364.[72] In his short reign, Jovian governed very much like a compromise candidate agreed on by partisans of both Constantius and Julian. He could be neither the austere, pagan philosopher that Julian had been nor an elaborately adorned and aggressively Christian emperor like Constantius. Instead, he struck a cautious middle position between his two predecessors. He dismissed some of the circle of philosophers and pagan intellectuals who had been traveling with Julian, but he kept on many of the other men Julian had advanced.[73] He also "restored some of the best men from all sides to office" by inviting back to court some of the moderate figures who had once served Constantius.[74]

Jovian's religious policy also split the difference between his two predecessors. Jovian quickly rescinded Julian's prohibition on Christians teaching and disbanded the regional priesthoods that Julian had created.[75] He did not, however, reinstate Constantius's ban on sacrifices, nor did he close the temples that Julian had opened.[76] Jovian instead endorsed a policy of deliberate religious toleration in which both traditional religion and Christianity could be practiced and supported by state resources.[77] This enabled Christians to recover from the financial and legal restrictions of Julian's reign, but it also meant that traditional religious practices remained essentially unrestricted. While Julian had not succeeded in revolutionizing the state, Jovian's compromises ensured that he had managed to turn back the clock to a pre-Constantinian world in which the empire officially permitted (and often financially supported) traditional religious activities. The balance Jovian set would become the new normal for most of the next two decades.

A GENERATION'S APOGEE

As the 360s dawned, the men born in the 310s entered the prime of their careers.[78] They were both well qualified and well positioned to occupy the highest offices and most prominent teaching positions the empire had to offer. This meant that the shuffling of people that occurred as Constantius gave way to Julian and Julian gave way to Jovian often involved members of the final pagan generation displacing one another as officials and imperial favorites. This dynamic process was very much unlike the period in the 340s and early 350s when these men first navigated the currents of imperial political life. By the 360s, they were known quantities with public identities that had already been defined. They now faced the challenge of plausibly reinventing themselves in ways that best suited each new political and cultural moment.

Themistius's experiences in the early 360s show how challenging this could be. In the 350s, Themistius had risen to prominence by using philosophical language and concepts to define the reign of Constantius. This so pleased the emperor that Constantius placed Themistius in the Constantinopolitan senate, put him in charge of recruitment as the senate expanded, and even issued a law that Themistius must be present if the senate wished to appoint anyone to certain offices in the state.[79] Themistius's influence in the capital also made him an important patron to whom friends from all over the Eastern empire turned when they needed tax or other administrative problems resolved.

Themistius's position changed abruptly when Julian took over. Julian had known Themistius before he became Caesar, and had apparently exchanged letters with him in the 350s.[80] Their relationship began to change as Themistius's public role expanded. When Julian was appointed Caesar, Themistius sent a message of congratulations that apparently repeated many of his standard lines about the philosophical nature of a good king, Julian's embodiment of all the best philosophical virtues, and the divine nature that Julian possessed. Julian responded by calling Themistius's rhetorical bluff.[81] Julian both denied that he possessed any divine nature and argued that Themistius was either misunderstanding or misrepresenting the ideas expressed by Plato and Aristotle.[82] He went further than this, however, and called into question the very conceit that Themistius repeatedly exploited when praising emperors. "I am sure," Julian writes, "that it was unlawful for you as a philosopher to flatter or deceive, but I am fully conscious that by nature there is nothing remarkable about me."[83] Julian goes on to criticize the very premise that a philosopher ought be called to a life of political action, citing Aristotle to prove that Themistius was misrepresenting Aristotle's ideas.[84] Julian then urges Themistius to recognize that Julian had "neither sufficient training nor natural talents above the ordinary" and to avoid "bringing reproach on philosophy" by raising expectations too high. Any successes that Julian achieves should be attributed not to any particular personal attributes he possesses but to God.[85]

While the *Letter to Themistius* was not an angry response, it did send a firm message. Julian knew the game that Themistius was playing, and would not respond to it with the fawning adoration that Constantius had displayed. For Themistius to remain influential under Julian, he would need to refashion himself. Things became even more complicated for Themistius when active hostilities broke out between Julian and Constantius. During the civil war, Themistius had strongly supported Constantius (as one would have expected of a man who lived in Constantius's capital and owed his career to the emperor). After Constantius's death, Themistius was not punished like the men tried at Chalcedon, but he lost a great deal of his influence and access to the emperor.[86] So, when Themistius delivered a panegyric of Julian in early 363, he spoke in Constantinople about an emperor who was staying in Antioch. If the speech ever reached Julian, it would have done so in written form.[87] Libanius's correspondence also shows the dimming of Themistius's star. After a steady stream of requests for help throughout the later 350s, Libanius stops calling on Themistius for favors in the reign of Julian. Instead, their letters reverted back to the sometimes prickly exchanges of preening intellectuals that typified their correspondence from the period just before Themistius's appointment to the senate.[88]

Themistius's position changed quickly following Julian's death. In January 364, Themistius gave an oration before Jovian celebrating the consulship of the emperor and his young son. At its outset, Themistius offers Jovian a gift of thanks "because you are restoring philosophy, which does not prosper among the masses at this present moment, to the palace once more and she stands near you with a more favored aspect."[89] The rest of the speech makes clear that the restoration of philosophy and the restoration of Themistius were one and the same. It contains Themistius's trademark claim that philosophy prevents him from saying anything that is untrue. Themistius proceeds to describe Jovian as divine law embodied and to explain the wisdom of some potentially divisive imperial policies.[90]

The oration has three major purposes.[91] It first presents Jovian's selection as emperor not as a messy compromise hashed out by two groups of officers but as a reflection of the singular will of the entire army.[92] It then defines his disastrous treaty with the Persians as a clear victory.[93] Finally, and evidently most importantly, it provides a long, philosophically flavored rationale for the policy of religious tolerance that Jovian recently put in place.[94]

The last aspect of the oration seems to suggest most clearly that Jovian had already returned Themistius to the position he had once enjoyed under Constantius. Themistius pretends that the call for tolerance is a plea he is making to Jovian, but he speaks about the policies in the present tense as if they had already been implemented.[95] Instead of advocacy for a new policy, Themistius seems to be building support for existing policies of religious tolerance. Indeed, it is quite possible that Jovian hoped that Themistius's strong ties to the Constantinopolitan senate could build senatorial enthusiasm for these ideas.[96]

Themistius's quick return to the center of imperial power following Julian's death can be seen in other contexts as well. A letter of Libanius speaks about Themistius being courted by "all the powerful" during the reign of Jovian.[97] Additionally, a letter of Gregory Nazianzen written in the mid-360s suggests that Themistius had regained the power to intervene effectively on behalf of litigants.[98] Themistius's renewed influence is easy to understand. His senatorial recruitment efforts had given him personal connections with many of the leading figures both in the Constantinopolitan senate and in the Eastern empire more broadly. As long as the emperor was not actively shunning him, Themistius's broad social connections made him a useful friend to have.

Themistius's orations and the letters addressed to him show his declining influence under Julian as well as its quick recovery under Jovian, but these materials do little to explain how such a figure's influence could rise and fall so quickly. Libanius's interactions with Julian give a good sense of how a member of the elite could try to choreograph his social advance. Libanius approached Julian in carefully calibrated ways that subtly suggested the sorts of services he could provide, but he also took care never to appear obsequious. Once Julian began to favor Libanius, the sophist used his influence with the emperor judiciously and balanced the services he rendered with the favors he requested.

Libanius had known Julian for some time before he came to power, perhaps dating back to the time that both men spent in Nicomedia in the late 340s.[99] They corresponded sporadically both before and after Julian was named Caesar.[100] Despite this, Libanius refrained from openly backing Julian during his usurpation. Part of this had to do with the fact that, while cordial, the relationship between Libanius and Julian was not particularly close before 362.[101] Libanius was not among the intellectuals invited to Constantinople by Julian in 361, and he either turned down or was never offered a place among the Antiochene ambassadors sent to Constantinople to congratulate the new Augustus.[102] He sent some letters to associates at the court in early 362, but it was Julian's entry into Antioch that summer that gave Libanius the best chance to build a closer relationship with the emperor.[103]

After Julian and his army crossed the border between Cilicia and Syria, they were met by a delegation sent by the province of Syria. Libanius accompanied this delegation but was not immediately recognized by the emperor.[104] When Julian learned that Libanius stood before him, Libanius claims that he "grasped my hand and would not let go, and he showered me with jokes."[105] Not long afterward, Libanius claims, Julian invited him to compose and deliver an oration.[106] Libanius gladly did this, but he also tried hard to keep a little bit of distance between himself and the emperor. Julian performed daily sacrifices in the garden of the imperial palace in Antioch, and he occasionally ventured out into the city to sacrifice at other shrines. People wishing to attract his attention would "go to any lengths to be sure that they were seen" at these moments,[107] but Libanius never turned up for any of the emperor's sacrifices.[108] Libanius claimed that he thought it rude to come when he was not invited, but he also made himself conspicuous by his absence.[109] This was a sound strategy, especially in light of Julian's rebuff of overtures from figures like Themistius who had enjoyed the favor of Constantius.[110] Libanius too had been richly rewarded by Constantius, and it was best that he not appear overeager.[111]

Libanius continued to refuse to turn up until the philosopher Priscus convinced the emperor to send him a personal invitation.[112] Julian first invited Libanius to lunch, then to dinner, and finally gave him an open invitation to visit whenever he liked.[113] When they met, Libanius says, their "sessions were discussions about literature and praises for things [Julian] had done well and criticism for those things he neglected."[114] Libanius claims to have asked Julian for "no villa, estate, or office," but he clearly had thought about how to make such requests in the future.[115] Libanius even asserts that Julian once said that "others loved his wealth, but I loved him."[116]

Libanius wanted his relationship with Julian to be seen in this way, but both men had uses for each other. Libanius agreed to serve Julian in whatever ways his emperor wanted without initially asking for much in return. While Libanius did request that Julian reinstate his imperial salary, which had been cut in the later 350s, the sophist understood that his access to Julian counted for far more in the long term than any gifts or privileges the emperor could immediately give. He concentrated on building relationships with the emperor and those who served around him while passing along requests for favors from his associates. He then banked the goodwill that these favors earned him.

In return, Julian asked Libanius to explain and defend the emperor's actions to leading Antiochenes during his stay in the city. Libanius delivered orations that attempted to pacify the emperor's anger and calm the city's anxiety when the army's arrival caused food shortages.[117] Julian invited Libanius to give an oration celebrating the emperor's consulship for 363, a speech that provided an occasion to present the emperor's biography and positive attributes to the city.[118] And Julian placed Libanius at the head of the commission that investigated the fire that destroyed the shrine to Apollo at Daphne.[119] As Julian set out for Persia, Libanius worked on orations that he hoped could calm the emperor's anger at his city.[120]

Following Julian's death, Libanius's influence declined nearly as quickly as that of Themistius rebounded. Though Libanius often speaks of this period as one where he was nearly paralyzed with grief and barely able to move from his bed, this is a literary conceit rather than a representation of reality.[121] It does seem to be true that Libanius stopped delivering orations during the summer and fall of 363, but his letters show that he had good reason to do so. As he had done in the aftermath of the Nicomedian earthquake, Libanius seems to have decided that his next project would consist of compositions that reflected on the tragic loss of Julian.[122] He evidently envisioned two orations that would celebrate the life and mourn the death of Julian. Given Julian's status and his controversial nature, this was a more complicated project than the monodies Libanius composed after the earthquake. It was also one that would take more time. The research for what would ultimately become *Orations* 17 and 18 consumed most of the fall of 363 and winter of 363/4.

Two letters from the fall of 363 show how carefully Libanius collected his materials. That October, Libanius wrote to Philagrius, an officer who had served under Julian and had been part of the retreating army.[123] The letter begins with a short greeting and then passes immediately to Libanius's request for Philagrius's campaign journals. Libanius states, "I suppose it is that you look down on me, since you have the story of the campaign written down and know that sophists will have to approach you when they have the urge to speak of its happenings."[124] In the interest of friendship, Libanius continues, "you will inform me of the bare facts; I will dress them in the robes of rhetoric. You would want your actions displayed to best advantage, and I wish not to be ignorant of what happened."[125] After this clear statement of rhetoric's power to adorn and embellish reality, Libanius then concludes with a brief note that Salvius, the letter carrier, be regarded as a friend. There is no mention at all of the grief that Libanius elsewhere claims paralyzed him throughout the summer.[126]

This differs from another letter written that November to Scylacius, a teacher of law. Like the letter to Philagrius, this letter requests information about Julian's campaigns. The tone of the request, however, is far different. The letter commences with a description of the paralyzing sadness Libanius felt when learning of Julian's death.[127] After making a vague allusion to attacks that he has had to endure, Libanius then moves to his proper request for "an account of the actions from my friends who have returned" from the campaign.[128]

The letters to Philagrius and Scylacius request essentially the same thing, but they go about it very differently. In approaching Philagrius, Libanius cannot play the role of the fragile, grief-stricken rhetor because he knows that competitors also seek the material that Philagrius possesses. In an age before print, Philagrius needed to be very selective when deciding who would get a copy of his diaries. If he suspected that Libanius would collapse into an emotional heap before completing the oration, Philagrius would certainly pass his diaries on to someone who would work more efficiently. Libanius takes a different tack with Scylacius. Earlier that fall they had exchanged letters speaking in overly dramatic terms about their sadness at Julian's death.[129] Libanius could continue the charade a month later without fearing that Scylacius might take him seriously. Both men were in on the rhetorical ruse and understood that this epistolary overdramatization of their sadness was just harmless exaggeration.

FAVORABLE POLICIES AND UNFAVORABLE RESULTS

Libanius's extensive correspondence from the reign of Julian shows the complexity of managing relationships amid the rapid changes that Julian initiated. Libanius broadly approved of many of Julian's policies, including nearly all of the initiatives that the emperor took to strengthen traditional religion, but he also frequently found himself compelled to ask that exceptions be made for friends and relatives who were adversely affected by them. Libanius intervened for colleagues who had lost influence after Constantius's death,[130] he worked to secure exemptions from curial service for friends despite Julian's desire to strengthen the councils,[131] and he advocated for Christian sophists like Prohaeresius who had lost their positions because of Julian's teaching laws.[132]

Most intriguingly, Libanius helped friends work around some of the very religious initiatives that he elsewhere praised. Shortly after Julian's death, Libanius characterized the emperor as "one who revived sacred laws ... raised up [the gods'] dwellings, erected altars, gathered together the priesthood that was languishing in obscurity, resurrected all that was left of the statues of the gods, [and] who sacrificed herds of cattle and flocks of sheep."[133] Despite this enthusiastic approval of Julian's policies, Libanius would repeatedly ask that his friends and family members be spared punishment when any of Julian's religious laws disadvantaged them.

In the spring of 363, for example, Libanius asked Alexander, the harsh governor of Syria, to help a man named Eusebius who was accused of trying to block the restoration of sacrifices at a festival. In his appeal, Libanius simultaneously expresses general support for Alexander's policy of encouraging sacrifices while asking that he decline to punish one who has "recently sacrificed, thinks what he has done is terrible, and once again praises abstinence from sacrifice."[134]

Libanius showed himself equally willing to help friends avoid the teeth of Julian's efforts to restore and rehabilitate temples and sacred statues. Both Constantine and Constantius had torn down some temples, but abandoned or poorly maintained temples would have been a much more widespread problem during their reigns. When a building came down or fell into disrepair it was only natural to reuse its pieces in new construction. After a generation of emperors neglecting temple maintenance, many building materials taken from old or demolished temples would have been reused in some of the new construction that the fourth century's prosperity enabled. Julian, however, expected that any piece of sculpture, masonry, or marble that once belonged to a temple would be restored to it, even if this meant tearing up the buildings that now included those architectural pieces.[135]

Despite this practical challenge, Julian's governors took seriously the emperor's efforts to repatriate the gods and restore their temples. In 362, Libanius wrote to Bacchius, a friend who had recently been named a pagan priest as part of Julian's revival. Libanius congratulates him for organizing a festival of Artemis that featured a sacred statue the governor had recovered from a private collection. Libanius encourages him to move forward with a project to restore a temple using material that the governor would take out of private hands. This, Libanius claims, pleased both the governor and the emperor "since some time ago he issued an edict for everyone to return what was in their possession."[136]

Libanius supported Julian's temple restorations and encouraged his friends to participate in them, but he recoiled when the repossessions of property these policies required affected people close to him. In the summer of 362, Orion, a former official who presided over the Arabian city of Bostra under Constantius, found himself targeted by people who are "hardly discrete in their desire for other people's property under the pretense of helping the gods."[137] Libanius wrote twice to Baleaus, the current governor of Arabia, asking him to intervene and prevent the further harassment of a man who "neither made war on the temples nor bothered the priests" under Constantius. This was important, he states, because Orion "was my friend in the days of his prosperity" and "now that things go badly with him I maintain the same attitude."

Libanius also wrote on behalf of other friends affected by these repossession efforts. In spring of 362 he asked the father of the governor of Cilicia to help a friend named Theodulus who had used materials taken by workers from a decrepit temple when he built a large villa outside of Antioch. Libanius wrote that he "desires no less than you priests that the temples be restored to their beauty, but I would not want this to happen at the expense of houses being destroyed." Theodulus's house "is beautiful and grand and it makes our city more beautiful." It should be spared demolition even if this meant that a ruined temple would not be restored.[138]

Libanius makes a similar appeal on behalf of the sons of the former praetorian prefect Thalassius, a man connected to Libanius's family by marriage.[139] Because of this relationship, Libanius claims that he would be a rogue who betrayed "those who should be my concern" if he did not write.[140] "The sons of Thalassius," Libanius admits, "converted a temple into a house, doing something that pleased the one then in power."[141] "I do not approve of it," Libanius affirms, "but these were the laws then," and since the sons of Thalassius have agreed to turn the house over to the people of Phoenicia, the matter should be settled without requiring them to rebuild the temple or repatriate any more of its property. "Though we are bound to rejoice at the restoration of the temples," Libanius cautions, "we must not surround the reform with an atmosphere of bitterness."[142]

These letters collectively show how interlocking social obligations and exchanges of favors complicated Libanius's support of Julian's policies.[143] In every case, Libanius expresses his enthusiasm for the resumption of sacrifices and the restoration of temples, but each of these letters also asks that the policies be disregarded in specific cases where they adversely affected Libanius's associates. These contradictory impulses make sense only when one considers the complicated social and political position in which Libanius found himself. Libanius had relationships with Euesbius, Orion, Theodulus, and the sons of Thalassius that demanded that he help them even if he disagreed with what they had done. In some cases, they or someone close to them had given similar assistance to Libanius in the past. In others, they could perhaps be expected to return Libanius's favor in the future. But one other point is also important to note. Although Libanius would not have done what these men apparently did, he also seems not to think the fault unforgiveable. Personal obligations clearly nuanced Libanius's commitment to Julian's sponsored revival of sacred practices.

. . .

The years between 361 and 364 presented a set of challenges unlike anything that men born in the 310s had experienced before. Most of their adult lives had consisted of a climb to the highest levels of an empire controlled by a Christian emperor. Many of those, like Themistius, who had risen to high positions under Constantius found themselves either cast out of office or dropped to a lower station under Julian. Others, like Libanius, who were less burdened by a close association with the old regime took their places.

Neither this shuffling of positions nor Julian's religious policies fundamentally changed the nature of the social and political system in which middle-aged elites functioned. The rise of newly favored figures under Julian also did little to break the ties that bound leading Romans to one another in the early 360s. As Libanius explains, it was only proper that the newly fortunate use their influence with Julian's associates to help those who had once offered help under Constantius. The system demanded this. What is more surprising, however, is the degree to which these obligations to associates took precedence over efforts to ensure the success of Julian's religious policies. On multiple occasions both during Julian's life and after his death, Libanius expresses great enthusiasm for Julian's restoration of temples, sacrifices, and festivals. This enthusiasm is certainly genuine, but Libanius also distinguished between the larger objective of restoring traditional religion and the specific ways that his friends were affected by policies designed to accomplish that goal. When officials tasked with recovering temple property turned up at the houses of Libanius's friends, relatives, and former students, Libanius responded by supporting the people he knew against a policy with which he sympathized.

This tendency to look out for the interests of friends even when they conflicted with Julian's religious reforms can be explained by more than the simple cronyism that the later Roman system encouraged. Julian was looking to institutionalize traditional religion in ways that were both unprecedented and somewhat alien. His paganism honored traditional gods with festivals and sacrifices at reconsecrated sacred sites, but it differed from the system into which the final pagan generation was born. In that system, festivals were common but not obligatory, priesthoods were decentralized, and the marble and bricks from decrepit temples could be quietly recycled. Most elites neither understood Julian's inflexibility nor sympathized with his efforts to legally disadvantage Christians because of what they believed. Many of the people born in the 310s wanted the temples open, but they did not want this process to be terribly disruptive.[144]

Ultimately the system moderated practical support for Julian's religious reforms in much the same way that it blunted opposition to

Constantius's anti-pagan policies. A man's place in the later Roman social, economic, and political order depended on his relationships with other people. Every shuffling of high office or change in imperial policy benefited some people and hurt others. Elites with a diverse and well-developed social network must always have known people on both sides of every major policy and personnel shift. They knew to ask favors of the fortunate and protect the interests of the less fortunate. This reality softened the blows abrupt change could cause. It slowed the practical implementation of new policies. And it buffered the passions of elites who strongly supported or opposed new directions. Julian needed far more than twenty months if he truly wanted to change a Roman world in which such men formed the social glue.

CHAPTER 6

The New Pannonian Order

The sudden death of the emperor Jovian in early 364 again reset the dynamics of the Roman state. A member of the family of Constantine had controlled at least a part of the empire from the appointment of Constantius Chlorus in 293 until Julian's death in the summer of 363. Jovian did not belong to this family, but he owed his position to a group of military officers who had been promoted by Constantius and Julian. The circumstances surrounding his selection as emperor, the tenuous nature of his position once he returned to Roman territory, and the short duration of his reign meant that he continued many of his predecessors' policies and retained most of the personnel they had appointed. When Jovian died, however, the consistory had more time to choose a successor who would have the freedom to operate independently. After trying and failing to convince more established figures to take the job, they settled on a Pannonian military officer named Valentinian. Following prompting from the army, Valentinian soon appointed his brother Valens as co-emperor. The two emperors then divided the empire between themselves.

Valentinian and Valens spent the next decade remaking the empire. Although slightly younger than the members of the final pagan generation we have been discussing, both emperors were products of the same imperial system that guided the men at the center of this study. They believed that the imperial system they had inherited from the Constantinian dynasty was a good thing that could be made more efficient and responsive. To do this, they systematically replaced Jovian's administrators with new men, many of whom came from their home region of Pannonia. They tried to tackle some of the corruption and opacity that had made the imperial system less responsive and transparent than it could be. They reversed some of Julian's financial initiatives and experimented with ways to reform the empire's finances in order to collect taxes more efficiently. And they broke with their Constantinian predecessors by largely deemphasizing policies concerning traditional religion. Although both emperors were Christian, the reversal of many of Julian's policies promoting traditional religion never became a particular priority for either emperor.

Themistius's position remained similar to what it had been under Jovian, but Libanius, Praetextatus, and Ausonius saw their fortunes change as Valentinian and Valens solidified their positions. The prominence and easy access to imperial authorities that Libanius enjoyed under Julian disappeared as the new emperors set up their regime. This change in fortune had the effect of limiting Libanius's loquaciousness. This was not, as some have suspected, a result of his fear of punishment, but because Libanius had less impressive accomplishments to advertise.[1] Ausonius's rise paralleled Libanius's fall. Valentinian's extended presence along the Rhine frontier caused him to tap Ausonius to tutor his son Gratian. Ausonius interacted directly with the emperor and accompanied the court as it moved along the frontier. While Libanius published less as his influence declined,[2] much of Ausonius's surviving literary output comes from the later 360s and 370s.

Unlike these two provincial teachers, Praetextatus was a Roman senator whose turn for high office came in 363. In the last months of his reign, Julian tapped Praetextatus to serve as proconsul of Achaea, a position that often served as an audition for a Roman urban prefecture. Valentinian had inherited him, but Roman senators like Praetextatus frequently rotated into and out of public service. If he disappointed the new emperor, Praetextatus could look forward to additional years of leisure (*otium*) like those that had separated his governorships in the 350s from his proconsulship.[3] Praetextatus, however, managed to impress Valentinian in 364 with his political acuity and skills. He was rewarded with an urban prefecture in 367–68. He then spent the rest of the reign of Valentinian and Valens making use of the social and political capital he had accumulated.

The rest of this chapter will explore the joint reign of Valentinian and Valens. It will begin by describing how the emperors came to power, and the immediate challenge posed by the revolt of Procopius, a relative of the former emperor Julian. It will then consider the way in which the co-emperors governed after Procopius's revolt, and, in particular, their efforts to bring Pannonians and other provincials into the highest levels of imperial administration. The discussion will finally turn to the diverse experiences of Libanius, Praetextatus, and Ausonius. Each of these figures is unique, but, collectively, they provide examples of the different paths that influential men took as two emperors tried to strengthen the system they had inherited while simultaneously turning over the personnel that manned it.

THE NEW DYNASTY

The story of Valentinian and Valens begins with the military career of their father, Gratian, an Illyrian who had risen from common soldier to a commander of the imperial guard and, ultimately, the military official in charge of Britain.[4] Gratian's service obligated his sons to enroll in the military, but his achievements also meant that, upon enrollment, they would not serve as common soldiers like he once had.[5] Instead, the young Valentinian accompanied his father when Gratian commanded forces in North Africa. His first known position was as a military tribune serving under Julian in the future emperor's campaign along the Rhine.[6] He may later have served as an officer in Mesopotamia under Constantius and possibly continued to serve once Julian supplanted Constantius as emperor, though this is less certain.[7] Valentinian came back into the army under Jovian, earning command of an imperial guard unit after heroic service outside of Rheims.[8] Valens, for his part, served as a member of the imperial guard from 359 until perhaps as late as 364.[9]

Although the future emperors belonged to the military side of the fourth-century Roman elite, they too benefited from the social mobility that the fourth-century imperial system produced. Valentinian and (to a lesser degree) Valens had been trained to excel within the imperial system through which their family had risen from obscurity. Unlike the younger Julian, they shared with their civilian peers a basic confidence in this system, an understanding of how to manage the personal ties that bound its members together, and a belief that attitudes toward traditional religion should not impede its function. These characteristics brought the two brothers to the height of imperial power and helped to determine some of their governing priorities.

Valentinian's acclamation as emperor followed the unexpected death of Jovian and a long debate in the imperial consistory. He was chosen more or less by default. Valentinian was stationed in Ancyra, which was near where the consistory was meeting, and he was familiar to the consistory's members because of his recent presence at court, and he fit the same demographic profile as Jovian.[10] He was, in the faint praise of Ammianus, "suitable ... and agreeable."[11] Almost immediately after Valentinian met up with the court, the army, which had lived through the recent deaths of three previous emperors, began calling for him to appoint a co-emperor. Valentinian took the call to heart. The next week he summoned his brother Valens and appointed him tribune in charge of the imperial stable. Then, three weeks later, Valens was proclaimed emperor with the general approval of the consistory and army.[12]

The two emperors spent the spring and summer of 364 working together to set the terms under which they would share the empire. In June, they split the army between them in a way that resembled a more sophisticated version of the military division before Julian's rebellion in 361.[13] In July, a similar division of administrative responsibilities occurred with Valentinian taking the Western districts (including Illyricum) and Valens the East. In August, they separated from each other. Valentinian went west to his provinces, Valens returned to the East, and each continued with the process of setting up their administrations.

The brothers staked their claim to imperial authority on a set of individual qualities. Valentinian presented himself as a strong, industrious, and militarily effective monarch,[14] while Valens emphasized the effective management skills that he developed through his administration of the family estate.[15] They issued coins advertising the security they provided and the restoration of prudent government they promised (see fig. 10).[16] The overriding characteristic that supposedly guided both of them was a brotherly concord that ensured that they would cooperate, defend each other, and never fall into civil war.[17] It also meant that they would be more forceful in responding to external threats to the empire, another cause for concern in light of Julian's Persian defeat and an Alammanic invasion of Gaul in 364/5.[18]

Imperial stability and muscular defense against barbarian threats had clear resonances in the popular mind. Successful emperors were supposed to do these things.[19] But Valentinian and Valens faced a different, less visible type of crisis as well. They had taken over an empire that could not pay the bills previous emperors had accumulated and could not cover the future promises that Julian and Jovian had made. Much of the blame lay with Julian. Julian had cut tribute payments in many different parts of the empire,[20] and he had also forgiven a large number of

FIGURE 10. Coins of Valentinian (*RIC* IX.5a, type ii Siscia) and Valens (*RIC* IX.15b, type 15 Siscia) championing the security and glory of the new order, A.D. 364–67. Courtesy of the author.

debts owed the treasury.[21] He led an army of perhaps sixty-five thousand people into Persia, spent a great deal of money supplying it, and promised significant bonuses to his troops during the campaign.[22] In addition to increasing expenses and cutting revenues, Julian reduced the total amount of property that the imperial government owned—an important resource that emperors could use to address food or revenue shortfalls.[23] He returned to temples the properties that Constantine had taken from them, he returned to the cities civic estates that Constantius had taken over, and he gave properties to friends as gifts.[24] But Julian's fiscal mismanagement represented only part of the problem. The two brothers also still needed to pay the donatives that Jovian had promised his soldiers as well as the gifts the troops expected of them as new emperors.[25]

Even supporters of Julian understood the severity of the situation. Ammianus compared the debts that Valentinian inherited to those left to the third-century emperor Aurelian (an allusion whose significance would be clearer if the books of Ammianus's history covering the reign of Aurelian had not been lost),[26] and Eutropius characterized Julian as "having a mediocre concern for the treasury."[27] The recognition that a fiscal emergency existed and the willingness to pay for its resolution were two different things, however. And while this crisis was a severe one, Valentinian and Valens could expect little patience from the people while they addressed it, and no gratitude if they raised taxes in order to weather it.[28]

The emperors saw the empire's fiscal situation as both an immediate crisis and a long-term structural problem. They began addressing it through a series of aggressive and unpopular actions. They immediately reinstated the crown gold tax that Julian had suspended—and expected cities to send it twice, once each for Jovian's accession and for their own.[29] They took back imperial control over the civic and temple estates that Julian had given to municipal and religious officials.[30] They removed the curia from the first stage of tax collection, entrusting this task to members of the staff of provincial governors, who could be punished more easily if things went wrong.[31] By 366, they issued a law requiring the melting into ingots of all gold coins tax collectors took in so that "every avenue of fraud shall be eliminated" for those collecting, conveying, and registering the taxes.[32]

The most unpopular part of their response consisted of levying large fines and collecting overdue debts. Ammianus characterizes Valens's father-in-law, Petronius, as one who "condemned the innocent and guilty equally" by charging them huge penalties for debts that reached "to the time of the emperor Aurelian."[33] Although Ammianus's comparisons of Petronius to figures active under Commodus might be a little extreme,[34] other sources confirm what Ammianus states about crippling bills for back taxes, expensive fines, and the confiscation of property given to friends by the emperor Julian.[35]

These actions helped the empire out of its fiscal crisis. The first years of their joint reign saw Valentinian and Valens issue an impressively large number of gold coins that nonetheless retained the same purity as previous issues.[36] More revenue was clearly coming in, but, unlike the successful repulsion of a barbarian invasion or the appointment of a capable co-emperor, Valentinian and Valens would never see their popularity increase because they managed to increase tax revenue. Instead, the opposite happened. Their fiscal measures proved so unpopular that they provoked another, more dangerous political crisis.

In September 365, Procopius, a cousin of the emperor Julian, staged a coup in which he seized on discontent caused by imperial fiscal policies and took control of the city of Constantinople. Procopius organized a small group of associates in the city and, in late September, managed to buy the support of the commanders of two military units passing through the capital. He turned up in the city on September 28, appeared before his purchased army of two thousand troops, and allegedly was proclaimed emperor while wearing purple slippers and holding a piece of purple cloth.[37]

Despite this farcical proclamation and his modest initial military force, Procopius quickly built substantial support in the capital and its surrounding provinces. He emphasized his family connection to the dynasty of Constantine whenever possible and presented himself as a figure who would bring back the happier conditions of earlier years. He went so far as to bring the wife and daughter of Constantius with him on campaign and mark his coins with an update of the Constantian-era legend "The Restoration of Happy Times" (see fig. 11).[38] By the late summer, he had begun to secure the diocese of Asia, and, that winter, his garrison held the city of Chalcedon against an attack by Valens and very nearly captured the emperor himself.[39] Procopius's successes were not to last, however. By the end of 365, the bulk of Valens's field army had met up with the emperor in Ancyra. The revolt collapsed in early 366 and concluded with Procopius's death that May 27.[40]

The failure of Procopius's revolt should not obscure how much the popular antipathy toward Valens and his officials had enabled the usurper to accomplish.[41] Procopius revealed to both Valentinan and Valens the need to entrust the implementation of their reformist policies to carefully selected, loyal, and capable officials. They had already begun to do this before the rebellion. Almost immediately after their accession, the two imperial brothers began to replace many of the key civilian officials who served under Jovian, Julian, or Constantius with administrators who owed either their positions or their advancement to the new emperors. Many of the deposed were governors who had gained their offices through somewhat dubious means or who had governed poorly.[42] But the emperors also removed mainstays like the praetorian

FIGURE 11. Coin of
Procopius advertising the
return of good times
(*Reparatio Fel. Temp.*), A.D.
365–66 (*RIC* IX.7 Heraclea).
Courtesy of the author.

prefect Salustius and the urban prefect Modestus, both of whom had
distinguished careers under Constantius, Julian, and Jovian.[43] In their
place, the emperors selected men like the prefect Caesarius and Flavius
Eutolmius Tatianus, individuals who had served at lower levels of
administration under previous regimes and owed their promotion to the
new emperors.

The emperors took particular interest in advancing the careers of
men from their home region of Pannonia who had been largely ignored
by the previous regimes.[44] Valens used family members like his father-in-
law, Petronius, as well as others who were chosen "because they had a

similar character and homeland" to the emperor.[45] Valentinian drew on a wider group of Pannonians that included men like Maximinus of Sopianae. Maximinus served successively as governor of Corsica, governor of Sardinia, governor of Tuscany, prefect of the Roman grain supply, vicar of the city of Rome, and praetorian prefect of Gaul between 364 and 371.[46] Each emperor also tapped underrepresented segments of the populations that they ruled. Valens drew administrative talent from the provincial elite of the Eastern empire, and Valentinian made efforts to incorporate the local Gallic aristocrats with whom he became familiar through his regular campaigning in the Roman northwest.[47] And both emperors developed a reputation for advancing lawyers to offices for which previous emperors had seldom thought them ideal candidates.[48]

Once in place, these new administrators tended to serve longer terms than their predecessors. Some officials stayed for seven or eight years in positions that had previously turned over every eighteen months.[49] Many of them also moved directly from office to office with little (if any) time off in between. These officials tended to be loyal, but Valentinian and Valens also prized administrative efficacy. As Petronius's mismanagement of affairs in Constantinople proved, the fiscal reforms that both emperors began in the 360s and that Valens continued to tinker with incrementally into the 370s could be dangerous if poorly implemented.

These reforms led the emperors to prize officials who could be counted on to do their jobs. Because of this, the emperors tried to bring only the most skilled and reliable people into office. As a first step, Valentinian and Valens cracked down on the sale of offices, a practice that sapped confidence in the administration.[50] Even more significant was their effort to create a centralized system designed to identify promising students who could serve as lower-level administrators. For most of the fourth century, these new bureaucrats had come to the attention of imperial officials through letters of reference written for them by teachers, friends, and former officials. In 370, the emperors issued a law designed to identify talented students and improve the training that they received. It ordered the office of tax assessment in Rome to compile an annual list of the city's students that would be sent to their regional offices so that the emperors might "learn the merits and education of the various students and may judge whether they may ever be necessary to Us."[51] In all likelihood, this formed the first, probably imperfect, step toward an empire-wide registry of student progress designed to find capable future bureaucrats.[52]

The reforming inclinations of the two emperors did not extend into religious matters. Valentinian intervened tentatively in episcopal succession disputes in the West, and Valens acted more aggressively against Nicene church leaders in the East, but neither emperor proved particularly interested in traditional religion.[53] They did act against people suspected of practicing divination and magic. Valentinian initiated a notorious sequence of treason trials that led to the execution of nine Roman senators and the exile of three others in 369.[54] Valens was responsible for a similar set of trials in 372 that resulted in more executions and the emergence of a short-lived but profoundly uncomfortable climate of fear in the East.[55] These investigations of magical practice, however, did not represent actions against traditional religion. Both targeted Christians and pagans who had engaged in practices that had long been illegal.

In fact, Valentinian and Valens took few measures to restrict the practice of traditional religion. This was important because Julian's dramatic recalibration of imperial religious policy in the early 360s had reversed all of the anti-pagan policies of Constantine and Constantius. Valentinian and Valens never tried to move imperial policy back to where Constantius had left it. While they reappropriated temple properties, they did not sanction the destruction of any temple buildings.[56] In fact, they were responsible for the continued rehabilitation and reconstruction of pagan temples in areas as diverse as North Africa and Greece.[57] Libanius states that "the imperial brothers" revived a ban on sacrifice, but the loss of any law doing this makes it impossible to determine what Libanius actually means and when this happened.[58] It is also unclear exactly what ban was revived. Libanius elsewhere says that Valens permitted incense offerings, allowed free access to temples, and paid no attention to the rituals and images of gods that continued to crowd public spaces. More interesting is Theodoret's comment that "the slaves of [pagan] error even went so far as to perform pagan rites . . . by revelers running wild in the forum."[59] If this is true, it is possible that the renewed ban on sacrifice was closer to the laws of the early 340s that prohibited sacrifice without specifying a penalty than it was to those of the mid-350s in which a severe penalty is mandated.

Two letters written by Libanius show what this world actually seemed like to pagans. Each was written early in the reign of Valens, before Libanius's collection of letters cuts off. One thanks a fellow Antiochene teacher named Eudaemon for praying for Libanius when he visited the healing shrine of Asclepius at Aegeae. This is notable because the sanctuary of Asclepius at Aegeae was one of the four temples that Eusebius says Constantine ordered destroyed. It was also a shrine mourned by Libanius and the father of one of his students in an exchange of monodies in 361.[60] In 364, however, the incubation shrine at Aegeae was again functioning and granting visions to pilgrims in much the same way as it had before Constantine.[61]

Another letter indicates that the temples continued to visually overwhelm people in 364. In this letter, Libanius thanks Theodorus, a friend serving as a provincial governor in Asia, for sending an image of Libanius's rhetorical idol Aelius Aristides.[62] The letter contains a long description of the portrait itself and a discussion of its similarity to other portraits of Aristides that Libanius had previously seen. As an aside, Libanius mentions that one such portrait looked to him like it was in fact one of Asclepius "similar to the way he is represented in Daphne." He "decided to place it in the temple of Zeus Olympius, near the great painting showing Apollo with his lyre, in between Asclepius and Hygeia[63] . . . which was lately restored to its place after being removed by people who intimidate us."[64] Although nothing is accidentally referenced in Libanius's letters, the casual mention of these images, their restoration, and their continued place in the temples suggests that the temples remained open and extravagantly decorated early in Valens's reign. Since there is no indication that either Valentinian or Valens was particularly concerned to change the situation, what Libanius describes in 364 likely remained essentially unchanged until after 375.[65]

LIBANIUS IN A MOMENT OF TRANSITION

Confessional politics had influenced the way that the elite social system functioned during the reign of Julian, but the administrative priorities of Valentinian and Valens presented members of the final pagan generation with a very different set of challenges. For all of his religious fervor, Julian had done little to interfere with the regular cycling of offices and honors that helped set the cadence of fourth-century elite life. The Pannonian emperors' reliance on a small cadre of loyal and capable administrators proved disruptive to those who had grown accustomed to the rhythms of the post-Constantinian system. Associates of Julian were replaced, but their replacements often did not belong to the social networks these men had cultivated for most of the past twenty years. As the newcomers remained in power for a long time, many nodes in these old social networks became less potent. The winners in the latest imperial reshuffling seemed like they would remain in office forever, and, more vitally, the losers saw little hope of climbing back up again.

Libanius found himself in this position following Julian's death. His situation had to do, in part, with the unique way that he had positioned himself during Julian's life and (especially) following Julian's death. Libanius had served as an important adviser and liaison during Julian's stay in Antioch and in the months following his departure. Under Julian, Libanius forwarded many individual requests for imperial assistance on behalf of associates, he served on the commission to investigate the burning of the temple of Apollo,[66] he spoke with the emperor to obtain a pardon for Antioch after the emperor's *Misopogon* lampooned the city,[67] and he composed orations that he hoped would chart a path toward respectful reconciliation between the city and its emperor.[68]

This association with Julian put Libanius in a difficult position under Valens, a situation made more difficult after the revolt of Procopius had heightened the emperor's suspicions of Julian's old associates.[69] Even before Valens's appointment in 364, however, Libanius expressed concern about a decline in his influence. He wrote twice to Salustius in 364 in order to check that his relationship with the praetorian prefect remained solid.[70] Similar letters were sent to Datianus and Themistius, both of whom had recently regained the influence they had lost under Julian.[71] Libanius had reason to worry. His friend Seleucus, a former courtier of Julian, had been fined and exiled in early 365.[72] Many of the intellectuals who had associated closely with Julian also suffered because of their connections to him. The physician Oribasius had his property confiscated,[73] the philosopher Priscus was arrested,[74] the rhetorician Himerius was exiled from the city of Athens,[75] and, most notoriously, the philosopher Maximus of Ephesus was fined, arrested, and pushed to the verge of suicide by the emperor's agents.[76] Maximus was briefly rehabilitated before he again fell under suspicion and was executed.[77]

Libanius differed from the group of intellectuals punished by Valens only because he had consummated his relationship with Julian at a later stage in the emperor's regime. Unlike Oribasius, Himerius, Priscus, and Maximus, Libanius had become close to the emperor only after he arrived in Antioch in 362. This gave Libanius a bit of space to recast his interaction with Julian in a slightly different light. In the previous chapter, we saw how Libanius presented Julian as a genuine friend with whom he discussed literature and to whom he offered "praises for things [Julian] had done well and reproofs for those things he neglected."[78] According to Libanius, theirs was not a friendship based on the gifts the emperor could give him but on the mutual respect and love that they shared with one another.[79]

These claims undoubtedly reflect something of how Libanius presented his relationship with Julian while the emperor lived, but the clearest and most frequent statements of the purity of Libanius's friendship with Julian appear in works like *Orations* 1, 17, and 18, all of which were written and released under Valens.[80] This is not a coincidence. Valens's officials focused in large part on Julian's favored intellectuals because they seemed to have profited immensely from their association with the profligate emperor. Libanius anticipated this type of charge and tried to blunt it by emphasizing how much he gained emotionally from Julian and how little he had benefited materially. He hoped that this would enable him to avoid the fates of his peers.

He would never be imprisoned, fined, or exiled, but Libanius did endure a difficult decade and a half under Valens. Libanius faced a series of intrigues and investigations that included a kidnapping attempt and a plot hatched by a military official close to Valens.[81] Even worse for Libanius, Valens proved unresponsive to his efforts to recapture the public prominence that he had enjoyed under Julian. Libanius mentions an epic oration praising Valens's Gothic campaigns of 367–69 that was so long that it required two different meetings for delivery. While Valens turned up for the first part of it, the second was never delivered, and Libanius was forced to send a written copy of it for the emperor to read at his leisure.[82] The speech failed to make the desired impression. Even more significant is the fact that Libanius's long string of published letters ends aburptly at the beginning of Valens's reign. This likely represents the conclusion of a published collection rather than an effort by Libanius to self-censor in order to avoid legal jeopardy, but it is still a significant development.[83] The publication of a collection of letters was the ultimate late antique act of self-fashioning and reputation management. Because his career seemed to have peaked under Julian, Libanius probably made the decision not to publish any additional letters so as not to advertise his diminished importance.[84] Indeed, most of the surviving material that Libanius composed during the reign of Valens reflects on and advertises past triumphs rather than Libanius's dimmer contemporary realities.

PRAETEXTATUS AND THE ART OF REMAINING RELEVANT

Not all of those who did well under Julian fared poorly under Valentinian and Valens. After bouncing through a series of governorships in the

350s, Praetextatus spent the late 350s and early 360s out of office and enjoying a spell of *otium*. In 362, however, Julian tapped him for the proconsulship of Achaea, a provincial governorship that promised its holders a higher level of access to the emperor.[85] Achaea was, of course, the province that contained Athens and most of the classical Greek heartland, but, in the fourth century, its governors were almost exclusively Latin-speaking (often pagan) aristocrats. Constantine had given the province a special status that allowed its proconsul to skip over the praetorian prefect and report directly to the emperor.[86] This made a proconsulship of Achaea one of the more desirable governorships. By the 340s, it comes to occupy a middle position in the hierarchy of offices held by prominent Italian senators. It ranked well above governorships like the governor of Tuscany and Umbria (the *corrector Tusciae et Umbriae*) and just below some of the prefect positions to which its holders often moved next. In this sense, the proconsulship of Achaea was not unlike that of Africa, another high-level governorship that figures like Petronius Probus and Olybrius held before becoming prefects.[87]

Julian tapped Praetextatus to serve as proconsul of Achaea on his own initiative without the input of other senior officials.[88] This was undoubtedly a sort of audition for higher office, but Praetextatus also fit the profile of the type of Achaean proconsul who might appeal to the emperor. He had, of course, held the necessary precursor offices and minor governorships. But Praetextatus also held a number of priesthoods at the time of his appointment (including, perhaps, a priesthood in the cult of Mithras that was dear to Julian).[89] He was also a well-educated man. He translated into Latin works of Greek poetry and a paraphrase of Aristotle written by Themistius.[90] While governor, he negotiated the return of the rhetorician Himerius, who had been barred from returning to Athens following Julian's death.[91]

Praetextatus was a perfect match for the Julianic intellectual and religious climate, but his administrative skill and personal savvy enabled him to remain influential under Valentinian and Valens. Praetextatus had real responsibilities when in office and also enjoyed the privileged access to the emperor that Achaean governors expected. This would prove particularly useful in 364 when Valentinian and Valens issued a law regulating certain nighttime rituals. The nature of this law has commonly been misinterpreted, often deliberately, as part of a historical tradition that goes back at least to the sixth-century pagan historian Zosimus. Zosimus describes this as a law crafted to hinder religious mysteries, a reading of the law mirrored both by the late antique interpreters and by many modern scholars.[92] When this law was issued, Zosimus explains, Praetextatus, a "man distinguished by every virtue," used his prerogative as proconsul of Achaea to speak to the emperor directly about its implications. Praetextatus explained that, as written, the law in question would "make life unbearable for Hellenes." Valentinian then abandoned the proposal and allowed everything to be done according to custom.[93]

Zosimus's story about Praetextatus's principled stand before the emperor mythologizes an imagined pagan hero much more than it describes Praetextatus's actual conduct. Fortunately, the probable text of the law in question survives in the *Theodosian Code*. In it, the emperors order that "no person during the night time should try to celebrate either wicked prayers or magic preparations or destructive sacrifices." They then decree a punishment for those who violate the order.[94] Although this law can be seen as a reiteration of an earlier law of Constantius restricting nocturnal sacrifices (*sacrificia nocturna*), it is actually quite different.[95] Instead of taking a new action against traditional religious practice, Valentinian and Valens reinforced a long-standing ban on magical practices and other secret rituals designed to cause harm to other people.[96] This is a very different sort of prohibition and one that is, perhaps, motivated primarily by the recent experience of two emperors who suspected that magicians may have caused the two of them to fall ill together during a recent visit to Constantinople.[97]

Valentinian and Valens were not trying to eliminate traditional religion or restrict religious mysteries,[98] but their intention did not preclude a governor interpreting the law they issued in 364 in this way. Praetextatus likely explained this to Valentinian. As proconsul of Achaea, he could tell Valentinian what the consequences of this law would be in his province. Valentinian, who was no religious zealot and privileged unproblematic administration over unnecessary religious conflict, would have been inclined to listen.[99] In fact, later in his reign, Valentinian came to be seen as a benefactor of traditional cults in Greece. Both Valentinian and Valens were given honors on the Sacred Way linking Athens and Eleusis, and each had statues erected to commemorate their benefactions to Delphi.[100] Praetextatus must have sensed that Valentinan would welcome a conversation about a law's unintended consequences. His communication with Valentinian then was not a pagan subordinate bravely confronting his Christian superior but a part of the regular communication between a senior administrator and his emperor.

Valentinian clearly appreciated both Praetextatus's skill and his candor. After Praetextatus stepped down from the Achaean proconsulship, he remained out of government service for less than two years. By 367, Valentinian had installed him as urban prefect of Rome, an office that capped many accomplished Italian senatorial careers, and one that Praetextatus would hold until at least September 368.[101]

As prefect, Praetextatus immediately walked into a simmering dispute between the Christians Damasus and Ursinus, both of whom claimed to be the rightful bishop of Rome.[102] Their dispute had begun in late 366 and erupted into street violence that led to 137 deaths and the exile of Ursinus.[103] The conflict had become so intense that Viventius, the urban prefect, had fled the city for a time out of concern for his own safety.[104] Indeed, Viventius's fate may have prompted the appointment of Praetextatus. Viventius was a Pannonian who was loyal, but not particularly capable.[105] Praetextatus was the opposite. He knew the city and had strong social connections to its most powerful figures. When called on to deal with the aftermath of the Roman rioting, he did so effectively. In early September 367, perhaps not more than a month after taking office, he supervised the return of all of those who were exiled following the fighting.[106] He then arranged the transfer of the basilica of Sicininus to Damasus around the beginning of 368.[107] When problems emerged again in January, he expelled the supporters of Ursinus from the city.[108] Unlike the Pannonian Viventius, the Roman Praetextatus seems to have been able to do this without prompting any more serious violence.[109]

Praetextatus also involved himself in other aspects of the religious and social life of the city. During his prefecture, he restored the Portico of the Consenting Gods in the Forum,[110] and he ordered the destruction of overhanging galleries and the walls of private homes that encroached on the sacred precincts of temples.[111] A letter of Symmachus may also suggest that he restored some public statues that had been taken down, though the language is sufficiently vague and the dating too imprecise to say whether this happened during Praetextatus's prefecture.[112] There is also the possibility that Praetextatus may have been responsible for the selection of the young Symmachus as a senatorial emissary to the court of Valentinian in 368.[113] If so, this helped to solidify a burgeoning social relationship with the young man that saw a steady exchange of letters and favors pass between them for much of the 370s and 380s.

Following his prefecture, Praetextatus settled into a life of aristocratic leisure interrupted occasionally by official duties that kept him in the public eye.[114] He served as a member of a number of senatorial embassies, including the successful delegation that asked Valentinian to curb the abusive investigations of Roman senators suspected of involvement in magic in 370.[115] As he had in 364, Praetextatus again confronted the emperor, asking him to stop the torture of senators and to ensure that their punishments matched those legally prescribed for the offenses with which they were charged.[116] Although Valentinian initially denied that any such extreme measures were being taken, he ultimately agreed to accept the limits the embassy proposed.

High-profile activities like this, however, were the exception for Praetextatus after he stepped down as prefect. He seems to have spent most of his time on his various estates. He remained involved in senatorial affairs, at one point even mediating a dispute between Symmachus and another senator,[117] but his direct engagement with Roman events was selective. Symmachus sometimes expressed (or feigned) great annoyance at Praetextatus's tendency to immerse himself in leisurely activities.[118] In the fourth century, members of the priestly college in Rome evidently divided their responsibilities in such a way that at least two were required to stay close enough to Rome that they could perform religious duties in the city.[119] In one letter, Symmachus recounts how he had changed his vacation plans because it was his month to serve, and states, "I do not intend to take my place when there is such negligence among the priests."[120] He then asks Praetextatus how long he intends to remain in Etruria, because "we are now beginning to complain that there should be something that takes precedence over your fellow-citizens for so long."[121]

Another letter criticizes Praetextatus's disengagement more explicitly. It follows a lull in their correspondence and uses this as a pretext to contrast Symmachus's priestly diligence with Praetextatus's *otium*. "The reasons for our mutual silence are different," it begins. "Concern for my pontifical duties constrains me, whereas the carefree leisure of [the resort of] Baiae constrains you." Symmachus continues by asserting that he does not say this to criticize Praetextatus's virtue. He is prompted because "we have many things to deliberate in the college; who gave you this leave of absence from public service?"[122]

One must exercise a bit of caution when considering how representative these letters are of Praetextatus's overall level of engagement with traditional cults.[123] The inscription with which his wife honored him following his death highlights his priesthoods and religious activities above his political offices.[124] Even if Symmachus's portrait is not complete, the letters do show that, like many members of the old senatorial elite, Praetextatus balanced his public service with extended periods of leisure activities. His service to Valentinian in 364 and again in 367–68 had shown him to be a gifted administrator who could serve effectively if called on, but his activities in the 370s show that he felt no obligation to serve perpetually. Unlike his Pannonian contemporaries, he had no interest in a full-time administrative career. He relished his time out of office and put it to use reading, writing, and "ruminating," though he remained willing to be called to service if circumstances demanded.

AUSONIUS AND THE RISE OF A PROVINCIAL ELITE

Praetextatus's status permitted him to engage selectively in public life, but people with less lofty backgrounds did not have that luxury. Unlike Praetextatus, Ausonius came from a family whose members had never held high office in the empire. As a middle-aged Gallic teacher, he seemed unlikely to embark on a career of this type until a combination of exceptional events in the later 360s offered him an unexpected opportunity to join the ranks of the empire's most powerful figures.

The circumstances leading to this were as exceptional as the promotion itself. Valentinian fell dangerously ill while on campaign in Gaul in 367, and when he recovered, he announced that his son Gratian, who was then eight years old, would serve as his co-emperor in the West.[125] As Ammianus describes it, Valentinian promised the army that the young boy would grow into a capable ruler because "the training which he acquires from the liberal arts will enable him to form an impartial judgment of right and wrong."[126]

Gratian now needed a reputable tutor, and because his elevation coincided with Valentinian's decision to base his court in Trier in 367,[127] Ausonius seemed a reasonable choice. Ausonius had long served as a professor of rhetoric in Bordeaux, Gaul's most renowned center of teaching. In addition, Ausonius's uncle Arborius had once served as tutor for one of the sons of Constantine.[128] Ausonius could be expected to understand what the position of imperial tutor entailed in a way that some of the local teachers in Trier perhaps could not.[129]

Ausonius astutely took full advantage of the opportunities that court presented to him. In addition to the literary education that Ausonius provided, Gratian also received on-the-job training in how to govern and administer the empire. This meant that when Valentinian took the army on a campaign against the Alamanni soon after Ausonius's arrival, the teacher and his student went along.[130] This proved a boon to Ausonius. Valentinian's campaigns inspired some of Ausonius's most important poetry, including two epigrams about the source of the Danube written at Valentinian's request, and Ausonius's *Mosella*, a poetic masterpiece that takes readers on a tour of the river and celebrates the peaceful countryside produced by Valentinian's campaigns.[131] In this long poem, Ausonius captures and advertises many of the same ideas of security and military prowess that Valentinianic propaganda emphasized.[132]

Ausonius did more than generate propaganda. He also interacted with the emperor and his soldiers in more relaxed, unofficial settings. He sent to Symmachus a playful poem on the number three that he wrote when "on active military service." The men in his bunk, he claims, "issued a challenge to drink . . . thrice three cups." The poem then was "begun during lunch and finished before dinner, which is to say while I was drinking and a little before I was to drink again."[133] In light of this, Ausonius warns Symmachus not to read the odd little poem unless he too has taken a drink or three.

Ausonius's playfully bantered with Valentinian as well. He mentions a number of works inspired by conversations and literary exchanges with the emperor.[134] The most interesting of these was the *Nuptial Cento*, a lewd poem composed from pieces of Vergil that Ausonius recombined to treat a new theme.[135] In a cover letter to his friend Paulinus, Ausonius explains that the poem "was written by command of . . . the sainted emperor Valentinian, a man, in my opinion, of deep learning." The emperor had once stitched together an amusing description of a wedding using only random snippets of Vergil, and then asked Ausonius to "assemble a similar poem on the same subject."[136] Few contemporaries thought of Valentinian as either a connoisseur of Vergil or a poet, but, for Ausonius, this exchange of centos offered an opportunity to develop a literary friendship with the emperor. Though the individual inclinations of Valentinian and Julian differed dramatically, Ausonius's initiatives resembled the efforts that Libanius made to build a literary friendship with Julian five years earlier.[137]

In Ausonius's case, the rewards of this friendship soon became apparent. Unlike Libanius, Ausonius received official titles and offices from his imperial friend. Following the composition of the *Mosella*, Ausonius seems to have secured an honorary position as a count (a *comes tertii ordinis*).[138] Then, by August 375, he had been made the member of the imperial consistory responsible for beautifying or revising the text of imperial legislation (the *quaestor sacri palatii*).[139] Even more significant was the effect that his presence at court had on his social standing. Libanius's short time as a confidant of Julian helped him build relationships with influential men he might otherwise never have met. Ausonius spent more time at court, and his influence ultimately far eclipsed that which Libanius had once enjoyed.

Symmachus's correspondence shows how efficiently Ausonius fashioned himself into a leading member of the Western elite. The correspondence between the two began around the time of Ausonius's appointment as imperial tutor, but their relationship developed into something much more familiar following the young Symmachus's embassy to the court of Valentinian in 368.[140] Symmachus spent much of 368 and 369 with Ausonius at court and on campaign with the emperor before returning to Rome by early 370.[141] He would never again see Ausonius in person, but a regular exchange of letters sustained their relationship for at least the next decade.

These letters reveal two friends who exchanged notes, texts, and favors. Intriguingly, given that Symmachus belonged to one of Rome's most well-established families, Symmachus's letters often rhetorically position Ausonius as a literary (and, at times, social) superior. This is certainly true in their first epistolary exchange, which begins with Symmachus fawning that Ausonius's "literary reputation made me wish to pay my respects to you, but I put off the task of writing for a long time out of modesty."[142] Later letters were less obsequious (or perhaps less sarcastic), but Symmachus always took care to acknowledge a sort of literary seniority in his friend. Ausonius was his master and parent who served as a literary mentor, a conceit that Ausonius indulged by calling Symmachus his son.[143] Indeed, as Michele Salzman has noted, it is not coincidental that these letters between Symmachus and his literary father come immediately after those between Symmachus and his biological father in the first book of his published letters.[144]

Tangible exchanges also joined the two men. Many of Symmachus's surviving letters to Ausonius involve recommendations of men traveling from Rome to the courts of Valentinian and Gratian. In keeping with the idea of Ausonius as his intellectual father, a number of them introduce intellectuals or other men of culture to Ausonius.[145] One recommended Palladius, an Athenian rhetorician who came to Ausonius armed with a declamation that "pleased the most eminent *literati*" in Rome and an endorsement from Symmachus that "he is as distinguished in rhetoric as in character."[146] Another recommended a philosopher named Barachus "whose true wisdom has the vigor of the ancient times."[147] A third "introduces an aspiring philosopher whose sense of decency will be apparent even at first glance."[148] A fourth was carried by a young rhetorician named Julian who, Symmachus claims, is among the rare ones to "associate eloquent speech and moral character in the arena of the courts."[149]

These letters reveal two distinctive but related things about Ausonius's jump from the local Gallic aristocracy to the imperial court. Like Themistius in the 350s, Ausonius seems to have aggressively presented himself as the leading intellectual at the court of Valentinian. This was, of course, deliberate. The middle-aged Gallic teacher now enjoyed a position of tremendous influence, but he had neither a family background nor a previous administrative career to match that of men like Symmachus and Praetextatus. Ausonius was a parvenu, but, unlike many of the Pannonians whom Valentinian brought into government, Ausonius's literary talent gave him a cultural authority that other elites recognized as legitimate.

When he came to court, Ausonius used this cultural capital to build useful alliances with members of more established senatorial families. Ausonius peppered Italian elites like Symmachus and Petronius Probus with letters and literary texts that hinted at but never explicitly acknowledged his influence with the emperor.[150] Ausonius and his correspondents kept their epistolary interactions largely confined to the literary sphere, where Ausonius's legitimate authority could not be questioned.[151] Ausonius played this game quite well. By the time of Valentinian's death in 375, he had built for himself a network of influential friends and associates who openly acknowledged his cultural authority and implicitly recognized his tangible influence. This was a significant trick that many of Valentinian's favorites never managed. It would serve Ausonius particularly well in the years following Valentinian's death.

. . .

The eleven-year joint reign of Valentinian and Valens shocked the social and administrative system in which men born in the 310s had been taught to function. The Pannonian emperors did not seek to dismantle this system. They instead tried to make it more effective and more efficient while simultaneously depending on it to solve the serious financial crisis that they had inherited from Julian and Jovian. The sensitivity of these tasks compelled the emperors to bring in a new group of loyal officials who had limited administrative experience. Once brought into the administration, these men also tended to stay in office longer than normal.

While the reforms of Valentinian and Valens did displace many men who had enjoyed positions of authority under Julian and Jovian, the picture is more complicated than this implies. Libanius, of course, became much less important after 364, but his experience was not universal. Themistius, who suffered under Julian but thrived under Jovian, remained an influential figure under Valens. Praetextatus, a member of the Italian senatorial order whose traditional offices were sometimes usurped by Valentinian's Pannonian associates, excelled under Valentinian because of his unique combination of high social position and practical political savvy. And the reign of Valentinian saw the provincial professor Ausonius remake himself into one of the most authoritative figures at the imperial court. The Pannonian emperors thrust the final pagan generation into a period of uncertainty and opportunity, but the Roman world remained largely governed by the same basic social rules that they had learned as children. These men knew how to adapt, survive, and even thrive despite these very real changes.

Both Valentinian and Valens had grown up within the system that framed elite life for the final pagan generation. They were, however, to be the last emperors who shared this idea about the need to work within the social consensus that the post-tetrarchic system had created. The younger emperors who followed them would be governed by a different set of ideas. They also would rule an empire that demanded different approaches. A generation gap loomed that the final pagan generation proved unprepared to bridge.

CHAPTER 7

Christian Youth Culture in the 360s and 370s

The death of the emperor Valentinian represents an appropriate moment to shift our focus from the final pagan generation to their children. These children cannot quite be considered the first Christian generation, but their attitudes about religious policy and service in the courts, imperial administration, and schools differed significantly from those of their parents. The great expansion of offices in the fourth century extended to provincial elites the administration of an empire that had once been run primarily by a narrow group of Italian senators and their households.[1] This was, in many ways, a part of the unique genius of these administrative reforms. They both increased the pool of talent on which the empire could directly draw, and bound these provincial elites to a shared imperial enterprise in a way that had not previously been possible. Teachers, advocates, and other figures who did not hold administrative positions also benefited. Both the demand for their services and the recognition they received increased as officials took greater interest in their activities. Provincial elites, whose horizons had once been largely confined to the councils of their home cities, could now aspire to positions that brought greater wealth, responsibility, and honor.

The final pagan generation brought up their children expecting that they would similarly embrace and thrive in this system. Many of their children did, but, by the 360s, it was becoming clear that some children of the post-Constantinian empire did not react to these opportunities in the way that their parents hoped. Unlike their parents, some elite youth of the 350s, 360s, and 370s came to suspect the rewards secular careers promised, and sought opportunities outside of them. In increasing numbers, they turned their backs on the lucrative jobs for which they were training, and embraced either service in the Christian church or, more controversially, a type of Christian ascetic life.

This was a process that began before the reign of Valentinian, and its full effects would not become clear until well after his death, but this youthful Christian reaction reached its most optimistic and energized state in the 360s and 370s. This chapter considers the origins and development of this youth culture from its earliest literary articulations through to the point at which young elites begin to embrace it as an alternative to the life their parents imagined for them. It begins by looking at possible causes and likely consequences of the first movements of members of the aristocracy from conventional careers into episcopal office in the 370s. It then turns to the cultural movement through which young men who had trained to pursue legal, administrative, or teaching careers chose instead to embrace a form of ascetic Christianity. A key catalyst of this development was Athanasius's *Life of Antony,* a text written to frame the Christian ascetic life in terms that were both appealing to elites and reassuring to the social world in which they lived. But the reality of embracing an ascetic life or a career in the church was much more complicated than this literary ideal suggested. Young elites struggled far more than Athanasius's literary Antony to escape the social and personal ties that bound them to the traditional Roman social order. Aspiring ascetics and aspiring bishops also faced strong criticism from parents, teachers, friends, and patrons. The chapter concludes by considering some of the strategies that enabled young Christian dropouts to withstand these social and personal pressures.

ELITE BISHOPS WITHIN AND OUTSIDE OF THE SYSTEM

The great expansion of imperial offices and the lucrative compensation that often came along with them powerfully linked elites to a shared imperial enterprise in the fourth century.[2] They willingly traded the limits that public service placed on their conduct for the rewards it promised. The men and women born in the 310s thrived in the imperial system and raised their children to take part in it as well. Most of the young born to senatorial and curial families in the 330s, 340s, and 350s aspired to the same types of offices, honors, and material rewards that their parents enjoyed. These were men like Symmachus, Ausonius's son

Hesperius, and Libanius's child Cimon. They went to schools and learned the same skills that their fathers once had. These students of the 350s and 360s built networks of peers through the same kinds of drinking parties, kidnappings, and hazing rituals that Libanius and his peers experienced in the 330s.[3] And they emerged from the classrooms fired by the same sorts of ambition that powered Libanius, Ausonius, Themistius, and Praetextatus through the 340s and early 350s. For young men like these, the social debts and obligations they owed to the family members and friends who helped them get established bound them to the imperial system just as tightly as they had their parents. Like their parents, they were products of a world designed to use their talents, reward their efforts, and control their reactions.

Some elite children proved more difficult to control. Much of this had to do with the emergence of new ways for demonstrating elite achievement that worked differently from the established municipal and imperial models. Elites had customarily taken little interest in service within the church. Clergy and even bishops had tended to be people of middling rank who could pursue careers in the church but lacked the background, means, or the social standing to hold high municipal or imperial office. Beginning in the 370s, however, men who had once served as teachers, advocates, and even imperial governors entered into bishoprics, a trend that accelerated as the fifth century approached.[4]

Ambrose offers perhaps the most familiar example of this new breed of bishop.[5] Ambrose came from a wealthy, senatorial, Christian family that owned extensive property and had built its fortune through service within the Constantinian imperial administration.[6] His father eventually rose to the position of praetorian prefect of Gaul, an office that he held at the time that Ambrose was born in 339.[7] He was executed not long after Ambrose's birth, and Ambrose grew up in Rome with his mother, brother, and a sister. Ambrose and his brother, Satyrus, prepared for the same sort of administrative career that their father once enjoyed. Satyrus first served as an advocate at the court of the praetorian prefect and then held a provincial governorship before dying prematurely in 374 or 375.[8] Ambrose followed a similar path. He began as an advocate, took a position as an assessor, and secured the governorship of Aemilia and Liguria in 370.[9]

Ambrose's governorship proved a pivotal moment in his career. His service as governor forced him to become involved in a conflict between Milanese Christians that threatened to boil over into a violent confrontation.[10] His actions so strongly impressed the Nicene Christian community in the city that, in 374, he agreed to become bishop of Milan.[11] Ambrose brought to the position the social and financial resources of a member of the senatorial elite. Ambrose was not Praetextatus, but he was far more impressive than his episcopal peers. As the heir to his father's large estate, he could personally underwrite a series of ambitious building and charitable projects that would reshape the Milanese Nicene church and its position in the city.[12] His early efforts included the construction of the church in which his brother was buried, and the regular distribution of gold coins to those receiving alms.[13] To this he added the confidence and connections of a member of the senatorial order facing down less accomplished and less socially distinguished Arian rivals.

Ambrose's status mattered because, as Neil McLynn has shown, Milan was a town whose leading figures tended to be products of the Constantinian imperial system.[14] No well-entrenched councillors or old-money senators stood above Ambrose in Milan. This enabled him to use his prominence to build a loyal and vocal following among the people of the city. They could be turned out when he needed their voices heard, but Ambrose had a particular talent for understanding when such a display might prove necessary and when its mere threat would suffice.[15] This made Ambrose a powerful figure whose influence was not circumscribed by the limits of an imperial office.

Ambrose himself notes that this was not the career that many would have envisioned for a former governor and the son of a prefect,[16] but the resources and social obligations of a late fourth-century bishop would have resembled those available to a member of the imperial elite. The emperor Constantine had given large amounts of money and substantial quantities of goods to the churches to support their sacred and charitable activities.[17] These funds had been cut off by Julian and were eventually restored by Jovian at only one-third the Constantinian rate.[18] Even at this reduced level, these imperial grants remained significant, and as the fourth century progressed, they were increasingly supplemented by private gifts.[19] As was the case with Ambrose, some bishops brought private financial resources with them when they joined the episcopacy.[20] The Christian tradition of charitable contributions further augmented the material resources a bishop controlled.[21] By the 370s, large urban churches controlled such sizable property portfolios that the middle-class bishops of the late third and early fourth centuries no longer had the administrative experience necessary to administer their finances.[22] Churches now needed bishops who knew how to manage large estates, diverse properties, and complicated political relationships. This led them increasingly to turn to talented members of the upper class to manage their affairs. In return, the churches offered these men a way to do recognizably elite activities in a new context of Christian service. The wealth and influence that came along with these positions even prompted Praetextatus to remark facetiously that he would convert to Christianity if the Christians would make him bishop of Rome.[23]

Mid-fourth-century bishops had developed powerful voices that allowed them to serve as effective patrons for their followers. Many of the middle-class bishops of the early fourth century managed to do this, but as Ambrose's later career shows, the elite bishops of the late fourth century could do far more than their predecessors. They came to the job already possessing social relationships with influential figures, familiarity with the imperial appeals process, knowledge of how to organize and conduct an embassy, and training in how to use the language of the cultured elite to advocate for friends and associates.[24] Those who had served as governors or advocates also had professional training that directly prepared them for the ecclesiastical courts in which they would hear civil lawsuits and mediate disputes between congregants.[25] Bishops now needed many of the same skills that helped prominent people maintain their place in the world outside of the church.

These elite church officers sought a type of success that depended only somewhat on the imperial system. This and their higher social status meant that they were less easily cowed by emperors than some of their socially middling predecessors had been. Nevertheless, many of the traditional metrics for elite achievement still applied to bishops.[26] Bishops publicly represented their communities in many of the same ways that leaders of city councils had, they continued to be responsible for managing estates in the way that large landholders did, and as episcopal visibility grew in the later fourth century, big-city bishops came to possess a title that carried with it an understood social prestige.[27] The prerogatives of office also enabled some bishops to look out for the financial and social interests of friends and members of their families.[28] Bishops were responsible for and answerable to congregations. They also needed buildings and administrative staffs to perform their duties. If they proved too problematic, emperors could marginalize bishops by separating them from all of these resources and supporters.[29] Emperors still possessed some tools to control the conduct of these men.

FRAMING ELITE ASCETICISM IN THE 360S AND 370S

The traditional metrics of elite achievement translated less easily to the ascetic life. Ascetics had been an important and influential part of Christian communities since the first century, but significant numbers of elites do not seem to have embraced Christian ascetic practices before the mid-fourth century.[30] Early fourth-century Syrian and Egyptian celibate or continent men and women tended to be people of middling status who lived in towns, participated in liturgy, and maintained a level of involvement in the lives of their families.[31] They were symbolically important figures whose renunciation of the world gave them authority, but their voices mattered far less than those of either bishops or the traditional civic elite. Two fourth-century Egyptian developments changed this. First, more radical forms of social renunciation emerged that pushed some ascetics to practice farther outside the physical and social spaces of Egyptian cities, towns, and villages. At the same time, a sequence of early fourth-century church conflicts caused various Egyptian ecclesiastical factions to compete for the support of celibates, virgins, and other ascetics. As the loyalties of Egyptian town-based ascetics split between competing Christian groups, bishops attempted to better regulate their activities out of concern that ascetics loyal to them might be slandered or induced to follow different ecclesiastical leadership.[32] Athanasius, the Nicene bishop who did this most aggressively, also began to celebrate the achievements of ascetics who moved away from settled areas. By the mid-fourth century, a number of different models of asceticism had developed. These included the community-based ascetic projects pioneered by Pachomius and his followers in the 320s and 330s and the solitary asceticism practiced by Antony.[33] Athanasius embraced these models, worked hard to show his support for the men who had developed them, and nurtured ties to their followers.[34]

Athanasius's support for the Pachomians and communal ascetic enterprises like theirs shows up repeatedly in mid-fourth-century sources,[35] but his most influential endorsement of a form of asceticism based outside of cities and towns comes in his landmark *Life of Antony*. This masterful text formed one of the centerpieces of a larger literary program that Athanasius wrote while he hid from imperial officials among the monks of northern Egypt in the later 350s.[36] In the *Life*, Athanasius claims a personal relationship with Antony, who had come to be seen as solitary monasticism's founder, and uses this to show Antony's endorsement of Athanasius's theological orthodoxy and institutional authority.[37] The *Life* structurally mimics earlier philosophical biographies in order to argue that the Christian ascetic pursuits of Antony represent a practical philosophy that surpassed both traditional Hellenic philosophy and, by implication, the Platonically tinged theology of Arius.[38]

The *Life* further marks Antony as a figure whose ascetic accomplishments far exceeded those of town-based Christian celibates. This is one of the *Life*'s more underappreciated purposes, but it is one that ultimately contributes significantly to the text's larger resonance. Athanasius's narration of Antony's life begins in a world in which celibate Christians exist only within the structures of village life. When Antony decided to embrace an ascetic life, he entrusted his younger sister to "known and trusted virgins" who then raised her in virginity.[39] Antony himself began his training by finding an old man in a neighboring village "who had trained in the solitary life from his youth." Antony then watched and imitated him.[40] Once he had learned all he could from this man, he moved on to learn from others like him. He began by visiting men who lived close to his own village, but Antony ultimately searched out everyone about whom he heard anything noteworthy. He visited each of them, observed their practices, and then, "gathering the attributes of each in himself," he returned to his own place of discipline.[41]

In Athanasius's telling, Antony's achievements went beyond the assembly of all of the existing best qualities of the ascetics who lived in Egyptian villages. Once he had learned and mastered all of these existing virtues, Antony pushed beyond the spatial limits of the villages and the spiritual limits village life set. Throughout the first stages of the *Life,* Athanasius's Antony moved progressively farther from settled life. He first moved to the tombs located on the fringe of his village,[42] and then withdrew three times more, each time venturing deeper into the desert, moving farther from settlements, and pioneering new spatial frontiers in ascetic practice.[43] As Antony expanded the boundaries of ascetic life, ascetic colonists followed him into the tombs and deserts beyond Egyptian cities and towns.[44]

Athanasius indicates that Antony further surpassed previous ascetics by completely disentangling himself from the rhythms and demands of village life. Throughout the text, Athanasius systematically breaks down the ties that linked Antony to the people with whom he shared relationships and the communities in which he lived. These were the very relationships that earlier generations of ascetics would traditionally have maintained and the same ones that bound the ambitious elite youths of the post-Constantinian empire to their schools and jobs. When Athanasius first introduces Antony, he describes him as the child of "well-born parents" who had "abundant possessions" and controlled over 300 *arourae* (nearly 200 acres) of fertile farmland.[45] Athanasius says nothing about Antony's hometown (aside from calling it a κώμης or village), but this amount of land would qualify Antony's father for membership in the local curia of all but the largest Egyptian cities.[46] Possession of this land brought with it specific financial obligations to the town, obligations that were not easily shed.[47] Antony also had obligations to other people. He was responsible for the care of his parents as they aged, for the raising of his younger sister until she married, and for the maintenance of the household slaves. Finally, in a fourth-century context, one could imagine that many people of Antony's financial and social position would be educated in a way that might equip them to pursue the lucrative careers in imperial service sought by many of his social peers. His property put him right in the middle of the ranks of city councillors like those who flocked to the schools of Libanius, Ausonius, and Themistius in search of new opportunities in imperial service.

A fourth-century audience would immediately recognize these social and family obligations as well as the ambitions that often excited men of Antony's station. This makes Athanasius's explanation of how Antony escaped them all the more remarkable. Athanasius quickly frees Antony from the career ambitions of many city councillors by indicating that Antony could not bear to learn letters and did not seek to build the relationships with classmates that laid the groundwork for an administrative career or effective curial service.[48] Athanasius next frees Antony of the obligation to take care of his parents by explaining that they both died by the time he reached age eighteen.[49] This left Antony responsible for his household (the house, land, and property, including any slaves), the curial obligations attached to it, and the care of his young sister. He entrusted his sister to virgins living in the town. His family properties "he gave to the people of the town so that no one would in any way trouble him or his sister."[50] This was consistent both with some third-century rescripts laying out provisions for the alienation of curial property and with fourth century legal provisions for the disposition of property belonging to clergy.[51] It was a perfectly legal but not particularly practical solution.

The first three chapters of the *Life of Antony* offer an idealized blueprint for how a member of the local elite could extricate himself from the personal relationships, financial obligations, and social aspirations that defined mid-fourth-century elite life. The rest of the work, in a sense, illustrates what one can achieve once these strictures are lifted. From the time that Antony disposed of his last possessions, he "devoted himself to the discipline rather than the household, attending to himself and patiently training himself."[52] This in turn led to a series of remarkable spiritual achievements that included successes in demonic combat, healings of the sick, and visions of the future.[53] But these spiritual achievements ultimately led Antony back to the world. When he returned, he managed an estate peopled by ascetic followers, corresponded with emperors, provided instruction to the entire city of Alexandria, and refuted the teaching of Greek philosophers.[54] Ultimately, Athanasius returns Antony to the world as a figure whose radical renunciation of conventional social and personal ties lent him a new, powerful type of authority whose value elites could immediately understand. Antony offered a better, more virtuous path to these ends, but the achievements of ascetics, like those of bishops, now could be understood in elite terms.

DROPPING OUT

The *Life of Antony* immediately resonated with elites far beyond the Egyptian environment in which it was composed. It proved wildly popular with them because it provided a compelling way to articulate in attractive, elite terms a movement that was already beginning to take root across the empire.[55] The popularity of the *Life* is broadly evident across a host of later fourth-century milieus. Latin translations appeared quickly, with the first coming perhaps in the early 360s and the second, by Evagrius, as early as 365 or 370.[56] In 375, Jerome wrote the *Life of Paul,* a clumsy, fictional imitation of the *Life* that mentions both the Greek original text and the Latin translation.[57] In 392, Jerome's *De viris inlustribus* (*On Illustrious Men*) mentioned the composition of the *Life of Antony* as one of the highlights of Athanasius's literary career and placed its translation into Latin among Evagrius's most memorable achievements.[58] In 380, Gregory Nazianzen began a homily on Athanasius with the wish that he might someday be able to commemorate the recently departed bishop in a work like the one Athanasius had written to celebrate Antony.[59] It is notable, of course, that all of these early translators and literary imitators belong to the generation that came of age in the 350s and 360s; they were the Christian children of the final pagan generation.

The *Life* did more than simply capture the literary imagination of these young men. In at least one case, it also inspired actions. In his

Confessions, Augustine tells about two courtiers of the emperor Valentinian who picked up the *Life of Antony* while killing time outside the city of Trier. Before the first of them had even finished reading it, Augustine recounts, "he conceived of the idea of taking up the same kind of life for himself and abandoning the world."[60] The two men then made a commitment to each other to walk away from their careers and support one another in an ascetic life.

A host of other authors writing in the 370s and 380s mention similar ascetic compacts between young elites. The young men who made these agreements to leave the world and embrace an ascetic life saw them as binding contracts that, once made, could not be broken.[61] In an early letter written to Theodore, one of the men with whom he made such an agreement, John Chrysostom, describes the reason for their choice.[62] "The things of this world," he writes, "are in their nature no better than dreams,"[63] while those who embrace God will spend eternity in peace, happiness, and joy.[64] Theodore, John continues, recognized all of this. He disregarded fine food, fancy clothes, and public processions with his attendants, never mentioned his prominent family, and never thought of wealth.[65] Instead, all he wished to do was run to the brothers he recognized as pursuing something far more noble than high birth. When Theodore moved away from the shadowy concerns of this world, he embraced a life dedicated to the glory of God.[66]

Even with the steadfast (and rather pushy) support of like-minded friends, disentangling oneself from the concerns of this world proved extremely difficult for young elites.[67] Chrysostom knew this from his own experience. Not long after he had completed his studies and began work as a lawyer, a fellow student named Basil decided to take up the life of the monks.[68] Chrysostom and Basil had studied with the same teachers and had always shown the same enthusiasm for learning.[69] The families of both men were equally wealthy and enjoyed the same social rank.[70] The paths of the two men diverged when they left school. Chrysostom began practicing law, angling for a bureaucratic appointment, and enjoying the pleasures of the city, while Basil embraced an ascetic life. As their friendship began to fray, Basil proposed that Chrysostom follow his lead in abandoning the concerns of the world. The two men would then move in together so that each could support the other.[71]

The partnership between Chrysostom and Basil ultimately fell apart when Basil was ordained. In fact, we know about Chrysostom's partnership with Basil primarily because Chrysostom felt compelled to write a defense of his own flight from church office in the first sections of his work *De sacerdote* (*On the Priesthood*).[72] But this was not always the reaction of young dropouts like Chrysostom when faced with the prospect of ordination. Chrysostom's earlier contemporaries Gregory Nazianzen and Basil of Caesarea looked to balance their commitment to an ascetic lifestyle with the demands of ordained ministry.[73] These two Cappadocians studied together in Athens and returned to their home region in the mid-350s hoping to balance their interest in asceticism with their obligations as members of the local elite. Basil was the son of a teacher in Caesarea, and he had been encouraged by an embassy of local magistrates to teach in his home city when he finished his education.[74] Gregory too had prepared for a teaching career that he was expected to begin when he returned to his home region of Nazianzus.[75] Both men had positioned themselves to assume these positions, and set off for Athens to get final training before returning home to begin their teaching careers.

When Gregory and Basil got to Athens, however, each had a difficult time adjusting to the city. Basil was hazed aggressively, though Gregory stepped in at one point to rescue him from a particularly heated encounter with some Armenians.[76] Even more challenging was the religious environment in the city. Gregory described it as so full of idols of the gods that it was hard not to be carried along by the popular embrace of traditional religion.[77] He and Basil worked together to counteract this. They lived together, went to church together, and became dear friends whose feelings for one another grew "ever warmer and stronger."[78] They supported one another in this difficult religious environment, and before they left Athens, the two friends made a pact to abandon their teaching careers and live an ascetic life together.

Basil returned from Greece, taught briefly in Caesarea, and traveled in the East for a time. Around 357 or 358, he decided to retreat to a family property in Pontus in order to live the life that he and Gregory had discussed.[79] He settled by himself across a river from the estate where the rest of the family spent time. He then wrote to Gregory, reminded him of their promise to live together as ascetics, and invited him to come to Pontus to join him.[80] Gregory wrote back in late 357 or early 358 admitting that he had lied when he promised to live in an ascetic partnership with Basil.[81] This was not an intentional lie, Gregory explains, because "the law that commands us to care for our parents trumped the law of our companionship and intimacy," and Gregory needed to put the needs of his family first.[82] After another series of letters, however, Basil convinced Gregory to come to Pontus in 359.

Gregory stayed for a short time, and then decided to return to his family and his teaching. He did not abandon asceticism but instead tried to fashion a type of ascetic practice that did not take him from his familial and social obligations.[83]

Gregory's desire to remain attached in some fashion to the larger elite social world placed him in a middle ground between the radical renunciations of Antony and the episcopal track of Ambrose. This was not a position that he would be allowed to occupy for long. If he would not fully renounce the world, the church had uses for him. In 361, Gregory seems to have been ordained into the priesthood.[84] He made a show of refusing the office and fled to Basil's retreat in Pontus, but his friend encouraged him to stop fighting the appointment.[85] Gregory returned home in early 362, and, later that year, Basil too was ordained.[86] The two young men then exchanged a series of letters in which they worked through how their new positions as priests could be reconciled with the ascetic pursuits that they wished to continue. This was, Gregory wrote, "not something that we aimed for," but since the ordination had happened with the blessing of the Holy Spirit, "we must put up with it."[87]

In a later letter, Gregory indicates that the ascetic brotherhood that bound him to Basil continued to join the two men now that they served the church. In 365, he responded to a letter sent by the bishop Eusebius of Caesarea that summoned him to a synod. Gregory thanked the bishop for the invitation but claimed that he could not "tolerate the insult that came, and which still comes, from your reverence against the most honorable brother Basil, whom from the beginning I have adopted and still have now as a partner in life, word, and the most exalted philosophy—and I find nothing at fault in my own judgment of him."[88] This initiated a series of exchanges in which Eusebius accused Gregory of being haughty and mean-spirited, while Gregory held firm that Basil must also be summoned to the synod.[89] When an invitation to Basil appeared to be forthcoming, Gregory then wrote to his friend and asked whether he thought "it good for me to be present, living and travelling together with you."[90] If so, Gregory continued, "then let's not run away from this" but take a stand so that "no one may seem more courageous than us and so that our many drops of sweat and labors do not suddenly come to nothing."[91]

Gregory and Basil's relationship evolved greatly in the period between 355 and 365, but the mutual support they offered one another remained an important element of it throughout this decade. What began as a scholastic friendship developed into a long-distance ascetic brotherhood before transforming again into an episcopal alliance. The apparent ease of this evolution obscures the important fact that both Basil and Gregory sought support from one another throughout this process. The challenges they faced in Athens are in some ways readily apparent to us, but both their embrace of asceticism and their path into the clergy presented their own difficulties that required emotional and tangible support.

PARENTS JUST DON'T UNDERSTAND

The families of both Basil and Gregory supported their decisions to embrace Christian service, but many of their peers were not so fortunate. Older elites did not always take kindly to the decisions of their children to become bishops or ascetics. Parents sometimes charged sons who entered the episcopacy with a betrayal of their obligations to their families. In 373, Amphilochius, a cousin of Gregory, a former student of Libanius, and the son of one of Libanius's classmates,[92] decided to abandon a career as an advocate and become bishop of Iconium.[93] His father, who had served as an advocate and teacher of rhetoric, was appalled and blamed Gregory for stealing his son and leading him astray.[94] He complains that he feels that his son "will not be present with [him] . . . he will not tend to [his] old age . . . he will not help out in day-to-day affairs as he usually does."[95] Gregory explains to his uncle that Amphilochius had made this decision on his own, and chastises his uncle for "bringing charges against me, as I am learning, and thinking that your son and my brother is being neglected or betrayed by me."[96] This is wrong, Gregory continues, because "I placed the hopes of life in him and assumed that he was the only support, the only good advisor, the only sharer of piety."[97] Gregory's letter shows the degree to which these young men supported each other when they made a choice that their elders opposed.

Gregory's own jump from a career as a teacher to one within the church helped him to understand and support Amphilochius's decision. He knew that, as a bishop, Amphilochius could continue acting as a friend and leader of his community while also giving service to the church. Libanius, Amphilochius's former teacher, had more trouble making sense of his student's embrace of episcopal office. Upon hearing of Amphilochius's decision, Libanius sent Amphilochius a letter that showed a subtle dismay about the choice. He explained that Amphilochius had once been an example of a student whose career refuted the criticism that Libanius had not trained any really successful students.[98] His work as an advocate had been admirable, and it served as an effective rejoinder to

Libanius's rivals, but Amphilochius no longer offered Libanius this possibility. As bishop, Libanius continued, Amphilochius could at least find a way to use his eloquence to excite an audience and get applause—a situation that at least salvaged some of his rhetorical talents.[99] By framing Amphilochius's new position in conventionally elite terms, this odd comment shows Libanius trying his best to explain a situation whose import he did not entirely understand.

Amphilochius's responsibility for his congregation, his connections to other influential men, and his continued occasions for practicing rhetoric offered a type of authority that his father and teacher could recognize. Young ascetics had less tangible influence and, therefore, often faced more resistance from friends, family members, and dependents when they left a conventional career path. When John Chrysostom told his mother about his decision to abandon a legal career in order to live an ascetic life alongside his classmate Basil, her "continual lamentations" hindered him. Chrysostom's father had died when he was young, and his mother reminded him of all that she had done to raise him.[100] She spoke of her efforts to manage the domestic slaves, to beat back the lawsuits of family members, and to defend her family against the threats of tax collectors.[101] She had not remarried so that Chrysostom might inherit his father's estate intact, and she reminded him that she used her own dowry and family resources in order to "spare no expense that was necessary to give him an honorable position."[102] She had clearly hoped that Chrysostom would succeed in the same way that many others of his age did. If he chose to turn away from the wealth and career success for which she had set him up, his mother asked one thing. In return for all that she had done, she wanted Chrysostom to "wait for her death" before he left home.[103]

Other figures faced even more difficult obstacles. People with particularly large estates or complicated domestic arrangements could find it extremely difficult to relinquish their property or step away from obligations to members of their household.[104] Later ascetic leaders even counseled men who wanted to join a monastery not to do so until dependent children, parents, or elderly slaves no longer needed their care.[105] Two of Chrysostom's contemporaries show what could happen to those who failed to disentangle themselves completely from the obligations and expectations of fourth-century society. His friend Theodore momentarily stepped away from the ascetic life when he fell in love with a woman named Hermione.[106] Even more significant was the case of an unnamed Phoenician man. His father, Urbanus, had worked as an assessor to the *comes Orientis* Modestus from 358 until 362 and had built up a substantial family fortune.[107] While Urbanus lived, his son "bid complete farewell to his studies in the schools" and retreated to the mountains to pursue "Christian philosophy." Urbanus's premature death forced the young man to return to the elite world his father had mastered. Someone needed to help administer the "great deal of money and many slaves and lands" his father had left. As the only surviving member of the family, this young man agreed to do so. He then "used to go all around the city, riding on horseback, accompanied by a large retinue" and became "inflamed by much luxury."[108]

There were many more men who, like Theodore and this Phoenician youth, abandoned their postadolescent flirtations with an ascetic life in the 370s when their parents left them the family property. This may, in fact, have even been true of the vast majority of the dropouts of the 370s. But their friends and peers often did not let them go easily. The Phoenician youth found himself continually confronted by his former ascetic brothers. He ignored them at first, but they persisted until "he would instantly dismount . . . and in time he displayed even greater reverence and respect towards them." Ultimately, Chrysostom explains, "they handed him over again to his former state of seclusion and devout contemplation."[109]

Chrysostom did the same thing to Theodore. When Theodore fell in love with Hermione, Chrysostom wrote to him that worldly affairs like wives, children, and domestic slaves only distracted the soul. He then commented that he found it strange of Theodore to be so unwilling to try to return to his discipline when others "are continually praying that they might have their member restored to them."[110] Chrysostom himself felt this same type of pressure when Basil repeatedly pressed him to abandon his mother and take up an ascetic life.[111]

Fourth-century Christian ascetics of all social stations recognized the power of these intensely personal appeals. This was, of course, the fundamental organizing principle of the Pachomian *Koinonia* and the subsequent cenobitic monastic foundations that evolved out of its pioneering model.[112] Some elites, like Pachomius's Egyptian protégé Theodore, did join the larger cenobitic communities that were springing up throughout the empire. But young elites like Chrysostom, Theodore, and the courtiers at Trier tended to avoid large institutional enterprises like the *Koinonia*. They instead formed small, collaborative enterprises that used social relationships like those members of the elite formed at school to provide positive reinforcement for certain behaviors that most of society did not endorse. Instead of creating a schoolboy camaraderie that reinforced one's commitment to the aspirations of traditional aristocratic life, these smaller ascetic groups existed to give young men the strength to pursue goals that diametrically opposed those endorsed by their parents, teachers, and many of their peers. They were, in Seth Schwartz's conception of a counterculture, embracing solidarity over reciprocity.[113] As modern sociologists have shown, creating this type of socially isolating community is one of the most effective ways to get people to adopt and maintain behaviors well outside of established social norms.[114] In the schools, these structures encouraged antisocial behaviors like rioting and excessive drinking that nonstudents shunned. In elite ascetic circles, they promoted a withdrawal from the social and material objectives to which most of their peers aspired.

The achievements these ascetic circles celebrated differed from those that marked a successful bishop and diverged dramatically from those that most members of the fourth-century Roman elite valued. The great success of the tetrarchic and Constantinian expansion of government bureaucracy derived from the emperors' unprecedented ability to link wealth, honor, and social prominence to participation in imperial political life. This created a social momentum that encouraged elites to aspire to certain types of achievement defined by the Roman imperial system. The ascetic circles created by Chrysostom's friends and the courtiers in Trier looked like nodes in an elite social network, but they exerted a different sort of social pressure. Instead of encouraging the pursuit of conventional success, they pushed young elites to drop out of the imperial system. These groups of friends explicitly framed their embrace of asceticism as a rejection of the system in which they had been trained to excel.[115] They spoke repeatedly about the folly of the rewards that system promised. They supported one another when unsympathetic friends and family members pushed them to return to it. And some of these men began to write extensively so that they could better articulate the alternative value structure that guided them.[116] As these ideas spread among young elites, they diluted the power of the social incentives that the empire used to guide elite conduct.

. . .

By the 380s, the growing interest in ascetic circles and episcopal service among young Christians created two subgroups of curial and senatorial figures over whom imperial officials had limited influence.[117] The young men who entered church offices remained somewhat engaged with the wider world. They were uninterested in offices and honors defined by the imperial system, but they remained plugged into elite social and cultural networks. They also depended on imperial resources and approval in order to effectively do their jobs. Unlike the men who entered episcopal service, the young ascetic dropouts often formed insular groups that monitored each other's behavior, criticized any aberrant tendencies, and rejected any worldly things that conflicted with their spiritual objectives. These were the first elites of the fourth century who immunized themselves against the rewards that imperial officials could offer and the punishments they could inflict.[118]

The empire seems initially not to have anticipated the challenges that these new types of bishops and ascetics presented. Since the later third century, emperors had worked to find ways to make more efficient use of the large numbers of talented members of the provincial elite. They did this by creating an expanded administrative apparatus that involved these men and sometimes richly rewarded their cooperation. Their efforts worked so well that some young men came to see the system their parents had so readily embraced as a "soul-destroying" thing to be resisted.[119] This was, in some ways, a natural reaction to a system that had done everything it was intended to do. But, as is often the case with such movements, the ideas that once motivated the radical renunciations of 360s, 370s, and 380s became a part of the mainstream. As more people came to accept the authority that these young Christian bishops and ascetics claimed, the Roman social and administrative system needed to find ways to contain their influence and direct their energies. As the 380s will show, the empire was not always successful.

Bishops, Bureaucrats, and Aristocrats under Gratian, Valentinian II, and Theodosius

While most of the elites who grew up in the 340s, 350s, and 360s did not follow the paths of Ambrose, Amphilochius, Basil, Chrysostom, and Gregory, their generation tended to be both more Christian and less wedded to the rhythms and protocols of elite life than their parents had been. Much of their experimentation occurred when the empire was safely in the hands of their elders, the emperors Valentinian and Valens, and a coterie of experienced advisers. Rebellion felt safe in the well-governed empire of one's parents.

The death of the emperor Valentinian in 375 began a period of transition during which the administrators of the 360s and 370s gave way to a younger generation. Valentinian and Valens were children of the 320s, and, like their slightly older peers Libanius, Ausonius, Themistius, and Praetextatus, the emperors were products of the late Roman administrative and social system. They had faith in its ability to bind ruler and ruled in mutually beneficial cooperation. By 375, however, the empire could no longer depend so heavily on men born in the 310s. Death was thinning their ranks quickly, and the number of them available to serve dropped significantly each year.[1] This presented a particular problem because experienced public servants were needed more acutely in the later 370s and early 380s than they had been for over a hundred years. The empire faced a set of challenges unlike anything it had experienced since the mid-third century. These included the threat posed to Roman cities by Gothic armies following the catastrophic military defeat at

Adrianople in 378, the rebellion of Magnus Maximus in the West in 383, the shift to a strongly pro-Nicene Christian emperor in the East, and the implementation of a series of provocative religious initiatives by the emperors Gratian and Theodosius in the early 380s. The new emperors required the experienced, steady hands of men like Ausonius, Themisitius, and Praetextatus, but they also needed to begin building up a stable of younger administrative talent to which the empire could eventually be entrusted.

This chapter considers the decade in which the Roman world experienced the transition from an empire dominated by men born in the 310s and 320s to one in which that generation's children began to direct the state. It proceeds differently than previous chapters. The history of this decade is so rich that it would overwhelm the generational narratives that emerge as the state begins to pass to a younger group of men. The chapter instead focuses on three distinctive moments in the reigns of Gratian, Theodosius, and Valentinian II that show how these younger emperors balanced the administrative style of the final pagan generation with the diverse attitudes and interests of a younger generation.

The first moment occurs between 375 and 380 and involves Ausonius's efforts to manage the transition from the regime of Valentinian I to that of Gratian. The second concerns Theodosius's enlistment of older members of the traditional elite like Themistius and younger dropouts like Gregory Nazianzen in a campaign to explain his policies to Constantinopolitan audiences during the difficult period between 379 and 383. The final moment occurs in 383 and 384 as the weak regime of Valentinian II mediates a conflict between older establishment figures like Praetextatus and younger Christians like Ambrose, while simultaneously trying to ensure the support of both groups. Taken together, these three moments show the gradual transition from an empire whose rulers depended primarily on traditional elite officeholders to one in which Christian figures who had once opted out of the imperial system felt empowered to insert themselves into its policy deliberations.

THE EMPIRE OF AUSONIUS

The earliest of these three moments centers on Ausonius. When the emperor Valentinian died unexpectedly in late 375, his careful succession planning exploded.[2] His sixteen-year-old son Gratian had been serving as his co-emperor and designated successor since 367, but Gratian was far from his father's army when Valentinian died.[3] Fearing either a rebellion or the possible domination of the state by a rival court faction, the army commanders and administrators who had been accompanying Valentinian I summoned his other son, the four-year-old Valentinian II, and proclaimed him Augustus.[4] When Gratian learned of this, he recognized the folly of contesting Valentinian II's proclamation. He soon acknowledged his brother as a legitimate emperor, but also ensured that the child did not have any specific territories or duties assigned to him.[5]

Valentinian I's core of supporters made these first moves, but they would not long hold the initiative. In a series of well-timed and expertly executed maneuvers, Gratian's advisers quickly removed nearly all of the most trusted members of his father's court. By early 376, Gratian reconfigured the court with a new circle of associates whose background and inclinations differentiated his new regime from that which had immediately preceded it. So Maximinus, the Pannonian who had managed Valentinian's investigation of the Roman senate in 370/1, was removed from his Gallic prefecture, tried, and executed.[6] Flavius Simplicius and Doryphorianus fell too, the latter in a horrific way that combined an extended stay in a Gallic dungeon with a merciful execution.[7] Many of the military commanders involved in Valentinian II's proclamation also found themselves sidelined. By mid-376, Gratian had purged the upper levels of the military and administration of all of his father's closest associates.

Gratian also attempted to create a new political climate by addressing senatorial concerns about judicial mistreatment under the preceding regime. A series of laws issued between February 376 and January 377 ensured that a court convened by the urban prefect of Rome would handle criminal cases involving senators, and senators themselves would be exempted from torture.[8] The rhetorical tone also changed. On January 1, 376, the senate heard an oration from Gratian that, Symmachus claims, "filled me with great hope and cheer," because Gratian now promised an age like those over which Nerva, Trajan, Antoninus Pius, and Marcus Aurelius presided.[9]

Two orations Symmachus subsequently gave in 376 show him gradually realizing how much the regime of Gratian really did differ from the one that preceded it. A little more than a week after the senate heard Gratian's oration, Symmachus delivered a speech ostensibly devoted to the proposition that the son of a senator should be praetor in 386. In reality, Symmachus seems mainly to have offered thanks for a new political climate in which the emperor ruled as a "princeps rather than a monarch" and did nothing to "crush the achievements of private citizens."[10] By the end of 376, Symmachus's optimism had overwhelmed any caution he had about attacking Valentinian's old order. In his *Pro patre,* an oration Symmachus gave to celebrate the selection of his father as consul, he speaks about a state collaboratively governed by the emperor and the senate.[11] He is pleased to note that figures like Maximinus, who had recently been removed, have no place in this configuration.[12] Symmachus's ever more confident denunciations of the figures responsible for past excesses show a senator gradually recognizing the dawning of a new age.

Ausonius played a large role in this imperial transformation. Gratian replaced Valentinian's men with a cast of characters largely assembled by Ausonius. Despite being in his sixties, Ausonius himself would become the most spectacular beneficiary.[13] He continued to serve as quaestor through 376, but he used his access to the young emperor to position himself, his relatives, and his associates for high offices in the new imperial order. Between 377 and 379, Ausonius held a prefecture of Gaul, a combined prefecture of Gaul, Italy, and Africa that he shared with his son, and a consulship.[14] He arranged for his ninety-year-old father to replace Valentinian's favorite Petronius Probus as proconsul of Illyricum in 377, almost certainly as part of the effort to keep those who had promoted Valentinian II in 375 on the sidelines.[15] His nephew Arborius served as the count of the sacred largesses (the *comes sacrarum largitionum*) in 379 and urban prefect of Rome in 380. His son-in-law Thalassius served as vicar of Macedonia in 377 and proconsul of Africa in 378.[16] Ausonius's son Hesperius took over as proconsul of Africa in March 376 before being promoted, apparently directly following the end of his term, to prefect of Gaul in 378.[17] He followed this with the joint prefecture of Gaul, Italy, and Africa that he shared with his father.[18] When his father retired as prefect of Gaul in late 379,[19] Hesperius continued on as prefect of Italy until 380.[20]

Ausonius's family members benefited from the turnover in personnel following Valentinian's death, but they were not the only ones. This shift was part of a larger transition away from the governing style of Valentinian toward one that sought to reconcile Gratian's imperial court and the Western senatorial aristocracy.[21] Some of the beneficiaries of this shift seem to have been selected for their symbolic value. Between April 16 and May 23, Maximinus was replaced as prefect of Gaul by Claudius Antonius, a correspondent of Symmachus, a family member of the future emperor Theodosius I, and the man who had preceded Ausonius as quaestor.[22] Maximinus had been responsible for many of the most abhorrent abuses of senatorial privileges during the Roman treason trials of the early 370s, and Antonius gave a speech at the height of the crisis in which he argued for senatorial prerogative to judge its own members.[23] Antonius's appointment, then, emphasized the new regime's break from the past.

Other early appointments by Gratian reinforced this. Gratian's first three urban prefects may all have been victimized by his father in the 370s. Terracius Bassus, who was charged but acquitted in the trials, served as urban prefect sometime after 374. Aradius Rufinus, who served as prefect in 376, may have been shut out of office by Valentinian, and his successor, Furius Maecius Gracchus, was the son of a senator executed by Valentinian.[24] In addition, Julius Hymetius, one of the men sent into exile following Valentinian's investigations, was recalled and honored with statues in Rome and Carthage in 376.[25] The symbolic importance of these appointments and honors could not be lost on contemporaries.

These selections also inaugurated a generational transition that began to populate the court with advisers closer in age to the emperor himself. Gratian and his associates (of whom Ausonius seems to have been one of the most important) replaced the core of his father's administration with a mixture of older men like Ausonius and others who were the age of his children. The reconciliation of the later 370s then did not simply involve the rehabilitation of senators mistreated by Valentinian. It was a more complicated process designed both to placate older, disaffected senators and to build new bonds of mutual obligation with younger men.

Although their social profile matched that of many of the aspirational elite of previous decades, two other features distinguished Gratian's early appointees. First, in large part because of the influence of Ausonius, a significant number of appointees were Gallic, a group not often represented among major officeholders before the 360s.[26] Equally interesting, however, is the clear emphasis on the social mobility of young, elite Christians like Hesperius, Thalassius, and Gracchus.[27] The selection of these men hints at the shape of a new, geographically diverse administrative structure in which younger Christians would play a leading role. These younger Christians belonged to the same generation as Ambrose and Chrysostom, but they did not participate in the Christian counterculture of the 360s and 370s. They were creatures of the establishment, the fourth-century version of fraternity brothers dressed in dinner jackets who walked impatiently by the hippies playing drums on the quad. They were selected not to challenge but to perpetuate the system to which Ausonius and men of his age had become so attached.[28] This was, however, an old man's vision of the future. As the 380s dawned, Ausonius settled into an active retirement in Gaul. Gratian moved south toward the Danube frontier and surrounded himself with a new, less capable group of advisers. As we will see momentarily, their competing interests and general incompetence ultimately destroyed the generational balance Ausonius tried to create.

YOUNGER MEN'S RULES

The Eastern empire felt similar stresses in the late 370s and early 380s, but the situation in the East presented much more dire risks than that in the West. In 376, the emperor Valens allowed large groups of Goths to cross into Roman territory.[29] Their numbers quickly overwhelmed the Roman administration's capabilities, and, by the summer of 377, the Goths rebelled.[30] In August 378, the Goths faced a Roman field army commanded by Valens, defeated it in open battle, and killed the emperor as well as perhaps two-thirds of his army.[31] The Eastern court and its army then needed to be quickly rebuilt while Goths wandered unchecked through the Balkans.

Gratian and his advisers selected a thirty-two-year-old Spaniard named Theodosius to confront these dual challenges in January 379. Theodosius was a westerner, selected by a Western court, and appointed by a Western emperor to deal with a problem in the Balkans, a peninsula that (except for its eastern corner) had been largely controlled by the West in the fourth century.[32] Many of his earliest appointees to the highest offices in the East were Spaniards and other Western Christians who were closer in age to the younger Theodosius than they were to Valens. While westerners made policy, easterners implemented it on the provincial level. Theodosius understood the need to build relationships with established Eastern elites, and he entrusted most of the governorships and midlevel administrative appointments to Eastern provincial notables.[33] This not only kept these figures invested in his regime but also helped to ensure that revenue continued to flow regularly from the provinces not threatened by the Goths.

The first years of his reign saw Theodosius aggressively court Eastern elites in other ways too. Soon after his appointment, he set up his court in Thessaloniki to prepare for a campaign against the Goths. While there, the new emperor received large numbers of petitioners asking for favors. Theodosius turned few of them down[34]—a perfectly natural response given his lack of familiarity with the cases and his need to build relationships with the Eastern elite.[35] These efforts to build support among leading figures in the East were essential, but, in 379 and 380, Theodosius placed far greater emphasis on military affairs. He had been selected to defeat the Goths militarily, and he was expected to do so quickly. Unfortunately, the war did not go as planned. Theodosius spent two full campaigning seasons without a decisive victory. He spent much of 379 rebuilding the Eastern field army destroyed at Adrianople, a task so complicated that he could not have made much progress that year.[36] In 380, his new field army was so soundly defeated in Macedonia that Gratian summoned Theodosius to a meeting in Sirmium and took control of eastern Illyricum back from him.[37] While Theodosius slunk back to Constantinople, Gratian's forces drove the Goths out of Illyricum in 381.[38] The Goths retreated to Thrace, territory still controlled by Theodosius, and ultimately agreed to a peace treaty with him in October 382 that allowed them to stay in the empire, essentially unpunished.[39]

When Theodosius returned to Constantinople in defeat in late 380, he realized that he could no longer promise a punishing and absolute victory over the Goths. An emperor who seemed obviously to fail in the specific objectives he set for himself was vulnerable, and Theodosius now needed to find another way to justify his regime. He decided to present himself as a religious, administrative, and social reformer who promised a better empire than that left by Valens. He had, in a sense, pivoted from a public persona centered on military success to one founded on domestic reform.

Theodosius's policies during those first months in Constantinople reflected this shift. He further developed a program of restoring property and privileges to those who had suffered losses under Valens,[40] and he began an expansion of the Constantinopolitan senate.[41] His first months in Constantinople saw Theodosius displace non-Nicene clergy from the city's main churches and replace them with Nicenes.[42] In May 381 he summoned the Council of Constantinople, an assembly that reaffirmed the new imperial commitment to the Council of Nicaea and, perhaps not coincidentally, preempted an ecumenical council that Gratian had planned to call later that year.[43] And because Theodosius now anticipated that he would be spending a great deal more time in Constantinople than he had probably once expected, he and his courtiers began a process of spatially, architecturally, and ceremonially defining the city as Theodosius's own imperial capital.[44]

Theodosius was trying to salvage an imperial project that seemed to be going wrong, and he turned to Themistius to help explain how all of these initiatives fit together. Themistius, of course, was quite good at this game. With the exception of his failed approach to Julian, he had used his philosophical credentials and his relationships with members of the Eastern senate to build productive partnerships with every emperor since Constantius. By the later 370s, Themistius had mastered the art of rhetorically presenting new imperial policies as the philosophically inspired actions of a wise sovereign while simultaneously using his network of associates to build practical support for them. As we have seen, there was always an implicit price for Themistius's assistance. He would gladly help, but he expected something in return.

Theodosius proved perfectly willing to work with and reward Themistius. Their collaboration began in the summer of 379, before Theodosius had even come to Constantinople. That summer Themistius joined a Constantinopolitan delegation sent to Thessaloniki to congratulate Theodosius on his accession. Themistius came late, delayed, he claimed, by an illness, but he arrived prepared to deliver a speech that defined the new regime as one that would restore balance, justice, and security to the empire.[45] The central point of his speech, however, was that Theodosius had been chosen to rule because his unique combination of martial virtue and success as a commander ensured that "those damned villains will suffer."[46] Theodosius had already crushed the Sarmatians, and, Themistius claims, the city of Constantinople was awaiting his return "bearing trophies of victory over the ill-starred" Goths.[47] In expectation of this, the city sent Themistius to award a crown of goodwill and promise a second crown of gold once the inevitable victory over the Goths had been achieved.[48]

Themistius acknowledges that this victory lay in the future,[49] but he does not hesitate to explain what it will mean for Theodosius and his capital. Theodosius's martial virtue created a situation where, although inferior to Gratian in terms of legal seniority, Theodosius serves as an effective father to the younger emperor.[50] Beneath this, of course, is the implicit contrast between Theodosius, who earned his position because of his great natural abilities, and Gratian, who simply was born to the right father. Themistius then transitions to his final point, an assertion that, under Theodosius's supervision, Constantinople will be made the true equal of Rome not just through the reaffirmation of orders of previous emperors but through further building, imperial patronage, and senate expansion.[51] This statement telegraphs Theodosius's future plans while also distinguishing the regime of Theodosius from that of Valens.[52] As Constantinopolitans remembered, it was rumored that Valens had threatened to demolish the capital and plow under its ruins following his Gothic campaign in 378.[53] Theodosius's commitment to expanding the capital then contrasted dramatically with the policy of the emperor who preceded him.

It would be lost on no one that Themistius's claims and future promises all depended on Theodosius's quick and resounding military victory over the Goths.[54] When these victories failed to materialize, Themistius again came forward to redefine the emperor as a political reformer instead of a military leader. In mid-January 381, two months after a humbled Theodosius returned to Constantinople, Themistius offered a different rationale for the emperor's reign. Themistius emphasizes some of the same themes that he had spoken about in 379, but the more aggressive claims of that summer are gone. Theodosius was no longer Gratian's superior, and he no longer seemed destined to inflict an overwhelming defeat on the Goths, at least immediately. Instead, Themistius explains the emperor's legitimacy in a new way without ever acknowledging the dramatic reversal in his military fortunes.

Themistius begins by dismissing "reports of wars and battles of men" as a task he cannot perform. He will instead "cull virgin blooms from the meadows of Plato and Aristotle" to honor a man who is both cultivated and skilled in war.[55] Theodosius, Themistius claims, derives his authority not from "beauty, physical stature, swiftness, nor might" but from the possession "in his soul of some form of resemblance to God," which shows itself in his justice and righteousness.[56] It is this combination, Themistius argues, that makes Theodosius a particularly formidable sovereign. This is because he has to turn his thoughts to how he should drive the barbarians from Roman lands and how he needs to regulate the areas of his empire that are not under threat from barbarians.[57] If this is done correctly, the barbarians will be defeated because "order is manifestly stronger than disorder, system than chaos . . . these are the weapons with which men conquer other men."[58] Theodosius's good governance of the empire, then, will bring about victory over the barbarians.

The body of the oration explains the ways in which Theodosius regularly shows his divinely inspired nature. Like Alexander the Great and Scipio Africanus, Theodosius governs with justice and shows mercy.[59] He grants requests made by subjects in need, forgives debts they owe to the state, and always seeks to do good.[60] He recalled exiles, restored property to the families of condemned men, and remitted death sentences yet to be carried out.[61] In his overall commitment to doing good each day, he equaled the emperor Titus and even surpassed the legendary Spartan statesman Lycurgus.[62] Left unsaid was the contrast between the age of Theodosius and that of the parsimonious Valens, whose reputation for excessive debt collection, prosecutions, and executions Constantinopolitans would not easily forget.

One other key feature distinguishes the argument made in *Oration* 15, Themistius's speech in 381, from that found in *Oration* 14, the speech of 379. While *Oration* 14 asserts Theodosius's superiority to Gratian in terms of age and experience, *Oration* 15 describes Gratian as one of "two helmsman" commanding the ship of state "on a voyage towards the storm which suddenly fell on it" (see fig. 12).[63] Both emperors are now philosophers, more skilled than the Platonist philosopher Antiochus of Ascalon and the Stoic philosopher Ariston of Chios, and they govern like a single king with a kingdom extending from the Rhine to the Tigris.[64] Themistius never mentions Theodosius's diminished position and his loss of command over Illyricum, but he nonetheless explains it away. Gratian did not demote Theodosius because of inefficacy. Instead, the shift in the conduct of the Gothic war represented nothing more than a policy decision taken by both emperors together. The audience was to believe that the empire remained in two pairs of capable hands, even if the tasks these hands took up shifted as time progressed.

The Gothic situation again changed in October 382 when Saturninus, the commander of imperial forces in Thrace, reached an agreement that ended the Gothic rebellion.[65] The Goths laid down their arms in return for land on which to farm, a degree of political autonomy, and an opportunity to serve in the Roman army.[66] Theodosius rewarded Saturninus's service by naming him consul for 383. This was a significant gesture. The year 383 was the fifth year of Theodosius's reign, and emperors since the late 360s had ordinarily assumed the consulship to celebrate their milestone anniversaries. Theodosius's decision to step aside resonated powerfully.

On January 1, 383, Themistius rose before the senate to praise Saturninus, Theodosius, and the peace treaty they crafted to end the Gothic threat. The oration used the idea of a philosophical king ruling according to the will of God to weave together a celebration of these three subjects.[67] Although he had expressed this idea on many previous occasions, Themistius still had significant work to do in this neatly organized speech. He needed to somehow make a peace treaty that left the

FIGURE 12. "Concord of the emperors" Theodosius and Gratian (*RIC* IX.27a Siscia [Theodosius] and *RIC* IX.45a Antioch [Gratian]). Courtesy of the author.

Goths who killed Valens essentially unpunished seem like a Roman victory. He had to emphasize again the importance of Theodosius's identity as a domestic reformer who had changed the empire's political climate.[68] And, crucially, Themistius sought to lay the rhetorical groundwork for Theodosius's planned proclamation of his son Arcadius as co-emperor (see fig. 13), an action that occurred later that January without the approval of Gratian and flew in the face of the claims of imperial concord that recent propaganda had emphasized.[69] Themistius managed to do all of this without losing sight of Saturninus, the person on whom the occasion ostensibly focused. This was a masterpiece of imperial propaganda that simultaneously communicated important policy

FIGURE 13. Arcadius
crowned by the hand of God
(*RIC* IX.15 Cyzicus),
January–August 383.
Courtesy of the author.
Photo by Nathaniel Watts.

decisions, tweaked the imperial image, and honored an important Theodosian supporter.

Just as Saturninus received the consulship as a reward for his work in
securing a Gothic peace, so too would Themistius receive a reward for
his service in the early 380s. Between the late summer of 383 and early
spring of 384, Theodosius appointed the old philosopher to serve as
urban prefect of Constantinople.[70] This was a controversial honor for

the sixty-six-year-old Themistius to accept, especially since he had once before rejected an appointment to the office.[71] But Themistius was older now and may have seen an urban prefecture as a fitting capstone to a career that had little time left to run.[72] Nevertheless, his decision to accept the office ultimately required Themistius to repeatedly defend the propriety of a philosopher serving in imperial administration.[73] This public criticism aside, Themistius's prefecture shows that Theodosius, like Gratian, generously compensated the service of old doyens of the imperial system with rewards drawn from it.[74] Both Theodosius and Themistius seemed happy with the deal they made.

THE ALTERNATIVE TRACK

The early Theodosian years saw younger Christians offering services to the emperor that led to different types of rewards. Gregory Nazianzen offers the most familiar, if not the most effective, example of such a figure. As we saw in the previous chapter, Gregory enjoyed (or perhaps endured) a peripatetic career in which he flitted from Cappadocian classrooms to the priesthood, from the priesthood to an ascetic retreat, from ascetic retreat to the episcopacy, and from the episcopacy back to a sort of retirement.[75] The high point of his career came in the summer of 379 when a council of Nicene bishops meeting in Antioch appointed Gregory bishop of Constantinople.[76]

Gregory arrived in the capital and began working to build support for the Nicene church in a city that had been dominated by non-Nicenes for most of its short history. Although Gregory had not been appointed by Theodosius, he carefully calibrated his words to curry favor with a Nicene emperor, who, in 380, was still trying to figure out whether his vision of a Nicene capital would be most easily created by co-opting the existing church establishment or building a new, Nicene one around Gregory.[77] Working with Gregory was not Theodosius's first choice, but when the incumbent bishop of the city turned down Theodosius's offer of imperial recognition in return for his agreement "to believe in Nicaea, unite the people, and establish peace," the emperor moved on to Gregory.[78] Gregory had little to offer Theodosius beyond his strong support for Nicaea and his willingness to advance the emperor's theological agenda, but Gregory embraced each task with great energy.

Some of the surviving works from his time in Constantinople show Gregory presenting Theodosius to his congregation in ways that correspond to the image of the emperor advanced in the senate by

Themistius. Gregory's *Oration* 33, for example, contrasts the moderate reign of Theodosius with the horrors of Valens and catalogs the maimings, executions, and exiles endured under the previous emperor.[79] In *Oration* 37, a sermon delivered to a congregation that included Theodosius himself, Gregory spoke out in favor of the emperor's laws "legislating piety," which helped restrain persecution and murder.[80] In a later work, Gregory also speaks of Theodosius "making his wishes into a written law of persuasion."[81] Left unsaid but impossible to ignore is the contrast with Valens, an emperor who did not persuade but coerced.[82]

Gregory's rhetoric may have matched that of Themistius, but his political skills fell far short of those deployed by his older senatorial contemporary. Admittedly, Gregory faced a number of difficult challenges. He had to determine how best to grow the Constantinopolitan Nicene community while also serving as one of its leading voices in larger imperial discussions. He did not manage either task particularly well. The threat of mob violence loomed over his relations with Constantinopolitan non-Nicenes from the very moment that Theodosius turned the Constantinopolitan cathedral over to him in December 380.[83] Gregory failed even more spectacularly in his efforts to lead Nicenes in the wider empire. Bishop Peter of Alexandria sent advisers to help Gregory manage the Constantinopolitan see in 380 before giving up on him and trying to arrange for the ordination of a rival. Even more damaging was Gregory's disastrous mishandling of the Council of Constantinople in the summer of 381. Theodosius had called the council in order to get a quick and strong statement of pro-Nicene theology that some dissident groups could also endorse.[84] He also expected that various church appointments (including that of Gregory to Constantinople) would be ratified by a broad collection of bishops. Ultimately he hoped that the council would craft a clear statement of Nicene theology and back it with a coherent leadership structure with which the emperor could work.

The council was proceeding as the emperor hoped until the death of Bishop Meletius of Antioch, its presiding office. Gregory took over for Meletius and absolutely botched the job. He showed no flexibility in doctrine and exacerbated a dispute about the selection of a new bishop of Antioch. His leadership failures quickly caused the council to bog down. Theodosius then summoned additional attendees from Egypt and Illyricum to resolve the impasse, but the Egyptians who arrived began to try to depose Gregory.[85] Ultimately, Gregory felt compelled to resign both as the council's presiding officer and as bishop of Constantinople.

Gregory was replaced as bishop of Constantinople by Nectarius, a Constantinopolitan senator and former government official who, like Gregory, traded his career within the imperial system for a position of honor in the church.[86] Gregory returned to Cappadocia and, aside from a brief tenure as bishop of Nazianzus, he spent much of the next few years defending his reputation and tending the personal relationships that continued to make him socially relevant.[87] Nectarius handled the capital's difficult terrain so well that he remained bishop until his death in 397. Nectarius's success should not mark Gregory as a failure. Gregory's career is strikingly diverse and seems unique at first glance. However, if one equates his sequence of episcopal offices with governorships and retitles his ascetic retreats as aristocratic *otium,* the shape of his career looks much more familiar. Gregory built friendships, maintained relationships, and exchanged favors with other elites just as Libanius or Ausonius did. He sought the same combination of honor and achievement that they did, but the track on which he chose to travel was an episcopal not an administrative one. If one sees him as an administrator of middling skill rather than as a bishop who failed spectacularly, Gregory's various positions and retirements take on a different meaning.

This helps us better understand Theodosius's interactions with Gregory and men like him in the early 380s. Theodosius understood the value of encouraging and rewarding men who could help him manage the empire. He saw that proven administrators like Nectarius could help him remake the theological landscape of the Eastern empire if they were brought into the episcopacy. Theodosius hoped that men like Gregory and Nectarius could serve as imperial administrators of a sort, but he also made sure that the things they managed remained largely separate from the tasks he depended on men like Themistius to do. Both Gregory and Themistius presented, defended, and implemented imperial policies, but each worked on a different part of Theodosius's agenda and defined a different part of his public persona. Maintaining the divisions between them was one of the greatest administrative successes of the early years of Theodosius's reign.

THE PATHS CONVERGE

While Theodosius separated the types of service he requested from and the rewards he granted to Themistius and Gregory, a series of imperial actions against traditional religion in the early 380s brought the interests of these two different types of elites into direct conflict. Unlike Valentinian and Valens, the younger emperors of the 380s had little interest in preserving the effective pagan-Christian détente that the imperial system and its custodians had supported since the death of Julian. Between 379 and 384, a series of measures were carried out to reduce the public presence of traditional religion. In the East, these largely consisted of laws designed to act against what were considered foundational elements of traditional religious practice. This began in December 381 with a law that prohibited diurnal and nocturnal sacrifices while also forbidding anyone to approach a temple.[88] Those who violated its terms were to be proscribed. A law issued in November 382 further clarified the situation. It concerned a temple that contained images that "must be measured by the value of their art rather than by their divinity."[89] These images, the emperor declared, were to be protected, and the temple that contained them was to remain open, "but in such a way that the performance of sacrifices forbidden therein may not be supposed to be permitted under the pretext of such access to the temple."[90] This was a radical change from the way that sacrifices and temples had been treated for most of the past two decades. In essence, these laws represented a final and full reversal of Julian's religious program.

Gratian took a different approach in the West. In 382, he undertook a series of actions that undercut the financial and practical foundations of traditional Roman religion. None of his actions are preserved directly in the *Theodosian Code,* but other sources discuss their main components.[91] Gratian sanctioned the removal of the Altar of Victory that had been placed in the Roman senate house by Augustus.[92] He ended some of the beneficial financial privileges enjoyed by the cult of the Vestal Virgins. He eliminated imperial funding for public cult rituals. And he confiscated the property that belonged to the traditional Roman cults, endowments that had funded rituals and maintained temples for centuries.[93] This final measure imperiled the very functioning of the traditional public cults of Rome. It is not clear whether Gratian appreciated the significance of these actions. He may simply have thought them symbolic measures that demonstrated his Christian piety, an important concern after Theodosius's anti-pagan legislative program and church council in Constantinople had established his own Christian leadership credentials.[94]

To most pagans and Christians living in the Western Roman Empire, the suspension of state support for public cults in the city of Rome would have mattered very little. For some members of the Roman senate, however, these actions fundamentally threatened the religious foundations of the Roman state. Part of this had to do with the idea that the state needed to pay for public rituals if those rituals were to represent true expressions of collective devotion.[95] There was also an extremely complicated practical problem caused by this new policy. The endowments and cultic estates that Gratian confiscated were immense and scattered throughout the empire. As late as 408, some properties owned by the college of pontiffs in Rome had yet to be reassigned.[96]

In 382, a delegation of some of the more traditionally minded senators traveled to Milan to describe for Gratian the consequences of his decrees. Symmachus headed the embassy—an honor that likely reflects the personal relationship he had established with Gratian during his time in Trier in the early 370s and his mastery of the "idiom of imperial communication," rather than his great religious convictions.[97] The embassy carried with it Gratian's pontifical robes, a tangible reminder of the cultic obligations that traditionally accompanied imperial power.[98] Perhaps also implicit in this was the reminder that even Constantius had fulfilled his pontifical obligations during the same visit to Rome in which he had ordered the removal of the Altar of Victory from the senate.[99]

In a blow to Symmachus and the traditionalists in the senate, the embassy never met the emperor. They were prevented from gaining access, Symmachus later explains, by *inprobi* (wicked men), a label that deliberately obscures the identity of the men responsible for this slight.[100] It is known that Ambrose had presented to Gratian a letter forwarded to him by Bishop Damasus of Rome and signed by "countless" senators who threatened not to attend meetings in the senate if Gratian reversed these measures, but this letter served only as an excuse for refusing an audience to the embassy.[101] The wicked men Symmachus refers to must have been courtiers, with the master of offices (the *magister officiorum*) Macedonius and his staff the most likely suspects.[102] The two bishops and a group of palatine officials had thus managed a successful act of obstruction that prevented Gratian from appreciating the full consequences of the measures he had taken against traditional religion. They had also sent a clear message to those accustomed to working through the imperial system that legitimate appeals brought forward through official channels could be frustrated by the informal and confused way in which information filtered through to Gratian. Young and middle-aged Christian courtiers could now tip the scales of imperial justice against any appeals that conflicted with the views of influential dropouts like Ambrose.[103]

This dysfunctional political situation changed with the revolt of Magnus Maximus, the commander in charge of Roman armies in Britain.[104] Maximus crossed to Gaul in the summer of 383, orchestrated the defection of Gratian's army, and trapped the emperor before he could return to Italy. Gratian was then executed by one of Maximus's subordinates. Maximus was a Spaniard like Theodosius, and because of the ill-concealed tension between the Eastern and Western courts, he evidently hoped that Theodosius would assent to his control of the West following Gratian's death.[105] To make this happen, however, Maximus needed to make some sort of arrangement with Valentinian II, Gratian's twelve-year-old half brother. Valentinian had been given an imperial title but no actual governing responsibilities following his father's death in 375. In the aftermath of Gratian's death, a collection of Italian and Pannonian elites tried to create a rival court around Valentinian before Maximus could force the boy to acknowledge his authority. This required setting up an effective administrative apparatus that could run Italy, Africa, and Illyricum in his name. It also meant securing sufficient military forces to prevent Maximus from crossing the Alps and taking control of Italy.

A disparate collection of figures coalesced around the effort. A group of senatorial aristocrats led by Petronius Probus but probably including Praetextatus and Symmachus helped assemble the administrative apparatus. The Frankish general Bauto, who apparently had control over the Western forces in Illyricum, provided the military support that would eventually close the Alpine passes to Maximus.[106] Ambrose led a mission to Maximus's court in Trier that was intended to buy enough time for the others to arrange affairs in Italy.[107] Valentinian II's coalition consisted of men who had mastered the imperial system and others who had opted out of it, but all worked toward the one common goal of sustaining a viable imperial court based in Italy. In the end, they managed to delay Maximus long enough that the Alpine passes could be sufficiently fortified to prevent a winter crossing into Italy.[108] They then convinced Theodosius to offer support to Valentinian II. His backing froze the conflict into a sort of cold war that lasted until 387.[109]

With the political situation stabilized, the men who had built Valentinian's new regime expected rewards. Bauto and Petronius Probus acquired a sort of permanent insider status with the new regime. Bauto directed military affairs—a position that he parlayed into a consulship in 385 and, eventually, into a marriage between his daughter and the son of Theodosius.[110] Petronius Probus served a final term as praetorian prefect from 383 to 384 and then apparently stayed on as a sort of informal adviser to the court until after its departure from Italy in 387.[111]

Others who rallied to support Valentinian received different sorts of rewards. Praetextatus and Symmachus each were named prefects for 384. Praetextatus took over for Probus as prefect of Italy, Illyricum, and Africa, while Symmachus assumed the urban prefecture in Rome. Praetextatus was also promised the consulship for the year 385. These were high honors, but the prefectures were also serious administrative positions that each man took up during a period of civil conflict.[112] The honor of being asked was a significant inducement, but, in exchange for their service, Symmachus and Praetextatus had agendas they wished to advance. Macedonius, the *inprobus* official who had sabotaged Symmachus's embassy to Gratian, and his associate Ammianus were put on trial in 384, with Symmachus serving as the presiding judge.[113] The two prefects also hoped to recover statues and other items taken from temples under Gratian, though strong Christian pressure ultimately compelled Symmachus to abandon the effort.[114] And Praetextatus, for his part, apparently led a group of distinguished senators in public processions in Rome at the Megalensian festival in 384.[115] Praetextatus and Symmachus evidently believed that their support for Valentinian II entitled them to high offices and gave them the freedom to roll back Gratian's anti-pagan policies.

In the summer of 384, not long after Symmachus took office as urban prefect, the senatorial traditionalists took their most dramatic step. Following a senate vote, Symmachus forwarded a senatorial motion asking that Valentinian reverse Gratian's anti-pagan policies of 382.[116] His request centered on a call that "all worship should be considered as one."[117] Symmachus ingeniously frames this as a solution to the very real political, military, and economic crises caused by divine disapproval of Gratian's religious policies.[118] Symmachus reminds his audience of the "Divine Mind's" distribution of distinctive divine guardians to protect the cities and nations within the empire. He then calls attention to the victories over Hannibal and Brennus's Gauls that Rome's gods had ensured,[119] and argues that the removal of the Altar of Victory from the senate negated this divine protection.[120] Symmachus judiciously left out a direct mention of the peace treaty of 382 that revealed Rome's inability to punish the Goths who had killed Valentinian II's uncle Valens, but the veiled reference to it would have been lost on absolutely no one. Symmachus paired this with a description of how Gratian's seizure of temple properties and his suspension of the privileges granted the Vestal Virgins were immediately followed by a serious food shortage in 383.[121]

Nearly everyone in the Roman world in 384 would have accepted Symmachus's premise that the divine directly influenced events within the empire. By making this connection explicit, Symmachus had transformed a pagan-Christian confessional conflict into a matter of state policy that had a direct impact on imperial security. As fourth-century Romans undoubtedly knew, the populace of the city of Rome had developed a nasty habit of burning down the houses of urban prefects in times of food shortages.[122] After the recent food shortage in 383, the senate was as justified in calling for a reevaluation of Gratian's religious measures as they would have been in requesting a reexamination of any other imperial law or policy that had demonstrably negative consequences for the senate and its city. Symmachus then simply called attention to a failed policy that needed to be abandoned in favor of one "which had preserved the empire for [Valentinian's] father."[123]

Symmachus certainly agreed with the argument he made, but it was neither a purely personal appeal nor was it driven by extreme religious piety. As had been the case in 382, Symmachus served as the eloquent mouthpiece for a larger group of senators, who, in 384, had neither the administrative position nor the eloquence that he possessed.[124] This made the appeal much more dangerous than if it had been an individual senator asking for a personal favor or a particularly pious figure asking for a religious dispensation. Indeed, it seems that Symmachus's argument had such force that some Christian members of Valentinian's court were inclined to assent to his request.[125] If the question were decided within the system as, for example, Praetextatus's call for Valentinian I to revise his ban on nocturnal rituals had been in 364, the senatorial appeal likely would have worked.

But Valentinian II was not his father, and 384 was not 364. Voices from outside the imperial administrative system mattered far more now—and they were quickly raised against the senate's petition. The most memorable of these belonged to Ambrose, a man who understood both the limitations of the system and the sort of influence that existed beyond it. When Ambrose learned of Symmachus's communication, he dispatched a letter that responded to what he anticipated Symmachus would say (or perhaps to what Symmachus had hoped to say in 382). This letter is remarkable both because Ambrose guessed incorrectly about the nature of Symmachus's request and because this mistake ultimately did not matter. In the end, Ambrose attacked asymmetrically in a way that Symmachus could not possibly counter.

Ambrose begins with a simple statement that the emperors serve God in the same way that all Romans serve the emperors. Because of this, the emperor cannot give money to support pagan rituals.[126] Ambrose then proceeds to dismiss an argument about the unfairness of placing restrictions on pagan activity.[127] Ambrose next shifts to the Altar of Victory itself. Replacing it would compel Christian senators to be "tainted with ashes from its altar" and would force them to endure a religious persecution launched by a Christian emperor.[128] After making this point, Ambrose stops addressing Symmachus's anticipated arguments and begins threatening consequences if Symmachus is allowed to prevail. Ambrose claims that the church will refuse to accept funds from an emperor who also pays for traditional religious activities, and suggests that Valentinian I would call down a rebuke from heaven if his son permitted a pagan altar in the senate.[129] More powerful than these consequences (which range from the unlikely to the comical) was the transition that preceded them. After terming the restoration of the altar a new persecution, Ambrose "appeals to [Valentinian's] faith as a minister of Christ" and asks that he refuse to commit sacrilege by signing on to such a decree.[130] This is, Ambrose continues, "a matter of religion" not a "civil matter," and, as bishop, he deserves both to be consulted and to be furnished with a copy of the *Relatio* so that he can formulate a fuller response.[131]

In the end, the fight came down not to rational arguments but crassly transactional politics. Ambrose had done more for Valentinian II than Symmachus or Praetextatus had—and he knew it. In the midst of this appeal to Valentinian's religious sensibilities, Ambrose asked him to remember the "legation recently entrusted to me," a comment that Neil McLynn has described as Ambrose calling in "the debt that had been incurred at Trier."[132] Ambrose's blatant reminder of his trip to Maximus's court and the security it earned the emperor persuaded the consistory to turn down the senate's petition. Ambrose had overpowered Symmachus, but he himself seems to have been somewhat uneasy about the purely political nature of his victory. When he received the text of Symmachus's *Relatio,* he then composed a point-by-point refutation of its main arguments.[133] This rhetorical exercise had no bearing on policy, but it did help to obscure the fact that Ambrose's actual arguments ultimately mattered far less than the personal leverage this unique political situation had given him.

Ambrose brilliantly realized that this obfuscation was necessary because he hoped to use the event to establish an important precedent. Both *Epistle* 17 and *Epistle* 18 worked from the principle that the Christian religious consequences of imperial policies were more important than any possible negative effects a legislative program might have. If taken to its logical end, this principle gave bishops the authority to decide when a particular policy had so much religious importance that its other consequences did not matter. Ambrose, the Christian leader who had abandoned an imperial career for the church, now claimed the power to veto policies produced by the imperial system he had left behind. The lines separating the appeals of elites who worked through the imperial administrative system and those pressed by the young Christian elites who had left it were now significantly blurred. For the first time since the reign of Diocletian, elites operating outside of the social and economic controls established by the Roman imperial system claimed the right to set its policies.[134]

. . .

Ausonius and the men around him who reconfigured imperial administration following the death of the emperor Valentinian could never have anticipated a situation like that which unfolded in 384. Their remaking of the court was a thoroughly conventional affair in which the Pannonians favored by Valentinian were replaced by a hybrid Gallic and Italian senatorial administration. They were a religiously and generationally diverse group, but they were all products of the conventional Roman administrative elite who accepted both the obligations and the rewards of later Roman imperial service. They were also deeply committed to reversing many of the anti-senatorial policies that Valentinian had promoted. Ausonius and his colleagues evidently hoped that, with this infusion of new talent, the imperial system could correct some of the imbalances that had developed in the early 370s.

By the early 380s, a combination of military reverses and weak emperors had dashed these hopes. If Ausonius hoped to be Gratian's Fronto, the last years of the young emperor's reign made him seem more like Seneca. By 380, Ausonius had moved into retirement, and Gratian had decamped from Gaul to northern Italy, where he fell under the influence of a collection of bickering advisers with competing interests. This prevented his regime from responding effectively to information about the needs of his subjects—a failure that eventually prompted his overthrow.

The situation in the East was even worse. The death of the emperor Valens and the destruction of much of the Eastern army at Adrianople presented his young successor Theodosius with a massive rebuilding project that proceeded in unexpected directions. For much of the 380s, Theodosius shifted his self-presentation in ways that corresponded to the success or failures of his military campaigns against the Goths. As he cast about for effective ways to explain why he should keep his job, Theodosius drew on a diverse group of supporters that included establishment figures like Themistius and church leaders like Gregory Nazianzen. Each performed tasks and received rewards keyed to their position within or outside of the imperial administrative system.

The fall of Gratian in 383 saw the wall between the Christian dropouts and elite establishment figures collapse. The frenzied attempt to quickly assemble an effective governing structure around Valentinian II indebted the new regime to a range of Italian and Illyrian military, senatorial, and ecclesiastical figures. When the immediate threat posed by Maximus had subsided, these men scrambled to seize as much power and influence as they could without regard for the lines that once separated ecclesiastical, military, and administrative rewards. Ambrose's assertion of an ecclesiastical veto over imperial policy represented only the most brazen attempt to redefine these boundaries in the leadership vacuum that surrounded the child emperor.

The particular weakness of Valentinian II compelled his advisers to allow figures who had opted out of the imperial administrative system to exercise influence over important decisions that occurred within it. These were admittedly exceptional circumstances, but even precedents set by weak imperial regimes often proved difficult to reverse. The challenge was compounded in the early 380s by the generational shift that Ausonius had tried to manage in the late 370s. The final pagan generation was fading out, and the empire was steadily passing into the hands of a younger generation that had less faith in and ties to the social and political regime of their parents. While many remained devoted to the imperial system, some, like Ambrose, prized religious goals over the stability and institutional inertia that their parents usually protected. The growing resonance of these outsider voices would soon come to threaten the broad religious and social consensus that the final pagan generation expected the imperial system to preserve.

CHAPTER 9

Old Age in a Young Man's Empire

All of the figures we have been following ended their public careers between 384 and 393. This is, in some ways, what we have been trained to expect of old men in the ancient world. It is often assumed that they graciously handed public functions over to a younger generation and quietly retreated into the life of their families.[1] Many members of the final pagan generation did pull back from public life to spend more time with their families as they entered old age, but focusing on this retreat offers an incomplete and distorted picture of their final decade. For every Ausonius who retired from public life following the usurpation of Magnus Maximus in 383, there is a Libanius who corresponded regularly with prominent officials and continued to give orations on public matters until right before he died. But even this basic dichotomy is an artificial one. Ausonius never fully disengaged from public life, and Libanius spent a great deal of time during his last years confronting health and family problems. Even as old men, these elites remained engaged in a wide variety of activities.

The world around them had clearly changed by the 390s. The eloquent councillor still mattered in an empire of young, assertive bishops and ascetics, but he mattered less than he did in 350. His network of associates, whose power and positions were defined by the post-Constantinian imperial system, remained potent, but it often lacked the diversity to influence imperial officials, who also listened to unconventionally authoritative people like Ambrose.[2] This mattered particularly when Christian leaders acted aggressively against traditional religion in the 380s and 390s. In those circumstances, the final pagan generation sometimes seemed as influential as the president of Polaroid in the age of the smartphone.

This chapter will look at the experience of being old in the period between 384 and 394. Praetextatus died at the decade's outset, Themistius fell silent soon after it began, and Ausonius spent the decade in retirement. This means that most of the discussion will focus on Libanius. The chapter starts by examining Roman ideas about old age and the degree to which these corresponded to late antique realities. It then looks at the personal challenges Libanius faced, the public roles that he continued to play, and the ways in which he advertised his continued authority. The discussion next turns to the Antiochene Riot of the Statues, a moment in 387 when Libanius and the old civic establishment worked alongside the new Christian ascetic and ecclesiastical leadership to secure an imperial pardon for the city's misbehavior. The chapter concludes by considering how Libanius responded to the anti-pagan laws and extralegal violence that shook Syria in the 380s and early 390s. Libanius was willing to speak out against these attacks, but only if his words did not threaten the wider social and political influence he still enjoyed. To the end, he and men like him preferred personal influence to confessional conflict.

RETIREMENT, 380S STYLE

When the sixty-six-year-old Themistius stood before the senate in January 383 to praise Theodosius's choice of the general Saturninus for consul, he began his oration with a plea for his audience's indulgence. "I have often thought to myself," he begins, "that since my body is worn out and old age advances, now is the time to lay aside my writing tablet and cease from further wearying the king's ears with my speeches."[3] But, Themistius continues, the occasion made it impossible "to hold myself back and, in Euripides' words, [I] 'do not disgrace my old age by intending to join the dance.'"[4]

Themistius's mention of the limits that his advancing age placed on his activity provides a dramatic introduction to a speech that presented Theodosius's disappointing Gothic peace treaty as a great Roman victory.[5] A modern audience might also find it absurd. By 383, Themistius had been an active contributor to policy conversations in Constantinople for the better part of thirty-five years and had risen regularly since 379 to speak in favor of Theodosian policies. Modern cynicism, however, sometimes obscures important late antique realities. Themistius did indeed use his advanced age for rhetorical effect at the beginning of *Oration* 16, but he also played on quite real perceptions about old age. After this triumphant speech before the senate in 383, we know of only three more speeches that Themistius gave. All of these concerned his brief tenure as urban prefect in 384, all respond to direct criticisms of him, and none of these defenses came after 385.[6] *Oration* 16 may seem like just another well-crafted speech in the long career of an imperial propagandist, but it actually began Themistius's final act.

Themistius probably already sensed this in 383. The comments he makes about old age eerily resemble a well-developed line of criticism directed against publicly engaged older men. In the second century A.D. the Athenian philosopher Juncus mocked old men "with the audacity to enter the agora" for "getting in the way and spoiling the common air of the city." When an old man appeared to speak, he was judged incapable of holding office because he was "bowed and withered, misshapen and feeble, and, in spirit, as the saying goes, he has become a child again."[7] Maximianus, a later Spanish poet, agreed. The old suffer "insults, contempt, and violent condemnation," he writes, "nor does anyone from all of those [who were once friends] offer any friendly deed."[8] These extreme statements bluntly express a common view that the ideal old age for a senator like Themistius consisted of retirement instead of continued public service. In a letter to the retired consul Pomponius Bassus, the Roman senator Pliny the Younger congratulates him on "a retirement that is worthy of your ripe wisdom. You live in a charming spot, you take exercise on both sea and land, you have plenty of good conversation, you read a great deal and listen to others reading." "That," the forty-three-year-old Pliny continues, "is just the way that a man should spend his later years after filling the highest magistracies . . . for we owe our early and middle adulthood to our country; our last years are due to ourselves."[9]

This was by no means the only view of how people lived out their final years. Plutarch, for example, argued quite strongly that older men should remain a vital and engaged part of society.[10] But Plutarch was an outlier. For most late Roman authors, retirement was an ideal as well as a thing guaranteed by law. As early as the reign of Augustus, all senators over the age of sixty-five were excused from attending senate meetings, an effective retirement age that Claudius lowered to sixty.[11] City councillors aged out of their civic obligations and responsibility for the poll tax at age seventy, an age that Constantine lowered to sixty in a law of 324.[12] In practice, these age limits seem to have been flexibly applied.

Younger men sometimes successfully managed to retire from exemptions before they actually reached the legal maximum age. The tendency by some to estimate their actual age probably meant that some others retired early without actually realizing it.[13]

Demographics help explain the social pressures pushing older men out of public life. Although we often think of the senate and city councils as bastions of elderly, experienced former magistrates, they were actually bodies made up primarily of young and middle-aged men. The minimum age for membership in the Roman senate in the imperial period was twenty-five. In the high empire, 14–16 percent of the senate was between twenty-five and twenty-nine years old, and an additional 25–28 percent was between thirty and thirty-nine. By contrast, only 11–13 percent was between sixty and sixty-nine, and perhaps as little as 5 percent was over age seventy.[14] The Constantinopolitan senate before which Themistius rose in 383 would have been even younger, as Theodosius's ongoing efforts to build its membership up to two thousand inevitably drew in primarily younger men.[15] Probably more than 90 percent of Themistius's audience in 383 was made up of men younger than him.

This helps to explain both the hostile senatorial reaction to Themistius's urban prefecture in 384, and his ultimate decision to retreat from public life soon after stepping down from this office. The urban prefecture was a senior office, but it was one often held by men like Symmachus, who were in their forties or fifties.[16] Not only was Themistius in his late sixties, but he had been offered the position when he was the appropriate age and had turned it down.[17] Younger senators could be forgiven for thinking that Themistius's turn for office had already passed. He was now just an old man standing in their way.

Themistius's usual volubility makes his retreat into silent retirement particularly striking, but other members of the final pagan generation also struggled to remain relevant as they confronted illness, family tragedy, and the death of close friends. Ausonius, for example, wrote a poem for his grandson's fifteenth birthday in which he thanks God for consenting "that, recovered, I may spend my old age brought back from the Fates' borderland and [that I may] behold this happy day and the stars I scarce hoped to see, I who was nearly mourned as one dead."[18] Early in the 380s, he ends a cover letter that accompanied a book of exhortation to another grandson who was preparing for school with an apology for the rough nature of the work. This feature should be overlooked, Ausonius explains, because "old men are twice children."[19]

Libanius, however, offers perhaps the most complete portrait of the challenges and opportunities that older elites confronted in the later 380s and early 390s. This has a great deal to do with the survival of a group of 272 letters that Libanius wrote between 388 and his death in 393.[20] These letters provide some of the most powerful and poignant statements about the experience of old age. In 390, for example, Libanius wrote to the philosopher Priscus, one of the philosophers who had joined the court of the emperor Julian in 361. The letter introduces the ninety-year-old Priscus to Hilarius, a much younger Antiochene philosopher who would soon travel to Greece.[21] In some ways, this was a standard letter of reference in which Libanius praises Hilarius, speaks about how his departure diminished Antioch, and likens him to the philosophers once patronized by Julian. In the middle of the letter, however, Libanius emphasizes the personal significance of Hilarius's departure. Libanius feels sad because "I have now reached the age of seventy-six and have not much time left. Hilarius will come back with a fine tale to tell [about meeting Priscus in Greece] . . . but, while delighting others, he will look in vain for me."[22]

The negative physical effects of old age that Juncus had once mocked had begun to bear down on Libanius by the time he wrote to Priscus. He experienced persistent migraines, and his eyesight had started to fail.[23] Libanius also felt other effects of being an old man in a young man's world. A governor in the late 380s encouraged a rival teacher to come to Antioch in an attempt to displace Libanius.[24] This attempt failed, but Libanius soon began to see the audiences for his public speeches change. They were not "as they used to be, formed of the governor and the great numbers that he used to bring from many provinces." Instead, Libanius began speaking to "an audience of friends" to which he felt he could speak more comfortably.[25] His audiences continued to decline, despite the calls by some friends that Libanius speak in public more frequently. In 393, Libanius wrote to Theophilus, one of his biggest backers, about a recent public performance he gave at the Antiochene Bouleuterion.[26] Theophilus had promised that an oration by Libanius would attract "a crowd of the most famous teachers followed by their students coming from the agora to the Bouleuterion."[27] Instead, "not one of them turned up at all" because, Libanius asserts, "I know that they want me dead."[28] Later in 393, Libanius claimed that he had been pushed out of the lecture rooms and compelled to work from home.[29]

The slowing of his teaching career was difficult for Libanius, but he struggled even more with the deaths of friends and family members whom he outlived. His younger brother died in 383 after a long decline in health.[30] The year 385 saw the death of his secretary, "whose writing assisted me greatly in my declamations, since it was much better than my own notes."[31] He later would face the death of a close friend's wife and that of Calliopius, the teaching assistant who kept Libanius's school running.[32] Even more difficult was the death, around 390, of "the woman who was the mother of my son."[33] She was a woman of servile status whom Libanius never names but with whom he partnered for almost forty years.[34] The difference in their social statuses meant that Libanius could not (or would not) clearly articulate his feelings for her. He does make clear, however, that her final illness was a long one that "caused her dreadful suffering" and took an emotional toll on him as well.[35]

No event affected Libanius more than the death of his son Cimon in 391. Cimon (whose birth name was Arabius) was born in the 350s, the illegitimate son of Libanius and his servant concubine.[36] Cimon's legal status barred him from inheriting Libanius's property, but Libanius nevertheless gave him a literary education designed to prepare him for a life of imperial service.[37] Libanius began agitating for Cimon to be legally recognized as his heir under Julian, but his effort did not succeed until the reign of Theodosius.[38] In the meantime, Cimon worked as an advocate at the court of the governor of Syria in the 370s and early 380s.[39] When he secured the right of inheritance, Cimon became liable for the curial obligations attached to his family property.[40] Libanius then began working with Cimon to find a way to gain an exemption. Cimon was named governor of Cyprus, but the senate canceled the appointment when the urban prefect Proculus failed to agree to it.[41] Against Libanius's advice, Cimon traveled from Antioch to Constantinople to appeal the senate's decision. The appeal failed disastrously, and members of the senate publicly mocked both Cimon and Libanius. Even worse, Cimon fell from his carriage on the way home, injured his leg, and then succumbed to an infection not long after returning to Antioch in 391.[42]

Libanius spoke often about how Cimon's death left him emotionally devastated. In his *Autobiography*, Libanius writes, "When I heard about [his fall] and saw him carried home, I felt the full force of his mother's death," and then was unable to even rise from the bed.[43] "As many a tear welled up in my eyes," Libanius continues, "the sight in one of them became weaker and I feared that it would go completely."[44] Libanius also mentions his grief at Cimon's death repeatedly in letters written in 391–93. In one of them, he even raises the medically dubious notion that his endless crying over it "has deprived me of my eyesight for the most part."[45] These constant claims of paralyzing grief have encouraged modern scholars to imagine that the death of Cimon "nearly broke him."[46]

One can understand why Libanius would react in this way to the deaths of his son, his brother, his partner, and so many close friends. At the same time, everything that Libanius writes in his letters and his *Autobiography* serves a rhetorical purpose.[47] These references to old age's physical, professional, and emotional challenges are no exception. One of his comments about crying so much that his eyes were "left in a pitiable state" comes at the beginning of a letter of introduction carried by Theophilus to the urban prefect Aristaenetus. The grief he felt following Cimon's death is just one of a long series of afflictions that Libanius says that Theophilus helped him overcome. Libanius then asks Aristaenetus to "write letters and commend" Theophilus "because of his kindness towards me."[48] Libanius's litany of misfortunes serves to vouch for the good character of Theophilus and sets up an elaborate request that Aristaenetus help Theophilus get established in the capital.

The most artful such use of the motif of paralyzing grief comes in a letter that Libanius wrote to Firminus in 392.[49] Firminus, a military official who recently took up the study of rhetoric, had apparently sent Libanius at least two letters that Libanius failed to answer. When he sent a third letter chastising Libanius for his silence, Libanius responded carefully in a way that both engages with the content of these two letters and apologizes for responding to them slowly. Libanius's apology begins, "How could I, who have been so moved by your change of career, ever despise—to use your own words—one who has given me this pleasure, so as not to write to you."[50] "You should have looked," he continues, "for some other reason [for my silence]." "Everyone has heard of the death of Cimon . . . now he is dead and I have sat in mourning for him, touching food under duress from my friends, who tell me that I must not embrace death and die as well. Letters arriving here I have received with tears, and I have been quite incapable of sending any."[51] After using his sadness at the death of his son and the claim of its nearly fatal effect on him to excuse his failure to return Firminus's letter, Libanius then concludes with a striking response. Under these circumstances, Libanius says, Firminus ought either to compose a funeral address about Cimon or stop accusing Libanius of being an unjust friend.[52] Although parts of the letter are touching and poignant when read in isolation, the letter offers no window into Libanius's soul. It serves instead as a devastating rhetorical counterattack that reasserted Libanius's dominant position in his epistolary relationship with Firminus.[53]

THE SYSTEM ABIDES

Libanius's letters to Firminus and Aristaenetus show the hazards of assuming that the final pagan generation fell into an old age like that romanticized by Pliny or derided by Juncus. Despite being in his midseventies, Libanius believed that he had recovered much of the influence within the Roman administrative and social system that he had once enjoyed. His collected letters from 388 to 393 show this. They do contain a litany of complaints, but all of them serve a rhetorical purpose.[54] These letters form an artfully composed and deliberately arranged collection assembled to show Libanius presiding over a network of friends and associates whose influence reached the highest levels of government.[55] The letters defined Libanius as a man of literary and social authority while simultaneously allowing him to present his own version of embarrassing events like Cimon's failed journey to Constantinople.[56] These were the works of a man who thought that he had triumphs to advertise.

This purpose becomes clear at the collection's outset in a letter written by Libanius to the praetorian prefect Flavius Eutolmius Tatianus.[57] Tatianus came from a pagan family in Lycia and held a string of high offices during the years when Valens ruled the East.[58] He had retired to his home in Sidyma following Theodosius's appointment, but Theodosius recalled him to service in early 388.[59] In 387, the usurper Magnus Maximus took control of Italy and forced the young emperor Valentinian II to flee to Thessaloniki.[60] Theodosius then began planning to lead an invasion of Maximus's territory that would likely take Theodosius away from Constantinople for a long period of time. He appointed Tatianus prefect of the East, made Tatianus's son Proculus prefect of Constantinople, and placed the two of them at the head of a team of experienced and effective administrators who could run the East while the emperor settled affairs in the West.[61] Along with Proculus, Tatianus served as the most important policy maker in the Eastern empire from 388 until Theodosius returned from the West in 391.[62]

Libanius defines his strong friendship with Tatianus in the very first sentence of the first letter in this collection.[63] The letter begins, "Your first letter reached me straightaway at the beginning of your term of office."[64] As the letter continues, it is clear that Libanius also wants to use the document to put to rest a series of rumors suggesting that Libanius had supported Maximus. Libanius mentions that Tatianus fell silent after that initial letter informing Libanius of his appointment, a silence that Libanius attributed to "the law that prevents those in your position" from writing to people suspected of disloyalty.[65] Libanius predicted that the letters would resume once the accusation died, and when it did, "the same day brought a letter from you."[66] This reflected a long friendship in which, Libanius claims, "one who had assisted me in my career lent his services in dealing with its accidents."[67] In less than thirty lines of text, this letter establishes Libanius as a figure of great importance who sits at the center of a strong epistolary network that reaches to the very top of the imperial court.

The rest of the collection reinforces these basic ideas.[68] Libanius includes twelve more letters to Tatianus, a highlight of which is a note thanking him for sending gifts of a diptych and goblet when Tatianus became consul in 391.[69] Many other leading figures also appear. There is a letter to Symmachus, Tatianus's consular colleague in 391; fifteen letters to Tatianus's son Proculus; and eight to Aristaenetus, Proculus's successor as urban prefect.[70] There are two letters to Rufinus, the court figure who deposed Tatianus and took his place as prefect of the East in 392; four letters to Richomer, a former consul and one of Theodosius's most trusted military commanders; four letters to Richomer's predecessor Ellebichus; and three letters addressed to the influential courtier Mardonius.[71] The collection thus displays Libanius's ties to a nearly complete roster of the top civilian administrators, military officers, and court officials who ran the Eastern empire between 388 and 393. He comes across as a figure who retained a thorough mastery of the later fourth-century imperial system until the end of his life.

This collection appears to offer a glimpse into Libanius's friendships with a diverse collection of the most influential men in the Roman world. There are pagans, Christians, and Jews,[72] city councillors who represent the old Roman administrative order, and imperial administrators, military officials, and Constantinopolitan senators who represent the new.[73] Despite their religious and social diversity, nearly all of the people who appear in this collection held positions and exercised authority defined by the fourth-century imperial system in which Libanius had long thrived. This was not, however, a network that reflected the growing influence of elite dropouts like Chrysostom. There are no ascetics in the second collection of Libanius's correspondence, and few bishops.[74] Libanius likely knew and interacted with many such figures (he may, for example, have taught Chrysostom), but whatever interactions he had with them did not reinforce the image of Libanius that the collection creates.[75] These men existed outside of the system that Libanius was claiming to master and were, then, irrelevant to the picture of Libanius that the letter collection paints.

THE RIOT OF THE STATUES

Chrysostom and his compatriots may have been irrelevant in the idyllic elite landscape that Libanius's letters depict, but they had become an extremely potent force in the real Syria of the later 380s and early 390s. No event shows this better than an explosion of urban violence that shook Antioch in early 387. Sometime that winter, the governor announced the imposition of a tax to be paid in gold that would fall on the leading members of the city.[76] The amount was so large, Libanius claims, that "the land could not meet the burden."[77] "The courtroom," Libanius continues, "was crammed with people—ex-governors, city councillors, advocates, retired military men," who became so distraught that they "began to make tearful supplication" so that they might be relieved of the burden.[78] Outside the courtroom, a crowd surrounded the residence of the governor, burned down part of the imperial palace in the city, and destroyed painted portraits and bronze statues of the imperial family.[79] The portraits and statues of the imperial family served as physical manifestations of the imperial presence in each city in the empire. Their toppling represented symbolic violence against the imperial family and was an act of rebellion for which the individual actors would be punished and the entire city held responsible. The rioters who toppled the statues were quickly executed, but the city was still left to fear collective punishment for its failure to control its citizens.[80]

The Riot of the Statues occurred when Theodosius was facing off against Magnus Maximus, and it immediately followed a leadership change in the Persian empire. These twin realities made a harsh punishment for the East's third-largest city rather unlikely.[81] Theodosius quickly arranged for an imperial commission to travel to the city in order to determine an appropriate reaction. Fearing a harsh verdict, many Antiochenes fled the city.[82] When Caesarius and Ellebichus, the two commissioners, arrived in Antioch, they questioned former imperial officeholders and members of the city council.[83] These interviews convinced the commissioners to be lenient with the city.[84] At the same time, a previous imperial order compelled the commissioners to arrest the members of the city council and hold them in confinement until a verdict from the emperor was received.[85] The councillors were rounded up, Caesarius set off to communicate his findings to Theodosius, and Ellebichus stayed in the city to monitor the situation. Caesarius reached Constantinople within six days, returned to Antioch not long after, released the city councillors, and announced that the city would receive nearly a full pardon.[86] According to Libanius, Ellebichus was as overjoyed as the rest of the Antiochenes.[87]

Though they shared the common purpose of saving Antioch, dropouts like Chrysostom and establishment figures like Libanius describe their efforts on behalf of the city in very different ways. Libanius saw the riot as an unfortunate event for which the councillors and former government officials in Antioch had no responsibility.[88] While they tried to discuss the tax rationally with the governor, an uncontrollable mob set off to find the Christian bishop Flavian. When they could not locate him, they began burning and destroying symbols of imperial power.[89] Christian rabble-rousers caused the violence, but Libanius assigns to himself a key role in resolving the crisis.[90] He claims that he sat with the commissioners and calmed them down so that they would be ready to hear the appeals of Antiochenes.[91] Ellebichus and Caesarius were among Libanius's correspondents, and Libanius had a particularly well-developed relationship with Ellebichus, for whom he had written a panegyric in 385.[92] While the commissioners were in town, Libanius claims to have argued Antioch's case, asked for imperial clemency, and convinced the commissioners to hear appeals from Antioch's leading citizens.[93] In his telling, Libanius tamed Ellebichus and Caesarius with "orations and tears,"[94] and "personally was held responsible" when the city was pardoned.[95]

Libanius indicates that the appeals for mercy coming from the Antiochene elite reached beyond the imperial commissioners. Perhaps influenced by senators who had ties to Antioch, the senate of Constantinople directly petitioned the emperor to spare the city.[96] Libanius contrasted the efforts of Antioch's leading citizens with the flight of Christians.[97] It was no surprise that when Theodosius's letter of clemency reached the city, it came through conventional channels. It went first to the imperial commissioners and then was read aloud by Ellebichus in the same courthouse in which the investigation began.[98] For elites like Libanius, lower-status Christian outsiders caused this crisis, elites (both pagan and Christian) working within the confines of the old imperial social and administrative system calmed it, and the ceremonial resolution of the crisis came in a public building used by imperial officials and civic notables.

The Antiochene Christian leadership described a completely different course of events. According to John Chrysostom, the traditional elites fled Antioch, and the new Christian establishment stepped up to save the city. Instead of the city council organizing appeals and sending embassies, the bishop Flavian traveled to Constantinople so that he might appeal to the emperor in person. Then, when Caesarius and Ellebichus arrived in the city, they were met not by Libanius and members of the council but by a flood of ascetics who "had been shut up for so many years in their cells." They came before the commissioners "ready to shed their blood" and "declared that they would not depart until the judges spared the entire city."[99] The amazing thing about this, Chrysostom continues, was that these men had once "forsaken the city, hastened away, and hid themselves in caves," but they returned to save it at a time when many of Antioch's most prominent residents fled.[100]

While Chrysostom credits the monks with saving the city from the immediate wrath of the commissioners, he explains that Flavian earns the most credit for its final salvation.[101] Flavian not only intervened with the emperor directly when in Constantinople,[102] but he even (supposedly) spoke with Ellebichus and Caesarius while they were on their way to Antioch.[103] In Chrysostom's telling, Flavian calmed the commissioners before they reached Antioch, the monks stayed their hand while they were there, and the bishop then "won renown with both God and man" by heroically convincing Theodosius to pardon the city.[104] Chrysostom even credits Flavian with sending his own emissary to the city so that the emperor's decision could be communicated through Christian channels before the imperial commissioners learned about it.[105] This triumph belonged entirely to the rising Christian church, its heroic bishop, and the Syrian ascetics.[106] According to Chrysostom, "those who were in power, those who were surrounded by great wealth, and those who possessed great influence with the emperor" deserved no credit for the city's pardon.[107]

Libanius and Chrysostom present two parallel accounts of the Riot of the Statues. Each describes the heroic actions of one part of the Antiochene community and refuses to give any credit to another, equally engaged part of the city. Both Libanius and Chrysostom deliberately omit the contributions of others, but it is likely that neither account fabricates the actions of the figures whose contributions it celebrates. When Theodosius and his advisers learned about the riot in Antioch, they seem to have understood that they needed to forgive the city in a way that acknowledged the influence of conventional elites like Libanius and less conventional figures of authority like Flavian. Theodosius made it known that he heard appeals from both Flavian and the Constantinopolitan senate. He sent an older pagan commissioner with a military background (Ellebichus) and a younger Christian civilian administrator (Caesarius) as his two investigators. And he approved as the Antiochene council voted to erect bronze statues honoring the two commissioners, and as its churches were filled with praises for the imperial clemency. Theodosius was not, as has sometimes been argued, signaling that only Christian actions prompted his decision to spare the city.[108] Instead, once Theodosius decided to pardon the Antiochenes, it was very much in his interest to allow as many Antiochenes as possible to take credit for convincing him to be merciful. He had given all of the influential figures in the city a gift of public recognition, and they now owed him debts of gratitude that he could call in should the civil war with Maximus take a bad turn.

THE SYSTEM, ITS DROPOUTS, AND THE TEMPLES

The Riot of the Statues prompted two very different coalitions of influential figures to work toward the same objective.[109] The religious policies of the mid-380s and early 390s forged a different dynamic. The ascetics and bishops celebrated by Chrysostom pushed imperial authorities toward ever more aggressive anti-pagan and anti-Jewish actions, while older men like Libanius worked within the confines of the imperial system to slow things down. These septuagenarians cared about the temples,[110] but they sought to protect them by working through the same formal and informal procedures that they used to blunt the effect of midcentury religious policies. In earlier decades, appeals to imperial officials and requests for special treatment limited the effect of both anti-pagan policies and Julian's pro-pagan religious reforms.[111] Unfortunately, the nature of the assaults on traditional religion had changed by the 380s, and actions taken within the confines of the old imperial social and administrative system now worked less well.

In the East in the 380s, the most devastating assaults on traditional religion came not from emperors and governors but from people working outside of the formal imperial administration. After a burst of legislative activity in 381 and 382 that prohibited diurnal and nocturnal sacrifices while also forbidding anyone to approach a temple,[112] the consistory remained largely silent on matters relating to traditional religion for the next decade. The only law to appear between 382 and 391 essentially reiterated prohibitions previously laid out. Theodosian policy, however, went beyond what legislation spelled out. The emperor issued no laws ordering the destruction of temples, but he tacitly sanctioned this activity in ways that challenged formal administrative models. The most notorious assaults came during the praetorian prefect Cynegius's inspection tour of Syria, Mesopotamia, and Egypt in 386–88. As a part of his official duties, Cynegius set out to survey his territory in the hope that he could identify ways to rebuild the strength of local curia. The nature of the tour changed quickly, however, as monks and bishops traveling along with him destroyed temples in Mesopotamia and Syria and sacked shrines in Egypt.[113] Cynegius certainly approved of these assaults, but his campaign was only a part of a larger sequence of events in which imperial administrators either encouraged or simply turned a blind eye toward Christian violence against non-Christian sacred sites. In 387, after Cynegius's tour moved into Egypt, an unnamed *comes Orientis* attempted to cut the sacred grove at Daphne outside of Antioch.[114] Then, in 388, a group of Christian monks and their bishop burned down a synagogue in the garrison town of Callinicum.[115]

All of this activity was done in such a way that the emperor could conveniently feign ignorance, but Christian thinkers understood what Theodosius aimed to do. Theodoret prefaces the segment of the fifth book of his *Ecclesiastical History* in which he discusses temple destructions with a celebration of Theodosius's unique achievement. No emperor, not even Constantine, had destroyed temples,[116] until Theodosius ordered the destruction of the "shrines of the idols" and "consigned [traditional rites] to oblivion."[117] Other Christians agreed with Theodoret. Prudentius, for example, saw the Theodosian-era temple destructions as the final step that prefigured a rush to the church.[118] John Chrysostom and Gregory Nazianzen claimed that the actions of Theodosius formed a sort of persuasion that would lead to traditional religion collapsing in on itself.[119] This was, of course, the path toward a Christian empire first proposed by Eusebius in the 320s, and the one that had guided imperial policy in the 340s and 350s. Now, however, the push took on a new form. Change was effected not by laws issued from the court but by actions taken by monks, bishops, and other Christians who operated outside its political constraints.

This was what particularly troubled Libanius. He knew how to mobilize his network of friends to protest against and slow down the implementation of anti-pagan measures that came through official channels. It was far more difficult to respond effectively to situations in which imperial officials like Cynegius encouraged extralegal actions taken by monks, bishops, and others outside the imperial system. This was asymmetrical religious warfare that Libanius and his peers were ill equipped to fight. They could not match the tactics of their opponents, but Libanius still responded as forcefully as he could.

Oration 30, a text that apparently dates to the period immediately following Cynegius's departure from Syria, serves as Libanius's first effort to respond to this new and troubling dynamic.[120] The speech begins with a *prooemium* in which Libanius claims to be a valued counselor who advises the emperor on policy matters. Libanius then describes how the current situation corresponds to the policies regarding temples set by the emperors who ruled during his lifetime. He starts with Constantine, an emperor whose embrace of Christianity caused "absolutely no alteration in the traditional forms of worship."[121] Libanius then moves to Constantius. He acknowledges that Constantius banned sacrifices, but he asserts that this happened simply because the weak emperor was dominated by his eunuchs and court attendants.[122] Julian restored sacrifice, but Valentinian and Valens restricted it again, permitting only the offering of incense.[123] Theodosius, Libanius claims, has upheld this policy. He has also "neither ordered the closure of temples nor banned entrance to them."[124] However, the "black robed tribe, who eat more than elephants . . . hasten to attack the temples with sticks and stones and bars of iron, and in some cases, disdaining these, with hands and feet. Then utter desolation follows." These were, of course, monks, who, Libanius later makes clear, were encouraged in these actions by bishops.[125] This is, Libanius asserts, not only an illegal action, but one that is "nothing less than war in peace time waged against the peasantry."[126] An effective emperor must stop it.

This short historical survey allowed Libanius to do two things. First, by comparing the mild and tolerant attitudes of Constantine with the actions taken by a weak successor who supposedly could not control the state, Libanius both establishes a set of ideal behaviors that a Christian emperor could exhibit and describes their opposite. Second, he implies that while Theodosius naturally possesses the virtues of Constantine, the current situation has gotten so out of control that he seems more like Constantius.[127] This is, Libanius makes clear, not a product of imperial policy but one of imperial will being ignored by others. And, he implies, the violent disregard of imperial policy constitutes a form of rebellion.

At the end of the oration, Libanius assures the emperor that no blame is cast his way, but he describes for him the destruction of a massive temple near the Persian frontier (possibly in Edessa).[128] This happened, Libanius claims, not because of the emperor's orders but because "of a scoundrel hated of the gods" who misled the emperor.[129] Although he is left unnamed, this person is likely Cynegius.[130] Libanius then spends the next three chapters of the oration expanding on the prefect's bad character and its detrimental effect on the emperor's policies. His rogue actions damaged the prestige of the emperor and diminished the resources available to him.[131] Theodosius also needs to understand that future campaigns like this will be met with a violent defense of the law that permits temples to remain standing.[132]

This oration neither anticipates nor reflects Theodosian policy.[133] It instead explains the danger of a situation in which the praetorian prefect initially charged with improving the fiscal situation of Eastern cities decided to destroy temples while touring the provinces under his authority.[134] This was, in Libanius's reconstruction, a product of Cynegius's own initiative, which worked against the interests of the emperor and threatened the imperial administrative apparatus that Theodosius superintended. It does not matter, of course, that Libanius deliberately blends what he thinks Theodosius's policies are with what he thinks they ought to be. Libanius identifies the prefect's corruption as an explanation for the temple raids and marks Theodosius's interest in good government as a possible way to address the problem. The oration then systematically defines the temple raids as a new sort of problem that threatens the regular operation of the empire, and uses a traditional appeal to the emperor to point out the problem. It also hints at the darker, more sinister possibility of armed resistance if Libanius's appeal is ignored.

Libanius's subsequent discussions of anti-pagan activity show that he had neither the stomach nor the resources necessary to lead any type of armed resistance. Instead, he continued to lodge complaints about anti-pagan initiatives from within the confines of the old imperial administrative process of appeal.[135] At the same time, it seems that the Theodosian administration became much more responsive to such appeals after Cynegius's death in 388. Some of these developments emerged from the new historical context. Theodosius's war with Maximus had recently heated up, and the emperor could not afford to have sectarian violence simmering while he was fighting in the West. His elevation of Tatianus and Proculus to their respective prefectures also replaced the Christian Cynegius with two pagan veteran administrators.[136] Everyone in the East must have understood that the old guard would again try to reassert its control over the Christian outsiders whose violence it had previously tolerated.

These changes meant that Libanius's efforts to protect traditional religious buildings began to have more success. The most developed such attempt came in *Oration* 49, a work composed not long after Tatianus's appointment in 388. Although this oration did not explicitly concern the treatment of traditional religious communities (the oration was in fact about the city councils), it again relied on a dynamic in which a just imperial policy of Theodosius is said to resemble that of an esteemed predecessor,[137] but its execution failed because of the corruption of Cynegius.[138] In the winter of 389–90, Libanius wrote about his opposition to a "pot-bellied governor's" plan to chop down the sacred grove of cypresses in the Antiochene suburb of Daphne. "I told him that I would invite the emperor to show concern for Daphne, or rather [I would ask him] to emphasize the concern that he felt already."[139] In response, the governor "sent a letter full of fabrications to his superiors in Phoenicia," but Libanius was vindicated after a series of complaints from the governor provoked only laughter when they reached the emperor and Tatianus.[140] The system had saved Libanius yet again.

Things began to get more difficult for figures like Libanius in the early 390s. By then, it had become clear that the laws of the early 380s had created an administrative nightmare in which people moved their traditional religious activities from temples to less publicly controllable locations and governors personally disobeyed laws they were supposed to enforce. In 391, Theodosius issued a new round of legislation designed to tighten enforcement of these anti-pagan measures. The first law reiterated the earlier ban on sacrifice and divination before expanding on what was meant by the prohibition of entry into temples.[141] The law also fined pagan judges and governors who were "devoted to profane rites and entered a temple," and penalized their staff if they did not immediately report an administrator who violated its terms.[142] The emperor and his advisers felt compelled to issue a longer elaboration of the same principles in November 392.[143] That law expanded the prohibition to include binding a tree with fillets, erecting altars of turf, and offering honors to gods within a household.[144]

These actions had little immediate effect on the massive infrastructure that continued to support traditional religious activity into the 390s. Many temples remained open and accessible even after a decade of legal restrictions and extralegal violence. In *Oration* 30, Libanius offers an impressive list of the major temples still intact in Antioch.[145] Even more intriguing is a letter he wrote to Richomer in 391. Libanius invites him to visit Antioch, where he could "set foot in Daphne, beloved of Apollo," and he asks the "gods, whose many temples we have in and around our city" to make this visit possible.[146] Beyond Antioch, the story is much the same. We cannot know the fate of the 2,393 temples counted in Alexandria in the early fourth century, but scattered pieces of evidence surviving from in and around the city suggest that quite a few remained intact and accessible in the 390s. There is also considerable evidence of a shift away from large, publicly accessible temples to smaller, house-based cultic centers, a process that began before the fourth century, continued throughout it, and likely ensured the survival of many such institutions into the fifth and even sixth centuries.[147] Beyond the major urban centers, cities with smaller or less vocal Christian communities saw little change in religious life in the early 390s. In Athens, for example, the temples remained open, and public sacrifice continued well into the fifth century.[148]

Imperial officials had even less success attacking other public elements of traditional religion. Images of the gods continued to crowd Roman cities. The first imperial law to address their prominence was sent to Africa in 399. It ordered that "idols should be taken down under the direction of the office staff after an investigation has been held."[149] But this law is not what it seems on first glance. While it calls for the removal of divine images, the law requires imperial officials to review any complaint about an image and then use their resources to take the image down. This prevented Christian leaders from destroying images on their own initiative and institutionalized a procedure for removal that could not be used in any large-scale fashion.[150] Its effect on the millions of images within the Roman world would have been negligible. Indeed, one suspects that this was the order's objective. Like Constantinian legislation against sacrifice, it endorsed the principle that images needed to be removed while creating an administrative process that made their removal extremely difficult.

Scattered pieces of later evidence suggest that the law had little appreciable effect. As late as the 480s there remained enough pagan statuary in Alexandria to keep a bonfire going for most of a day, and this included neither the statues in the Tychaion (which remained in place in the seventh century)[151] nor any found in private collections.[152] The situation was similar elsewhere. Maximus of Turin wrote during the reign of Theodosius's son Honorius that, "apart from a few religious people, hardly anyone's field is unpolluted by idols, hardly any property is kept free from the cult of demons. Everywhere the Christian eye is offended, everywhere the devout mind assailed; wherever you turn you see either the altars of the devil or the profane auguries of the pagans."[153]

Traditional festivals proved even more enduring. Despite some efforts to designate a limited number of traditional holidays that would continue to have legal standing in the 380s and 390s, many prominent ones like the Lupercalia continued into the later fifth century in Rome and persisted until at least the tenth century in Constantinople.[154] The surviving works of Libanius attest to a large number of ongoing festivals in Antioch in the period.[155] Many smaller festivals also survived the push of the 390s. At a council in Carthage in 401, for example, North African bishops called for the elimination of banquets in which Christians participated alongside pagans in activities "brought together by pagan error."[156] The African call to abolish traditional festal banquets was brusquely denied in a law of 399.[157] By 408, however, the consistory and emperor had come around. They then prohibited "convivial banquets in honor of sacrilegious rites" and "granted to bishops . . . the right to use *ecclesiastica manus* to prohibit such practices."[158] Governors who chose not to enforce this law were to be fined twenty pounds of gold. Again, however, the persistence of events like the Athenian Panathenaic procession suggests that even these efforts fell short of their intended mark.[159] The cities of the empire remained nearly as full of the sights, sounds, and smells of the traditional gods in the 390s as they had been in the 310s.

. . .

Libanius certainly noticed the new direction in which imperial policy had moved in 391 and 392. Had he lived past 393, he might have again tried to use his influence to moderate the application of these laws. But he also lived in an empire that still had hundreds of thousands of open temples, in a city that had tens of thousands of images of the gods publicly displayed, and at a time when the streets regularly filled with processions and festivals honoring the traditional gods. Traditional religion remained very much alive throughout the empire.[160] One can then understand why Libanius's concern about laws restricting traditional religion was only one among many things that demanded his attention in his last years.

Nothing shows his wide-ranging concerns better than a reply that Libanius wrote to a message sent by a pagan called Hierophantes around 390.[161] Libanius's letter, a masterful piece of epistolary literature, serves as an extended pun on Hierophantes's name (which means essentially "chief priest"). In it, Libanius offers a long list of maladies that is bracketed by requests for Hierophantes's religious assistance. He begins by asking Hierophantes to bless him, and then fills the middle of the letter with a list of every possible complaint that he could imagine.[162] He complains about the outrages taken against pagan statues, the diminished station of rhetoric, his bad relations with governors, his physical infirmity, and his grief at the loss of so many friends. He then tells Hierophantes that "these things and others like them . . . will cease now that your letter has come to me." Libanius concludes by asking that Hierophantes bring even more divine assistance by "speaking with the gods on my behalf."[163]

This letter shows that Christian attacks on the gods clearly bothered Libanius, but the temples were only one item in a long list of things that concerned him in the early 390s. As he approached the end of his life, Libanius worried about his health, battled loneliness, continued to fight for public recognition as a teacher, and worked hard to remain close to leading local and imperial officials. Despite the drama this letter manufactures, most of Libanius's later writings advertise his continued activity, his ongoing relationships with powerful individuals, and the wider influence that these things gave him. He would defend the temples (sometimes successfully and sometimes not), but he never intervened in ways that risked damaging his other concerns or diminishing his reputation.

Those elites born in the 310s who were still alive in 393 shared many of the concerns that Libanius expressed in his letter to Hierophantes. It is impossible to know how most of them reacted to their retirement, how connected they still felt to their old friends, or what they thought about Cynegius's temple destructions and Theodosius's later religious policies. Libanius and Ausonius are the elite men born in the 310s whose words from the 390s still survive in any quantity, and only Libanius speaks at any length about these sorts of things. It is clear, however, that many of these figures did not match the drooling, disabled, and senile caricatures once drawn by Juncus. Their numbers were much diminished, and their influence had receded, but the final pagan generation remained engaged in the public life of the empire on their own terms well into the 390s.

At the same time, public life had changed. While these older men exercised authority in much the same way as they had since the early 340s, the young men who dropped out of the imperial system in the 360s and 370s honed ever more efficient techniques for influencing an empire that had become increasingly receptive to the calls of Christian leaders. The successes of these younger men do not necessarily mean that the efforts of men like Libanius failed. As the aftermath of the Riot of the Statues shows, the exercise of influence in the late empire was seldom a zero-sum game. Effective emperors like Theodosius understood that the imperial system worked best when it created conditions under which many different groups could simultaneously claim credit for positive outcomes. This meant that Libanius could go to his grave with the idea that the last five years of his life showed him to be one of the empire's most influential elder statesmen. He had, of course, lost some significant battles related to temples and the career of Cimon, but he had also been allowed impressive victories that offset these reverses. For Libanius and many other members of the final pagan generation, these years represented nothing less than the successful conclusion of long, well-rounded public and private lives. They would likely have been surprised to learn that anyone could see their golden years any differently.

CHAPTER 10

A Generation's Legacy

This book began with the destruction of the magnificent Alexandrian temple of Serapis by a Christian mob following a burst of urban rioting in 392. The Christian historian Rufinus saw the Serapeum destruction as the culmination of an eight-decade process during which Christianity moved from a persecuted religion to one that supplanted traditional religion.[1] For Rufinus, this made perfect sense. When the Serapeum destruction was paired with the recent Theodosian legal restrictions on sacrifice, it seemed that the path to an empire free from sacrifice and functioning temples now lay open. One needed only to wait for the churches to fill with the inevitable flood of converts.[2]

Other Christians agreed. In a homily delivered soon after the temple fell, Theophilus, the bishop of Alexandria, claimed that the temple destruction represented a throwing down of "the remnants of idolatry" and a purification of a site long cherished by Christians.[3] Later representations of Theophilus celebrated the Serapeum destruction as the defining moment of his career. An early fifth-century Alexandrian chronicle included a picture of Theophilus standing atop a statue of Serapis (see fig. 14), a visual parallel that linked his anti-pagan efforts to those of earlier Hebrew prophets.[4] The notion that a bishop should act aggressively against traditional religious sites eventually became so ingrained in the fifth-century Alexandrian Christian community that Theophilus came to serve as a prototype of ideal episcopal behavior.[5] Some ascetic communities also quickly adopted the idea that

FIGURE 14. Theophilus standing atop
bust of Serapis, from a fifth-century
Alexandrian world chronicle. From
Bauer and Strzygowski, *Eine
Alexandrinische Weltchronik* (Vienna,
1905), fig. VI verso.

ascetics should act aggressively against traditional religion and its practitioners.[6]

Pagan authors similarly idealized the actions of figures who resisted Christian attacks on the Serapeum. Olympus, a Cilician philosopher who had come to Alexandria in order to worship Serapis, led the defense. He guided the defenders through regular worship and superintended a final ceremony through which Serapis abandoned his temple.[7] Rufinus attacked him as "a philosopher in name and garb only" and the "leader of a criminal and impudent band." Pagan sources, however, celebrated him as a "man who was not human but entirely godlike."[8] Other pagan teachers who participated in the defense also saw the Serapeum destruction as a defining moment in their lives. The grammarians Helladius and Ammonius both spoke proudly to the Christian historian Socrates Scholasticus about their roles in fighting Christians during the Serapeum siege. Ammonius complained about the abuse done to traditional religion before the violence started, and Helladius bragged about killing nine Christians with his own hands during the defense of the temple.[9] Even figures with no direct connection to the fighting were remembered primarily because of their ties to the Serapeum. The philosopher Antoninus once predicted that "the temples would become tombs" because of the move by Christians to place the bones of martyrs on former cultic sites. Although Antoninus died before the Serapeum assault, Eunapius says that the event confirmed his reputation "for great foresight because he had said to everyone that the temples would become tombs."[10]

All of these celebrations of Serapeum attackers and defenders come from a future that the final pagan generation did not live to see. It is only in the first years of the fifth century that opinion began to coalesce around the idea that heroes were made during those desperate days. None of those heroes belonged to the final pagan generation. Men like Praetextatus, Ausonius, Libanius, and Themistius were remembered less for the faiths they defended than for the public and literary careers they enjoyed. When Praetextatus died in 384, authorities ordered a period of public mourning in the city of Rome and paid for a public funeral.[11] His wife Paulina composed a poem in his memory that celebrated both his public career and his sacred offices. She explained that the priestly duties were more important, but they were nevertheless intimately connected to the offices he held and the public service he rendered.[12] The commemorations of Praetextatus went beyond his immediate family. The Vestal Virgin Coelia Concordia petitioned for permission to erect a statue honoring him in part because he had been a priest of Vesta.[13] Symmachus, for his part, forwarded to the emperor a senatorial request that the state erect a statue of Praetextatus in the Forum, an honor that Praetextatus shared with only five known contemporaries.[14] Symmachus asked the emperor to write something honoring Praetextatus, "for praise is all the more illustrious if it comes from a celestial judgment."[15] His peers saw Praetextatus as a well-rounded senator whose exemplary cultic service complemented and enhanced his broader public achievements.

This contrasts with a Christian polemical tradition that characterized Praetextatus as a pagan zealot whose service to traditional cults negated his political achievements. At its center was the *Carmen contra paganos* (*CCP*),[16] an anonymous Christian poem that attacked the social, moral, and intellectual standing that Praetextatus enjoyed in Rome by mocking the traditional religion to which he was so closely attached.[17] The poem attacks the mourning in which the city engaged following Praetextatus's death as "madness" that obscured his identity as a religious charlatan who offered sacrificial foods, gave gladiatorial games, and seduced Christians from the faith.[18] In the end, his painful death from dropsy was insufficient punishment for a man who "while seeking the honors of nobility by [his] magic arts" instead was "rewarded with a tiny tomb."[19]

The *Carmen contra paganos* tried to diminish Praetextatus by removing service to traditional cults from the set qualifications that one needed to be seen as a truly exemplary senator. It seems largely to have failed to convince. By the 430s, Praetextatus appears as one of the central figures in Macrobius's *Saturnalia*.[20] Macrobius, a Christian, wrote this antiquarian dialogue to educate his son Eustachius and serve "as a literary repository . . . of things worth remembering" derived from traditional Roman literary and religious culture.[21] Macrobius sets the discussion during the Saturnalia of 382,[22] at a gathering of leading Roman senators and scholars that first assembled at Praetextatus's house. The participants included the senators Praetextatus and Symmachus as well as a collection of other famous learned men. Macrobius apologizes at the dialogue's outset for including a few characters from the generation after that of Praetextatus—a statement that suggests that he sees Praetextatus as the dialogue's central figure.[23] It has been argued, with good reason, that Macrobius puts Praetextatus forward as the character who expresses Macrobius's own views within the text.[24] At the same time, it is clear that Macrobius focuses on Praetextatus not because of his reputation as a pagan militant but because he represented the most authoritative and "the most learned" of the old Roman elite. By the time that

Macrobius wrote, there remained no question about who Praetextatus was. Perhaps better than anyone else, Praetextatus epitomized the complete range of interests and achievements that marked the most successful members of the late fourth-century Roman senatorial elite.

No other member of the final pagan generation had his reputation attacked quite as aggressively as Praetextatus, but later authors did try to use the legacies of other men born in the 310s to reflect popular perceptions of the elite world to which they belonged. Later authors spend less time manipulating the legacy of Themistius and Ausonius, but in their cases too a general consensus developed that they represented fixtures of the imperial system against whom younger, less conventional contemporaries sometimes pushed. In later Arabic traditions, Themistius comes to be linked with Julian (of all people) as the wise counselor who advised Rome's last philosophical emperor before the empire descended into Christian irrationality.[25] Later Christian chroniclers like Barhebraeus agreed that Themistius served as a rational adviser to emperors and credited him with advising the emperor Julian against persecuting Christians.[26] In each case, however, his memory was directly tied to his role as an adviser working within a functioning fourth-century imperial system guided by reason and not religious persuasion.

Ausonius's legacy is similarly defined, though, in a twist, he sometimes serves as a foil to the famous Christian dropout Paulinus of Nola. A series of letters exchanged between Ausonius and Paulinus of Nola sometimes circulated separately from the rest of Ausonius's corpus. These show Ausonius's dismay at Paulinus's decision to abandon a secular career and embrace an ascetic life.[27] The significance of Paulinus's renunciation of the world is then underlined by his response to the criticisms of an older, establishment figure. Although he too was a Christian, Ausonius came to represent a member of the conventional elite who thrived by working within the bounds of the fourth-century imperial system. Paulinus then represents a new Christian order against the aristocratic ideals recognizably embodied by Ausonius.

Libanius left perhaps the most intriguing legacy. Soon after Libanius's death in 393, Eunapius celebrated his remarkable personal charm and praised his unrivaled skill as a letter writer.[28] Eunapius saw Libanius as more than a stylistic exemplar, however. "He also had a talent for administering public affairs and, in addition to the formal orations, he would confidently undertake and easily compose certain other works more suited to please an audience in the theater."[29] This "left in the minds of all men the profoundest admiration for his talents."[30]

Eunapius had read a great deal of Libanius's writings, and it is not surprising that the Libanius he describes strongly resembles the master of late imperial social and political life who inhabits Libanius's letters.[31] Later authors seem to agree. By the fifth century, Libanius symbolized the rhetorical education that underpinned the fourth-century imperial system. He also began to play a role in literary traditions that describe the significance of the decisions made by Basil, Gregory Nazianzen, and John Chrysostom to abandon secular careers and take up ascetic and episcopal service. In each case, Libanius is used as a sort of foil whose connection to the Christian dropouts suggested sure worldly success on their part. Because they were trained by Libanius, their decision to leave the world behind becomes even more significant.

Libanius's prominence in the biographical tradition attached to John Chrysostom shows this dynamic particularly well. Chrysostom is connected to Libanius by Socrates Scholasticus in the fifth century. Socrates had previously introduced Libanius as an influential figure who gained a great deal of influence in Antioch during the reign of Julian.[32] Socrates introduces Chrysostom as an Antiochene "who was the son of Secundus and a mother named Anthousa . . . he was an inner circle student of the sophist Libanius and a listener of the philosopher Andragathos."[33] When he was about to start work in the courts, he considered "the restless and unjust life of those who practiced law," and embraced the ascetic life.[34] Chrysostom may indeed have studied under Libanius, but the Antiochene sophist is mentioned here to prove that Chrysostom did not embrace asceticism as a fallback but had chosen to pursue it instead of a potentially lucrative worldly career.

Socrates's contemporary Sozomen offers an added twist to this story that eventually became part of many later Byzantine retellings. Sozomen, like Socrates, agrees that Chrysostom studied under Libanius and then abandoned his legal career, but he adds another detail that further reinforces the dramatic choice that Chrysostom made. "When the sophist was on his deathbed," Sozomen writes, "he was asked by his friends who should take his place. 'It would have been John,' he replied, 'if the Christians had not stolen him.'"[35] This detail, which Sozomen introduces to emphasize both the significance of Chrysostom's sacrifice and the great power of his oratory, develops into a standard part of later Byzantine accounts of Chrysostom's early life.[36]

Another tradition, first found in Socrates Scholasticus but repeated nearly verbatim by church historians into the late Byzantine period, connects Libanius to the education of Basil and Gregory. "When they were youths," Socrates writes, "they were pupils of the most famous sophists Himerius and Prohaeresius at Athens and, after this, they studied together under Libanius in Antioch in Syria."[37] Although they were qualified to teach rhetoric, Socrates continues, "abandoning the world, they selected the monastic life."[38] This tradition is extremely unlikely to be true, but it too is picked up by Sozomen and later Byzantine writers who use Libanius to emphasize what Basil and Gregory gave up when they dropped out of the fourth-century imperial system.[39]

If one moves beyond the historiographical tradition, one finds an even more remarkable engagement with this symbolic Libanius. This comes in the form of a forged epistolary collection that supposedly contains a series of twenty-one letters between Libanius and Basil.[40] The collection itself takes an interesting form. Seventeen of its letters are complete forgeries, and the other four lift and then adapt text from genuine Libanian letters or other documents.[41] The conversations are structured in such a way as to show Basil besting Libanius rhetorically while also framing an argument for the intellectual superiority of Christianity.[42] The collection presents Libanius as a sophistic master, while Basil comes across as a man who possessed far greater rhetorical gifts but turned away from them to pursue higher, Christian knowledge.[43] Thus it illustrates in a novel way the significance of Basil's decision to abandon rhetoric and drop out of the later fourth-century imperial system.

Lieve Van Hoof has recently called attention to a sixth-century source that suggests how this collection may have been understood in antiquity.[44] Zacharias Scholasticus's *Life of Severus* describes a conversation in which Severus, the future bishop of Antioch, who was then training to be a lawyer, expressed great admiration for Libanius's style.[45] Zacharias suggested that Severus should read the epistolary exchange between Basil and Libanius. After he had done so, Severus "started praising Basil's letters to Libanius aloud, and also Libanius' replies to them, in which Libanius admitted that he had been surpassed by Basil." One of Zacharias's friends then commented, "[Severus] will be a brilliant bishop, like the holy John."[46]

The comparison between Severus and John Chrysostom that the *Life of Severus* makes may seem odd, but it resonates on a number of different levels. Both Severus and Chrysostom had obvious connections to Antioch and equally obvious stubborn streaks, but the text here implies something deeper and much more profound about the role that this letter collection played in changing the trajectory of Severus's life. Severus came to the Basil and Libanius letters as a law student infatuated with the world of rhetoric and imperial power that Libanius had mastered. By the time he finished reading the collection, he had instead embraced the ascetic and episcopal counterculture of Basil and Chrysostom. Even into the 520s, then, Libanius continued to embody conventional success in the imperial system, while the dropouts of the 360s and 370s retained their significance as emblems of a different social order. The generational divide between the men born in the 310s and those born in the 330s and 340s remained just as noticeable in the 520s as it did in the 380s.

This points to a story of the fourth century that ancients recognized quite clearly but modern historians have been hesitant to tell. The fourth century has come to be seen as the age when Christianity eclipsed paganism, and Christian authority structures undermined the traditional institutions of the Roman state. Modern historians have highlighted the rising influence of bishops, the emergence of Christian ascetics, the explosion of pagan-Christian conflict, and the destruction of temples. This is one fourth-century story, but it is neither the story that the final pagan generation would have told nor the one that later generations told about them. Their fourth century was the age of storehouses full of gold coins, elaborate dinner parties honoring letter carriers, public orations before emperors, and ceremonies commemorating officeholders. These things occurred in cities filled with thousands of temples, watched over by myriads of divine images, and perfumed by the smells of millions of sacrifices. This fourth century was real, and the men who lived through it told its story in ways that mesmerized later Byzantine and Latin audiences. These later men and women found the fourth century of Libanius, Ausonius, and Themistius as fascinating as they did that of Christian dropouts like Chrysostom, Basil, and Paulinus. It is time that we too remember the exciting, enchanting, and ultimately ephemeral age of gold these figures so artfully documented.

Notes

INTRODUCTION

1. Rufinus, *HE* 11.22.
2. No term accurately captures the diversity of religious approaches of devotees of traditional Mediterranean religion better than "pagans." "Pagan" has sometimes been shunned as pejorative, but I remain inclined to agree with Alan Cameron's recent assessment of it as a descriptive, nonpejorative category in the fourth century (*The Last Pagans of Rome,* [Oxford, 2010], 14–31, with a thorough discussion of previous scholarship). Douglas Boin, "Hellenistic 'Judaism' and the Social Origins of the 'Pagan-Christian' Debate," *JECS* 22 [2014]: 167–96, has recently shown how, within a Christian context, the term drew on Hellenistic Jewish concepts to differentiate true Christians from outsiders. Despite this, it is clear that pagans had no name for themselves in the period and did not conceive of themselves as any sort of unified confession (a point proven quite effectively by I. Sandwell, *Religious Identity in Late Antiquity: Greeks, Jews, and Christians in Antioch,* [Cambridge, 2007]). As we will see, pagans had a tremendous diversity of beliefs and practices. Not all pagans were polytheists, they had no common creed, and they observed or ignored gods, rituals, and festivals according to their own individual inclinations. For the purposes of this study, "pagans," however imprecise the term, is preferable to a longer phrase along the lines of "non-Jewish devotees of traditional Mediterranean gods."
3. Rufinus, *HE* 11.22.
4. This passage deliberately evokes earlier descriptions of Christian martyrs. For the use of martyrdom ideas in Christian historiography, see E. Castelli, *Martyrdom and Memory: Early Christian Culture Making* (New York, 2004).
5. Rufinus, *HE* 11.22.
6. Rufinus, *HE* 11.23.
7. Rufinus, *HE* 11.29.

8. The challenges of reconstructing these events have been analyzed repeatedly in the past decade. See, for example, C. Haas, *Alexandria in Late Antiquity: Topography and Social Conflict* (Baltimore, 1997), 161; N. Russell, *Theophilus of Alexandria* (London, 2007), 7–10; S. Davis, *The Early Coptic Papacy* (Cairo, 2004), 64–65. The most comprehensive recent treatment of the sources for this event is that of J. Hahn, *Gewalt und religiöser Konflikt: Studien zu den Auseinandersetzungen zwischen Christen, Heiden, und Juden im Osten Römischen Reiches* (Berlin, 2004), 85–97. Rufinus's treatment (*HE* 11.22–30) was assembled from two earlier sources in the first years of the fifth century. His account of the riot and destruction of the cult statue drew on a Palestinian account written by a Sophronius (a point first raised in J. Schwartz, "La fin du Sérapeum d'Alexandrie," in *American Studies in Papyrology*, vol. 1, *Essays in Honor of C. Bradford Welles* [New Haven, CT, 1966], 98–111), and his description of the transfer of relics to the site derives from a Theophilan source (on this, see T. Orlandi, "Uno scritto di Teofilo di Alessandria sulla destruzione del Serapeum?," *PP* 23 [1968]: 295–304). Mention of the event is made in Theodoret (*HE* 5.22), Sozomen (*HE* 7.15), Socrates (*HE* 5.16), Eunapius (*VS* 472–73), and a range of lesser-known Coptic and Greek Egyptian texts. For these, see the discussion of E. Watts, *Riot in Alexandria* (Berkeley, 2010), 190–207.

9. For discussions of the sack of Rome and its implications, see Socrates, *HE* 7.10; Sozomen *HE* 9.9 (though cf. *HE* 9.6, where he reproduces Socrates); Jerome, *Ep.* 128; Orosius 7.39–41; Philostorgius, *HE* 12.3. Note as well the comments of G. Chesnut, *First Christian Histories: Eusebius, Socrates, Sozomen, Theodoret, and Evagrius* (Macon, GA, 1986), 206–7. For an extensive discussion of the ways in which contemporaries came to understand the significance of the sack of Rome, see M. Salzman, *The "Falls" of Rome: The Transformations of Rome in Late Antiquity* (forthcoming); and Salzman, "Apocalypse Then? Jerome and the Fall of Rome in 410," in *Maxima debetur magistro reverentia,* ed. P.B. Harvey, Jr., and C. Conybeare, Biblioteca di Athenaeum 54 (Como, 2009), 175–92.

10. These events will be discussed in more detail in chapters 8 and 9.

11. This is described in more detail in chapter 3.

12. For pagan survivals, see M. Whitby, "John of Ephesus and the Pagans: Pagan Survivals in the Sixth-Century," in *Paganism in the Later Roman Empire and Byzantium,* ed. M. Salaman (Krakow, 1991), 111–31. Note too the discussion of the devotees of traditional religion in the Mani at the time of its reconquest by Basil I (Constantine Porphyrogenitus, *De admin. imp.* 50 [165.v]). These Eastern examples make me skeptical of the broader applicability of a model advanced by Alan Cameron (*Last Pagans,* 783ff.) that suggests a disappearance of traditional religious practices in the West in the fifth century. For continued activity among elites in the fifth-century West, see M. Salzman, "The End of Public Sacrifice: Changing Definitions of Sacrifice in Post-Constantinian Rome and Italy," in *Ancient Mediterranean Sacrifice,* ed. J. Wright Knust and Z. Várhelyi (Oxford, 2011), 167–83, at 175–77. See too the archaeological findings that suggest continued pagan sacrificial activity in fifth- and sixth-century Italy published by C. Goddard, "The Evolution of Pagan Sanctuaries in Late Antique Italy (Fourth-Sixth Centuries A.D.): A New Administrative and Legal

Framework; A Paradox," in *Les cités de'Italie tardo-antique (IVe-VIe siècle)*, ed. M. Ghilardi, C. Goddard, and P. Porena (Rome, 2006), 281–306.

13. This is the famous case of Harran, a city that still had active temples when visited by al-Mas'udi in the tenth century. For discussion of this visit and its implications, see K. van Bladel, *The Arabic Hermes: From Pagan Sage to Prophet of Science* (Oxford, 2009), 70–79.

14. For further discussion of this, see chapter 2, as well as the unpublished paper by Peter Brown, "Constantine, Eusebius, and the Future of Christianity."

15. For persecution in the Eastern part of the empire in the 310s, see S. Mitchell, "Maximinus and the Christians in A.D. 312: A New Latin Inscription," *JRS* 78 (1988): 105–24.

16. The number of Christians in the empire at this time is the subject of considerable controversy, though it is clear that Christians were a minority comprising perhaps 10 percent of the Roman population in the 310s and had grown to more than 50 percent of the population by the 390s. For a survey of possible numbers, see R. Stark, *The Rise of Christianity: A Sociologist Reconsiders History* (Princeton, NJ, 1996), 4–13. Note in particular the diachronic study of R. Bagnall, "Religious Conversion and Onomastic Change," *BASP* 19 (1982): 105–24.

17. These extant histories are those of Festus and Eutropius. On them, see R. W. Burgess, "Eutropius V.C. *'Magister Memoriae?,'*" *CP* 96 (2001): 76–81. For Festus, see G. Kelly, "The Roman World of Festus' Brevarium," in *Unclassical Traditions*, vol. 1, ed. C. Kelly, R. Flower, and M. Stuart Williams (Cambridge, 2010), 72–89. Praxagoras the Athenian wrote a history of the reign of Constantine that survives only in Photius's epitome (Photius, *Bibl.* Cod. 62; and see T. D. Barnes, *Constantine: Dynasty, Religion and Power in the Later Roman Empire* [London, 2011], 195–97). The slightly younger Nicomachus Flavianus wrote a history that is now entirely lost. It has been argued that this was a substantial work, but this claim has recently been called into question by Alan Cameron (*Last Pagans*, 627–90).

18. The parents' generation is represented by the histories of Eusebius and Lactantius. The views of their children color the works of Ammianus and Eunapius.

19. See, for example, Elder's pathbreaking study *Children of the Great Depression: Social Change in Life Experience* (Chicago, 1974). As was the case for the children of the Depression, the regular rhythms of daily life shaped the later worldviews and conditioned the behaviors of people born in the 310s far more than any one dramatic event.

20. For the identity of these subjects, see T. Dumas, "A Woodstock Moment—40 Years Later," *Smithsonian Magazine*, August 13, 2009.

21. While nationwide attendance figures for college football games contested in 1969 are impossible to determine, the University of Michigan alone drew 70,183 to its season-opening victory over Vanderbilt that September 20.

22. Sly and the Family Stone's "Everyday People" was number one from late February to early March.

23. According to *Cashbox*, the Archies' "Sugar, Sugar" was the top-selling single in the United States in 1969. Sly and the Family Stone was the top Woodstock act, but only the fifth-best selling single. The next best-selling single from

a Woodstock performer was Credence Clearwater Revival's "Green River," at number nineteen. (*Cashbox* magazine, December 27, 1969, http://www .cashboxmagazine.com/archives/60s_files/1969YESP.html).

24. *Cashbox,* December 23, 1967. *Billboard* ranks it thirty-third.

25. Laura Ingalls Wilder would have been 102 when Woodstock occurred; someone born on the date of Constantine's accession would have been 86 when the Serapeum was destroyed.

26. The precise date of Praetextatus's birth is not known, and the range of possibilities runs from 314 to 324. The reason for my belief that a date in the mid-320s is not plausible is addressed further in chapter 3.

27. For a discussion of the status of Praetextatus's likely ancestors, see M. Kahlos, *Vettius Agorius Praetextatus: A Senatorial Life in Between* (Rome, 2002), 20–23.

28. This was a translation of an Aristotelian paraphrase by Themistius. He also apparently translated Greek poetry into Latin, though we do not know what poems in particular. For discussion of this and the possibility of other works by Praetextatus, see Kahlos, *Praetextatus,* 134–37.

29. Symmachus, *Letters* 1.44–55.

30. E.g., Macrobius's *Saturnalia,* a fictional discussion that supposedly takes place in his home. For discussion of this, see chapters 1 and 10.

31. *CIL* 6.1779 = Dessau 1259.

32. For the attribution of this poem to Praetextatus, see Cameron, *Last Pagans,* 273–319.

33. Peter Brown, *Through the Eye of a Needle* (Princeton, NJ, 2012), 14–18.

CHAPTER 1. GROWING UP IN THE CITIES OF THE GODS

1. On this aspect, see now D. Kalleres, *City of Demons: Violence, Ritual, and Christian Power in Late Antiquity* (Berkeley, 2014).

2. The list reads: "At Alexandria one finds in Quarter A: 308 temples, 1,655 courts, 5,058 houses, 108 baths, 237 taverns, 112 porticoes. In Quarter B: 110 temples, 1,002 courts, 5,990 houses, 145 baths, 107 taverns. In Quarter Γ: 855 temples, 955 courts, 2,140 houses, ... baths, 205 taverns, 78 porticoes. In Quarter Δ: 800 temples, 1,120 courts, 5,515 houses, 118 baths, 178 taverns, 98 (porticoes). In Quarter E: 405 temples, 1,420 courts, 5,593 houses, ... baths, 118 taverns, 56 porticoes. Thus the total number of temples is 2,393 (in fact, 2,478); of courts 8,102 (in fact, 6,152); of houses, 47,790 (in fact, 24,296); of baths, 1,561; of taverns, 935 (in fact, 845); of porticoes, 456" (quoted from P. M. Fraser, "A Syriac Notitia Urbis Alexandrinae," *JEA* 37 [1951]: 103–8). The list has a somewhat odd provenance, but there is no reason to think that it has been corrupted or that its contents are inaccurate.

3. For a thorough discussion of the Serapeum site and its history, see J. S. McKenzie, S. Gibson, and A. T. Reyes, "Reconstructing the Serapeum in Alexandria from the Archeological Evidence," *JRS* 94 (2004): 73–121. For the Roman temple in particular, note too J. S. McKenzie, *The Architecture of Alexandria and Egypt, 300 BC–AD 700,* (New Haven, CT, 2007), 195–202.

4. Rufinus (*HE* 11.23) gives the most extensive contemporary description.

5. Eunapius, *VS* 471–73.

6. D. Frankfurter, *Religion in Roman Egypt: Assimilation and Resistance* (Princeton, NJ, 1998), 36–37; *P.Oxy* XXXVI.2782. See too F. Dunand, "Le petit Serapieion romain de Louqsor," *BIFAO* 81 (1981): 115–48, at 135–48.

7. Most such temples have been identified in rural areas, but they could (and probably did) function in much the same way in an urban environment. In the city of Rome, for example, one finds temples and shrines in neighborhoods and even in grain warehouses. See, for example, S. Panciera, "Nuovi luoghi di culto a Roma dale testimonianze epigrafice," *Archeologia laziale* 3 (1980): 202–13. For Egypt in particular, see Frankfurter, *Religion in Roman Egypt,* 39, who discusses examples known from Luxor, Deir el-Medina, Ras el-Soda, and elsewhere.

8. L. de Ligt, *Fairs and Markets in the Roman Empire* (Amsterdam, 1993), 117–18, 250–52.

9. For one among a myriad of examples, see the caves of Pan in Attica, discussed in G. Fowden, "City and Mountain in Late Roman Attica," *JHS* 108 (1988): 48–59

10. K. Bowes, *Private Worship, Public Values, and Religious Change in Late Antiquity* (Cambridge, 2008), 28–30.

11. These were crucial given the degree to which religious rituals like the *lustratio* and offerings of first fruits defined rural space, time, and social hierarchy. For this, see Bowes, *Private Worship,* 33–35.

12. Bowes, *Private Worship,* 34–36.

13. Bowes, *Private Worship,* 38–45.

14. Bowes, *Private Worship,* 36.

15. Ps.-Libanius, *Alexandrian Tychaion* 4–6. For this document and translation, see C. Gibson, "Alexander in the Tychaion: Ps.-Libanius on the Statues," *GRBS* 47 (2007): 434–57.

16. On the Acropolis, see R. Krumeich and C. Witschel, eds., *Die Akropolis von Athen im Hellenismus und in der römischen Kaiserzeit* (Wiesbaden, 2010).

17. For broken objects, see, for example, the pottery listed in *ID* 128. I thank Fritz Graf for mentioning this to me.

18. Rufinus, *HE* 11.22–23.

19. Zacharias Scholasticus, *Vit. Sev.* 33. For discussion, see E. Watts, *Riot in Alexandria* (Berkeley, 2010), 234–43.

20. For traditional Compitalia festivals, see Dionysius of Halicarnassus, *Roman Antiquities* 4.14. For Augustan additions, see Ovid, *Fast.* 5.143–46. For the continuity of the compital shrines across the imperial period, see S. Panciera, "Tra epigrafia e topografia –I.," *Archeologia Classica* 22 (1970): 131–63; Bowes, *Private Worship,* 235 n. 89. *CIL* 6.30960 provides an inscription commemorating a repair in Rome in 223. The *Curiosum urbis Romae* indicates that the official responsible for these shrines continued to exist into the fourth century.

21. Bowes, *Private Worship,* 27–29.

22. A. Kaufmann-Heinimann, "Religion in the House," in *A Companion to Roman Religion,* ed. J. Rüpke (Oxford, 2007), 188–201, at 200.

23. P. Allison, *The Insula of Menander at Pompeii,* vol. 3, *The Finds: A Contextual Study* (Oxford, 2006).

24. On these, see L. Stirling, *The Learned Collector: Mythological Statuettes and Classical Taste in Late Antique Gaul* (Ann Arbor, MI, 2005), 29–90.

25. *P.Ryl.* 630, 504–5. For discussion of this larger document, see J. Matthews, *The Journey of Theophanes* (New Haven, CT, 2006).

26. Romans were able to distinguish between cult objects and decorative representations of the gods, but the rationale for making such a determination is sometimes not entirely clear to a modern reader. For a discussion of this particular problem, see C. Ando, *The Matter of the Gods: Religion and the Roman Empire* (Berkeley, 2010), 21–42.

27. While a calendar stands as the most notable element of this richly illustrated compilation, the document actually contained sixteen different sections. On the *Codex Calendar of 354*, see the definitive study of M. Salzman, *On Roman Time: The Codex Calendar of 354 and the Rhythms of Urban Life in Late Antiquity* (Berkeley, 1990).

28. Salzman, *On Roman Time*, 117–20.

29. Salzman, *On Roman Time*, 119.

30. For this hierarchy, see Salzman, *On Roman Time*, 120.

31. For a list of these gods, see Salzman, *On Roman Time*, 130–31. For imperial holidays, fully sixty-nine were devoted to members of the house of Constantine. An additional twenty-nine days honored earlier emperors or actions taken by them (Salzman, *On Roman Time*, 132).

32. Two were in March, one in April (a joint festival with the god Serapis), and one in August. October saw a four-day-long festival devoted to Isis that ran from October 28 to 31. The first three days of November too were devoted to festivals concerned with specific aspects of the cult. For the Isaic festivals, see the table in Salzman, *On Roman Time*, 170.

33. The Isaic festivals seem to have entered the Roman calendar under the later Julio-Claudians. On this, see M. Malaise, *Les conditions de pénétration et de diffusion des cultes égyptiens en Italie* (Leiden, 1972), 221–44.

34. For the place of these festivals in a sort of common Roman religious calendar shared by pagans and Christians in the fourth century, see M. Salzman, "Religious *Koine* and Religious Dissent in the Fourth Century," in *Blackwell's Companion to Roman Religion*, ed. J. Rüpke (Oxford, 2007), 109–24.

35. See, for example, the blending of the celebration of the Kalends of January and the *ludi Compitales* (Salzman, *On Roman Time*, 80 nn. 75–76; M. Meslin, *La fête des kalendes de janvier dans l'Empire Romain* [Brussels, 1970]).

36. Salzman, *On Roman Time*, 120.

37. Achilles Tatius, *Leucippe and Clitophon* 5.2.1. The translation is based on that of Gaselee in the Loeb Classical Library (hereafter LCL).

38. It is worth noting here David Frankfurter's discussion (*Religion in Roman Egypt*, 58–65) of the downsizing of major religious festivals and the resiliency of minor ones in late antique Egypt.

39. Apuleius, *Metamorphoses* 11.7. For processions more generally, see the excellent discussion of P. Harland, "Christ-Bearers and Fellow Initiates: Local Cultural Life and Christian Identity in Ignatius' Letters," *JECS* 11 (2003): 487–97.

40. Apuleius, *Metamorphoses* 11.7–9.

41. Apuleius, *Metamorphoses*, 11.9.

42. For the varied level of religious enthusiasm among participants, see Salzman, "Religious *Koine,*" 112.

43. Both are described in *Metamorphoses* 11.9.

44. For some examples of the things found in public streets, see Juvenal, *Sat.* 3.269–77 (discussing chamber pots emptied out of windows) and 1.131 (for people urinating around statues), as well as Galen, *De san. tuenda* 1.11 (on cadavers and rotten food in the city).

45. Tertullian, *De idolatria* 11. For discussion, see S. Harvey, *Scenting Salvation: Ancient Christianity and the Olfactory Imagination* (Berkeley, 2006), 38.

46. Harvey, *Scenting Salvation,* 30.

47. Harvey, *Scenting Salvation,* 34–35.

48. D. Potter, "Odor and Power in the Roman Empire," in *Constructions of the Classical Body,* ed. J. Porter (Ann Arbor, MI, 1999), 169–89.

49. Harvey, *Scenting Salvation,* 33. Plutarch, for example, says that the manufacture of cyphi, a sleeping draught, combined sixteen different sweet-smelling ingredients (Plutarch, *Isis and Osiris* 80A). For the cost see Athenaeus, *Deino.* 15.688.

50. On sacrifice in antiquity more generally, see now the magisterial work of F.S. Naiden, *Smoke Signals for the Gods: Ancient Greek Sacrifice from the Archaic through Roman Periods* (Oxford, 2013).

51. Naiden, *Smoke Signals,* 79.

52. On the relative rarity of blood sacrifice in the fourth century, see S. Bradbury, "Julian's Pagan Revival and the Decline of Blood Sacrifice," *Phoenix* 49 (1995): 331–56, though Michele Salzman has recently argued that, in Italy at least, blood sacrifice remained an important part of elite practice in the fourth century (Salzman, "The End of Public Sacrifice: Changing Definitions of Sacrifice in Post-Constantinian Rome and Italy," in *Ancient Mediterranean Sacrifice,* ed. J. Wright Knust and Z. Várhelyi [Oxford, 2011], 176–77). On the range of acceptable ways that one could offer sacrifices to the gods, see Lucian, *On Sacrifices* 12.

53. Harvey, *Scenting Salvation,* 37.

54. Plutarch, *Isis and Osiris* 79C (LCL, trans. Babbitt).

55. Plutarch, *Isis and Osiris* 79D.

56. Plutarch, *Isis and Osiris* 80A. On the formulation of cyphi, see above.

57. Harvey, *Scenting Salvation,* 40–41.

58. Harvey, *Scenting Salvation,* 42.

59. Tertullian, *Ad uxorem* 6.1.

60. On this point, see É. Rebillard, *Christians and Their Many Identities in Late Antiquity, North Africa, 200–450 CE* (Ithaca, NY, 2012), chap. 1.

61. B. Rawson, *Children and Childhood in Roman Italy* (Oxford, 2003), 103.

62. C. Laes, *Children in the Roman Empire* (Cambridge, 2011), 50.

63. N. Morley, *Metropolis and Hinterland: The City of Rome and the Italian Economy, 200 B.C.–A.D. 200* (Cambridge, 1996), 39–54; W. Scheidel, "Germs for Rome," in *Rome the Cosmopolis,* ed. C. Edwards and G. Woolf (Cambridge, 2003), 158–76, at 175–76; and Scheidel, "Human Mobility in Roman Italy, I: The Free Population," *JRS* 94 (2004): 1–26, at 15–19.

64. For diseases in the Roman world, see W. Scheidel, *Death on the Nile: Disease and the Demography of Roman Egypt* (Leiden, 2001); and Scheidel, "Demography, Disease, and Death," in *The Cambridge Companion to Ancient Rome,* ed. P. Erdkamp (Cambridge, 2013), 45–59.

65. In August and September the city of Rome regularly endured malaria outbreaks. For the rhythm of disease in Rome, see B. Shaw, "Seasons of Death: Aspects of Mortality in Imperial Rome," *JRS* 86 (1996): 100–139. For elites fleeing the cities in the summer, see, for example, Libanius, *Or.* 1.77 (on his two summers in Bithynia); Symmachus, *Ep.* 1.8 (on the quiet of his retreat in Campania).

66. For accidents, consider the case of Libanius's son Cimon, who died of gangrene following a carriage accident. This is described in more detail in chapter 9.

67. Laes, *Children in the Roman Empire,* 44.

68. B. Shaw, "'With whom I lived': Measuring Roman Marriage," *Ancient Society* 32 (2002): 195–242. See as well the concise discussion of Laes, *Children in the Roman Empire,* 44–47.

69. Laes, *Children in the Roman Empire,* 47.

70. At any rate, so says Aristotle (*Hist. an.* 588a5).

71. Laes, *Children in the Roman Empire,* 65–66.

72. For a general introduction to the *Parentalia,* see R.H. Green, *The Works of Ausonius* (Oxford, 1991), 298ff.

73. Ausonius, *Parentalia* 29.

74. *Parentalia,* 13.5–7.

75. K. Bradley, "Wet-Nursing at Rome: A Study in Social Relations," in *The Family in Ancient Rome: New Perspectives,* ed. B. Rawson (London, 1986), 201–29; S. Crespo Ortiz de Zarate, *"Nutrices" en el imperio romano,* 2 vols. (Valladolid, 2005–6); Laes, *Children in the Roman Empire,* 69–83. For lower-class women relying on wet nurses, see *CIL* 6.19128. For the possibility that upper-class women would still breastfeed their own children, see Aulus Gellius (quoting Favorinus), *Noctes Atticae* 12.1.1–23; Zacharias Scholasticus, *Vit. Sev.* 19.

76. Soranus, *Gyn.* 2.19.

77. Quintilian, *Inst.* 1.1.4–5.

78. Laes, *Children in the Roman Empire,* 72; Suetonius, *Augustus* 94.6.

79. For this age, see Laes, *Children in the Roman Empire,* 81; Oribasius, *Lib. inc.* 38–23 (two years old); Macrobius, *Somn. Scip.* 1.6.62 (thirty-four months old); Quintilian, *Inst.* 1.15–16.

80. Tacitus, *Dial. or.* 28–29.

81. Dio Chrysostom, *Or.* 4.74.

82. Laes, *Children in the Roman Empire,* 76.

83. Pliny, *Ep.* 6.3.1.

84. For these incidents, see Laes, *Children in the Roman Empire,* 76. For Nero and Domitian, see Suetonius, *Nero* 50 and *Domitian* 17.

85. R. Cribiore, *The School of Libanius* (Princeton, NJ, 2007), 118–19.

86. For the role of the pedagogue in regulating the conduct of a student, see Cribiore, *School of Libanius,* 31

87. Libanius, *Or.* 58.7 (all translated passages of *Or.* 58 are based on Norman's translation, with slight modifications where necessary).

88. Libanius, *Or.* 58.7.

89. Libanius, *Or.* 58.10.

90. Libanius, *Or.* 58.8.

91. Libanius, *Or.* 58.9.

92. For beatings by pedagogues, see Martial, *Ep.* 10.62.10.

93. Libanius, *Or.* 58.11.

94. For these, see Laes, *Children in the Roman Empire,* 119.

95. Augustine, *Serm.* 62.18.

96. This is *Oration* 58, a speech that tries to fix the damage this incident did to Libanius's standing among Antiochene pedagogues by shamelessly pandering to them. Pandering aside, however, it does provide one of the best descriptions of what pedagogues wanted to hear about their role in the upbringing and education of a child.

97. Because one's teacher was customarily called a father, Ausonius plays a bit of an artful game with the dueling concepts of intellectual and biological fatherhood in this poem. For the notion of intellectual fatherhood and its relationship to biological fatherhood, see the Ps.-Platonic *Theages,* 127–28. On the purpose of the *Theages,* see H. Tarrant, "Socratic *Sunousia:* A Post-Platonic Myth?," *Journal of the History of Philosophy* 43.2 (2005): 131–55. Arborius's teaching of his nephew is not a unique situation; there were many people in late antiquity who got their education from family members (e.g., the case of Paralius, described in Zacharias, *Vit. Sev.* 14–15; the case of Hypatia, in Socrates, *HE* 7.15).

98. Ausonius, *Parentalia* 3.8–10.

99. Ausonius, *Parentalia* 5.9–10.

100. Ausonius, *Parentalia* 2.4.

101. It has been conventional to downplay the emotional attachments between parents and children in antiquity (e.g., Laes, *Children in the Roman Empire,* 100), though this paradigm is now beginning to be questioned. For relationships between fathers and sons, see M. Salzman, "Symmachus and His Father: Patrimony and Patriarchy in the Roman Senatorial Elite," in *Le trasformazioni delle "élites" in età tardoantica,* ed. R. Lizzi Testa (Rome, 2006), 357–75. It is worth noting too that Ausonius would eventually arrange for his father to be appointed proconsul of Illyricum in 377, when his father was ninety. For discussion, see chapter 8.

102. This was on ninth day after birth for a boy and eighth day for a girl (Plutarch, *Roman Questions* 288C-E). For discussion of this, see Laes, *Children in the Roman Empire,* 66.

103. For discussion of the rituals, see Laes, *Children in the Roman Empire,* 66–67; P. Garnsey, "Child Rearing in Ancient Italy," in *The Family in Italy: From Antiquity to the Present,* ed. D. Kertzer and R. Saller (New Haven, CT, 1991), 51–54.

104. Tertullian equates the naming ceremony with "private and social solemnities such as those of the white toga, of espousals, of nuptials" (*De idolatria* 16.1). Although sacrifices were offered on such occasions, Tertullian agreed that

Christians could participate in them because their primary purpose was to honor a person, not the gods.

105. See the discussion of Salzman, "Religious *Koine*," 112, 121.

106. For Tertullian's view of these festivals, see *De idolatria* 13. On the late antique Parentalia, see F. Dolansky, "Ritual, Gender, and Status in the Roman Family" (PhD diss., University of Chicago, 2005), chap. 2; Dolansky, "Honoring the Family Dead on the Parentalia: Ceremony, Spectacle, and Memory," *Phoenix* 65 (2011): 125–57.

107. For the duration and other details, see Ovid, *Fasti* 2.533–82. For the Vestals' involvement, see Salzman, *On Roman Time,* 160. For the wreaths, see Ovid, *Fasti* 2.537. Most of these individual activities seem to have been concentrated into the festival's final day. Less is said about the eight days preceding it.

108. Ovid, *Fasti,* 2.631–33.

109. Valerius Maximus 2.1.8. On nonfamily members, see Martial 9.55; Tertullian, *De idolatria* 10. These are all Western Roman festivals, but while some of these festivals were not celebrated in the East, others like them were. For the continuation of similar funerary rites by both Christians and pagans in the fourth century, see Salzman, "Religious *Koine*," 114–16.

110. Ausonius, *Parentalia,* praefatio in prosa 9–10 (trans. Evelyn-White).

111. Tacitus, *Dial. or.* 29.

112. "In the case of children we employ the pleasing myths to spur them on, and the fear-inspiring myths to deter them. . . . [They] are incited to emulation by the myths that are pleasing, when they hear the poets narrate mythical deeds of heroism, such as the Labours of Heracles of Theseus, or hear of honours bestowed by gods, or, indeed, when they see paintings or primitive images or works of sculpture which suggest any similar happy issue of fortune in mythology; but they are deterred from evil courses when, either through descriptions or through typical representations of objects unseen, they learn of divine punishments, terrors, and threats" (Strabo, *Geog.* 1.2.8, LCL trans.).

113. For discussion, see A. C. Dionisotti, "From Ausonius' School Days? A Schoolbook and Its Relatives," *JRS* 72 (1982): 83–125, at 86–88. On the *Hermeneumata,* see R. Cribiore, *Gymnastics of the Mind* (Princeton, NJ, 2001), 15–16, 85–86; E. Dickey, *The Colloquia of the Hermeneumata Pseudo-dositheana* (Cambridge, 2012).

114. Dionisotti, "Ausonius' School Days," 90–91.

115. Dionisotti, "Ausonius' School Days," 12r1–10.

116. Dionisotti, "Ausonius' School Days," 12r11–12v13.

117. Dionisotti, "Ausonius' School Days," 12v14.

118. Dionisotti, "Ausonius' School Days," 12v18–14r42.

119. Dionisotti, "Ausonius' School Days," 14v43–16r 69

120. J. Pucci, "Ausonius' *Ephemeris* and the *Hermeneumata* Tradition," *CP* 104 (2009): 50–68.

121. Ausonius, *Ephemeris* 2.10–20.

122. For Julian's effort and its effect, see E. Watts, *City and School in Late Antique Athens and Alexandria* (Berkeley, 2006), 64–78; and chapter 5 in this book.

123. Macrobius's text is discussed in more detail in chapter 10.

124. Macrobius, *Saturnalia* 1.praef. 10–11, trans. P. Davies (New York, 1969). For calendars as a part of the curriculum more generally, see Salzman, *On Roman Time*, 14–16.

125. Symmachus, *Ep.* 2.53; the translation is that found in Salzman, *On Roman Time*, 15.

126. On this timing, see Dolansky, "Ritual, Gender, and Status," chap. 2.

127. *De idolatria* 2 (*ANF* trans.).

128. *De idolatria* 2.

129. *De idolatria* 3–11.

130. *De idolatria* 13–23.

131. *De idolatria* 12.

132. *De idolatria* 24.

CHAPTER 2. EDUCATION IN AN AGE OF IMAGINATION

1. For this line of thought, see P. Brown, *Power and Persuasion in Late Antiquity* (Madison, WI, 1992), 122. M. Bloomer ("Schooling in Persona: Imagination and Subordination in Roman Education," *ClAnt* 16.1 [1997]: 57–78, at 59–63) has described the particular role that *fictio personae* played in developing a student's conception of gentlemanly behaviors.

2. Plutarch, *Moralia* 7E.

3. Portions of this section were previously published in E. Watts, "Christianization," in *Late Ancient Knowing: Explorations in Intellectual History,* ed. C. Chin and M. Vidas (Berkeley, forthcoming).

4. For a discussion of Decius's law, see J.B. Rives, "The Decree of Decius and the Religion of the Empire," *JRS* 89 (1999): 145–47.

5. É. Rebillard, *Christians and Their Many Identities in Late Antiquity, North Africa, 200–450 CE* (Ithaca, NY, 2012), 53.

6. Libanius, *Or.* 5.43–53.

7. As the Eusebian description of Philip the Arab suggests (*HE* 6.34), third-century events even enabled Christians to imagine a Christian emperor. For a critical discussion of this Eusebian portrait, see H. Pohlsander, "Philip the Arab and Christianity," *Historia* 29 (1980): 463–73.

8. As R. Van Dam points out (*The Roman Revolution of Constantine,* [Cambridge, 2007], 10), Christians had always imagined that pagan, Roman rule would be replaced by Christ's "heavenly and angelic empire" not a Christian, Roman one. For this notion, see, for example, Eusebius, *HE* 3.20.4.

9. For the variety of accounts of Constantine's conversion, see, for example, the discussion of G. Fowden, "The Last Days of Constantine: Oppositional Versions and Their Influence," *JRS* 84 (1994): 146–70; D. Potter, *Constantine the Emperor,* (Oxford, 2013), 294–95. For a thorough discussion of subsequent stories about Constantine in medieval legendary material, see S.N.C. Lieu, "Constantine in Legendary Literature," in *The Cambridge Companion to the Age of Constantine,* ed. N. Lenski, 2nd ed. (Cambridge, 2010), 298–321.

10. Potter, *Constantine,* 111–14; T.D. Barnes, *Constantine: Dynasty, Religion and Power in the Later Roman Empire* (London, 2011), 62–64.

11. For the tetrarchic succession scheme and the challenge Constantine's proximity to his father's court presented, see S. Corcoran, "Before Constantine," in Lenski, *Cambridge Companion to Constantine*, 14–58, at 40–41 and 54; Barnes, *Constantine*, 49–51.

12. For Constantine's place in the succession discussions, see D. Potter, *The Roman Empire at Bay, AD 180–395* (London, 2004), 340; Potter, *Constantine*, 114; Barnes, *Constantine*, 56–60, 64–66.

13. The background and nature of the conflict between Constantine and Maxentius has received regular and extensive scholarly attention. For discussions, see, among many others, H.A. Drake, *Constantine and the Bishops* (Baltimore, 2000), 165–78; T.D. Barnes, *Constantine and Eusebius* (Cambridge, MA, 1981), 28–43; Potter, *Constantine*, 115–22.

14. For date and circumstances, see Barnes, *Constantine*, 67–68.

15. For the earlier engagements with Severus, see Lactantius, *Mort. pers.* 26.5; Zosimus 2.10. For Galerius's attack, see Lactantius, *Mort. pers.* 26.11; Zosimus 2.10. Against the idea that Severus was killed immediately (found in both sources), see Barnes, *Constantine and Eusebius*, 299 n. 14. For discussion, see Potter, *Constantine*, 115–19; Barnes, *Constantine*, 68–70; N. Lenski, "The Reign of Constantine," in Lenski, *Cambridge Companion to Constantine*, 59–90, at 63.

16. An important component of this was building strong relationships with the elite in Rome. For discussion, see Potter, *Constantine*, 131–33.

17. Barnes, *Constantine*, 71 speaks aptly of the "dismal" alternative of ruling only the territory Constantine inherited from his father. It is worth noting, however, that Maxentius's coinage show him deftly trying to build up popular enthusiasm and civic patriotism in the areas under his control. Their reverses show prominent local temples and read, "Conserv Urb Suae" (e.g., *RIC* 113, 116, 121a, 124, 125 [Aquileia]; *RIC* 194a, 195, 202, 209, 210, 258 [Rome]; *RIC* 91, 95, 100, 101, 103, 106 [Ticinum]). On Maxentius's building program in Rome, see too E. Marlowe, "*Liberator urbis suae*: Constantine and the Ghost of Maxentius," in *The Emperor and Rome: Space, Representation, and Ritual*, ed. B. Ewald and C. Noreña (New Haven, CT, 2010), 199–219.

18. On Constantinian coinage from this period, see Potter, *Constantine*, 136.

19. *Panegyric Latina* VI (7).2; cf. C.E.V. Nixon and B. Saylor Rogers, *In Praise of Later Roman Emperors: The Panegyrici Latini* (Berkeley, 1994), 28–29. For discussion, see Barnes, *Constantine*, 72–73; Potter, *Constantine*, 123–28; Lenski, "Reign of Constantine," 66–67. Constantine's embrace of this fictional genealogy lasted longer than is often noticed. Well into the 310s Claudius Gothicus is called the *nepos* (grandfather) of Constantine on public inscriptions and is honored in an issue of coins in 317/318 as one of the three divinized emperors to whom Constantine has direct ties (e.g., *RIC* 7.26B [Thessalonica]; *RIC* 7.43 and 7.112 [Rome]).

20. This number is drawn from *Panegyric Latina* XII (9).3.3, 5.1.

21. For Licinius's plans, see Barnes, *Constantine*, 80.

22. Eusebius, *VC* 1.26.

23. H. Dey, *The Aurelian Wall and the Refashioning of Imperial Rome, AD 271–855*, (Cambridge, 2011), 285–91 has recently called into question the

degree to which Maxentius is responsible for repairs to the walls. While it is true that previous scholarship may have overestimated the amount of repairs Maxentius undertook, the extreme dependence that his regime had on the defenses of Rome makes it implausible that he is not responsible for many of the repairs attributed to him.

24. Part of Maxentius's unpopularity stemmed from the taxes his political position forced him to assess Italians. For discussion, see Barnes, *Constantine and Eusebius*, 37; Barnes, *Constantine*, 82.

25. *Pan. Lat.* XII 3.3 gives Maxentius an army of one hundred thousand, a figure almost certainly inflated for rhetorical reasons.

26. On Constantine's northern Italian campaign, see Potter, *Constantine*, 137–42; Barnes, *Constantine*, 80–82; Lenski, "Reign of Constantine," 69.

27. Eusebius, *VC* 1.27. All passages from the *Life of Constantine* quoted in this chapter derive from the NPNF translation.

28. Eusebius, *VC* 1.29; cf. Lactantius, *Mort. pers.* 44.5–6; *Pan. Lat.* VI [7].21.3–7. There exists an immense literature on Constantine's vision and its significance. I rely here on P. Weiss, "The Vision of Constantine," trans. A.R. Birley, *JRA* 16 (2003): 237–59, as well as the subsequent discussions of Barnes, *Constantine*, 74–80; Lenski, "The Reign of Constantine," 67; and H.A. Drake, "The Impact of Constantine on Christianity," in Lenski, *Cambridge Companion to Constantine*, 111–36, at 114. See, among many others, J. Long, "How to Read a Halo: Three (or More) Versions of Constantine's Vision," in *The Power of Religion in Late Antiquity*, ed. A. Cain and N. Lenski (Aldershot, 2009), 227–35; R. Van Dam, "The Many Conversions of the Emperor Constantine," in *Conversion in Late Antiquity and the Early Middle Ages*, ed. K. Mills and A. Grafton, (Rochester, NY, 2003), 127–51; O. Nicholson, "Constantine's Vision of the Cross," *VC* 54 (2000): 309–23; B. Bleckmann, "Pagane Visionen Konstantins in der Chronik der Johannes Zonaras," in *Constantino il Grande dall'antichita all'umanesimo*, vol. 1, ed. G. Bonamente and F. Fusco (Macerata, 1992), 151–70; R. Macmullen, "Constantine and the Miraculous," *GRBS* 9 (1968): 81–96.

29. Eusebius, *VC* 1.29

30. Lactantius places the vision immediately before the battle of the Milvian Bridge. Eusebius is vague about the timing. Potter (*Constantine*, 142), Barnes (*Constantine*, 80), and K.M. Girardet, "Das Christentum im Denken und in der Politik Kaiser Konstantins d. Gr.," in *Kaiser Konstantin der Grosse*, ed. K.M. Girardet [Bonn, 2007], 29–53, at 32–42) suggest a range of dates before the battle of the Milvian Bridge.

31. For the battles in northern Italy, see Potter, *Constantine*, 138–42.

32. Lactantius, *Mort. pers.* 44.3–5. See too Drake, *Constantine and the Bishops*, 180; Lenski, "Reign of Constantine," 69.

33. For a more comprehensive discussion of the battle of the Milvian Bridge, see now the intriguing study of R. Van Dam, *Remembering Constantine at Milvian Bridge*, (Cambridge, 2011). See too the survey of W. Kuhoff, "Die Schlacht an der Milvischen Brücke: Ein Ereignis von weltgeschichtlicher Tragweite," in *Konstantin der Große: Zwischen Sol und Christus*, ed. K. Ehling and G. Weber (Darmstadt, 2011), 10–20.

34. E.g., Lactantius, *Mort. pers.* 44.

35. For this view, see, among others, Barnes, *Constantine and Eusebius,* 271; C. Odahl, *Constantine and the Christian Empire* (New York, 2004), 106; and Lenski, "Reign of Constantine," 71.

36. Lactantius, *Mort. pers.* 48. On the "Edict of Milan," see O. Seeck, "Das sogenannte Edikte von Mailand," *ZKG* 10 (1891): 381–86; Barnes, *Constantine and Eusebius,* 318 n. 4; Drake, *Constantine and the Bishops,* 193–98; Drake, "Impact of Constantine," 121–23; A.D. Lee, "Traditional Religions," in Lenski, *Cambridge Companion to the Age of Constantine,* 159–79, at 171; Potter, *Constantine,* 145–49; and Barnes, *Constantine,* 93–97.

37. Eusebius, *HE* 9.9. For discussion of Daia's attitudes toward Christianity, see P. Stephenson, *Constantine: Roman Emperor, Christian Victor* (New York, 2010), 159.

38. On the various revisions of Eusebius's *Ecclesiastical History,* see T.D. Barnes, "The Editions of Eusebius' *Church History,*" *GRBS* 21 (1980): 191–201; R.W. Burgess, "The Dates and Editions of Eusebius' *Chronici Canones* and *Historia Ecclesiastica,*" *JTS* 48 (1997): 471–504.

39. Eusebius, *HE* 9.11.9 (NPNF trans.). On Licinius's religious attitudes in this period, see too Lactantius, *Mort. pers.* 46; Potter, *Constantine,* 147–48.

40. The text and context of Galerius's edict is found in Lactantius, *Mort. pers.* 33–34.

41. Lactantius was certainly one of these, helped in part by time spent at the court of Constantine. For discussion, see B. Digeser, *The Making of a Christian Empire* (Ithaca, NY, 2000), chap. 2; Digeser, "Lactantius and the 'Edict of Milan': Does It Determine His Venue?" *StPatr* 31 (1997): 287–95.

42. Potter, *Constantine,* 172–82.

43. For Constantine and the Donatist controversy, see Drake, *Constantine and the Bishops,* 212–21; Drake, "Impact of Constantine," 116–21; Potter, *Constantine,* 193–203.

44. Potter, *Constantine,* 176–77.

45. For the progression of the war against Licinius, see Barnes, *Constantine,* 103–6; Potter, *Constantine,* 207–14; Lenski, "Reign of Constantine," 72–77.

46. The famous Constantinian "Letter to the Eastern Provincials" (reproduced by Eusebius at *VC* 2.24–42 and partially preserved in Egyptian papyrus fragment *P.London* 878) can be read as a sort of announcement of this new regime. See Barnes, *Constantine,* 108.

47. This is a point made expertly by Peter Brown in the unpublished paper "Constantine, Eusebius, and the Future of Christianity," a study that explores the way that Eusebius's *Ecclesiatical History* charts the emergence of a Roman Empire in which Christianity becomes fully visible by the time of Constantine.

48. For Constantine's endorsement, see his *Oration to the Assembly of the Saints* 11 and the discussions of Drake, "Impact of Constantine," 128, and Barnes, *Constantine,* 113–20.

49. Constantine had apparently already done this in the West in 312. He was forced, in 320, to remind his prefect that these privileges should not be abused by appointing men with civic financial obligations to clerical positions unless they were replacing clerics who had died (*CTh* 16.2.3).

50. Eusebius, *VC* 2.46. For discussion, see T.D. Barnes, *Athanasius and Constantius* (Cambridge, MA, 1993), 176–78; Barnes, *Constantine,* 135–36; Brown, *Power and Persuasion,* 90; Brown, *Poverty and Leadership in the Later Roman Empire* (Hanover, NH, 2002), 26–32.

51. These were *manumissio in ecclesia* and *episcopalis audientia.* For discussion, see Barnes, *Constantine,* 134. For *episcopalis audientia* in particular, see *CTh* 1.27.1 and 2; *Sirmondian Constitution* 1; Drake, *Constantine and the Bishops,* 322–25; and the broader discussions of C. Rapp, *Holy Bishops in Late Antiquity* (Berkeley, 2005), 242–44; and J.C. Lamoreaux, "Episcopal Courts in Late Antiquity," *JECS* 3 (1995): 143–67.

52. For the percentage of Christians in the empire in 315, see R. Bagnall, "Religious Conversion and Onomastic Change in Early Byzantine Egypt," *BASP* 19 (1982): 105–24—numbers also consistent with the model of Christian growth proposed by R. Stark, *The Rise of Christianity* (Princeton, NJ, 1996), 11–13. Note as well M. Edwards, "The Beginnings of Christianization," in Lenski, *Cambridge Companion to Constantine,* 137–58, at 137–38.

53. Eusebius's *Life of Constantine* was composed after Constantine's death. As such, it is less a record of purely Constantinian ideas than a representation of ideas shaped both during and immediately after Constantine's reign.

54. Eusebius, *VC* 2.44.

55. Eusebius, *VC* 2.45; see Barnes, *Constantine,* 109–10.

56. Eusebius, *VC* 2.45.

57. For discussion, see chapter 1.

58. Deuteronomy 12.2 (NRSV trans.). I thank Jeremy Schott for calling my attention to this similarity to Deuteronomy.

59. F. Millar, *The Emperor in the Roman World (31 BC–337 AD)* (Ithaca, NY, 1992), 266, 271.

60. The ways in which a law could be made are described in *CJ* 1.14.3, an address made to the Western senate by Valentinian III in 426, and *CJ* 1.14.8, a law of 446 describing procedures. For discussion, see J. Harries, "The Roman Imperial Quaestor from Constantine to Theodosius II," *JRS* 78 (1988): 148–72; and J. Matthews, *Laying Down the Law* (New Haven, CT, 2000), 171–72.

61. The consistory and its composition are discussed in detail in J. Harries, *Law and Empire in Late Antiquity* (Cambridge, 1999), 38–42. While its composition would have been slightly different in the time of Constantine, the consistory had settled into this form by the reign of Constantius II. The counts of the consistory lacked any other defined office.

62. On this process, see E. Watts, "Justinian, Malalas, and the End of Athenian Philosophical Teaching in AD 529," *JRS* 94 (2004): 174–75.

63. See, for example, the situations described in Ammianus 28.1 and Zosimus 4.3, both discussed in chapter 6.

64. Emperors were quite aware of the possibility of governors choosing not to enforce laws (e.g., *CTh* 16.10.13.1).

65. Eusebius, *VC* 4.23.

66. Eusebius, *VC* 4.54.

67. Eusebius, *VC* 3.54; Sozomen, *HE* 2.5. Palladas 10.90 may refer to this confiscation, though, if the dating is correct, the absence of any Egyptian

mention of these actions in later Coptic and Greek sources working to justify confiscations of temple property in Alexandria in the 390s is an odd anomaly (for these discussions, see E. Watts, *Riot in Alexandria* [Berkeley, 2010], 191–205). For Palladas as a potential source for these confiscations, see K. Wilkinson, "Palladas and the Age of Constantine," *JRS* 99 (2009): 26–60, at 51–56; Barnes, *Constantine*, 129–31. I do not follow Barnes (*Constantine*, 199) in seeing *P.Lond.* 163 IX.13–22 as evidence for confiscations of temple property. Even if this text is connected to Constantine (which is debatable), the comment about instructions to officials "to avoid the spoliation of shrines" seems to suggest protection of temple property rather than "the confiscation of riches they had accumulated over the centuries" (as argued by Barnes, *Constantine*, 130).

68. Eusebius, *VC* 3.55.

69. On these temple destructions, see Potter, *Constantine*, 276; Lee, "Traditional Religions," 174. For the possibility that Aegeae was chosen because of its links to the great persecution, see R. Lane Fox, *Pagans and Christians* (New York, 1986), 671–72.

70. Libanius, *Or.* 30.6.

71. Eusebius, *VC* 2.60; a point reinforced by Barnes, *Constantine*, 110.

72. Bradbury, "Constantine and the Problem of Anti-Pagan Legislation in the Fourth Century," *CP* 89 (1994): 131–32. For other assessments of this question, see Lee, "Traditional Religions," 172–74. Against the idea of a law banning sacrifice, see Lane Fox, *Pagans and Christians*, 667; J. Curran, *Pagan City and Christian Capital: Rome in the Fourth Century* (Oxford, 2000), 175–85.

73. S. Bassett, *The Urban Image of Late Antique Constantinople* (Cambridge, 2004); cf. Potter, *Constantine*, 261–62; Stephenson, *Constantine*, 201–3. For the meaning of these statues in Constantinople in later periods, see C. Mango, "Antique Statuary and the Byzantine Beholder," *DOP* 17 (1963): 53–75, at 59–63.

74. For the engineering challenges associated with taking down a temple, see, for example, Theodoret, *HE* 5.21, a case where the soldiers and others assembled to destroy a temple struggled to figure out how to do so (I thank Adam Schor for this reference). The fact that Theodoret characterizes the appearance of a man who knew how to take down the temple as a miracle suggests that demolition experts would usually be required for such an operation.

75. On the nature of the Serapeum site, see the excellent treatment of J.S. McKenzie, S. Gibson, and A.T. Reyes, "Reconstructing the Serapeum in Alexandria from the Archeological Evidence," *JRS* 94 (2004): 73–121.

76. Potter, *Constantine*, 276.

77. For the monody, see the summary offered in Libanius, *Ep.* 695. For other discussions, see Libanius, *Epp.* 727, 1300, 1342.

78. As noted above, Palladas might provide the unique exception to this.

79. Zosimus 4.36.

80. E.g., *CTh* 16.10.1.

81. *CIL* 11.5265. Constantine did set the condition that "this temple dedicated to our name should not be defiled by the deceits of any contagious superstition"—probably a reference to sacrifices. See Lee, "Traditional Religions," 175; Potter, *Constantine*, 281. For the Hispellum rescript, see now the contribu-

tion of G. Cecconi, "Il rescritto di Spello: Prospettive recenti," in *Costantino prima e dopo Costantino*, ed. G. Bonamente, N. Lenski, and R. Lizzi Testa (Bari, 2012), 273–90.

82. As Tertullian's *De idolatria* shows, some Christians had always held jobs that required them to perform actions that, strictly speaking, were inconsistent with their faith. It is possible that Constantine may not have viewed the religious obligations of his job all that differently from the third-century incense seller whose trade supported pagan practices in which he never directly participated.

83. This inscription is J. Baillet, *Inscriptions grecques et latines des Tombeaux des Rois Syringes à Thebes* (Cairo, 1920–26), no. 1265. For discussion of Nicagoras and the context of his trip, see G. Fowden, "Nicagoras of Athens and the Lateran Obelisk," *JHS* 107 (1987): 51–57; Barnes, *Constantine*, 193.

84. Photius, *Bibl.* Cod. 62; and Barnes, *Constantine*, 195–97.

85. Libanius alludes to these actions in *Oration* 30. Because this oration contrasts the strong Christian emperor Constantine with his son (who, in Libanius's view, acted against paganism because he was unable to control his court), it is possible that Libanius is deliberately obscuring Constantine's actions. It is equally possible, however, that Libanius did not know specifically what policies Constantine initiated. For the thematic elements of *Oration* 30, see chapter 9.

86. For broader treatments of ancient education, see H. Marrou, *Histoire de l'éducation dans l'Antiquité* (Paris, 1956); T. Morgan, *Literate Education in the Hellenistic and Roman Worlds* (Cambridge, MA, 1998); and R. Cribiore, *Gymnastics of the Mind: Greek Education in Hellenistic and Roman Egypt* (Princeton, NJ, 2001).

87. When one argues largely from empirical evidence, the most compelling estimates of literacy rates in the high imperial period suggest that between one-tenth and one-third of the population could write and read simple documents. For the lower figure, see W. Harris, *Ancient Literacy* (Cambridge, MA, 1989), 256–83. For a different approach and ultimate assessment of the question, see, for example, A. Hanson, "Ancient Illiteracy," in *Literacy in the Roman World*, ed. J.L. Humphrey (Ann Arbor, MI, 1991), 159–98, as well as the other essays in that volume.

88. What follows is a description of the ideal path a student followed. The realities of late antique education were often more complicated, however. Grammar schools, for example, also taught elementary letters as well as rhetoric. See A.C. Dionisotti, "From Ausonius' School Days? A Schoolbook and Its Relatives," *JRS* 72 (1982): 83–125, at 98–101.

89. Instruction in grammar could begin as early as age seven or eight (cf. R. Kaster, *Guardians of Language: The Grammarian and Society in Late Antiquity* [Berkeley, 1988], 11), but a later age may be more typical. Libanius, for example, finished his grammatical training at thirteen (R. Cribiore, *The School of Libanius in Late Antique Antioch* [Princeton, NJ, 2007], 31).

90. See, for example, R. Cribiore, *Writing, Teachers, and Students in Graeco-Roman Antiquity* (Atlanta, 1996), nos. 160 and 379.

91. For an especially thorough discussion of the *progymnasmata*, see Cribiore, *Gymnastics of the Mind*, 221–30. For the exercises as a sort of primer for the

lifestyle of the cultivated, see R. Webb, "The Progymnasmata as Practice," in *Education in Greek and Roman Antiquity,* ed. Y. L. Too (Leiden, 2001), 289–316.

92. One student, Euphemius, enrolled under Libanius at age eleven (Libanius, *Ep.* 634 = Cribiore *Ep.* 16; for the age of eleven, see Cribiore, *School of Libanius,* 240). Eunapius famously joined a school of rhetoric at age sixteen (*VS* 485), perhaps a bit later than usual. Libanius made this jump at age fourteen.

93. For this limit, see *CTh* 14.9.1.

94. Cribiore, *School of Libanius,* 31.

95. This seems to be the role played by Eusebius and Thalassius in Libanius's school. For a description of their role, see *Epp.* 905–9 and 922–26 as well as *Oration* 31. For discussion, see A. Norman, *Libanius: Autobiography and Selected Letters* (Cambridge, MA, 1990), 2:454–61; Cribiore, *School of Libanius,* 33–37.

96. Cribiore, *Gymnastics of the Mind,* 226–30.

97. Ausonius, *Protrepticus* 73. He later claims that this is what allowed him to advance to the quaestorship, prefecture, and consulship (91).

98. *Or.* 1.24, trans. Norman. While he certainly studied hard, Libanius is here being somewhat disingenuous; this segment of *Oration* 1 uses its description of Libanius's student experiences to model ideal student behaviors.

99. For illness from toil, see *Ep.* 462. On lazy students becoming fat, see *Or.* 23.20, 34.12, and 38.6. For discussion, see Cribiore, *School of Libanius,* 17.

100. "The Muses have their amusements . . . nor does the sour schoolmaster's domineering voice always harass boys, but spells of rest and study keep each their appointed times. For an attentive boy to have read his lessons willingly is enough, so to rest is lawful" (*Protrepticus* 1–6, trans. Evelyn-White).

101. *Protrepticus* 29–33.

102. It is reasonable to suspect the accounts of regular beatings of students by teachers of rhetoric and grammar. Ausonius, for example, remarks that the schools "resound with the sound of lashes" (*Protrepticus* 24), but comments that he only encouraged his students with "mild warnings and gentle threats" (70).

103. *Oration* 34 refers to an epithalamium that Arcadius had heard Himerius deliver earlier. The epithalamium does not survive.

104. For this recruitment process, see Cribiore, *School of Libanius,* 112–17.

105. Ausonius called his uncle Arborius "father" on a number of occasions and, in his *Parentalia,* even playfully contrasts the academic fatherhood of Arborius with the status enjoyed by his biological father (*Parentalia* 3.1–10; *Professores* 16.5). He uses the same honorific for others who taught him (e.g., Staphylius, called "a father and an uncle, both in one, like a second Ausonius, like a second Arborius" in *Prof.* 20.4–6).

106. E.g., Libanius, *Epp.* 931, 1009, 1070, 1257; Ausonius, *Epp.* 23; 26; 28. For a discussion of these terms, see P. Petit, *Les étudiants de Libanius* (Paris, 1957), 35–36; and Cribiore, *School of Libanius,* 138–43.

107. Students asked that teachers use their influence to help their families (Libanius, *Ep.* 359), they asked them to suggest that their parents raise their allowances (Libanius, *Ep.* 428), and they helped ensure that their teachers' literary works found the right audience (Ausonius, *Epp.* 23, 24).

108. These are *Orations* 44 and 45.

109. Among many other references, see Eunapius, *VS* 483.

110. Libanius, *Or.* 18.13–14 indicates that such a restriction was placed on Julian.

111. Libanius watched this happen to a classmate while he was a student (*Or.* 1.21). Himerius alludes to this student violence a number of times, most notably in *Orations* 16, 65, and 66.

112. Libanius, *Or.* 1.11

113. Libanius, *Or.* 1.19. Himerius, in *Or.* 69, alludes to serious injuries that may have resulted from student violence. For discussion, see R. Penella, *Man and the Word: The Orations of Himerius* (Berkeley, 2007), 69.

114. *Or.* 3.22. Other scholastic riots in the fourth century may have been motivated by a similar desire to win prestige for teachers. See, for example, Eunapius, *VS* 483; Himerius, *Or.* 67; and Libanius, *Or.* 1.21, on the great riot.

115. Libanius, *Or.* 1.19, trans. Norman (adapted).

116. Augustine, *Conf.* 5.8.

117. This oath was either "coerced" (as in the case of Libanius) or given willfully (as Eunapius experienced). Libanius (*Or.* 1.16) describes being abducted and held against his will. Himerius (*Or.* 48.37) describes something similar. For the more agreeable experience of Eunapius, see *VS* 485–87.

118. *Or.* 69.8. Himerius here welcomes students from Cappadocia, Galatia, and Lydia, and a group from Egypt. *Oration* 35 seems to be a similar address welcoming transfer students.

119. Himerius, *Or.* 69.7; Gregory Nazianzen, *Or.* 43.16. This ritual is known as well from Eunapius, *VS.* 486 and Olympiodorus of Thebes, fr. 28 = Photius, *Bibl.* Cod. 80.177f.

120. Gregory describes the performance as "seeming very fearful and brutal to those who do not know it, [but] it is to those who have experienced it quite pleasant and humane, for its threats are for show rather than real" (*Or.* 43.16, NPNF trans.). Eunapius, who was quite ill when he arrived in Athens, suggests that it was nonetheless a physically draining experience (*VS* 486).

121. Olympiodorus, fr. 28.

122. Gregory, *Or.* 43.16.

123. The necessity of wearing a student cloak while engaged in basic rhetorical study is suggested by Eunapius, *VS* 487. This was not only an Athenian convention. Heraclas in Alexandria was forced by his teacher to wear a *tribōn* (Eusebius, *HE* 6.19.12–14).

124. For assistant teachers, see E. Watts, *City and School in Late Antique Athens and Alexandria* (Berkeley, 2006), 49–53; Cribiore, *Gymnastics of the Mind,* 28.

125. The student leaders have different names in ancient sources. Their role in the school is not particularly clear, nor is it evident that they were distinct from the upper-level students. Olympiodorus (fr. 28), for example, mentions that newly initiated students had to pay them a fee upon the commencement of their studies. On this hierarchy in conventional schools as well as the privileges attached to the head of a teacher's *choros,* see Cribiore, *School of Libanius,* 201; and Libanius, *Ep.* 886.

126. In fourth-century Athens, for example, it was common for first-year students to be ganged up on whenever they argued a point (Gregory Nazianzen, *Or.* 43.17). Zacharias Scholasticus (*Vit. Sev.* 47) records a similar situation in the law schools of Berytus in the later 480s.

127. For more on this relationship, see chapter 7.

128. Eunapius, *VS* 487.

129. E.g., Synesius, *Ep.* 139 to Herculianus.

130. Libanius, *Or* 58.33; cf. Cribiore, *School of Libanius,* 104.

131. Cribiore, *Gymnastics of the Mind,* 21–34.

132. For discussion of Libanius's various locations, see R. Cribiore, "Spaces for Teaching in Late Antiquity," in *Alexandria Auditoria of Kom el-Dikka and Late Antique Education,* ed. T. Derda, T. Markiewicz, and E. Wipszycka (Warsaw, 2007), 143–50, at 145–46; cf. Cribiore, *School of Libanius,* 30; and now C. Shepardson, *Controlling Contested Places: Late Antique Antioch and the Spatial Politics of Religious Controversy* (Berkeley, 2014), 31–41. Libanius mentions the bathhouse at *Or* 1.55 and describes the space in the city hall at some length in *Or.* 22.31 and 5.45–52. For the temple and his use of his own house in Antioch, see *Or.* 1.101–4.

133. *Or.* 22.31, trans. Norman.

134. The remains are described and analyzed in detail by G. Majcherek, "The Late Roman Auditoria," in Derda, Markiewicz, and Wipszycka, *Alexandria Auditoria,* 11–50.

135. Majcherek, "Late Roman Auditoria," 23–25. These remains seem to correspond to the space in which Zacharias Scholasticus describes an Alexandrian class (*Amm.* 92–99).

136. Majcherek, "Late Roman Auditoria," 25.

137. For Aphrodisias, note R.R.R. Smith, "Late Roman Philosopher Portraits from Aphrodisias," *JRS* 80 (1990): 127–55, at 151–53. For the possible identification of the Atrium House as a school, see K. Welch, "Some Architectural Prototypes for the Auditoria at Kom el-Dikka and Three Late Antique (Fifth Century AD) Comparanda from Aphrodisias in Caria," in Derda, Markiewicz, and Wipszycka, *Alexandria Auditoria,* 115–34.

138. This evidence, much of which predates late antiquity, is masterfully discussed by Cribiore, *Gymnastics of the Mind,* 29–32.

139. Ausonius says nothing about the religious self-identification of any of the teachers he describes in the *Professores,* but Arborius's invitation to Constantinople, probably to teach Constantine's nephew Dalmatius, suggests that he may have been a Christian. For this, see R.P.H. Green, *The Works of Ausonius* (Oxford, 1991), 352–54.

140. This was especially true of the philosophy classrooms of the time. For mythology and its role in teaching, see Hermogenes, *Progymnasmata.*

141. Plutarch, *Moralia* 7E.

142. The first payment they receive from every student is "consecrated both to the honour and to the name of Minerva" (Tertullian, *De idolatria* 10, *ANF* trans.).

143. Gregory Nazianzen, *Or.* 43.21. For the nature of fourth-century Athenian life, see Watts, *City and School,* 48–78.

144. Though, again, his uncle may have been Christian.

145. For more on the rhetorical nature of Libanius's *Autobiography,* see L. Van Hoof, "Libanius' *Life* and Life," in *The Cambridge Companion to Libanius,* ed. L. Van Hoof (Cambridge, 2014).

CHAPTER 3. THE SYSTEM

1. Magnentius rebelled in Gaul in 350 and controlled its territory until his death in 353. His control over Italy was more tenuous and lasted a shorter time. Neither Ausonius nor Praetextatus is known to have had deep involvement in his regime.

2. Among the problems exacerbated by the third-century crisis were brigandage (e.g., *P.Oxy.* 1408), city damages caused by civil war (e.g., Herodian 8.2.3–4.8), and rural population loss (e.g., CIL 3.12336).

3. The catalyst for this seems to have been a currency reform launched by the emperor Aurelian that broke the rough peg that had kept the value of the silver coinage and gold coinage in line with one another. For discussion of the relative stability that this peg ensured, see D. Rathbone, "Monetisation, Not Price Inflation, in Third Century AD Egypt," in *Coin Finds and Coin Use in the Roman World,* ed. C.E. King and D.G. Wigg (Berlin, 1996), 321–39. For Aurelian's reform and its effects, see D. Potter, *The Roman Empire at Bay, AD 180–395* (London, 2004), 273; C. Howgego, *Ancient History from Coins* (London, 1995), 126; and the slightly different assessment of K. Harl, *Coinage in the Roman Economy, 300 BC–700 AD* (Baltimore, 1996), 143–48.

4. See E. Lo Cascio, "The Function of Gold Coinage in the Monetary Economy of the Roman Empire," in *The Monetary Systems of the Greeks and Romans,* ed. W.V. Harris (Oxford, 2008), 160–73, for the breakdown of stability in the Roman imperial coinage system of the third century and its effects into the fourth century. For the distorting effects of third-century debasements, see, for example, *P.Ryl.* 607.

5. S. Corcoran, *The Empire of the Tetrarchs,* 2nd ed. (Oxford, 2000) remains the definitive study.

6. This process of imperial subdivision had begun in the third century (e.g., CIL 3.6783, which dates a provincial division to the reign of Gordian III), but Diocletian got particular credit for creating smaller, more efficiently administered provinces (e.g., Lactantius, *Mort. pers.* 7.4). The fourth-century Verona list catalogs nearly one hundred Roman provinces. For discussion, see T.D. Barnes, *The New Empire of Diocletian and Constantine* (Cambridge, MA, 1982), 195–225; and, for the earlier third century, B. Malcus, "Notes sur la révolution du système administratif romain au IIIe siècle," *OpRom* 7 (1969): 213–37. For the emergence of new, separate administrative districts in Asia and Dacia as early as the late second century, see C. Roueché, "Rome, Asia and Aphrodisias," *JRS* 71 (1981): 103–20, at 117 n. 98; G. Bowersock, *Martyrdom and Rome* (Cambridge, 1995), 85–98; and D. Potter, "Procurators in Asia and Dacia under Marcus Aurelius: A Case Study of Imperial Initiative in Government," *ZPE* 123 (1998): 270–74.

7. This process had clearly begun by the first decade of the fourth century (F. Millar, *The Roman Near East, 31 B.C.–A.D. 337 AD* [Cambridge, MA, 1993],

191–92). Eusebius gives a couple of indications of *duces* whose positions are defined in these terms (*MP* 13.1–3; *HE* 9.5.2)

8. For the dating of this process to the 290s, see Millar, *Roman Near East,* 193.

9. So, for example, Diocletian and his colleagues adapted and expanded the role of praetorian prefect from the figure who commanded the praetorian guard into a sort of imperial chief of staff (A.H.M. Jones, *The Later Roman Empire, 284–602* [Norman, OK, 1964], 371). Constantine would further develop this office into a civilian administrator who ranked above the governors and controlled a defined territory. On this process of development, see C. Kelly, "Bureaucracy and Government," in *The Cambridge Companion to the Age of Constantine,* ed. N. Lenski (Cambridge, 2006), 185–87; T.D. Barnes, *Constantine: Dynasty, Religion and Power in the Later Roman Empire* (London, 2011), 158–63, presents this office as evolving throughout the reign of Constantine but not as a deliberate result of reform by the emperor.

10. There were five prefects as early as the 330s, though their territories and duties were not yet fixed. On this, see Barnes, *Constantine,* 161; Kelly, "Bureaucracy and Government," 186.

11. P. Heather, "New Men for New Constantines?" in *New Constantines: The Rhythm of Imperial Renewal in Byzantium, 4th–13th Centuries,* ed. P. Magdalino (Aldershot, 1994), 11–34, at 18–21.

12. For the number of military officials and their staffs, see Jones, *Later Roman Empire,* 597–601.

13. This is best seen in the decree issued by the prefect of Egypt in 297 describing the new system. On it, see A.E.R. Boak and H.C. Youtie, *The Archive of Aurelius Isidorus in the Egyptian Museum, Cairo and the University of Michigan (P. Cair. Isidor.)* (Ann Arbor, MI, 1960), no. 1.

14. See, for example, *Syro-Roman lawbook.121* in *Fontes iuris romani antejustiniani,* vol. 2. ed. S. Riccobono et al. (Florence, 1940–43), no. 791. For discussion of this assessment process, see Millar, *Roman Near East,* 194–97.

15. Jones, *Later Roman Empire,* 451–60.

16. R. Bagnall, *Currency and Inflation in Fourth Century Egypt,* Bulletin of the American Society of Papyrologists Supplement, no. 5 (Chico, CA, 1985), 19–25. Bagnall dates the reform to 296 based on arguments first advanced by William Metcalf. For an alternative date of 293, see Harl, *Coinage in the Roman Economy,* 148–51.

17. Existing coins remained in circulation with their values adjusted to reflect the new standards. See Bagnall, *Currency and Inflation,* 19–20; K. Erim, J. Reynolds, and M. Crawford, "Diocletian's Currency Reform: A New Inscription," *JRS* 61 (1971): 171–77.

18. For the fate of the tetrarchic silver coinage, see Harl, *Coinage in the Roman Economy,* 148–62.

19. See Bagnall, *Currency and Inflation,* 31–34, 41, 44. For a discussion of the decrease in the purity of the *nummus* between 305 and 341, and the decrease in its value relative to the *solidus,* see Harl, *Coinage in the Roman Economy,* 162–71, esp. table 7.2.

20. For a survey of the various debasements of the silver coinage and the relationship of its value to that of gold coins, see Bagnall, *Currency and Inflation,* 27–48.

21. The cutoff point at which one secured exemptions was a moving target. In 364, Valentinian and Valens permitted advancement in rank only after the fulfillment of curial duties and the understanding that one's son would remain eligible for them. For discussion of the changing limits both before and after 364, see Heather, "New Men," 25–27.

22. The *comes Africae.* For his career, see Ammianus 30.7. For the rise of Balkan soldiers in this period, see the discussion of D. Potter, *Constantine the Emperor* (Oxford, 2013), 7–19.

23. *PLRE* 1.400; *CIL* 3.12900. On the possibility of a visit with Constans, see C. Aull, "Imperial Power in the Age of Valentinian I, 364–375 CE" (PhD diss., Indiana University, 2013), chap. 1.

24. Eunapius, *VS* 487.

25. On the career of Prohaereius, see E. Watts, *City and School in Late Antique Athens and Alexandria* (Berkeley, 2006), 48–78.

26. For a discussion of the income and its distribution across those working in various ministries, see Jones, *Later Roman Empire,* 572–96. Libanius received some of his compensation as an in-kind payment of goods produced by an imperial estate, though he was once pressed by the praetorian prefect to repay it in gold (Libanius, *Ep.* 1254).

27. P. Brown, *Through the Eye of a Needle* (Princeton, NJ, 2012), 15.

28. *CIL* 8.22660; Epiphanius, *De mensuris et ponderibus* 53. This had long been a practice for very large purchases made with a large number of high-value coins, but it seems not to have been used for smaller transactions. For discussion, see M. Hendy, *Studies in Byzantine Monetary Economy, c. 300–1450* (Cambridge, 2008), 338–43; Harl, *Coinage in the Roman Economy,* 166; A.H.M. Jones, "The Origin and Early History of the Follis," *JRS* 49 (1959): 34–38.

29. *Anonymous de rebus bellicis* 2.1–2, trans. Brown. For this passage and its broader context, see Brown, *Through the Eye of a Needle,* 15; J. Banaji, *Agrarian Change in Late Antiquity* (Oxford, 2001), 46–49; Banaji, "Economic Trajectories," in *Oxford Handbook of Late Antiquity,* ed. S. Johnson (Oxford, 2012), 598–624, at 598–601. The increase in the circulation of gold in the fourth century may be due to the discovery of a new source of gold around 350, an idea explored in an unpublished paper by G. Bevan and R. Burgess.

30. Olympiodorus, fr. 41.2. For an analysis of the utility of these numbers, see Brown, *Through the Eye of a Needle,* 16–17; and W. Scheidel, "Finances, Figures, and Fiction," *CQ* 46 (1996): 222–38. The current value of this income is calculated based on a gold price of $1,270 per ounce (the market price on February 9, 2014) and a rough equivalence of twelve modern ounces for each Roman pound.

31. *Life of Melania* 15. This was 1,666 pounds of gold, worth $12.7 million at current gold prices.

32. *Life of Melania* 17.

33. Olympiodorus, fr. 41.1. Archaeological evidence suggests that here again Olympiodorus exaggerates, but only somewhat.

34. Brown, *Through the Eye of a Needle,* 185–98; Banaji, "Economic Trajectories," 601–7. For aristocratic home construction in the period, see C. Machado, "Aristocratic Houses and the Making of Late Antique Rome and Constantinople," in *Two Romes: Rome and Constantinople in Late Antiquity,* ed. L. Grig and G. Kelly (Oxford, 2012), 136–58.

35. Paulinus of Pella, *Eucharisticon* 143–46, LCL trans., slightly modified.

36. Ausonius, *Ep.* 5.41–50, LCL trans., modified.

37. The poem is the *Griphus,* discussed further in chapter 6.

38. *Epigram* 48, entitled "Mixobarbaron liberi patris signo marmoreo in villa nostra omnium deorum argumenta habenti."

39. Ausonius, *Epigram* 87.

40. As Ausonius himself does in his poems about the German servant girl Bissula.

41. As Heather suggests ("New Men," 27), the skills needed to succeed in this system remained inaccessible to the poorer members of Roman society.

42. For this local elite, see now Brown, *Through the Eye of a Needle,* 3–11.

43. On these privileges, see P. Brown, *Power and Persuasion in Late Antiquity* (Madison, WI, 1992), 53–54; Libanius, *Or.* 28.

44. Brown, *Through the Eye of a Needle,* 22–23; Heather, "New Men," 12–18.

45. On the *Album* of Timgad, see A. Chastagnol, *L'album municipal de Timgad* (Habelt, 1978). By the 360s, *clarissimi, spectabiles,* and honorary *illustres* had lost their exemptions. On this, see Heather, "New Men," 26; Jones, *Later Roman Empire,* 528–29, 741–43; Libanius, *Or.* 49.5–6.

46. Libanius's grandfather, for example, was stripped of his property by Diocletian in 303 after he and other leading citizens of Antioch raised a militia in order to beat back a rebellious Roman army that attacked the city. This penalty for taking up arms was decreed even though the Antiochenes were fighting for Diocletian against the usurper Eugenius (Libanius, *Or.* 11.158–62, 19.45–46, and 20.18–20).

47. Ammianus 30.7. For Sirmium as a possible settling place, see Aull, "Valentinian," chap. 1, on the basis of the location of the emperor Gratian's birth. See as well N. Lenski, *Failure of Empire: Valens and the Roman State in the Fourth Century* (Berkeley, 2002), 41.

48. Jerome, *Chron.* 242–43. For discussion of this complicated affair, see Watts, *City and School,* 64–76.

49. On the case of Symmachus, see C. Sogno, *Q. Aurelius Symmachus: A Political Biography* (Ann Arbor, MI, 2006), 68–76; Alan Cameron, *The Last Pagans of Rome* (Oxford, 2012), 58, 76. Unlike relative outsiders such as Gratian, Symmachus also would have been better protected because of what Cristiana Sogno once called his Roman "senatorial cocoon" (pers. comm., March 2013).

50. For this particular problem among young elites, see as well chapter 4.

51. R. Cribiore, *The School of Libanius in Late Antique Antioch* (Princeton, NJ, 2007), 198–200.

52. The stay could last for hours or, in some cases, multiple months. The expectations and rules of the "letter event" where the letter is delivered is dis-

cussed thoroughly by B. Storin, "The Letters of Gregory Nazianzus: Discourse and Community in Late Antique Epistolary Culture" (PhD diss., Indiana University, 2012).

53. For a less charitable view of this system in action, see Ammianus 14.6. On patronage in late antiquity more generally, see P. Garnsey, "Roman Patronage," in *From the Tetrarchs to the Theodosians*, ed. S. McGill, C. Sogno, and E. Watts (Cambridge, 2010), 33–54.

54. For Libanius's interactions with Miccalus, see R. Cribiore, *Libanius the Sophist: Rhetoric, Reality, and Religion in the Fourth Century* (Ithaca, NY, 2013), 190–98, as well as the critical portrait of Miccalus that Libanius offers in *Oration 63*.

55. This is *Ep.* 98. On Spectatus's career, see *PLRE* 1: Spectatus 1.

56. *Ep.* 97.

57. *Ep.* 99.

58. This controversy is described more fully in a second letter Libanius sent to Themistius in the winter of 360–61. For the confusion about the debt, see Libanius, *Ep.* 252.2–3. For Themistius's role in the senate at this time, see chapter 4.

59. Libanius's friendship with Olympius, from whom he would ultimately receive an inheritance, is discussed in some detail in *Oration 63* and treated in Cribiore, *Libanius the Sophist*, 190–93.

60. *Ep.* 97.2. For Olympius, see *PLRE* 1: Olympius 3. In 360, Olympius was an Antiochene senator who had served as governor of Macedonia in 356.

61. *Ep.* 97.4.

62. Miccalus had yet to inherit any family property. Without a position in imperial service, he had no income of his own with which to support a wife.

63. *Ep.* 97.5. There is more to this request than Libanius lets on. Olympius apparently had no interest in marriage and controversially had surrounded himself with chaste servants who lived in quasi-ascetic spiritual marriages (*Or.* 63.31). For discussion, see Cribiore, *Libanius the Sophist*, 197–200.

64. *Ep.* 98.3–4, trans. Bradbury.

65. Given Miccalus's later conduct (on which, see below), this is less surprising than it may seem at first glance.

66. Libanius, *Ep.* 704. For his marriage, see Libanius, *Or.* 63.30–35. This governorship may actually have been secured more because of the influence of Priscianus, under whom he served as an assessor in Euphratensis, than through this trio of Libanian associates in Constantinople. As *Ep.* 149 shows, Libanius facilitated Miccalus's introduction to Priscianus as well.

67. Libanius, *Ep.* 154.2–3, trans. Bradbury.

68. *Ep.* 175.5, trans. Bradbury.

69. τῇ μὲν οὖν πατρίδι μικρὸν ἔμπροσθεν ἐφάνη καὶ τοῖς ἄλλοις Φοίνιξι καὶ ῥήτωρ ἐνομίσθη (*Ep.* 693.4).

70. Libanius's student Hyperechius offers a good example of a young man who expected higher offices than he was ever likely to receive. For an example of his disappointment when offered only a middling office, see Libanius, *Ep.* 1441.

71. A perfect example of an established figure investing in a rising star is Praetextatus's sponsorship of Symmachus for an imperial embassy in 368. On this, see Sogno, *Symmachus*, 6.

72. Libanius, *Epp.* 1001, 1002, 1023.

73. John Lydus, *De mens.* 4.2. The date of Praetextatus's birth is uncertain. A reference in the *Carmen contra paganos* (line 67) that states that its subject was an ephebe for sixty years cannot be taken as a definitive statement of Praetextatus's age (contra Barnes, *Constantine*, 127). This imprecision is matched by a similarly round number of years of purity following Praetextatus's *taurobolium* (line 62). In addition, a more precise number of years would throw off the meter of the line. It is preferable to follow M. Kahlos, *Vettius Agorius Praetextatus: A Senatorial Life in Between* (Rome, 2002), 17, who places Praetextatus's birth somewhere between 314 and 319, with the later years in this range perhaps most likely.

74. If, as has been argued, his role in this ceremony was that of a minor, this would be the first event in his career, and he would have been about ten years old when it happened. For this interpretation of Lydus's passage, see J. Rüpke, *Fasti sacerdotum* (Oxford, 2008), 948 n. 1. Kahlos, *Praetextatus*, 17–20, argues that Lydus may here refer to a different Praetextatus, but I find Rüpke's argument persuasive.

75. A number of surviving inscriptions preserve all or part of the *cursus honorum* of Praetextatus (*CIL* 6.1777 and 1778 = Dessau 1258 omit his earliest offices; *CIL* 6.1779 = D 1259 gives a full *cursus honorum*). Unlike many other career inscriptions of Roman notables, that of Praetextatus lists his sacred offices separately from those *in re publica vero*. For the dating of the priesthoods, see Rüpke, *Fasti sacerdotum,* no. 3468. For a possible explanation of the separation of priesthoods and other offices, see Cameron, *Last Pagans,* 139–41. For the political offices, see Kahlos, *Praetextatus,* 28–31.

76. For these ages, see Kahlos, *Praetextatus,* 29. *CTh* 6.4.1 mandates a minimum age of sixteen for a quaestor.

77. Both *CIL* 6.314a and 6.318 record praetors who already held priesthoods. Iunius Priscillianus Maximus held two priesthoods while praetor in the 290s (*PLRE* 1.589). For discussion, see Cameron, *Last Pagans,* 137.

78. Rüpke (*Fasti sacerdotum,* 948) places his time as *corrector* before 350, though that is nothing more than a rough estimate. His father may well have held the office between 307 and 312. For this, see J. Matthews, *Western Aristocracies and Imperial Court, A.D. 364–425* (Oxford, 1975), 26. For the likelihood that Praetextatus secured this position because his family owned land in the region, see Kahlos, *Praetextatus,* 30.

79. This is something of an exceptional appointment. Men of lower status usually governed Lusitania. On this, see Kahlos, *Praetextatus,* 31.

80. See Sogno, *Symmachus,* 2–6, for the ways in which young men could use friendships to find their way onto embassies.

81. For priesthoods seen in this way, see M. Salzman, *The Making of a Christian Aristocracy* (Cambridge, MA, 2002), 134–35; and Cameron, *Last Pagans,* 150–51.

82. For the duties of the praetorship in the fourth century, see *CTh* 6.4.3, 16; Cameron, *Last Pagans,* 137; A. Chastagnol, *Le sénat romain à l'époque imperial* (Paris, 1992), 243–47.

83. The bulk of laws about quaestors and praetors in the *Theodosian Code* regulates the obligations of officeholders to put on these games (*CTh* 6.4.1–34).

84. Olympiodorus, fr. 41 provides the range of costs. For the nature of these games, see Brown, *Through the Eye of a Needle*, 65–69, 116–19.

85. For the selection of animals, see Symmachus, *Epp.* 6.43 and 9.141 (crocodiles); 2.72 (bears); 2.76 (lions); 2.46 (Saxon prisoners to fight as gladiators). This broad collection of animals was not unique to the officeholders in the city of Rome. Libanius indicates that the Syriarch brought together a similarly diverse collection of fauna.

86. Libanius's letters indicate competition for the best athletes (*Ep.* 1183) and animals (*Ep.* 1400; cf. Symmachus, *Ep.* 2.76). He elsewhere complains about having to replace animals at short notice when imperial officials requisitioned those he had secured for a Syriarch so that they could instead be used for an imperial festival (*Ep.* 218). Sponsors of games in Rome certainly faced similar challenges.

87. Symmachus, *Ep.* 2.81. See Brown, *Through the Eye of a Needle*, 118; Cameron, *Last Pagans*, 712–42. On the preparations for Memmius's games, see Sogno, *Symmachus*, 77.

88. *CIL* 6.1780.

89. *CIL* 6.1779.

90. Praetextatus and his wife wrote poems expressing their affection for one another and arranged for them to be inscribed on a four-sided monument (*CIL* 6.1779). About Paulina, Praetextatus wrote: "Paulina, the partnership of our heart is the origin of your propriety; it is the bond of chastity and pure love and fidelity born in heaven. To this partnership I entrusted the hidden secrets of my mind; it was a gift of the gods, who bind our marriage couch with loving and chaste bonds" (trans. Lefkowitz and Fant).

91. C. Sogno, "Roman Matchmaking," in McGill, Sogno, and Watts, *From the Tetrarchs to the Theodosians*, 55–71.

92. This lost work is noted by Boethius (*De int.* pp. 3–4) and is a significant project not much shorter than the original text. For discussion, see now Cameron, *Last Pagans*, 543.

93. For this, see R.H. Green, *The Works of Ausonius* (Oxford, 1991), 352–54.

94. Ausonius 1.1.17.

95. Ausonius 1.1.23 explains that he held teaching appointments in Gaul for thirty years before he was summoned to court to teach the emperor's son Gratian.

96. Ausonius, *Professores* 24.

97. He was a "fellow student and master and colleague" (condiscipulum atque magistrum collegamque) (*Professores* 3.1).

98. *Professores* 19 and 20.

99. Her father, Attusius Lucanus Talisius, died before her marriage to Ausonius (*Parentalia* 10).

100. On the wealth and prominence of Ausonius's family, see H. Sivan, *Ausonius of Bordeaux: Genesis of a Gallic Aristocracy* (London, 1993), 49–72.

101. For their Paphlagonian origins, see Themistius, *Or.* 2.28d and 27.333c-d; J. Vanderspoel, *Themistius and the Imperial Court* (Ann Arbor, MI, 1995), 31–32.

102. On the family's modest wealth, see Themistius, *Or.* 2.28d, 23.291d.

103. For honors to Themistius's grandfather, see *Or.* 5.63d and the discussion of this passage in Vanderspoel, *Themistius,* 32–33. For Eugenius's reputation in Constantinople, see *Or. Const.* 22b-23b, 28d.

104. Vanderspoel, *Themistius,* 34–35, on the basis of *Or.* 27.332d-333a.

105. *Oration* 23, delivered in 357, indicates that Themistius had been in Constantinople for twenty years (for the 357 date, see the discussion of Vanderspoel, *Themistius,* 35). Beginning the study of philosophy at the age of twenty was not atypical (Proclus, for example, began serious philosophical study in his early twenties), and there is no reason to suppose a date earlier than 337 for Themistius's arrival in the city. On the view that Themistius was not native to Constantinople, see too R. Penella, *Private Orations of Themistius* (Berkeley, 2000), 1–2 (argued on the basis of *Or.* 17.214).

106. Libanius arrived in Nicomedia in 344, and he does not seem to have become well acquainted with Themistius until around 350 (suggested by Libanius, *Ep.* 793). This may suggest that Themistius left the city before Libanius arrived, but one cannot take this evidence as definitive. For Themistius's time in Nicomedia, see too Vanderspoel, *Themistius,* 42–49.

107. *Or.* 24.302, trans. Penella.

108. *Or.* 24.303.

109. *Or.* 24.303.

110. Vanderspoel, *Themistius,* 48, sees Nicomedian sophists as his rivals.

111. Lucian's *Eunuchos* gives an exaggerated, but not entirely unrealistic version of the ancient job talk and selection process.

112. He taught Plato's *Laws* to the future emperor Julian in Constantinople in that year (Julian, *Letter to Themistius* 257d-258d). For discussion of the date, see P. Heather and D. Moncur, *Politics, Philosophy, and Empire: Select Orations of Themistius* (Liverpool, 2001), 43.

113. *Or.* 24.302d, though the context perhaps suggests that one should question somewhat the significance of the assertion.

114. The date of 347 has been proposed on the basis of *CTh* 11.36.8, a law that places Constantius in Ancyra on March 8, 347. For arguments in favor of this date, see Vanderspoel, *Themistius,* 48, 73–77; Heather and Moncur, *Politics, Philosophy, and Empire,* 4, 69–71. Even if, as Vanderspoel suggests, Themistius at that time resided in Ancyra and gave this speech as part of the imperial adventus to the city, he still relied on well-placed friends to secure him that honor. It is perhaps just as likely that, like Libanius's friend Bassus's visits to various governors, Themistius traveled to the emperor in order to deliver a prepared panegyric.

115. *Or.* 21.244b. The name of his wife is unknown, as is the identity of her father (though Vanderspoel, *Themistius,* 41, suggests it might have been Maximus of Byzantium).

116. Libanius, *Ep.* 575 (on the son); Themistius, *In Arist. phys.* 6.2 (for multiple children). For discussion, see Vanderspoel, *Themistius,* 40–42; Penella, *Private Orations,* 40–43.

117. Marriages between philosophical families were not uncommon in late antiquity. See, for example, the marriage between Aedesia and Hermeias (Damascius, *Vit. Is.* 56).

118. In the fourth century, both Himerius and Augustine translated their professional success as rhetoricians into marriage arrangements of this kind. Himerius came from a wealthy Bithynian family but married into the Athenian intellectual dynasty of Minucianus and Nicagoras after he had established himself as a rhetorician in Athens (*Or.* 7.4, 8.21). Augustine came from a curial family in Thagaste but translated his appointment to the chair of rhetoric in Milan into a marriage arrangement with a young heiress that he would later break off.

119. *Or.* 21.244.

120. *Or.* 11.158–62, 19.45.46, 20.18–20. For discussion of this rebellion and its consequences, see G. Downey, *A History of Antioch in Syria* (Princeton, NJ, 1961), 330. For his family background, see J.H.W.G. Liebeschuetz, *Antioch: City and Imperial Administration in the Later Roman Empire* (Oxford, 1972), 1–2; J. Wintjes, *Das Leben des Libanius* (Rahden, 2005), 43–62.

121. Libanius, *Or.* 1.2.

122. *Or.* 1.5 (games of Panolbius). For discussion of these activities and their significance in fourth-century Antioch, see S. Bradbury, *Selected Letters of Libanius* (Liverpool, 2004), 1–2, 27; G. Downey, "The Olympic Games of Antioch in the Fourth Century A.D.," *TAPA* 70 (1939): 428–38; Liebeschuetz, *Antioch*, 136–44.

123. Libanius, *Epp.* 217, 218, 219, 544, 545. The unnamed cousin served as Syriarch from 356 until at least 360, at which point the expense of the position exceeded his resources. For the obligations of the Syriarch, see Liebeschuetz, *Antioch*, 141–44.

124. *Or.* 1.4.

125. *Or.* 1.6, LCL trans.

126. *Or.* 1.5.

127. This was Celsus, who drew on Libanius's connections to get animals and performers for the games (e.g., Libanius, *Ep.* 1400). See Liebeschuetz, *Antioch*, 141.

128. *Or.* 1.12.

129. *Or.* 1.11–12.

130. For discussion of Athenian student life, see chapter 2.

131. A point that he makes repeatedly in *Or.* 1.17–24. This section of the *Oration* seems more to prescribe how a student ought to behave than to describe how Libanius actually did behave.

132. *Or.* 1.24–25. For the context, see Watts, *City and School,* 45–46.

133. *Or.* 1.25.

134. *Or.* 1.25. For student violence in situations like this, see chapter 2; and E. Watts, *Riot in Alexandria* (Berkeley, 2010), 28–52.

135. *Or.* 1.25–26.

136. *Or.* 1.29.

137. *Or.* 1.30, LCL trans.

138. *Or.* 1.31.

139. *Or.* 1.32–35.

140. *Or.* 1.36. This was Flavius Dionysius, *consularis Syriae* 329–35.

141. *Or.* 1.37.

142. *Or.* 1.44; Eunapius, *VS* 495 describes the pederasty charge. Robin Lane Fox has discussed the possible nature of this charge in an unpublished paper. For more discussion of this pederasty accusation, its plausibility, and the use of sexual innuendo in invective, see Cribiore, *Libanius the Sophist,* 46–48 (pederasty) and 78–79 (sexual accusations in invective).

143. For the rhetorical nature of this text, see now Van Hoof, "Libanius' *Life* and Life," in *The Cambridge Companion to Libanius,* ed. L. Van Hoof (Cambridge, 2014).

144. *Or.* 1.48. Libanius says comparatively little about the two years he spent in Nicaea.

145. *Or.* 1.48.

146. *Or.* 1.74.

147. This is *Oration* 59. On it, see P.-L. Malosse, "Libanios, Discours 59: Texte, traduction et commentaire" (PhD diss., Montpelier, 1998).

CHAPTER 4. MOVING UP IN AN AGE OF UNCERTAINTY

1. In effect, they now legally held *patria postestas,* a status that gave them legal authority over most members of the household. For the general applicability of this traditional Roman concept after 212, see A. Arjava, "Paternal Power in Late Antiquity," *JRS* 88 (1998): 147–65. Note, however, K. Cooper's excellent discussion of shifting familial dynamics in late antiquity (*The Fall of the Roman Household* [Cambridge, 2007]) and the way that they influenced the understood prerogatives of older men.

2. On details of this system, see N. Lenski, "The Reign of Constantine," in *The Cambridge Companion to the Age of Constantine,* ed. N. Lenski (Cambridge, 2006), 59–90; T. D. Barnes, *Constantine: Dynasty, Religion and Power in the Later Roman Empire* (London, 2011), 164–68.

3. On the possibility that Constantius initiated this massacre, see R. Burgess, "The Summer of Blood: The Great Massacre of 337 and the Promotion of the Sons of Constantine," *DOP* 62 (2008): 5–51, at 42.

4. *PLRE* 1.3–4: Ablablius 4. On his fall, probably as a result of some trickery by people at court, see Eunapius, *VS* 464; Zosimus 2.40.3; Jerome, *Chron.* s.a. 338.

5. Rome was held for much of June by Nepotianus (a member of the family of Constantine) before being retaken by forces loyal to Magnentius. The massacre that Nepotianus ordered after taking the city means that all historical sources take a hostile view of him, a fact that makes any reconstruction of the causes and initial popularity of his rebellion quite difficult. Vetranio, the figure who took control of Illyricum before Magnentius could do so, is portrayed as a usurper by Aurelius Victor (*Caes.* 41–42), but Philostorgius (*HE* 3.22) and Ammianus (21.8.1) suggest that Vetranio was instead a sort of placeholder for Constantius. His proclamation as Augustus was planned so as to keep Illyricum from Magnentius. This seems the best way to understand Vetranio's decision to mint coins with Constantius's portraits on the obverse and Concordia Militum on the reverse alongside coins with his own portrait and the identical reverse of Concordia Militum at the mints under his control in Siscia (these are *RIC*

VIII.284 and 286 [Constantius] and *RIC* VIII.274, 277, 281 [Vetranio]). It also explains his willingness to turn his territories over to Constantius when Constantius arrived in December 350, and his subsequent comfortable retirement on an estate. For more details on this reading of events, see T. D. Barnes, *Athanasius and Constantius* (Cambridge, MA, 1993), 101–5; Vanderspoel, *Themistius and the Imperial Court* (Ann Arbor, MI, 1995), 85.

6. On Gallus's proclamation as Caesar, see Ammianus 14.1.1; Eutropius 10.12.2; Aurelius Victor, *Caes.* 42.9; Philostorgius, *HE* 3.25.

7. Magnentius was defeated at the battle of Mons Seleucus. He committed suicide on August 10, eight days after the battle.

8. For Gallus's problems, in particular with the populace of Antioch, see Ammianus 14.7; and J. Matthews, *The Roman Empire of Ammianus* (Ann Arbor, MI, 2007), 406–8. For his execution, see Ammianus 14.11.

9. On the usurpation of Silvanus, see Ammianus 14.5–6. For discussion of Silvanus's background and the possible circumstances leading to his revolt, see J. Drinkwater, *The Alamanni and Rome, 213–496 (Caracalla to Clovis)* (Oxford, 2007), 151–53, 211–15.

10. For these charges, see Athanasius, *Festal Letter* 4.5; *Defense against the Arians* 60.4; *Festal Index* 3; Barnes, *Athanasius and Constantius,* 21–22.

11. Socrates, *HE* 2.22; Rufinus, *HE* 10.20; Philostorgius, *HE* 3.12; Theodoret, *HE* 2.8. For discussion of this, see E. Watts, *Riot in Alexandria* (Berkeley, 2010), 180; Barnes, *Athanasius and Constantius,* 63–70, 89–91.

12. This is described in Athanasius's *Defense before Constantius* (*Apol. ad. Const.* 6–11), a version of events clearly edited to reflect well on Athanasius. Athanasius claims that this was done informally, and, though accusers produced a copy of a letter Athanasius had written to Magnentius, Athanasius denied that he ever exchanged any letters with the usurper (9, 11). For discussion of Athanasius's interaction with Magnentius, see Barnes, *Athanasius and Constantius,* 102–4.

13. Athanasius, *Apol. ad. Const.* 10.

14. Barnes, *Athanasius and Constantius,* 102–5, 279 n. 37.

15. Athanasius, *Hist. Ar.* 51.4. For discussion, see Barnes, *Athanasius and Constantius,* 104.

16. Ammianus 30.7. For Gratian's career, see N. Lenski, *Failure of Empire: Valens and the Roman State in the Fourth Century* (Berkeley, 2002), 38–41.

17. Ammianus 14.5, trans. Hamilton. For punishments after fall of Gallus, see Ammianus 15.3. For those following the rebellion of Silvanus, see Ammianus 15.6. For a critical discussion of Ammianus's presentation of the political climate, see Matthews, *Roman Empire of Ammianus,* 33–39.

18. For discussion, see Barnes, *Athanasius and Constantius,* 109–19.

19. *CTh* 16.10.2, trans. Pharr. Here again there is no evidence of anyone actually being prosecuted for violating this law.

20. All of this occurs in Maternus's *De errore profanarum religionum,* a work dated between 343 and 350. For this work, see now J. Lössl, "Profaning and Proscribing: Escalating Rhetorical Violence in Fourth Century Christian Apologetic," in *The Purpose of Rhetoric in Late Antiquity: From Performance to Exegesis,* ed. A. J. Quiroga Puertas (Tübingen, 2013), 71–90 and 74–75, for Maternus's exhortation to the emperors.

252 | Notes to Pages 87–89

21. Maternus, *De errore* 16.4, trans. Forbes.

22. Maternus, *De errore* 20.7, trans. Forbes.

23. Maternus, *De errore,* 16.4–5, trans. Forbes.

24. The manuscripts of the *Theodosian Code* date this law, *CTh* 16.10.4, to 346, but its addressee, the praetorian prefect Taurus, held office from 355 to 361. The dating of the addressee is more convincing based on the evident contextual relationship to *CTh* 16.10.6.

25. For sacrifices continuing, see, for example, Ammianus 19.12. On the difficult implementation of these laws, see S. Bradbury, "Constantine and Anti-Pagan Legislation in the Fourth Century," *CP* 89 (1994): 137.

26. Note Bradbury, "Anti-Pagan Legislation," 136–37.

27. *CTh* 16.10.3, November 1, 342. The law effectively attempts to reclassify as entertainment some of the most popular temple functions. On this intention of the law, see M. Salzman, "Religious *Koine* and Religious Dissent in the Fourth Century," in *Blackwell's Companion to Roman Religion,* ed. J. Rüpke (Oxford, 2007), 116–18.

28. On the Caesareum transfer, see C. Haas, *Alexandria in Late Antiquity: Topography and Social Conflict* (Baltimore, 1997), 210. Constantius also transferred to Christian ownership a basilica that once contained a subterranean Mithraeum (Rufinus, *HE* 11.22; Sozomen *HE* 7.15).

29. It seems that six are known (the temples at Cyzicus, Aegeae, Arethusa, Heliopolis, Gaza, and Alexandria). For discussion, see T. D. Barnes, "Christians and Pagans in the Reign of Constantius," in *L'Église et l'empire au IVe Siècle,* ed. A. Dihle (Geneva, 1989), 301–43, at 325–28; P. Heather and D. Moncur, *Politics, Philosophy, and Empire: Select Orations of Themistius* (Liverpool, 2001), 52 n. 26.

30. E.g., Libanius, *Epp.* 724, 763, 1364.

31. They were not the only ones. As R. von Haehling has shown (*Die Religionszugehörigkeit der hohen Amtsträger des römischen Reiches seit Constantins I. Alleinherrschaft bis zum Ende der theodosianischen Dynastie* [Bonn, 1978]), a large majority of the people who served under Constantius can be identified as non-Christian.

32. E.g., Themistius, *Or.* 6.74b-c, 76 a-b. For discussion, see Heather and Moncur, *Politics, Philosophy, and Empire,* 25.

33. Themistius, *Or.* 5. This oration was designed to generate support for a policy that the emperor Jovian wanted to implement. Themistius almost certainly supported the policy, but this speech was also a piece of political propaganda that must be read cautiously. For discussion, see Heather and Moncur, *Politics, Philosophy, and Empire,* 144.

34. Libanius, *Or.* 30.7.

35. Libanius, *Ep.* 283.3–4.

36. Libanius, *Epp.* 695, 727, 1342. The monody is impossible to date, but the correspondence praising it comes from the reign of Julian. It is notable that Eusebius credits Constantine not Constantius with destroying the temple (see chapter 2).

37. Ammianus 16.10; Symmachus, *Rel.* 3.7. For discussion of this visit, see Salzman, "Religious *Koine*," 109–10.

38. Libanius's comment that "whoever does not long for the abyss will choose to hide the speech" about Gallus suggests that people understood that there were social and professional consequences for antagonizing emperors even if there were no legal prohibitions on speech. For a larger discussion of freedom of expression in late antiquity, see E. Watts, "Freedom of Speech and Self-Censorship," *Revue Belge*, forthcoming.

39. For dating, see chapter 3.

40. This identity is claimed immediately, at *Or.* 1.1a. For discussion, see Heather and Moncur, *Politics, Philosophy, and Empire*, 73–77.

41. For discussion, see Vanderspoel, *Themistius*, 88–89.

42. *Demegoria Constantii* 19b, trans. Heather and Moncur, with slight modifications; all translated passages of the *Dem. Const.* are based on the translation of Heather and Moncur.

43. *Dem. Const.* 20a.

44. *Dem. Const.* 20c.

45. *Dem. Const.* 21b.

46. As stated in *Dem. Const.* 20c. For discussion, see Heather and Moncur, *Politics, Philosophy, and Empire*, 4–5.

47. This perspective on his reign is particularly seen in later discussions like those of Ammianus (14.5) and Libanius (*Or.* 30.7), but these were written by men who lived through the period. They likely reflect contemporary suspicions as well as later attitudes.

48. This speech is *Oration 4*.

49. On this oration and the possibility that the ending of our text was delivered separately, see J. Vanderspoel, "A Tale of Two Cities: Themistius on Rome and Constantinople," in *Two Romes: Rome and Constantinople in Late Antiquity*, ed. G. Kelly and L. Grig (Oxford, 2012), 223–40.

50. Heather and Moncur, *Politics, Philosophy, and Empire*, 117.

51. Heather and Moncur, *Politics, Philosophy, and Empire*, 117; Matthews, *Roman Empire of Ammianus*, 231–35.

52. Ammianus 16.10; Symmachus, *Rel.* 3.7. On these colleges and Constantius's actions related to them, see Alan Cameron, *The Last Pagans of Rome* (Oxford, 2012), 33; contra J. Rüpke, *Fasti sacerdotum* (Oxford, 2008), 58.

53. Ammianus 16.10.

54. For discussion of this passage, see J. Francis, "Late Antique Visuality," in *Shifting Cultural Frontiers in Late Antiquity*, ed. D. Brakke, D. Deliyannis, and E. Watts (Aldershot, 2012), 139–49, at 143–46.

55. For the purpose and dating of the speech, I here follow the arguments of Heather and Moncur, *Politics, Philosophy, and Empire*, 114–25.

56. Themistius, *Or.* 3.41b (all translated passages of *Or.* 3 are based on the translation of Heather and Moncur).

57. *Or.* 3.42d.

58. *Or.* 3.45b.

59. *Or.* 3.45b.

60. *Or.* 3.46c.

61. I thank Michele Salzman for this view of the purpose of Constantius's visit.

254 | Notes to Pages 92–95

62. The prefect, Memmius Vitrasius Orfitus, erected a temple of Apollo during his time in office (*CIL* 6.45 = D 3222).

63. Vanderspoel, "A Tale of Two Cities," argues that these features of the speech were not part of the oration given in Rome, largely on the basis of the positive reaction Romans seem to have had to the speech.

64. On the administrative transformation from a proconsul to prefect, see G. Dagron, *Naissance d'une capitale* (Paris, 1974), 213–39.

65. On the senatorial expansion and equivalence, see Heather and Moncur, *Politics, Philosophy, and Empire*, 122–23; P. Heather, "New Men for New Constantines?," in *New Constantines: The Rhythm of Imperial Renewal in Byzantium, 4th–13th Centuries*, ed. P. Magdalino (Aldershot, 1994), 11–33.

66. Against the view that the transfers of senators from Rome to Constantinople began in the later 350s, see A. Skinner, "The Early Development of the Senate of Constantinople," *BMGS* 32 (2008): 128–48.

67. He alludes to this trip in *Or.* 34.13.

68. Libanius, *Ep.* 40.1, trans. Bradbury.

69. *CTh* 6.4.12. The specific office mentioned here is the praetorship, the key office that began the public career of senatorial youths.

70. On their relationship in this period, see the overview in J. Wintjes, *Das Leben des Libanius* (Rahden, 2005), 135–43. I am less inclined than he to see a rivalry between the two men during the later 350s.

71. *Ep.* 476. See the discussion in Wintjes, *Libanius*, 139.

72. E.g., *Epp.* 40, 62, 70, 76, 86, 252.

73. The panegyric is *Oration* 59. For text and discussion, see P.-L. Malosse, *Libanios, Discours 59: Texte, traduction et commentaire* (Montpelier, 1998).

74. Eunapius suggests that charges of pederasty may have driven Libanius from Constantinople, charges examined critically by R. Cribiore, *Libanius the Sophist: Rhetoric, Reality, and Religion in the Fourth Century* (Ithaca, NY, 2013), 46–47. For more discussion, see chapter 3.

75. *Or.* 1.77.

76. A plague forced him to leave in the summer of 350. A food shortage did the same in 351 (*Or.* 1.77).

77. *Or.* 1.80–85. For discussion, see Wintjes, *Libanius*, 99–100.

78. *Or.* 1.86. Cribiore (*Libanius the Sophist,* 48) rightly highlights the similarities between Libanius's narration of his return to Antioch and Aristides's discussion of his return to Smyrna in the *Sacred Tales*.

79. *Or.* 1.86, trans. Norman.

80. For Gallus, see *Or.* 1.88, 91. For the promised salary see *Or.* 1.92.

81. On this arrangement, see S. Bradbury, *Selected Letters of Libanius* (Liverpool, 2004), 7.

82. *Or.* 1.94.

83. *Or.* 1.95.

84. *Or.* 1.96–97. Libanius here deliberately downplays his closeness to Gallus, the figure on whom he thought his return to Antioch would depend.

85. *Or.* 1.101–2. The broader Antiochene setting is described in Libanius, *Or.* 22.31; *Or.* 5.45–52; cf. Cribiore, *School of Libanius*, 44.

86. For a description of the Antiochene classrooms in which Libanius taught, see *Or.* 5.45–52.

87. E.g., Libanius, *Ep.* 454.

88. For these demographic figures, see Laes, *Children in the Roman Empire,* 50–56; and chapter 1.

89. Possibly as many as half of Roman men had lost their fathers by the age of twenty-five, and, by the age of forty, most were fatherless. For discussion, see Arjava, "Paternal Power," 148.

90. Eugenius died in 355, and Themistius's son in 357. The death of his wife cannot be dated securely, but it must have occurred by 359, the probable date of Libanius, *Ep.* 241. For the death of Themistius's father, see Vanderspoel, *Themistius,* 89; Penella, *Private Orations of Themistius* (Berkeley, 2000), 10. For the wife and son, see Vanderspoel, *Themistius,* 40–42.

91. For his wife and child, see *Dem. Const.* 22. For the presence of his fathers, see *Dem. Const.* 23.

92. This type of reaction cannot be taken for granted. As men reached middle age, those with living fathers sometimes injudiciously complained that their fathers were hanging on for too long and, as a result, depriving them of their inheritance (e.g., John Chrysostom, *In Coloss.* 1.3).

93. *Or.* 20.233. Claims like these should not be taken at face value when they serve a clear rhetorical purpose, but they should not be discounted entirely either.

94. *Or.* 20.233.

95. *Or.* 20.237.

96. *Or.* 20.237.

97. *Or.* 20.236.

98. The estate is described in *Oration* 20. The location of "this piece of land that did not have a very Hellenic name" is probably in Eugenius's native Paphlagonia. For this, see Penella, *Private Orations,* 56 n. 11. All translated passages of *Or.* 20 are based on Penella's translation.

99. On some level, it seems that Themistius may have wanted to follow his father into a country retirement—he even composed a short oration (*Or.* 30) that equates farming and philosophical virtue—but he could never make the pursuit of this sort of "philosophical leisure" a full-time activity without abandoning the city.

100. E.g., Libanius, *Epp.* 115, 126.

101. For this date, see Libanius, *Ep.* 575; Penella, *Private Orations,* 42.

102. *Or.* 32.363. For this oration preceding the death of his son, see Vanderspoel, *Themistius,* 41–42; and Penella, *Private Orations,* 42–43.

103. *Or.* 32.356.

104. This is something of a trope in letters of consolation following the death of a spouse or child (e.g., Procopius of Gaza, *Epp.* 102, 125). Compare Himerius, *Or.* 8; and E. Watts, "Himerius and the Personalization of Monody," forthcoming.

105. Libanius, *Ep.* 575.1.

106. Libanius, *Ep.* 241.1, trans. Norman.

107. Libanius, *Ep.* 241.4.

108. This *scholion* is included and translated by A.F. Norman, *Libanius: Autobiography and Selected Letters* (Cambridge, MA, 1992), 1:498.

109. *Or.* 1.117–18, trans. Norman.

110. Nicomedia's earthquake was August 24, 358. Eusebius died in 359 (*Epp.* 263, 1406). Phasganius, his uncle, died in late 359 (*Ep.* 96), and his mother died later that year. On this strategy more generally, see L. Van Hoof, "Libanius *Life* and Life," in *The Cambridge Companion to Libanius,* ed. L. Van Hoof (Cambridge, 2014).

111. Ammianus 17.7.

112. Tsunami: Libanius, *Or.* 61.15; fire: Libanius, *Or.* 61.15; Ammianus 17.7.

113. Ammianus 17.7.7, trans. Hamilton.

114. The road is described by Libanius as "crescent shaped and shady, winding around the edge of the bay" (*Or.* 61.21). This road would certainly have been cut in the aftermath of the quake and tsunami.

115. "Quosdam domorum inclinata fastigia intrinsecus servabant intactos, angore et inedia consumendos" (Ammianus 17.7.6). It is interesting that Ammianus here specifies death by starvation. Not only does this assume that many victims had water in their homes that they consumed while waiting for rescue, but it also means that the agony lasted for many, many days—not just the two or three that dehydration would take.

116. E. Watts, "Historical Context: The Rhetorical Use of Suffering in Libanius' Monodies, Letters, and Autobiography," in *The Cambridge Companion to Libanius,* ed. L. Van Hoof (Cambridge, 2014). For the oration itself and its similarity to a monody penned in the second century by Aelius Aristides, see G. Karla, "Die Klage über die zerstörte Stadt Nikomedeia bei Libanios im Spiegel der Mimesis," in *Theatron: Rhetorical Culture in Late Antiquity and the Middle Ages,* ed. Michael Grünbart, Millenium Studies 13 (Berlin, 2007), 141–56.

117. This letter is *Ep.* 388. Strategius is Strategius Musonianus (*PLRE* 1.611–12). His friendship with Aristaenetus is alluded to in *Epp.* 326, 537, and 561.

118. *Ep.* 388.1, trans. Norman.

119. *Ep.* 388.2.

120. *Ep.* 388.5.

121. The charges are described in *Ep.* 636. The letter is a rhetorical gem. For a discussion of its literary qualities, see J. H. W. G. Liebeschuetz, *Antioch: City and Imperial Administration in the Later Roman Empire* (Oxford, 1972), 19.

122. For the oration on Phasganius, now lost, see *Ep.* 283.1.

123. His influence is suggested by *Or.* 1.116.

124. E.g., *Ep.* 389.3. For discussion, see Bradbury, *Selected Letters,* 187.

125. Discussed in *Epp.* 28, 258, 740.

126. *Ep.* 258.3, trans. Bradbury. On Libanius's relationship with Olympius, see Cribiore, *Libanius the Sophist,* 190–94; and chapter 3.

127. On this marriage, to Panolbius's grandson Bassianus, see Libanius, *Ep.* 1409.

128. *Ep.* 115.2.

129. For discussion of this, see Norman, *Selected Letters,* 2:22–23, note a.

130. *Ep.* 115.3–4.

131. *Ep.* 115.5.

132. *Ep.* 126.

133. The *comes rei privatae* was a natural person to whom someone in Libanius's position would appeal because he was the one who signed off on all transfers of imperial property granted by the emperor. For discussion, see *CTh* 10.8.2 and the analysis of J. N. Dillon, *The Justice of Constantine: Law, Communication, and Control* (Ann Arbor, 2012), 183.

134. Libanius, *Ep.* 192.

135. Ausonius's surviving writings suggest that he spent the 350s teaching in Gaul. Praetextatus's governorship of Lusitania is impossible to date but precedes his proconsulship of Achaea, an office he assumed in 362 (*CIL* 6.31929).

CHAPTER 5. THE APOGEE

1. Libanius, for example, has 1,269 surviving letters as well as 12 orations dating from the period between 355 and 365. For a survey of Julian's writings while in Antioch, see S. Elm, *Sons of Hellenism, Fathers of the Church* (Berkeley, 2012), 269–335. These include a range of materials but, most notably, his *Caesars* (written in December 362), the *Hymn to King Helios* (composed a few days after the *Caesars* [Elm, 287]), the *Misopogon* (datable to January 363), and the *Contra Galilaeos* (written between late 362 and early 363 [Elm, 301, on the basis of Libanius, *Or.* 18.178]).

2. Reign of Julian as sole emperor: November 3, 361–June 26, 363. Reign of Vitellius: April 12–December 24, 69.

3. On *Oration 2*, see Elm, *Sons of Hellenism,* 63; G. Bowersock, *Julian the Apostate* (Cambridge, MA, 1978), 37; P. Athanassiadi-Fowden, *Julian and Hellenism* (Oxford, 1981), 63–68.

4. Ammianus 20.4, trans. Hamilton; cf. Libanius, *Or.* 12.58–61; Zosimus 3.8.3; Julian, *Letter to the Athenians* 279. For discussion, see Elm, *Sons of Hellenism,* 63; J. Matthews, *The Roman Empire of Ammianus,* 2nd ed. (Ann Arbor, MI, 2008), 93–103.

5. Ammianus 19.6. Zosimus 3.8.3 sees Constantius using Amida as an excuse to weaken Julian. Matthews, *Roman Empire of Ammianus,* 94–96, provides a balanced analysis of the real implications of Constantius's losses at Amida, his need for reinforcements, and Julian's reasons for concern.

6. Ammianus 20.4.

7. For discussion, see D. Potter, *Roman Empire at Bay, AD 180–395* (London, 2004), 502–6. I thank an anonymous reader for the Press for calling my attention to this.

8. Florentius (*PLRE* 1: Flavius Florentius 10), the praetorian prefect of Gaul, was in Vienne and refused to come when summoned by Julian. Lupicinus (*PLRE* 1: Flavius Lupicinus 6), the *magister equitum,* was in Britain and could not be consulted. On this, see as well Julian, *Letter to the Athenians* 279–81.

9. Ammianus 20.4.14, LCL trans. On this account, see too Matthews, *Roman Empire of Ammianus,* 97–98.

10. Both Ammianus and Libanius (*Or.* 12.61, 13.33) claim that Julian accepted this acclamation with reluctance, a position that Julian echoes in his *Letter to the Athenians* (279–82). Opinions about the truth of this claim vary.

For a summary and discussion of the various viewpoints, see Elm, *Sons of Hellenism*, 63 n. 6.

11. See chapter 2.

12. Ammianus 20.5.

13. *Letter to the Athenians* 284, LCL trans.

14. Julian's offer and Constantius's response are preserved in Ammianus 20.8–9. Julian sent messengers to the major cities of the south and east of the empire charged with spreading word both of the military victories that he had won as Caesar and of the power-sharing offer he made to Constantius. For this policy, see C. Ando, *Imperial Ideology and Provincial Loyalty in the Roman Empire* (Berkeley, 2000), 195–200. For its logistics, see Potter, *Empire at Bay*, 506.

15. This is most clearly expressed in his *Letter to the Athenians* 270–72 and echoed again at 276. On the *Letter to the Athenians*, see now the excellent treatment of Elm, *Sons of Hellenism*, 75–80.

16. *Letter to the Athenians* 272.

17. On the actions of the Roman senate, see K. Ehling, "Kaiser Julian, der Senat und die Stadt Rom," *ZPE* 137 (2001): 292–96.

18. On this strategy, see Ammianus 21.8; Matthews, *Roman Empire of Ammianus*, 100–105; Potter, *Empire at Bay*, 508.

19. Ammianus 21.7.

20. Even Ammianus (21.7.3) had no doubt about this.

21. The dubious loyalty of Italy is clear from the rebellion of Aquileia in mid-361 (Ammianus 21.11).

22. Ammianus 22.2.

23. Ammianus 22.5, trans. Hamilton.

24. Ammianus (22.5, trans. Hamilton) somewhat overdramatizes things. While he may not have been conducting the energetic public sacrifices that characterized his reign between 361 and 363, Julian had been openly consulting the gods since the time of his proclamation as Augustus (e.g., Eunapius, *VS* 475–76; *Hist.*, fr. 21). For Julian's interest in traditional religion while a student, see also Eunapius, *VS* 473.

25. About his summons from Athens to command in Gaul and the likelihood that he would not succeed, Eunapius wrote, "As Caesar he was dispatched to Gaul, not so much to rule there as with the intention that he should perish by violent means" (*VS* 476, LCL trans.)—a comment that echoes a rumor to which Ammianus also alludes (at 16.11). For an example of his risky tactics, see Ammianus 16.2 and 16.12.28, 36–41.

26. E.g., *To the Cynic Heraclios* 231B–234C; *Letter to the Athenians* 272.

27. For the trials at Chalcedon, see Ammianus 22.3, as well as the discussion of Bowersock, *Julian*, 66–78; Potter, *Empire at Bay*, 515.

28. Ammianus 22.3. Pentadius, who had investigated Julian's brother Gallus and been present at his execution, was acquitted. Palladius, Taurus, Florentius, Euagrius, Saturninus, and Cyrinus were exiled. Ursulus, Apodemius, Paul, and Eusebius were executed. Of these four, Ammianus says that only the execution of Ursulus was a mistake.

29. Those punished for working against Gallus included Palladius, Pentadius, Apodemius, and Paul. Paul, however, had also antagonized Julian when he

kept watch on him for Constantius in 359. For a counterpoint to Ammianus see the (no-more-reliable) comments of Libanius, *Or.* 18.153, which praise Julian's restraint.

30. For a list of figures affected by the leadership change, see G. Dagron, *Naissance d'une capitale* (Paris, 1974), 234 n. 26.

31. Ammianus reports that the barber made "in every day twenty men's allowances of bread and a proportionate amount of fodder for his beasts . . . as well as a substantial annual salary and many profitable prerequisites" (22.4). Libanius says that Constantius employed "a thousand cooks, as many barbers, and even more butlers" (*Or.* 18.130)—a comment that should be taken as an exaggerated representation of popular opinions rather than an accurate number.

32. Bowersock, *Julian*, 72. Nothing like the complaints voiced by John Lydus in the sixth century survives from the bureaucrats laid off by Julian, but similar sentiments were certainly expressed privately. For a discussion of Lydus's complaints and their larger bureaucratic context, see C. Kelly, *Ruling the Later Roman Empire* (Cambridge, MA, 2004), 12–15 (on Lydus's complaints), 220–21 (on Julian's purge).

33. On the philosophical character of Julian's court and its reflection in the works written in Constantinople during his time there, see Elm, *Sons of Hellenism*, 88–143.

34. Elm, *Sons of Hellenism*, 92.

35. For this idea and its genesis, see chapter 2.

36. For discussion, see chapter 4.

37. *CTh* 16.10.6. For discussion of this law and its context, see chapter 4. Libanius claims that Julian's intervention brought back sacrifices and festivals "which only a few old men were left to remember" (*Or.* 1.119), but this claim is plainly not true and contradicted by statements that Libanius makes elsewhere. For Julian and sacrifices, see S. Bradbury, "Julian's Pagan Revival and the Decline of Blood Sacrifice," *Phoenix* 49 (1995): 331–56. On the persistence of sacrifices in the West well beyond this date, see M. Salzman, "The End of Public Sacrifice: Changing Definitions of Sacrifice in Post-Constantinian Rome and Italy," in *Ancient Mediterranean Sacrifice*, ed. J. Wright Knust and Z. Várhelyi (Oxford, 2011), 174–77. Note too Neil McLynn's discussion of the *taurobolium* (N. McLynn, "The Fourth Century *Taurobolium*," *Phoenix* 50 [1996]: 312–30).

38. E.g., the prefect Anatolius, described by Eunapius as regularly sacrificing under Constantius (*VS* 490). Libanius's remarks to Julian and those serving under him about people "who sacrificed even when it was forbidden" (e.g., *Ep.* 1351) suggest that some people's behavior may have been influenced by these laws. On problems with accepting claims like this uncritically, see I. Sandwell, *Religious Identity in Late Antiquity: Greeks, Jews, and Christians in Antioch* (Cambridge, 2007), 7–8, 91–120.

39. See chapter 4.

40. Julian, *Ep.* 60 (Hertlein = *Ep.* 21 Wright = *Ep.* 60 Bidez-Cumont).

41. Rufinus, *HE* 11.22.

42. *Misop.* 346B. On this, see the discussion of Matthews, *Roman Empire of Ammianus*, 439–41; Bowersock, *Julian*, 81. For the relics of Babylas, see now the discussion of C. Shepardson, *Controlling Contested Places: Late Antique*

Antioch and the Spatial Politics of Religious Controversy (Berkeley, 2014), 58–91.

43. Zonaras 13.12 suggests that at least some of the pieces were used to construct a Christian church. For discussion of other temples destroyed under Constantius, see T.D. Barnes, "Christians and Pagans in the Reign of Constantius," in *L'Église et l'empire au IVe Siècle,* ed. A. Dihle (Geneva, 1989), 301–43, at 325–28; P. Heather and D. Moncur, *Politics, Philosophy, and Empire: Select Orations of Themistius* (Liverpool, 2001), 52 n. 26.

44. As David Potter has shown (*Roman Empire at Bay,* 509), Julian did in fact see a place for Christianity in this new world—but as a component of a broader, polytheistic religious system in which Christ was one among many divine figures (cf. Julian, *Caesars* 336A-B).

45. For discussion of Julian's ideas on the duties of these priests, see Elm, *Sons of Hellenism,* 321–24.

46. *Letter to a Priest* 288D.

47. *Letter to a Priest* 290D. For discussion of philanthropy in Julian's priesthood, see Elm, *Sons of Hellenism,* 322; P. Athanassiadi-Fowden, *Julian and Hellenism* (Oxford, 1981), 187–89. For a different view of Julian's motivations, see Bowersock, *Julian,* 87–89.

48. *Letter to a Priest* 291C.

49. Julian, *Ep.* 63 (Hertlein = *Ep.* 20 Wright = *Ep.* 89a Bidez-Cumont). Cf. Julian, *Ep.* 62 (Hertlein = *Ep.* 18 Wright = *Ep.* 88 Bidez-Cumont).

50. Note, for example, Libanius, *Epp.* 757, 770.

51. Libanius, *Ep.* 1351

52. Julian, *Misopogon* 362A-B.

53. The refusal to offer sacrifice was at the heart of many cases brought against early Christians, and these cases were dismissed if a Christian could show evidence that he had sacrificed. Whether or not he believed in Christ was legally irrelevant. The same was true of the Constantinian and Constantian laws against traditional religion, all of which regulated activities not ideas.

54. The need to distinguish between the famous Julianic law against Christian teachers and the law found in the *Theodosian Code* has been described by E. Watts, *City and School in Late Antique Athens and Alexandria* (Berkeley, 2006), 68–76; Elm, *Sons of Hellenism,* 139–43; J. Matthews, *Laying Down the Law* (New Haven, CT, 2000), 274–77; and T. Banchich, "Julian's School Laws: *Cod. Theod.* 13.3.5 and *Ep.* 42," *Ancient World* 24 (1993): 5–14. For the idea that this law could potentially be applied against pagan teachers too, see J. Stenger, *Hellenische Identität in der Spätantike* (Berlin, 2009), 101–10. There are, however, no clear cases of this actually happening.

55. *CTh* 13.3.5, trans. Pharr, with slight modifications.

56. Latin: "si quisque docere vult."

57. *CTh* 13.3.5, trans. Pharr, with slight modifications.

58. Moral uprightness had long been an important qualification for teachers (e.g., Quintilian, *Inst. or.* 12.1.1, though the notion itself far preceded him).

59. For Ammonius and this tendency in other late antique philosophical circles, see E. Watts, "Doctrine, Anecdote, and Action: Reconsidering the Social History of the Last Platonists (c. 430-c. 550 CE)," *CP* 106 (2011): 226–44.

60. Banchich, "Julian's School Laws," 13. Given the administrative challenges of creating the register of teachers mandated by *CTh* 13.3.5, the second law was likely issued in the late summer.

61. Julian, *Ep.* 42 (Hertlein = *Ep.* 36 Wright = *Ep.* 61 Bidez-Cumont), LCL trans., with slight modifications.

62. This reflects Julian's own biography. The future emperor was first taught classical texts by Christian teachers. Some of these, like Mardonius, were teachers capable of refined thought (for Mardonius, see *Misopogon* 252A–254C; and Bowersock, *Julian*, 24). Others, like the eunuchs who kept guard over Julian in Cappadocia, were less able (Eunapius famously derides them in *VS* 473). These men carefully constructed their lessons to prevent the prince from thinking seriously about the pagan content of the texts he was reading. This was only undone when Julian was allowed to begin studying classical philosophical texts with the pagan Maximus of Ephesus. Then, in response to the "correct" training he received in that school, Julian became a convert to paganism. See Libanius, *Or.* 12.34 and 13.12 for a discussion of Julian's conversion and its significance. See also Bowersock, *Julian*, 29ff.

63. E.g., R. Lamberton, *Homer the Theologian* (Berkeley, 1986).

64. As I. Sandwell has shown (*Religious Identity*, 132–46), by the end of the fourth century, Christians had come closer to demarcating which beliefs and behaviors were and were not properly Christian, but, even then, there was no practical consensus among Christians. Pagans, for their part, had not really undertaken any similar efforts. In the 360s, however, neither group had really gotten very far in this process.

65. Prohaeresius was the most prominent (see Watts, *City and School*, 68–77), but other sources indicate that it was widely applied (e.g., Jerome, *Chron.* 242f.; Gregory of Nazianzen, *Or.* 4.12; Socrates, *HE* 3.5–6; Sozomen, *HE* 5.12; Theodoret, *HE* 3.4.2 and 5.1).

66. Elm, *Sons of Hellenism*, 271–73.

67. Ammianus 25.3. For a thorough discussion of Julian's Persian invasion and the sources for it, see Matthews, *Roman Empire of Ammianus*, 140–79.

68. Ammianus 25.5; Matthews, *Roman Empire of Ammianus*, 183–87. Themistius, *Or.* 5.65b-67a offers a different perspective. See Heather and Moncur, *Politics, Philosophy, and Empire*, 150–52, for a way to possibly bridge the difference between the two accounts.

69. For this selection as a product of the disagreement between supporters of Constantius and those of Julian, see Ammianus 25.5.2. This is Saturninus Secundus Salutius, the prefect of the East from 361 to 367.

70. He was a *protector domesticus* under both emperors (Ammianus 21.16.20) and had accompanied Constantius's body back to Constantinople. He was promoted to *primicerius domesticorum* by Julian in 363 (Ammianus 25.5.4).

71. Ammianus 25.7. For a more charitable view of the peace treaty, see Themistius, *Or.* 5.66a. For discussion, see Matthews, *Roman Empire of Ammianus*, 185–87. For the status of Armenia and Iberia as key components of this treaty, see N. Lenksi, *Failure of Empire: Valens and the Roman State in the Fourth Century* (Berkeley, 2002), 167–85.

72. Ammianus 25.10.13; Matthews, *Roman Empire of Ammianus,* 188.

73. Even the men he dismissed (like Maximus of Ephesus) were not punished. Among those Jovian kept on were the senior commanders Arintheus, Victor, and Dagalaifus.

74. Themistius, *Or.* 5.67b.

75. *CTh* 13.3.6.

76. Themistius describes Jovian's policy as "opening up the temples … allowing lawful sacrifices" (*Or.* 5.70b). It is not clear if these permitted sacrifices included blood sacrifices or only incense and libations (for discussion see Heather and Moncur, *Politics, Philosophy, and Empire,* 156), though at least one source claims that blood sacrifice (restored by Julian) remained licit through the reign of Valens (Epiphanius, *Adv. haer.* 51.22.9–11). Theodoret (*HE* 4.21) claims that nocturnal sacrifices continued at Alexandria and Petra under Valens, but he explains that Jovian restricted sacrifices only to have Valens again remove that restriction. There is no independent evidence supporting Theodoret's claim about Jovian.

77. Themistius, *Or.* 5.67c–70c. Themistius frames this policy of toleration as one that promotes religious competition, a kind of spiritual capitalism that improves matters for everyone.

78. Most senior appointments were held by men in their forties or early fifties (T. Parkin, *Old Age in the Roman World* [Baltimore, 2003], 116–17). In 360, Libanius was forty-six, Themistius was forty-three, Praetextatus between forty and forty-five, and Ausonius was in his midforties.

79. For discussion of Themistius's career in the 350s, see chapter 4.

80. Julian, *Letter to Themistius* 253c, 257d, 259c, 260a, 266a. On this relationship, see Heather and Moncur, *Politics, Philosophy, and Empire,* 139. For a broader discussion of Julian's interactions with Themistius, see Elm, *Sons of Hellenism,* 96–106.

81. The date of Julian's response is somewhat controversial. Heather and Moncur (*Politics, Philosophy, and Empire,* 139) and S. Bradbury ("The Date of Julian's *Letter to Themistius,"* *GRBS* 28 [1987]: 235–51) place Julian's *Letter to Themistius* in 355. T.D. Barnes and J. Vanderspoel ("Julian and Themistius," *GRBS* 22 [1981]: 187–89) and Elm (*Sons of Hellenism,* 106) suggest that Julian sent a revised version of the letter of 355 following his break with Constantius—a position that may be supported by the letter's placement among documents written during Julian's time as emperor in the MS Vossianus Graecus 77. On the Arabic evidence for Themistius's correspondence with Julian, see J. Watt, "Themistius and Julian: Their Association in Syriac and Arabic Tradition," in *The Purpose of Rhetoric in Late Antiquity: From Performance to Exegesis,* ed. A.J. Quiroga Puertas (Tübingen, 2013), 161–76. I have not yet seen S. Swain, *Themistius, Julian and Greek Political Theory under Rome* (Cambridge, 2013).

82. E.g., *Letter to Themistius* 253, 257a, 258d, 260d-263b.

83. *Letter to Themistius* 254b, LCL trans.

84. *Letter to Themistius* 263c.

85. *Letter to Themistius* 266d-267a. If the *Letter to Themistius* was revised and reissued after 360, this section was almost certainly added to it at this later date.

86. The *Suda* (2.690) says that Themistius held an urban prefecture of Constantinople under Julian, but this is unlikely. Themistius does not mention this among the list of offices he provides in *Or.* 34, and says at 34.13 that he had not previously held office. For discussion of a possible urban prefecture, see J. Vanderspoel, *Themistius and the Imperial Court* (Ann Arbor, MI, 1995), 111–13; Heather and Moncur, *Politics, Philosophy, and Empire*, 44–47. For Themistius's later service as urban prefect, see chapters 8 and 9.

87. This is the panegyric mentioned by Libanius in *Epp.* 818.3 and 1430. For the possible circumstances, see Vanderspoel, *Themistius*, 130–31.

88. E.g., *Epp.* 793 and 818, both related to a comment that Libanius supposedly made about Themistius.

89. *Or.* 5.63c, trans. Heather and Moncur.

90. *Or.* 5.64a (philosophical freedom to speak only truth), 5.64b (Jovian as divine law embodied).

91. For discussion, see Heather and Moncur, *Politics, Philosophy, and Empire*, 150–58.

92. *Or.* 5.64d-66a.

93. *Or.* 5.66a.

94. *Or.* 5.67c-70c.

95. Vanderspoel (*Themistius*, 148–53) sees the oration as advocacy for policies not yet in place, a view countered by Heather and Moncur, *Politics, Philosophy, and Empire*, 154–58.

96. Heather and Moncur, *Politics, Philosophy, and Empire*, 157–58.

97. Libanius, *Ep.* 1455.

98. Gregory, *Ep.* 24.

99. This is certainly possible, though, in *Or.* 18.14, Libanius claims that Julian was forced to swear an oath not to study under him in Nicomedia and was forced instead to read Libanius's works when they circulated in written form.

100. The earliest letter (*Ep.* 13) dates to 353. Three more letters (*Epp.* 35, 369, 493) were written to Julian while he was Caesar.

101. In *Ep.* 369.9–11 Libanius complains of not being among the circle of Julian's associates who received gifts when Julian was named Caesar.

102. Libanius claims that he was too sick to participate in the embassy (*Ep.* 697), which, given his frequent use of sickness as a rhetorical device explaining away inactivity, may or may not be true. Antioch's embassy was the last to arrive, a fact that evidently irritated Julian (*Misop.* 367C). For more discussion of the embassy see P. Petit, *Libanius et la vie municipale à Antioche au IVe siècle après J. C.* (Paris, 1955), 416ff.

103. Libanius's initial approach to members of Julian's court seems to have yielded middling results. The letter of congratulations (*Ep.* 701) he sent in early 362 to Julianus, the emperor's maternal uncle, appears not to have elicited any response (based on the tone of *Ep.* 725). He seems to have had better luck reaching out via Seleucus, another associate of the emperor who later accompanied Julian on his Persian campaign (e.g., *Ep.* 697).

104. *Ep.* 736.1.

105. *Ep.* 736.1.

106. This speech was *Oration* 13. For Libanius's adamant claim that Julian made this request of him, see *Ep.* 736.2; *Or* 1.120.

107. *Or.* 1.122.

108. This included special occasions like the time that Julian planned to climb to a mountain temple of Zeus (Ammianus 22.14), a trip Libanius claimed illness prevented him from taking (*Ep.* 739).

109. *Or.* 1.122–24.

110. Another such figure is Prohaeresius, a favorite of the emperor Constans. For his fate under Julian, see Julian, *Ep.* 2 (Hertlein = *Ep.* 14 Wright = *Ep.* 31 Bidez-Cumont); and the discussion of Watts, *City and School,* 64–76.

111. There were two types of risks associated with appearing overeager. Either Julian would think that Libanius was insincere (as he thought about Themistius and Prohaeresius) or Libanius's peers might see in him a person willing to do anything to gain imperial attention (e.g., *Ep.* 797). One must also keep in mind that Libanius is writing about these things after Julian's death in a way that presents his career under Julian in a way that conforms with later ideas about what behavior was proper. This account, like all others drawn from Libanius's work, must be read somewhat critically.

112. *Or.* 1.122–24.

113. *Or.* 1.124.

114. *Or.* 1.125. Libanius's use of *sunousia* here indicates his attempt to make these meetings seem like the intimate conversations of true friends rather than occasions for flattery (for this meaning of *sunousia,* see Watts, *City and School,* chap. 6). Here again, Libanius is implicitly contrasting his interactions with Julian with those characteristic of typical sophist-emperor relationships.

115. *Or.* 1.125. The return of his grandfather's property, seized by the fisc in 303, was apparently a big issue because both Or. 1 and *Ep.* 1154 make the point that Libanius never asked Julian for this.

116. *Or.* 1.125.

117. For Libanius's various interventions, see *Or.* 1.126; 15.20; 16.21; 18.195. For discussion, see Petit, *Vie municipale,* 109.

118. Described at *Or.* 1.127–30. This was *Oration* 12, the third panegyric of Julian delivered that day, but, in Libanius's telling, the most successful.

119. *Ep.* 1376.

120. These are *Orations* 15 and 16. For discussion of their relationship to the *Misopogon,* see L. Van Hoof and P. Van Nuffelen, "Monarchy and Mass Communication: Antioch A.D. 362/3 Revisited," *JRS* 101 (2011): 166–84, at 178–83.

121. This is against the more literal reading of R. Cribiore, *Libanius the Sophist: Rhetoric, Reality, and Religion in the Fourth Century* (Ithaca, NY, 2013), 161–64. For discussion of why Libanius adopts this pose, see E. Watts, "Historical Context: The Rhetorical Use of Suffering in Libanius' Monodies, Letters, and Autobiography," in *The Cambridge Companion to Libanius,* ed. L. Van Hoof (Cambridge, 2014). For examples of Libanius's overly dramatic discussion of this period, see *Or.* 1.135 ("My first impulse was to look to my sword, for life would be harder to bear than any death"); *Ep.* 1424.2 ("From the day that I heard the news, I have been practically dumb with respect to speaking and I have stopped writing").

122. For Nicomedia, see chapter 4. If *Oration* 17.37 is to be believed, Libanius was working on *Oration* 15 at the time of Julian's death. Or. 15.1 also seems to suggest a revision in the text to account for Julian's recent death. On this point, see Van Hoof and Van Nuffelen, "Monarchy and Mass Communication," 180–82. *Orations* 15, 17, and 18 together take up 308 Loeb pages. For the sake of comparison, *Orations* 19, 20, 21, 22, 23, 30, 33, and 45 (which date to 386 and 387) total 330 Loeb pages. If anything, Libanius's productivity increased immediately following Julian's death.

123. Philagrius (*PLRE* 693) is mentioned in Ammianus 21.4.2. Norman dates this letter to October, 363, which seems plausible.

124. *Ep.* 1434.2, trans. Norman.

125. *Ep.* 1434.4, trans. Norman.

126. For this view, see Norman, *Libanius: Autobiography and Selected Letters* (Cambridge, MA, 1990), 2:207 note a. The casual nature of this letter led Norman to suppose that Libanius had now fully recovered, though, as described below, the depression itself seems to be a literary fiction.

127. *Ep.* 1220.1.

128. *Ep.* 1220.7.

129. Libanius had written to Scylacius, a teacher in Berytus, in October, at roughly the same time that he contacted Philagrius. The letter, which again claims that Libanius will "console myself with the letters that I write to you," is *Ep.* 1431.

130. E.g., *Ep.* 763.

131. For Julian's initiatives strengthening councils and Libanius's support of them, see *Or.* 17.27; 18.146–48. For attempts to secure exemptions for friends under Julian, see, for example, *Ep.* 704.

132. *Ep.* 275. For a possible rivalry between Libanius and Prohaeresius, see *Suda* Λ 486, Π 2375.

133. *Or.* 17.9, trans. Norman. For discussion of the dates of Libanius's *Monody* and other speeches following the death of Julian, see now P. Van Nuffelen, "Earthquakes in A.D. 363–368 and the Date of Libanius, *Oratio* 18," *CQ* 56.2 (2006): 657–661.

134. *Ep.* 1411.1, trans. Bradbury. For discussion of Eusebius's situation, see Cribiore, *Libanius the Sophist*, 158–59.

135. Julian, *Ep.* 80 (Bidez-Cumont = *Ep.* 29 Wright = *Ep.* 1 Papadopoulos-Kerameus). Libanius, *Or.* 18.126, however, comments that people who built homes using temple materials "began to contribute money" to the effort.

136. *Ep.* 712.3, trans. Bradbury.

137. *Ep.* 763.6, trans. Bradbury.

138. *Ep.* 724, trans. Bradbury.

139. For Thalassius's relationship with Libanius, see chapter 4. Bassianus, one of Thalassius's sons, had also studied under Libanius (e.g., *Ep.* 155).

140. *Ep.* 1364.2.

141. *Ep.* 1364.7.

142. *Ep.* 1364.6; cf. the similar comments in *Ep.* 757.

143. They also, incidentally, highlight how difficult it is to use these letters to assess the nature or strength of his religious convictions. These were fundamentally

documents that displayed Libanius's personal relationships and influence rather than his religious feelings.

144. E.g., Libanius, *Ep.* 1364.6–7.

CHAPTER 6. THE NEW PANNONIAN ORDER

1. L. Van Hoof, "(Self-) Censorship or Self Fashioning? Gaps in Libanius' Letter Collection," *Revue Belge,* forthcoming.

2. There is no reason to suppose that Libanius produced less in the period, despite the fact that less material survives. For this, see Van Hoof, "(Self-) Censorship"; Van Hoof, "Libanius' Letter Collection," in *Late Antique Epistolography,* ed. C. Sogno, B. Storin, and E. Watts (Berkeley, forthcoming).

3. For the balance between *negotium* and *otium,* see, for example, the discussion of Matthews, *Western Aristocracies and Imperial Court, A.D. 364–425* (Oxford, 1975), 17.

4. Gratianus I (*PLRE* 1.400–401). His career is discussed in Ammianus 30.7; Symmachus, *Or.* 1.3; Aurelius Victor, *Epit.* 45.2. For analysis, see N. Lenski, *Failure of Empire: Valens and the Roman State in the Fourth Century* (Berkeley, 2002), 36–39, 46–47; C. Aull, "Imperial Power in the Age of Valentinian I, 364–375 CE" (PhD diss., Indiana University, 2013), 18–20, 45–47; and chapter 3.

5. For the obligation to serve, see Lenski, *Failure of Empire,* 45.

6. For him accompanying his father, see Symmachus, *Or.* 1.1. For the tribune position in Gaul in 357, see Ammianus 16.11. Sozomen defines the position as the *tribunus* of the *Ioviani legio* (*HE* 6.6). Given that Valentinian was thirty-six at the time, it is likely that he had already served in some less senior positions that are not recorded in surviving sources.

7. Philostorgius, *HE* 7.7; for service under Julian, see also Theodoret, *HE* 3.16. Against the story of service and exile under Julian, see, however, Lenski, *Failure of Empire,* 49–50; Lenski, "Were Valentinian, Valens, and Jovian Confessors before Julian the Apostate?" *ZfaC* 6 (2002): 94–117.

8. For this incident, see Ammianus 25.10; Symmachus, *Or.* 1.6.

9. Socrates, *HE* 3.13, 4.1; John of Antioch, fr. 179. For discussion of why this service may be suspect, see Lenski, *Failure of Empire,* 52.

10. For the importance of his Pannonian background, see Lenski, *Failure of Empire,* 20–21. For further discussion, see Aull, "Valentinian," 41 n. 80.

11. Ammianus 26.1

12. Ammianus 26.4.

13. For a discussion of this division, see Lenski, *Failure of Empire,* 307–9. For its connection to the possible establishment of cohorts of *iuniores* and *seniores,* see R. Tomlin, "*Seniores-Iuniores* in the Later Roman Field Army," *AJPh* 93 (1972): 253–78. I thank Charles Aull for this reference.

14. See, for example, the thrust of Symmachus, *Or.* 1 and 2. For discussion of this feature of Valentinian's propaganda, see Aull, "Valentinian," chap. 1; C. Sogno, *Q. Aurelius Symmachus: A Political Biography* (Ann Arbor, MI, 2006), 9–17.

15. Themistius, *Or.* 8.113d; echoed in Ammianus 31.14.

16. Imperial security was emphasized in coins like *RIC* IX. Siscia 15b, the reverse of which reads, SECVRITAS REI PUBLICAE. The restoration of good governance was widely celebrated in issues like *RIC* IX. Antioch 2d, the reverse of which reads, RESTITUTOR REI PVBLICAE.

17. For *concordia* in their reigns, see Themistius, *Or.* 6. Note too the coinage and other forms of propaganda discussed by Lenski, *Failure of Empire*, 28–32.

18. As Lenski (*Failure of Empire*, 159–63) notes, the peace treaty in 363 concluding Julian's Persian war seems designed to undo many of the Roman gains made by Galerius in 299. For the Alamanni, see Ammianus 26.5.

19. See Aull, "Valentinian," 80–88.

20. The tribute reduction in Gaul was a whopping 68 percent; Ammianus 16.5, 18.1.

21. Ammianus 25.4; Julian, *Ep.* 73.

22. For the cost of the campaign, see Ammianus 30.8; Libanius, *Or.* 18.168–70. For bonuses, see Ammianus 24.3; Zosimus 3.13. For a larger discussion of this, see Lenski, *Failure of Empire*, 289–90.

23. As Julian himself did when he shipped food from imperial estates to Antioch in order to alleviate a shortage. Julian, *Misop.* 369A-B.

24. Temple estates: *CTh* 5.13.3, 10.1.8; civic estates: Ammianus 25.4; Libanius, *Or.* 13.45; *CTh* 10.3.1; *CJ* 11.70.1; and, more generally, A.H.M. Jones, *The Later Roman Empire, 284–602* (Norman, OK, 1964), 732–73; J.H.W.G. Liebeschuetz, *Antioch: City and Imperial Administration in the Later Roman Empire* (Oxford, 1972), 149–61; gifts to friends: Eutropius 10.16.

25. Lenski, *Failure of Empire*, 290.

26. Ammianus 30.8. For the significance of earlier imperial exempla to Ammianus's representations of fourth-century figures, see more generally G. Kelly, *Ammianus Marcellinus: The Allusive Historian* (Cambridge, 2008), 297–302.

27. Eutropius 10.6.

28. The emperor Domitian, for example, provides a textbook example of how little credit emperors got for their management of economic crises. He proved an adept manager of the economy who kept to a budget and reversed the currency debasements of his predecessors, but his need for increased revenue prompted conflicts with the senate that led in part to his unpopularity with senators.

29. This was the *aurum coronarium*, a vital source of revenue that largely paid for donatives to soldiers. See R. Duncan-Jones, *Money and Government in the Roman Empire* (Cambridge, 1994), 7–8; Lenski, *Failure of Empire*, 289–91; and the counterview of Aull, "Valentinian," 68 n. 51. For multiple embassies, see Eunapius, *Hist.*, fr. 31; Libanius, *Epp.* 1184–86, 1436, 1439.

30. *CTh* 5.13.3, 10.1.8 (temple properties); *AE* 1906.30 (civic estates).

31. Lenski, *Failure of Empire*, 297, on the basis of *CTh* 12.6.7.

32. *CTh* 12.6.12; cf. Lenski, *Failure of Empire*, 300. The issue at hand was the possibility that officials might embezzle gold by shaving the edges off the *solidi* they collected. K. Harl, *Coinage in the Roman Economy, 300 BC–700 AD* (Baltimore, 1996), 159–60, argues, however, that something more nuanced must have happened in practice because the process of continual reminting would be extremely wasteful.

33. Ammianus 26.6.7. For discussion, see Lenski, *Failure of Empire*, 291.

34. E.g., Cleander, a notorious figure presumably mentioned earlier in the history by Ammianus and is compared to Petronius at 26.6.8. For Cleander's career, see Dio 62.12–13; *Historia Augusta, Commodus*, 6, 7.

35. E.g., Basil, *Ep.* 21; Eunapius, *VS* 478.

36. Lenski, *Failure of Empire*, 291. Much of this is certainly due to increased revenue generation, though, as G. Bevan and R. Burgess have recently argued (unpublished paper delivered at Shifting Frontiers X, March 2013), some of this is perhaps due to a new source for gold becoming available at the time.

37. Ammianus 26.6.15; Themistius, *Or.* 7.91a-c. Our accounts of this are filled with obviously farcical elements. For discussion, see Matthews, *The Roman Empire of Ammianus* (Ann Arbor, MI, 2007), 193–95; Lenski, *Failure of Empire*, 73.

38. For Faustina on Procopius's campaigns, see Ammianus 26.9.3. Most of the reverses of his coins read, REPARATIO FEL TEMP (RIC IX. Constantinople 17a, 17b, 18, 19; Cyzicus 6, 7; Heraclea 7; Nicomedia 1, 8, 10a-g). This evokes coins issued in the 340s and 350s under Constans, Constantius, and Julian (while Caesar). For this early issue, see H. Mattingly, "FEL. TEMP. REPARATIO," *NC* 93 (1933): 182–201, as well as G. Richardson, "The 'Barbarian/Hut' Cententionalis and Vergilian Iconography," *Vergilius* 54 (2008): 70–96.

39. Ammianus 26.7–8 (on Procopius's movements into Asia) and 26.8.2–3 (on Chalcedon).

40. Ammianus, 26.9.9; Philostorgius 9.5; Zosimus 4.8.4. Later ecclesiastical historians recount a gruesome execution of Procopius in which he is torn in half by the force of two small flexing trees, but Lenski (*Failure of Empire*, 81) rightly dismisses this as a fiction.

41. Procopius's usurpation rested on a thin familial link to the family of Julian, an even thinner claim that Julian had named Procopius his successor before setting off for Persia, and the much more compelling fact that Procopius was not Valens. On his familial ties to Julian, see Lenski, *Failure of Empire*, 69. For rumors of his appointment as Julian's successor, see Ammianus 23.3; Philostorgius 9.5; Zosimus 4.4. For discussion of this rumor, see F. J. Wiebe, *Kaiser Valens und die heidnische Opposition* (Bonn, 1995), 11–20.

42. The historian Aurelius Victor (made governor of Pannonia II after publication of his historical work) is a possible example of the former. Alexander of Heliopolis, a harsh governor of Syria under Julian, is an example of the latter.

43. For summaries of their careers, see *PLRE* 1: Saturninius Secundus Salutius 3 and Domitius Modestus 2.

44. For discussion, see Matthews, *Western Aristocracies*, 32–55; Lenski, *Failure of Empire*, 56–67.

45. Ammianus 26.10. This refers to Serenianus, his first *comes domesticorum*. Lenski, *Failure of Empire*, 61.

46. *PLRE* 1: Maximinus 7. He was *praeses Corsicae* in 364, *praeses Sardiniae* sometime between 364 and 366, *corrector Tusciae* in 366, *praefectus annonae* from 368 to 370, *vicarius urbis* from 370 to 371, and praetorian prefect of Gaul from 371 to 376. For discussion of his career, see Lenski, *Failure of Empire*, 58. For the senatorial nature of these offices, see Matthews, *Western Aristocracies*, 39.

47. For discussion, see Lenski, *Failure of Empire*, 60–62, 67.

48. E.g., Eupraxius, made urban prefect by Valentinian. For discussion, see Lenski, *Failure of Empire*, 64; Matthews, *Western Aristocracies*, 62.

49. Among them were Sophronius (*magister officiorum*, 369–78), Fortunatianus (*comes rei privatae*, 370–77), and Modestus (praetorian prefect of the East, 369–77). Extended tenures exist for lower offices as well. Lenski (*Failure of Empire*, 62–63) notes, for example, that only four proconsuls of Asia served between 366 and 378, with tenures that were up to four times the expected length. This was a senatorial office that usually rotated each year or two. For a complaint about this tendency, see Ammianus 31.14.2.

50. Peculation led to the dismissal of a number of officials early in the reign of Valentinian, including the ex-consul Mamertinus (Ammianus 27.2).

51. *CTh* 14.9.1, trans. Pharr. Although the surviving copy of the law is addressed to the urban prefect in Rome, provisions in the law seem to have been observed in other cities as well. See, for example, Libanius, *Or.* 1.169–70; and Lenski, *Failure of Empire*, 270.

52. It is worth noting, however, that letters from teachers (like those featured in R. Cribiore, *The School of Libanius in Late Antique Antioch* [Princeton, NJ, 2007], app. 1) still probably formed the basis for the measurement of student achievement in this new, centralized system.

53. For Valentinian's interests, see Aull, "Valentinian," 163–80. For Valens's actions against religious dissenters, see Lenski, *Failure of Empire*, 211–13. The climate of his later reign produced a call for tolerance from Themistius in an oration that has unfortunately been lost. Mention of it is found in Socrates, *HE* 4.32.1; Sozomen, *HE* 6.36–37. For discussion, see C. Ando, "Pagan Apologetics and Christian Intolerance in the Ages of Themistius and Augustine," *JECS* 4 (1996): 171–207, at 176–82.

54. For discussion, see Matthews, *Western Aristocracies*, 56–63.

55. Lenski, *Failure of Empire*, 213–32, has effectively refuted the arguments of others (e.g., Wiebe, *Kaiser Valens*) that these incidents involved a pagan opposition party. Lenski is certainly correct to see them as somewhat excessive responses to very conventional imperial concerns. For the climate of fear, see, for example, John Chrysostom, *In Act. apost. hom.* 38.5 (speaking about magical books floating in the Orontes River); Ammianus 29.2.

56. For the reappropriation of temple property, see *CTh* 5.13.3; 10.1.8.

57. For North Africa, see Aull, "Valentinian," 189–90, citing G. Sears, "The Fates of the Temples in North Africa," in *The Archeology of Late Antique Paganism*, ed. L. Lavan and M. Mulryan (Leiden, 2011), 229–62, at 232–36.

58. Libanius, *Or.* 30.7.

59. Theodoret, *HE* 4.21, NPNF trans. Epiphanius (*Adv. haer.* 51.22.9–11) makes a similar claim that nocturnal sacrifices continued at Alexandria and Petra under Valens. Theodoret spends much of book 4 creating a narrative in which the heretical Valens permits all religious activity but that of Nicene orthodox leaders. He also claims (at 4.21) that Jovian restricted sacrifices only to have Valens again remove that restriction. There is no independent evidence supporting this last claim.

60. For the destruction at Aegeae, see chapter 2. For the monodies, see chapter 4.

61. Libanius, *Ep.* 1300.

62. This letter is *Ep.* 1534.

63. The placement of Aristides between Asclepius and Hygeia is appropriate given his frequent discussions of his health and healings.

64. *Ep.* 1534.4, trans. Norman.

65. For discussion of the policies of Valentinian and Valens, see Lenski, *Failure of Empire,* 216–18.

66. *Ep.* 1376.

67. *Or.* 16.1–2. On the possibility that Libanius has fabricated this, however, see L. Van Hoof and P. Van Nuffelen, "Monarchy and Mass Communication: Antioch A.D. 362/3 Revisited," *JRS* 101 (2011): 166–84, at 178 n. 72.

68. These speeches are *Orations* 15 and 16. For discussion of their relationship to the *Misopogon,* see Van Hoof and Van Nuffelen, "Monarchy and Mass Communication," 178–83.

69. For this larger climate of hostility, see Zosimus 4.1–2; and the discussion above.

70. These letters were *Epp.* 1185 and 1298.

71. *Epp.* 1184, 1186.

72. *PLRE* 1: Seleucus 1. The exact nature of his position under Julian is unclear. For his punishment in 365, see Libanius, *Epp.* 1473, 1508.

73. Eunapius, *VS* 498.

74. Eunapius, *VS* 479.

75. Himerius, *Or.* 8. The exact circumstances are unclear, but the exile had ended by 365. For *Oration* 8 more broadly, see E. Watts, "Himerius and the Personalization of the Monody," forthcoming.

76. Eunapius, *VS* 478–79.

77. For his rehabilitation, see Eunapius, *VS* 479. For his subsequent arrest and execution, see Eunapius, *VS* 480–81; Ammianus 29.1.

78. *Or.* 1.125, trans. Norman.

79. *Or.* 1.125.

80. The first part of the *Autobiography* (*Oration* 1) appeared around 374. For discussion of this text, see L. Van Hoof, "Libanius' *Life* and Life," in *The Cambridge Companion to Libanius,* ed. L. Van Hoof (Cambridge, 2014). *Oration* 17 is harder to date, though it likely appeared in 364 (H.-U. Wiemer, *Libanios und Julian: Studien zum Verhältnis von Rhetorik und Politik im vierten Jahrhundert n. Chr.* [Munich, 1995], 255). *Oration* 18 may be dated as late as 368. For this late date, see P. van Nuffelen, "Earthquakes in AD 363–368 and the Date of Libanius, *Oratio* 18," *CQ* 56.2 (2006): 657–61.

81. For a description of some of these, see *Or.* 1.136–38.

82. The oration is lost, but the incident is described at *Or.* 1.144. Lenski, *Failure of Empire,* 94, suggests that Valens may not have known Greek well enough to understand the speech.

83. Scholars have long argued that the gap between the earlier and later phases of Libanius's collected letters reflects a deliberate act of self-censorship in the face of Valens's investigations (e.g., Wiebe, *Kaiser Valens,* 154; S. Bradbury,

Selected Letters of Libanius [Liverpool, 2004], 11). As Lieve Van Hoof ("[Self-] Censorship") has argued, this explanation for the notable lacuna in his letter collection is not sustainable.

84. For this idea, see E. Watts, B. Storin, and C. Sogno, introduction to *Late Antique Epistolography* (Berkeley, forthcoming). On Libanius in particular, see Van Hoof, "Libanius' Letters," in that volume. As Van Hoof explains, manuscripts suggest that the letters from 355–65 and 388–93 circulated together as one collection in the middle Byzantine period. At the same time, the letters from 355–65 highlight different characters, develop different themes, and address different aspects of Libanius's career than do the letters from 388–93 (the characteristics of that group of letters are discussed in chapter 9). I suspect, though it is impossible to prove, that these may once have been conceived of (and possibly even distributed as) two distinct letter collections, which were later merged in the manuscript tradition.

85. For Praetextatus's proconsulship, see M. Kahlos, *Vettius Agorius Praetextatus: A Senatorial Life in Between* (Rome, 2002), 31–35.

86. Constantine's upgrading of this office (which previously had been defined as a *corrector*) can be seen almost immediately in his selection of Vettius Cossinius Rufinus, a former *corrector*, as the first proconsul. The staff of the proconsul also came to look more like that of a prefect than that of a *corrector*. For discussion, see Jones, *Later Roman Empire*, 106–7, 129; Kahlos, *Praetextatus*, 34.

87. While I note the comments of Kahlos, *Praetextatus*, 32, I am persuaded by H. Bloch, "A New Document of the Last Pagan Revival in the West, 393–394 A.D.," *HThR* 38 (1945): 199–244, at 204, who sees real significance in holding the Achaean proconsulship. Although both were prestigious positions, Achaea differed from Africa in the religious identities of the men who held its proconsulship. Whereas Petronius Probus, Olybrius, and many of the other senators who became prefects after serving as proconsul of Africa were Christian, nearly all of the proconsuls of Achaea whose confessional inclinations can be determined were pagan. Olybrius (*PLRE* 1.640–42) was proconsul of Africa in 361. His next office was urban prefect of Rome in 369–70. Petronius Probus (*PLRE* 1.736–40) was proconsul of Africa in 358 and then held the praetorian prefecture of Illyricum in 364. Johannes Hahn (unpublished paper) counts four Achaean proconsuls who were certainly pagan, another who might have been, and finds no clear evidence for a fourth-century Christian proconsul of Achaea.

88. Ammianus 22.7.6. See Kahlos, *Praetextatus*, 32. This occasionally somewhat random appointment process was a tendency of Julian's about which people complained (e.g., Libanius, *Or.* 18.180). I thank an anonymous reader for pointing this out.

89. Some of these are mentioned in *CIL* 6.31929 and detailed more extensively in the verse epitaph written for Praetextatus by his wife (part of *CIL* 6.1779). For discussion of Praetextatus's Mithraism, see Kahlos, *Praetextatus*, 79–80.

90. Praetextatus's interests extended to translations of Greek poetry (*CIL* 6.1779) and Themistius's commentary on the *Analytics* of Aristotle (mentioned by Boethius, *De interpret. ed. sec.* 1.289).

91. For Himerius's exile, see Himerius, *Or.* 8. Praetextatus's role in his return likely prompted Himerius to write *Or.* 51, unfortunately now lost.

92. Zosimus describes the law at 4.3.2. The Gothic king Alaric's *Breviarium*, which contains both the original law and an interpretation of it, similarly expands the law's prohibitions to include nocturnal religious practices, explaining, "Anyone who celebrates nocturnal sacrifices or invokes demons with incantations will be punished with capital punishment." For the equation of *CTh* 9.16.7 and the events described in Zosimus, see most recently Kahlos, *Praetextatus,* 34–35, 83–84.

93. κατὰ τὰ ἐξ ἀρχῆς πάτρια (Zosimus 4.3.3).

94. "Impp. valent. et valens aa. ad secundum pf. p. ne quis deinceps nocturnis temporibus aut nefarias preces aut magicos apparatus aut sacrificia funesta celebrare conetur. detectum atque convictum competenti animadversione mactari, perenni auctoritate censemus. dat. v. id. sept. divo ioviano a. et varroniano coss." (*CTh* 9.16.7). The exact relationship of this law to what Zosimus describes is unclear. What survives in the *Code* is a copy from the East, which may suggest that the Western law was not enforced in the territory under Valentinian's control but remained on the books in the east. Alternatively, this might be a second law that clarifies imperial intent issued after the earlier law described by Zosimus was rescinded. For analysis of these details and their significance for any reconstruction of this incident, see Kahlos, *Praetextatus,* 83–84; contra R. von Haehling, *Die Religionszugehörigkeit der hohen Amtsträger des römischen Reiches seit Constantins I. Alleinherrschaft bis zum Ende der theodosianischen Dynastie* (Bonn, 1978), 165–66.

95. The Constantian law, *CTh* 16.10.5, reads: "Idem a. ad cerealem praefectum urbi. aboleantur sacrificia nocturna magnentio auctore permissa et nefaria deinceps licentia repellatur. et cetera. dat. viiii kal. dec. constantio a. vi et caes. ii conss."

96. For a different reading of this law, see Lenski, *Failure of Empire,* 217–18; Wiebe, *Kaiser Valens,* 241–46.

97. Ammianus 26.4.4; Themistius, *Or.* 6.72b. For a discussion of the climate of suspicion these illnesses caused, see Lenski, *Failure of Empire,* 25. It is notable that the *Theodosian Code* law is addressed to Salustius, whom Zosimus (4.1.1) credits with calming Valentinian's suspicions about sorcery. Unlike traditional religious activities, magical practices remained a legislative concern for the emperors throughout their reigns, as *CTh* 9.16.8–10 shows.

98. Kahlos, *Praetextatus,* 83.

99. For this view, see Aull, "Valentinian," 180–91.

100. For the Sacred Way, see *IG*² II-III 5204; for Delphi, *AE* 1949.87.

101. On his urban prefecture, see Kahlos, *Praetextatus,* 35–38. The *Theodosian Code* gives a rough sense of the length of his prefecture. *CTh* 8.14.1 shows him in the position by August 18, 367; and *CTh* 1.6.6, the last law addressed to him, dates to September 20, 368. The actual term of office certainly extended beyond both of these dates. The last law addressed to Volusianus, Praetextatus's predecessor, dates to May 15, 367; and the first to Olybrius, his successor, dates to January 1, 369.

102. For Praetextatus's role in this conflict, see Kahlos, *Praetextatus,* 115–21.

103. For the dispute, see *Collectio Avellana* 1.5–13. For this violence, see also Sozomen, *HE* 6.23; Ammianus 27.3. Ammianus gives the figure of 137 dead; the *Collectio Avellana* 1.7 counts 160.

104. Ammianus 27.3.12–15.

105. Ammianus 26.4.4. His previous experience had involved the legal examination of people who had served under Julian, and his somewhat more successful intervention in a church dispute in Milan in 364. For discussion of that, see Aull, "Valentinian," 171–73; N. McLynn, *Ambrose of Milan: Church and Court in a Christian Capital* (Berkeley, 1994), 25. I thank Charles Aull for calling this previous service to my attention.

106. *Collectio Avellana* 5, dated by *Collectio Avellana* 1.10 to September 367. For discussion of the context, see Aull, "Valentinian," 173–78.

107. *Collectio Avellana* 6, dated to somewhere between November 367 and January 12, 368.

108. *Collectio Avellana* 7, January 12, 368.

109. Ammianus writes that he "quieted the disturbance caused by the quarrels of the Christians. After the banishment of Ursinus, profound peace reigned, a state of affairs extremely welcome to the citizens of Rome" (27.9, trans. Hamilton). The *Collectio Avellana* (1.12) speaks about a subsequent massacre by partisans of Damasus, though this is nowhere else mentioned.

110. CIL 6.102 = ILS 1259. For discussion of this, see M. Salzman, ed. and trans., *The Letters of Symmachus: Book 1* (Atlanta, 2011), 92; Kahlos, *Praetextatus*, 91–96; Matthews, *Western Aristocracies*, 22.

111. Ammianus 29.9. For discussion of this context, see Aull, "Valentinian," chap. 5; Kahlos, *Praetextatus*, 94–95.

112. Symmachus, *Ep.* 1.46. This action may or may not have been connected to an imperial edict. For various interpretations of this, see H.P. Kohns, *Versorgungskrisen und Hungerrevolten im spätantiken Rom* (Bonn, 1961), 157; R. Lizzi Testa, *Senatori, popolo, papi: Il governo di Roma al tempo dei Valentiniani* (Bari, 2004), 373–74. Note especially the concise summary and discussion of Salzman, *Letters of Symmachus*, 99–100.

113. For this, see Sogno, *Symmachus*, 6.

114. For this period of *otium*, see Kahlos, *Praetextatus*, 43–8.

115. For this embassy, see the discussion of Matthews, *Western Aristocracies*, 62; Kahlos, *Praetextatus* 40–41.

116. Ammianus 28.1.24–25.

117. Symmachus, *Ep.* 1.55.

118. E.g., Symmachus, *Ep.* 1.53.

119. For discussion of this, see F. Van Haeperen, *Le collège pontifical (3e s. a.C.-4e s. p.C.): Contribution à l'étude de la religion publique romaine* (Rome, 2002), 209–10; and Salzman, *Letters of Symmachus*, 107–8.

120. Symmachus, *Ep.* 1.51, trans. Salzman.

121. Symmachus, *Ep.* 1.51, trans. Salzman.

122. Symmachus, *Ep.* 1.47, trans. Salzman.

123. The inclusion of these particular letters in Symmachus's published letters likely came about in part because of Symmachus's opposition to a proposal that a statue honoring Praetextatus be erected following his death. As Michele

Salzman argues (*Letters of Symmachus,* 94–96), these particular letters may be designed to challenge the perception of Praetextatus as a sort of holy man. On this point, see too Kahlos, *Praetextatus,* 156.

124. CIL 6.1779 = *ILS* 1259, lines 13–15. See too the discussion of Kahlos, *Praetextatus,* 124–79.

125. Ammianus 27.6. For discussion of this incident, see too H. Sivan, *Ausonius of Bordeaux: Genesis of a Gallic Aristocracy* (London, 1993), 99–101.

126. Ammianus 27.6.8, trans. Rolfe. Valentinian's decision to proclaim a child Augustus was, in the minds of some, overstepping traditional limits. For discussion of this, see M. McEvoy, *Child Emperor Rule in the Late Roman West, 367–455* (Oxford, 2013), 49–50.

127. Ausonius was likely summoned in late 367 or 368. For 368, see A. Coşkun, *Die gens Ausoniana an der Macht: Untersuchungen zu Decimius Magnus Ausonius und seiner Familie* (Oxford, 2002), 37–43. For the 367 date, see Sivan, *Ausonius,* 101 n. 33. Others date his summons as early as 364, though this seems unlikely.

128. The uncle in question is Aemilius Magnus Arborius (*PLRE* 1: Arborius 4), his maternal uncle. I disagree with Sivan (*Ausonius,* 54) that Arborius taught one of the emperor Julian's siblings. For discussion, see chapter 2.

129. Charles Aull has pointed out to me that Ausonius was chosen over Usulus and Harmonius, both of whom are known to have been teaching in Trier at the time (Ausonius, *Ep.* 10).

130. Ammianus 27.10.10. For discussion, see Sivan, *Ausonius,* 104–5.

131. For the epigrams on the Danube, see Sivan, *Ausonius,* 105. The initial composition of the *Mosella* is usually placed somewhere between 368 and 370/71, with a second edition in 378/9. For discussion, see Salzman, *Letters of Symmachus,* 44; D. Shanzer, "The Date and Literary Context of Ausonius' *Mosella*: Ausonius, Symmachus, and the *Mosella,*" in *The Discipline of the Art,* ed. P. Knox and C. Foss (Stuttgart, 1997), 284–305.

132. See, for example, the presentation of Valentinian in Symmachus, *Or.* 2 and 3, as well as the discussion of Aull, "Valentinian," 133–50; Sivan, *Ausonius,* 108; Sogno, *Symmachus,* 3–17.

133. Ausonius, *Griphus ternarii numeri,* praef.

134. These included the epigrams on the Danube (*Epig.* 28, 31) and the *Versus Paschales* (Ausonius 3.2). For discussion, see Sivan, *Ausonius,* 109–10.

135. On the cento more generally, see S. McGill, *Virgil Recomposed: The Mythological and Secular Centos in Antiquity* (Oxford, 2005), with chap. 5 focusing on Ausonius's cento in particular. For a discussion of cento techniques, see too K. Pollmann, "Sex and Salvation in the Virgilian Cento of the Fourth Century," in *Romane Memento: Virgil in the Fourth Century,* ed. Roger Rees (London, 2004), 79–96.

136. Ausonius, *Cento nuptialis,* praef. As McGill suggests (*Virgil Recomposed,* 92–94), the wedding of Gratian and Constantia, the daughter of Constantius, may have been the occasion that prompted the exchange.

137. For this process, see chapter 5.

138. Sivan, *Ausonius,* 108. The honor is listed first on Ausonius's *cursus* in *Praef.* 35, and the *Gratiarum actio* 2.11 indicates that Ausonius held the rank before being promoted to *quaestor* in ca. 374.

139. On Ausonius's appointment, see R.H. Green, *The Works of Ausonius* (Oxford, 1991), 695–706. On the office of the *quaestor* in this period, see J. Harries, "The Roman Imperial Quaestor from Constantine to Theodosius II," *JRS* 78 (1988): 148–72. As Harries (158) indicates, it is unlikely that Ausonius had much to say about the actual content of the laws, only the style in which they might be expressed.

140. I follow the argument of S. Roda (*Commento storico al libro IX dell'epistolario di Q. Aurelio Simmaco* [Pisa, 1981], 291–92; echoed by Sogno, *Symmachus*, 6; and Salzman, *Letters of Symmachus*, 37) that Symmachus, *Ep.* 9.88 is addressed to Ausonius and precedes Symmachus's arrival at court in February 368.

141. For 368 as the time on campaign, see Salzman, *Letters of Symmachus*, xxiv-xxv. For 369, see Sogno, *Symmachus*, 14. For a return to Rome in 370, see Salzman, *Letters of Symmachus*, xxvi n. 74, based on *Ep.* 9.112.

142. *Ep.* 9.88, trans. Salzman.

143. *Dominus:* Symmachus, *Ep.* 1.15; *parens:* Symmachus, *Ep.* 1.33; *filius:* Ausonius, *apud Symmachum, Letter* 1.32.4. For discussion, see Salzman, *Letters of Symmachus*, 38.

144. Salzman, *Letters of Symmachus*, 38.

145. For letters of reference from Symmachus to Ausonius that do not fit this model, see *Epp.* 1.17, 1.19. 1.22. It must be remembered that the published letters have been deliberately chosen to convey distinct impressions of both Symmachus and Ausonius. In short, these were included because they presented both men in ways that made thematic sense.

146. *Ep.* 1.15. Once he arrived at court, Palladius would advance quickly, rising to *comes sacrarum largitionum* in 381 and *magister officiorum* in 382 (though both offices were ultimately held under the supervision of Theodosius I). For his career, see *PLRE* 1: Palladius 12.

147. *Ep.* 1.29, trans. Salzman.

148. *Ep.* 1.41, trans. Salzman.

149. *Ep.* 1.54, trans. Salzman.

150. Ausonius, *Ep.* 12 is addressed to Petronius Probus. It serves as a cover letter for two manuscripts that Probus requested as well as a short poem that Ausonius wrote in the margin. On this relationship, see Sivan, *Ausonius*, 114–15. For the letter itself and an allusion to Catullus contained in it, see Alan Cameron, *The Last Pagans of Rome* (Oxford, 2012), 365; R. Nisbet, *Collected Papers on Latin Literature* (Oxford, 1995), 83.

151. For this as a stylistic tendency in other letters exchanged between literary figures, see Cameron, *Last Pagans*, 383–88.

CHAPTER 7. CHRISTIAN YOUTH CULTURE IN THE 360S AND 370S

1. For this development, see P. Heather, "New Men for New Constantines?," in *New Constantines: The Rhythm of Imperial Renewal in Byzantium, 4th–13th Centuries*, ed. P. Magdalino (Aldershot, 1994), 11–34; as well as the discussion in chapter 3.

2. This is described in chapter 3.

3. For the hazing of entering students in the 350s and 360s, see Gregory Nazianzen, *Or.* 43.17; Eunapius, *VS* 486. For the earlier experiences of Libanius in the 330s, see chapter 2.

4. For discussion of this tendency and its beginnings in the 370s, see P. Brown, *Through the Eye of a Needle: Wealth, the Fall of Rome, and the Making of Christianity in the West, 350–550 AD* (Princeton, NJ, 2012), 120–34; M. Salzman, *The Making of a Christian Aristocracy* (Cambridge, MA, 2002), 133; N. McLynn, *Ambrose of Milan: Church and Court in a Christian Capital* (Berkeley, 1994), 1–52. Some Christian provincial elites had already made this jump before the 350s (the most notable being the father of Gregory Nazianzen, discussed below), but this remained a relatively rare situation.

5. Ambrose is the most familiar but is not exactly typical. In her exhaustive survey of Western senators who became bishops, Michele Salzman (*Making of a Christian Aristocracy*, 132–34) counts only three more, all of whom took office decades after Ambrose did.

6. The family may once have had Alexandrian roots. For this categorization of Ambrose's family, see Brown, *Through the Eye of a Needle*, 124.

7. *PLRE* 1: Ambrosius 1. The date of Ambrose's birth is alternately placed in 334 or 340, based on Ambrose, *Ep.* 59, a letter describing a usurper's invasion of Italy when Ambrose was fifty-three. This is either the invasion of Magnus Maximus in 387 or that of Eugenius in 393. Brown (*Through the Eye of a Needle*, 123) places his birth in 339. This would make sense if the death of his father is connected to Constans's defeat of Constantine II in a civil war in 339. I thank an anonymous reader for this suggestion.

8. *PLRE* 1: Uranius Satyrus. Advocate: Ambrose, *De exc. Sat.* 49; provincial governorship: *De exc. Sat.* 58; death: *De exc. Sat.* 30–32.

9. For his earlier career, see *PLRE* 1: Ambrosius 3. For the date of his governorship around 370, see Brown, *Through the Eye of a Needle*, 122.

10. This is described in Rufinus, *HE* 11.11. See too the thorough analysis of McLynn, *Ambrose of Milan*, 1–13.

11. Jerome, *Chron.* 374; Paulinus, *V. Amb.* 3.3–9; Sozomen, 6.24; Socrates, 4.30; Rufinus, *HE* 2.11. For discussion, see Brown, *Through the Eye of A Needle*, 122–23; McLynn, *Ambrose of Milan*, 1–52.

12. Although his father had been a prefect, this position was likely not enough to ensure a breakthrough into truly exclusive senatorial circles. For the position of ex-prefects like Ambrose's father, see Brown, *Through the Eye of a Needle*, 562 n. 12; McLynn, *Ambrose of Milan*, 31–37; P. Porena, "Trasformazioni istituzionali e assetti sociali: I prefetti del Pretorio tra III e IV secolo," in *Le trasformazioni delle "elites" in età tardoantica*, ed. R. Lizzi Testa (Rome, 2006), 325–56, esp. 334–46.

13. Brown, *Through the Eye of A Needle*, 123; McLynn, *Ambrose of Milan*, 69–71.

14. McLynn, *Ambrose of Milan*, 220–25. On the diversity of the people settled in and around the city in the fourth century, see as well Matthews, *Western Aristocracies and Imperial Court, A.D. 364–425* (Oxford, 1975), 183–86.

15. For discussion, see Brown, *Through the Eye of A Needle*, 125–26.

16. Ambrose, *De officiis* 1.14.

17. Note, for example, Eusebius, *Vit. Const.* 2.46; Athanasius, *Defense against the Arians* 60.2. For discussion of this trend, see T. D. Barnes, *Athanasius and Constantius* (Cambridge, MA, 1993), 176–79; P. Brown, *Power and Persuasion in Late Antiquity* (Madison, WI, 1992), 90, as well as Brown, *Poverty and Leadership in the Later Roman Empire* (Hanover, NH, 2002), 26–32; and the discussion in chapter 2.

18. For this shift, see A. H. M. Jones, *The Later Roman Empire, 284–602* (Norman, OK, 1964), 898–99; N. Lenski, *Failure of Empire: Valens and the Roman State in the Fourth Century* (Berkeley, 2002), 240 n. 161; C. Aull, "Imperial Power in the Age of Valentinian I, 364–375 CE" (PhD diss., Indiana University, 2013), chap. 6; Theodoret, *HE* 4.4.1.

19. C. Rapp, *Holy Bishops in Late Antiquity: The Nature of Christian Leadership in an Age of Transition* (Berkeley, 2005), 215–19; Brown, *Poverty and Leadership,* 32.

20. Rapp, *Holy Bishops,* 199–200. For the sale of property, see Rapp, 212–15, as well as L. W. Countryman, *The Rich Christian in the Church of the Early Empire: Contradictions and Accommodations* (New York, 1980), 114–18. Many bishops did not fit this category, with Athanasius a prime example (suggested by Rufinus, *HE* 10.15; Socrates, *HE* 1.15; Sozomen, *HE* 2.17.5–31; Gelasius of Cyzicus 3.13.10–14). For regulation of this practice, see *CTh* 12.1.59; and the discussion of Aull, "Valentinian," chap. 6.

21. Brown, *Poverty and Leadership,* 18–24, 96.

22. While this is true of some of the larger cities, most bishops elsewhere remained socially middling figures. On this, see C. Sotinel, "Les évêques italiens dans la société de l'Antiquité tardive," in *Le trasformazioni delle "élites" in età tardoantica,* ed. R. Lizzi Testa (Rome, 2006), 377–406, at 388–95.

23. Jerome, *C. Ioa. Hierosol.* 8. For discussion, see Salzman, *Making of a Christian Aristocracy,* 132.

24. For embassies, see Brown, *Power and Persuasion,* 104–8; Ambrose, *Ep.* 51.2. For letter writing, see R. Rémondon, "L'Église dans la société égyptienne à l'époque byzantine," *ChrÉg* 47 (1972): 254–77; and the examples described by Brown, *Poverty and Leadership,* 89–90.

25. For relevant laws, see *CTh* 1.27.1 and 2; *Sirmondian Constitution* 1. On the *episcopalis audientia,* see Rapp, *Holy Bishops,* 242–44; Brown, *Poverty and Leadership,* 68; and the more extensive discussion of J. C. Lamoreaux, "Episcopal Courts in Late Antiquity," *JECS* 3 (1995): 143–67. Note as well H. A. Drake, *Constantine and the Bishops: The Politics of Intolerance* (Baltimore, 2000), 322–25. For the view that these courts primarily worked to mediate disputes, see J. Harries, *Law and Empire in Late Antiquity* (Cambridge, 1999), 191–211; Rapp, *Holy Bishops,* 243–52.

26. S. Elm, *Sons of Hellenism, Fathers of the Church* (Berkeley, 2012), 483.

27. For bishops as public advocates, see, among others, Rapp, *Holy Bishops,* 156–60; Brown, *Power and Persuasion,* 137–40; Alan Cameron and J. Long, *Barbarians and Politics at the Court of Arcadius* (Berkeley, 1993), 71–102; J. H. W. G. Liebeschuetz, "Why Did Synesius Become Bishop of Ptolemais?," *Byzantion* 56 (1986): 180–95; as well as Liebeschuetz, *Barbarians and Bishops:*

Army, Church, and State in the Age of Arcadius and Chrysostom (Oxford, 1990), 105–38, 228–35. For the complexity of church finances, see Rapp, *Holy Bishops,* 215–33.

28. This can be seen most memorably in the complaints leveled by the family of Cyril of Alexandria after his successor turned them out of positions in the church hierarchy. For discussion of this, see M. Gaddis, *There Is No Crime for Those Who Have Christ* (Berkeley, 2005), 319; E. Watts, *Riot in Alexandria: Tradition and Group Dynamics in Late Antique Pagan and Christian Communities* (Berkeley, 2010), 217–18.

29. It was, of course, difficult but not impossible for a bishop to maintain ties with a church once he had been forced into exile. See, for example, the case of the Alexandrian bishop Timothy Aelurus between 460 and 475 (for discussion, see Watts, *Riot in Alexandria,* 226–29). Interestingly, it seems that the church staff remained in place regardless of the bishop.

30. For early Christian advocacy of the renunciation of property see, for example, Matthew 19.21. For Christianity and its fostering of a culture of "overachievement" that encouraged such things, see R. Lane Fox, *Pagans and Christians* (New York, 1987), 336–40.

31. The earliest Egyptian allusion to significant numbers of men and women fitting this description is found in Canon 7 of the *Canons of Hippolytus* (ed. R. G. Coquin, *PO* 31.2, 273–323). Canon 38 of the same document appears to lay out rules governing the interaction of male celibates and women in a domestic context, another suggestion that the group of people to which it applies lived in towns. The Sons and Daughters of the Covenant are the better-known Syrian institution. One of the earliest descriptions of them occurs in Aphrahat's *Sixth Demonstration* (primarily 6.8), but they are perhaps best known from the *Rabbula Canons* (on which see A. Vööbus, *Syriac and Arabic Documents Regarding Legislation Relative to Syrian Asceticism* [Stockholm, 1960], 34–50). For such figures owning and administering property, see the later fourth-century Canon 102 in the *Canons of Athanasius* and *P.Lips.* 43. Note too the discussion of S. Elm, *Virgins of God* (Oxford, 1994), 239.

32. For bishops promoting greater isolation of town-based ascetics, see both the Pseudo-Athanasian *Canons* and Athanasius's fragmentary *Letter to Virgins* (published in L-T. Lefort, "Athanase: Sur la virginité," *Le Muséon* 42 [1929]: 297–374), as well as the discussions of Elm, *Virgins of God,* 331–38; D. Brakke, *Athanasius and Asceticism* (Baltimore, 1998), 34–35. For such figures being recruited by other groups, see Athanasius, *Ep. ad monachos* 1 (Opitz, ii, 181f.); Epiphanius, *De haer.* 68.4; and the discussion of Brakke, 19–20.

33. On Pachomian communities, see P. Rousseau, *Pachomius: The Making of a Community in Fourth-Century Egypt,* 2nd ed. (Berkeley, 1999); Watts, *Riot in Alexandria,* 95–107.

34. For Athanasius's support for the Pachomians, see Brakke, *Athanasius and Asceticism,* 111–29; Watts, *Riot in Alexandria,* 106.

35. Watts, *Riot in Alexandria,* 177, 222–23.

36. This was during Athanasius's third exile, which lasted from 356 to 362. For details on it, see Barnes, *Athanasius and Constantius,* 118ff.; Watts, *Riot in Alexandria,* 181.

37. Athanasius recounts Antony's repeated and strong denials of any association with Melitians and Arians (*Vit. Ant.* 67, 68), his heroic resistance to Arian government officials (86), his visit to Alexandria in support of Athanasius (69–71), and his request that Athanasius be entrusted with one of his two cloaks (91). For a reappraisal of what can be recovered about the historical Antony, and how this relates to the textual portrait of the monk, see the exciting new book of Peter Gemeinhardt: *Antonius der erste Mönch: Leben, Lehre, Legende* (Munich, 2013).

38. See, for example, E. Watts, "Three Generations of Christian Philosophical Biography," in *From the Tetrarchs to the Theodosians,* ed. S. McGill, C. Sogno, and E. Watts (Cambridge, 2010), 127–29.

39. Τὴν δὲ ἀδελφὴν παραθέμενος γνωρίμοις καὶ πισταῖς παρθένοις δούς τε αὐτὴν εἰς παρθενίαν ἀνατρέφεσθαι (*Vit. Ant.* 3.1).

40. *Vit. Ant.* 3.3.

41. *Vit. Ant.* 4.2. This evokes what earlier authors said Pythagoras had done (e.g., Iamblichus, *Pyth.* 3–4). On the comparisons between the *Life of Antony* and earlier Pythagorean biographies, see S. Rubenson, "Antony and Pythagoras: A Reappraisal of the Appropriation of Classical Biography in Athanasius' *Vita Antonii,*" in *Early Christianity in the Context of Antiquity,* ed. D. Brakke, A. Jacobsen, and J. Ulrich (Berlin, 2006), 191–208; A. Priessnig, "Die literarische Form der spätantiken Philosophenromane," *ByzZeit* 30 (1929): 23–30; and Priessnig, "Die biographishe Form der Plotinvita des Porphyrios und das Antoniosleben des Athanasios," *ByzZeit* 64 (1971): 1–5; P. Cox, *Biography in Late Antiquity: A Quest for the Holy Man* (Berkeley, 1983), 50–55.

42. *Vit. Ant.* 8–9.

43. This process is described in *Vit. Ant.* 45–50.

44. *Vit. Ant.* 44.

45. Ἀντώνιος γένος μὲν ἦν Αἰγύπτιος, εὐγενῶν δὲ γονέων καὶ περιουσίαν αὐτάρκη κεκτημένων (*Vit. Ant.* 1.1), an idea reiterated at *Vit. Ant.* 1.4.

46. Membership in a town council in the period when Athanasius was writing may have required only capital of 300 *solidi* and an income of around 25–30 *solidi* a year (*Novella of Valentinian III* 3.4; cf. Brown, *Through the Eye of a Needle,* 6; Jones, *Later Roman Empire,* 738–39). Antony's family owned approximately 200 acres of land. It is impossible to know the exact income Antony's supposed estate would have generated, but the rent for two-thirds of an acre of Egyptian land planted with vines could be as much as 3 *solidi* (T. Hickey, "Aristocratic Landholding and the Economy of Byzantine Egypt," in *Egypt in the Byzantine World,* ed. R. Bagnall [Cambridge, 2009], 288–308, at 296).

47. On curial obligations, see chapter 3.

48. *Vit. Ant.* 1.

49. *Vit. Ant.* 2.

50. Ὁ δὲ Ἀντώνιος, ὥσπερ θεόθεν ἐσχηκὼς τὴν τῶν ἁγίων μνήμην καὶ ὡς δι' αὐτὸν γενομένου τοῦ ἀναγνώσματος, ἐξελθὼν εὐθὺς ἐκ τοῦ κυριακοῦ τὰς μὲν κτήσεις ἃς εἶχεν ἐκ προγόνων ἄρουραι δὲ ἦσαν τριακόσιαι εὔφοροι καὶ πάνυ καλαί, ταύτας ἐχαρίσατο τοῖς ἀπὸ τῆς κώμης, ἵνα εἰς μηδ' ὁτιοῦν ὀχλήσωσιν αὐτῷ τε καὶ τῇ ἀδελφῇ

(*Vit. Ant.* 2.4). For the difficulties in getting rid of the properties associated with an estate, see as well Matthews, *Western Aristocracies*, 153.

51. For third-century parallels, see *P.Oxy* 1405. For clergy, see *CTh* 12.1.59.

52. *Vit. Ant.* 3.1.

53. The importance Athanasius attached to removing these ties is made clear in *Vit. Ant.* 5, when the first things that the devil uses to tempt Antony are memories of his possessions and concerns for his sister.

54. Corresponds with emperors: *Vit. Ant.* 81; teaching in Alexandria: *Vit. Ant.* 69–71; debating philosophers: *Vit. Ant.* 72–80.

55. The long-term popularity of the text should be clear simply from the number of manuscripts and translations in which it is preserved. There are over 160 Greek manuscripts as well as late antique or medieval translations into Latin, Coptic, Syriac, Armenian, Georgian, Slavonic, and Ethiopic. For a discussion of the main editions, see T.D. Barnes, "Angel of Light or Mystic Initiate? The Problem of the *Life of Antony*," *JTS* 37 (1986): 354–68, at 357–58.

56. For the earliest Latin translation, see G. Garitte, *Un témoin important de la vie de S. Antoine: La version inédite latine des Archives de S. Pierre a Rome* (Rome, 1939). For that of Evagrius, see *PL* lxxiii, cols. 125–70 = *PG* xxvi, cols. 833–976 (= *BHL* 609).

57. *PL* xxiii, col. 18. For Jerome's interest in trying to outdo Athanasius, see T.D. Barnes, *Early Christian Hagiography and Roman History* (Tübingen, 2010), 183.

58. Jerome, *De viris inlustribus* 87, 125.

59. *Or.* 21.5.

60. *Confessions* 8.6, trans. Pine-Coffin, with slight modifications. Some have speculated that one of the courtiers may have been Jerome, but there is no concrete evidence for Jerome's identification. For the possibility, see P. Courcelle, *Recherches sur les "Confessions" de saint Augustin* (Paris, 1950), 181; Matthews, *Western Aristocracies*, 50. For doubts about this, see Barnes, "Mystic Initiate," 359.

61. *Ad Theodorum lapsum* 2.3.

62. For Chrysostom's arrangements with Theodore and Maximus, see Socrates, *HE* 6.3, as well as the discussion of D. Hunter, *A Comparison between a King and a Monk/Against the Opponents of the Monastic Life* (Lampeter, 1988), 8–9.

63. *Ad Theodorum lapsum* 1.9, NPNF trans. This is a common sentiment in Chrysostom's works. See *Ad Theodorum lapsum*, 1.13; *Contra Eutropium* 1.1.

64. *Ad Theodorum lapsum* 1.11.

65. *Ad Theodorum lapsum* 2.1; cf. Chrysostom, *Oppugnatores* 3.6; *Comparatio* 1.

66. *Ad Theodorum lapsum* 1.12; cf. Chrysostom, *Comparatio* 1.4.

67. For the notion of Chrysostom as a sort of student radical, see the comments of J.H.W.G. Liebeschuetz, *Ambrose and John Chrysostom: Clerics between Desert and Empire* (Oxford, 2011), 139.

68. τὸν μακάριον τὸν τῶν μοναχῶν μεταδιώκειν βίον καὶ τὴν φιλοσοφίαν τὴν ἀληθῆ (*De sacerdote* 1.2).

69. *De sacerdote* 1.1.

70. *De sacerdote* 1.1.

71. *De sacerdote* 1.2.

72. This is explained in *De sacerdote* 1.6. For dating and discussion of this, see Hunter, *Comparison*, 8–9; R.E. Carter, "The Chronology of Saint John Chrysostom's Early Life," *Traditio* 18 (1962): 357–64, at 362.

73. Elm, *Sons of Hellenism*, 42–59, 147–212, provides an excellent analysis of the context for Gregory's ordination and the way in which he attempted to balance ideals of Christian philosophical retreat, submission to the will of his father, and continued public engagement in the wider world.

74. Basil, *Ep.* 210.2. For discussion, see P. Rousseau, *Basil of Caesarea* (Berkeley, 1994), 61–62.

75. B. Storin, "The *Letters* of Gregory Nazianzus: Discourse and Community in Late Antique Epistolary Culture" (PhD diss., Indiana University, 2012), 20–22.

76. Gregory Nazianzen, *Or.* 43.16.

77. Gregory Nazianzen, *Or.* 43.21.

78. Gregory Nazianzen, *Or.* 43.19. The characterization of Athens dramatically overstates things. All cities in the empire remained full of idols in the 350s. For the possibility that Gregory is also overstating his connection with Basil, see D. Konstan, "How to Praise a Friend: Gregory Nazianzus's Funeral Oration for St. Basil the Great," in *Greek Biography and Panegyric in Late Antiquity*, ed. T. Hägg and P. Rousseau (Berkeley, 2000), 160–79.

79. For this timeline, see Rousseau, *Basil of Caesarea*, 66.

80. Rousseau, *Basil of Caesarea*, 63–64, 71–72; Basil, *Ep.* 223.5 also describes Basil's living situation. Basil's letter to Gregory is lost, but Gregory's response survives (Gregory, *Ep.* 1).

81. Gregory, *Ep.* 1.1, trans. Storin.

82. *Ep.* 1.2, trans. Storin.

83. Rousseau, *Basil of Caesarea*, 66; Storin, "Letters of Gregory," 21.

84. Gregory repeatedly terms the ordination a "tyranny" (e.g., *Or.* 1.1; *Or.* 2.6; *Carm.* 2.1.11.345). Elm, *Sons of Hellenism*, 42–59, however, demonstrates that it was nothing of the sort but instead a step that Gregory likely expected and probably welcomed.

85. Elm, *Sons of Hellenism*, 183–201, expertly demonstrates that this refusal, flight, and eventual acceptance fit within a series of classical topoi. One should not take Gregory's account of them at face value.

86. Rousseau, *Basil of Caesarea*, 67; Gregory, *Ep.* 8.

87. Gregory, *Ep.* 8.1–4, trans. Storin.

88. Gregory, *Ep.* 16.4, trans. Storin. The bishop in question is Eusebius of Caesarea, a prelate whom both Gregory and Basil suspected was not orthodox (Gregory, *Or.* 43.28; Rousseau, *Basil of Caesarea*, 135).

89. Gregory, *Epp.* 17 and 18 show how tense the exchanges became.

90. Gregory, *Ep.* 19.7, trans. Storin.

91. Gregory, *Ep.* 19.1, trans. Storin.

92. His father was *PLRE* 1: Amphilochius 2.

93. On Amphilochius, see J. Maxwell, *Christianization and Communication in Late Antiquity* (Cambridge, 2006), 37–39.

94. Gregory, *Ep.* 63.3.

95. Gregory, *Ep.* 63.1, trans. Storin.

96. Gregory, *Ep.* 63.3, trans. Storin.

97. Gregory, *Ep.* 63.3, trans. Storin.

98. Libanius, *Ep.* 144.2, trans. Norman.

99. *Ep.* 144.2–3.

100. Palladius, *Dial.* 5. For Chrysostom's family situation, see Hunter, *Comparison*, 3; J.N.D. Kelly, *Golden Mouth: The Story of John Chrysostom* (Ithaca, NY, 1995), 4; A.H.M. Jones, "Saint Chrysostom's Parentage and Education," *HTR* 46 (1953): 171–73.

101. *De sacerdote* 1.2.

102. *De sacerdote* 1.2.

103. *De sacerdote* 1.2.

104. Note, for example, the cases of Paulinus and, later, that of Melania and Pinianus (for discussion, see Brown, *Through The Eye of a Needle*, 184–85, 209–10 [Paulinus] and 294–98 [Melania and Pinianus]).

105. For example, Barsanuphius and John, *Epp.* 571 and 572, which caution Aelianus not to dispose of his property before taking care of his dependents. On this, see as well J. Hevelone-Harper, *Disciples of the Desert: Monks, Laity, and Spiritual Authority in Sixth-Century Gaza* (Baltimore, 2005), 122–23.

106. *Ad Theodorum Lapsum* 1.14.

107. *PLRE* 1: Urbanus 3.

108. *Ad Theodorum lapsum* 1.17, NPNF trans.

109. *Ad Theodorum lapsum* 1.17, NPNF trans.

110. *Ad Theodorum lapsum* 2.4, NPNF trans.

111. *De sacerdote* 1.2.

112. This system of mutual support is laid out in the Pachomian biographical traditions (B. 105, 127–29; G^1 120b-c). For discussion, see Watts, *Riot in Alexandria*, 99–107.

113. Developed in S. Schwartz, *Were the Jews a Mediterranean Society? Reciprocity and Solidarity in Ancient Judaism* (Princeton, NJ, 2010), 1–20.

114. This would be a consequence of a situation where, to draw on the formulation of Rodney Stark, "interpersonal attachments to members [of the circle] overbalanced their attachments to non-members" and pushed them into a position unlike one readily accepted by outsiders (Stark, *The Rise of Christianity: A Sociologist Reconsiders History* [Princeton, NJ, 1996], 16). For this model, see as well J. Lofland and R. Stark, "Becoming a World-Saver: A Theory of Conversion to a Deviant Perspective," *American Sociological Review* 30 (1965): 862–75.

115. This is nowhere made more explicit than in Chrysostom's *Oppugnatores* 3.3–4, 11–18, where he outlines a system of Christian education based on ascetic principles. For discussion of this, see Hunter, *Comparison*, 32–36; and the forthcoming discussion of Jan Stenger.

116. For this view, see Chrysostom, *Oppugnatores*, book 1, as well as the discussion of R.L. Wilken, *John Chrysostom and the Jews: Rhetoric and Reality in the Late Fourth Century* (Berkeley, 1983), 26.

117. For the claim that priests had an obligation to resist imperial authorities when laws of God were at stake, see Liebeschuetz, *Ambrose and John Chrysostom*, 91–94, 148–52.

118. No one expresses this view better than John Chrysostom when he states that the monk who is free of worldly attachments "will address kings with exceedingly great power" (*Oppugnatores* 2.8). For a deeper analysis of the intersection between freedom of expression and ascetic achievement, see the extensive treatment of Liebeschuetz, *Ambrose and John Chrysostom*.

119. Chrysostom, *Ad Theodorum lapsum* 1.1. Cf. *Oppugnatores* 3.6 and the analysis of F. Leduc, "La thème de la vaine gloire chez Saint Jean Chrysostome," *Proche-Orient Chrétienne* 29 (1969): 3–32.

CHAPTER 8. BISHOPS, BUREAUCRATS, AND ARISTOCRATS UNDER GRATIAN, VALENTINIAN II, AND THEODOSIUS

1. On mortality rates, see, for example, B. Frier, "Roman Life Expectancy: Ulpian's Evidence," *HSCP* 86 (1982): 213–51; W. Scheidel, "Emperors, Aristocrats, and the Grim Reaper: Towards a Demographic Profile of the Roman Elite," *CQ* 49 (1999): 254–81; T. Parkin, *Old Age in the Roman World: A Cultural and Social History* (Baltimore, 2003), 36–56.

2. For his death, see Ammianus 30.6.

3. Ammianus 30.10; Zosimus 4.19; *Epit. de Caes.* 46.10. On Gratian's position and the possibility that he was actually administering Gaul while his father campaigned in Illyricum, see G. Kelly, "The Political Crisis of AD 375–6," *Chiron* 43 (2013): 357–406, at 366–67.

4. Ammianus 30.10. For the possibility of court rivalry and not fear of rebellion, see Kelly, "Political Crisis," 368, 374.

5. For Gratian's delay in recognizing Valentinian II, see Kelly, "Political Crisis," 370.

6. Ammianus 28.1.57.

7. Ammianus 28.1.57. For discussion, see J. Matthews, *Western Aristocracies and Imperial Court, A.D. 364–425* (Oxford, 1975), 65. On the possibility that the retirements of Maximinus and some of the leading courtiers who sponsored the proclamation of Valentinian II all happened at once and served as a sort of mutual disarmament of two court factions, see Kelly, "Political Crisis," 385–87.

8. *CTh* 9.1.13, 1.6.7, and 9.35.3.

9. *Ep.* 1.13, written to Ausonius, who would have taken particular interest in the reception given to this speech of his student. For discussion, see C. Sogno, *Q. Aurelius Symmachus: A Political Biography* (Ann Arbor, MI, 2006), 25–26; Matthews, *Western Aristocracies*, 67; M. Salzman, ed. and trans., *The Letters of Symmachus: Book 1* (Atlanta, 2011), 41–43. For Symmachus's echo of Pliny here, see G. Kelly, "Pliny and Symmachus," *Arethusa* 46.2 (2013): 261–87.

10. "Ideo magnus, ideo praeclarus es, quia primum te mavis esse quam solum . . . et quasi amari imperatoribus tantum liceret, privatorum merita presserunt" (Symmachus, *Or.* 5, trans. Sogno). For discussion, see Sogno, *Symmachus*, 23–24. Symmachus speaks of the reception of this speech in *Ep.* 1.44, to Praetextatus.

284 | Notes to Pages 170–171

11. The *Pro patre* is *Oration 4*. For discussion, see Sogno, *Symmachus*, 25; Matthews, *Western Aristocracies*, 67.

12. On Maximinus and his downfall, see Symmachus, *Or.* 4.11; *Ep.* 10.2.3 (addressed to Gratian).

13. As Kelly ("Political Crisis," 392) notes, Claudius Antonius not Ausonius immediately takes over as prefect of Gaul. As noted below, however, the symbolism of that appointment was very important to the reconciliation with the senate that Gratian wished to achieve and thus may not be an accurate representation of the relative authority of the two men. I am also less willing than Kelly to dismiss the appointment of Ausonius's son Hesperius as proconsul of Africa in 376 as evidence of Ausonius's influence at that time.

14. For discussion of Ausonius's career in this period, see H. Sivan, *Ausonius of Bordeaux: Genesis of a Gallic Aristocracy* (London, 1993), 132; Matthews, *Western Aristocracies*, 69–70.

15. PLRE 1: Iulius Ausonius 5.

16. Matthews, *Western Aristocracies*, 69–71.

17. *PLRE* 1: Decimius Hilarianus Hesperius 2. A. Coşkun (*Die gens Ausoniana an der Macht: Untersuchungen zu Decimius Magnus Ausonius und seiner Familie* [Oxford, 2002], 136–40) has argued that Hesperius's prefecture began as early as 377, but I am persuaded by Salzman's argument against this (*Letters of Symmachus*, 145).

18. Ausonius, *Praef.* 4.35–36.

19. Ausonius must have retired from the prefecture of Gaul by December 3, 379, when Siburius, his successor, received *CTh* 11.31.7.

20. He is last attested in this office by *CTh* 10.20.10, dated to May 14, 380.

21. Kelly ("Political Crisis," 376–77) perceptively notes that Gratian's reconciliation with the senate began before he knew what the regime of Valentinian II planned to do. As such, it was a preemptive effort by Gratian to ensure that no senators entertained the thought of accepting a rival court organized around Valentinian II.

22. *PLRE* 1: Fl. Claudius Antonius 5. The window of dates is suggested by *CTh* 9.19.4 (addressed to Maximinus and dated to April 16, 376) and *CTh* 13.3.11 (addressed to Antonius and dated to May 23). For correspondence with Symmachus, see *Ep.* 1.89–93. For discussion of Antonius's career, see Salzman, *Letters of Symmachus*, 161–62; Matthews, *Western Aristocracies*, 65.

23. Described by Symmachus, *Ep.* 1.89. For the identification of the oration named in the letter, see R. Lizzi Testa, *Senatori, popolo, papi: Il governo di Roma al tempo dei Valentiniani* (Bari, 2004), 225–48, 432–33; Salzman, *Letters of Symmachus*, 164 n. 2.

24. Matthews, *Western Aristocracies*, 66.

25. *ILS* 1256. For discussion, see Matthews, *Western Aristocracies*, 65.

26. This point has been extensively discussed. See, for example, M. Salzman, *The Making of a Christian Aristocracy* (Cambridge, MA, 2002), 102–3; Matthews, *Western Aristocracies*, 69–76; Sivan, *Ausonius*, 13–22.

27. Gracchus was apparently a Christian convert. For this tendency in Gratian's appointments, see Salzman, *Making a Christian Aristocracy*, 103 and app. 4.

28. For a clear statement of Ausonius's attachment to the idea of imperial service binding younger generations in much the same way that it bound his peers, see *Protr. ad nepotem* 94–100.

29. Described at Ammianus 31.3–4; Eunapius, fr. 42; Socrates, *HE* 4.34; Sozomen, *HE* 6.37. For discussion, see P. Heather, *Goths and Romans, 332–489* (Oxford, 1991), 128–35; R.M. Errington, *Roman Imperial Policy from Julian to Theodosius* (Chapel Hill, NC, 2006), 59–62; M. Kulikowski, *Rome's Gothic Wars* (Cambridge, 2007), 123–38.

30. For this revolt and the possible involvement of the Greuthungi as well as the Tervingi, see P. Heather and D. Moncur, *Politics, Philosophy, and Empire: Select Orations of Themistius* (Liverpool, 2001), 200. Kulikowski, *Rome's Gothic Wars*, 131–32; Matthews, *Western Aristocracies*, 89.

31. Ammianus 31.7–13; Heather, *Goths and Romans*, 143–47; Kulikowski, *Rome's Gothic Wars*, 139–43.

32. For the assignment of much of Illyricum, traditionally under Western control, to Theodosius, see Sozomen, *HE* 4.1–2. There is no consensus about how much of Illyricum Theodosius had been given in 379. Heather ("Liar in Winter: Themistius and Theodosius," in *From the Tetrarchs to the Theodosius,* ed. S. McGill, C. Sogno, and E. Watts [Cambridge, 2010], 185 n. 1) suggests that Theodosius took just the eastern part. For the possibility of it being the whole diocese and not just part, see R.M. Errington, "Theodosius and the Goths," *Chiron* 26 (1996): 1–27, at 23–26.

33. Matthews, *Western Aristocracies*, 115.

34. Zosimus 4.25.1; 4.28.1–4 implausibly says that no petitions were denied.

35. Heather, "Liar in Winter," 195–96. For the lack of familiarity with cases, see Ammianus 30.9.3. For parallel developments following Constantine's victory over Licinius, see Heather, "New Men for New Constantines?," in *New Constantines: The Rhythm of Imperial Renewal in Byzantium, 4th–13th Centuries,* ed. P. Magdalino (Aldershot, 1994), 11–33.

36. Heather and Moncur, *Politics, Philosophy, and Empire*, 206.

37. Heather and Moncur, *Politics, Philosophy, and Empire*, 207, on the basis of Themistius, *Or.* 15. See too the discussion of N. McLynn, "Moments of Truth: Gregory Nazianzus and Theodosius I," in McGill, Sogno, and Watts, *From the Tetrarchs to the Theodosians*, 215–39, at 226–27.

38. Heather and Moncur, *Politics, Philosophy, and Empire*, 207.

39. For the treaty and events leading to it, see Errington, "Theodosius and the Goths," 1–27; Heather and Moncur, *Politics, Philosophy, and Empire*, 208–12; Heather, "Liar in Winter," 203–13; Errington, *Roman Imperial Policy*, 63–65; Kulikowski, *Rome's Gothic Wars*, 152–53. Note too Heather's suggestion ("Liar in Winter," 203–4) that Gratian may also have endorsed the terms of this treaty.

40. Heather, "Liar in Winter," 194–98; N. McLynn, *Ambrose of Milan: Church and Court in a Christian Capital* (Berkeley, 1994), 107; *CTh* 10.10.12–15; Libanius, *Or.* 1.186, 196; Themistius, *Or.* 15.192d, 194d.

41. Themistius, *Or.* 34.xiii; Heather, "Liar in Winter," 195.

42. *CTh* 16.1.2 is often seen as a key moment in this. For a thorough discussion of how the handover worked in practice, see McLynn, "Moments of Truth," 222–31.

43. For the Council of Constantinople, see, among many others, McLynn, "Moments of Truth," 232–39. For this as possible preemption of Gratian, see Heather and Moncur, *Politics, Philosophy, and Empire*, 215; McLynn, *Ambrose of Milan*, 123–46.

44. B. Croke, "Reinventing Constantinople," in McGill, Sogno, and Watts, *From the Tetrarchs to the Theodosians*, 241–64.

45. For his illness, see *Or.* 14.180c; restoring balance and justice: *Or.* 14.181a.

46. *Or.* 14.181c, trans. Heather and Moncur.

47. *Or.* 14.181d, trans. Heather and Moncur.

48. *Or.* 14.181d-182a.

49. He speaks at *Or.* 14.181b about Theodosius making "fighting spirit return to the cavalry and the infantry . . . while he makes farmers a terror to the enemy"—an indication that he knew that the emperor was still assembling an army. On this, see too the comments of Errington, *Roman Imperial Policy*, 63.

50. *Or.* 14.183a. Heather and Moncur (*Politics, Philosophy, and Empire*, 228 n. 68) see a careful rhetorical balancing here, though Vanderspoel's diagnosis of signs of tension between the two emperors (*Themistius and the Imperial Court* [Ann Arbor, MI, 1995], 197) seems the best way to explain this deliberate rhetoric.

51. *Or.* 14.183a-184a.

52. Vanderspoel, *Themistius*, 198.

53. Socrates, *HE* 4.38. There is no way that this was a serious threat, but the Constantinopolitan Socrates's memory of it probably reflects the city's deep unease about Valens and his intentions.

54. There is debate about how much of Themistius's profile reflects Theodosius's own plans about how to deal with the Gothic threat. Errington, "Theodosius and the Goths," 8–9, sees *Oration* 14 as a projection of senatorial hopes not Theodosian policy. Against this, see Heather and Moncur, *Politics, Philosophy, and Empire*, 223–24.

55. *Or.* 15.184b-185b; this and all passages of *Or.* 15 come from the translation of Heather and Moncur.

56. *Or.* 15.188c-189a.

57. *Or.* 15.186b.

58. *Or.* 15.197b.

59. *Or.* 15.191d.

60. *Or.* 15.192b-c.

61. *Or.* 15.192d.

62. *Or.* 15.193a-c.

63. *Or.* 15.194d-195a.

64. *Or.* 15.195b (Antiochus and Ariston); 15.198b (single kingdom).

65. Like Themistius, Saturninus had lost influence under Julian because of his ties to Constantius and was sent into exile following the Chalcedon trials (Ammianus 22.3). He recovered his position under Valens because he was serving as *comes* in 373 (Basil, *Ep.* 132) and *magister equitum* at Adrianople. He was one of the few commanders to survive the battle. He thrived under Theodosius and remained influential into the early years of the fifth century (see

Zosimus 5.18; Socrates, *HE* 6.6; Sozomen, *HE* 8.4; all three mention that Gaïnas asked that Saturninus be turned over to him in 400). For his full career, see *PLRE* 1: Flavius Saturninus 10.

66. The terms of this treaty have been widely discussed. See, for example, H. Wolfram, *History of the Goths,* trans. T. Dunlap (Berkeley, 1988), 133–35; G. Wirth, "Rome and Its Germanic Partners in the Fourth Century," in *Kingdoms of the Empire: The Integration of Barbarians in Late Antiquity,* ed. W. Pohl (Leiden, 1997), 13–56; Heather and Moncur, *Politics, Philosophy, and Empire,* 259–64; Kulikowski, *Rome's Gothic Wars,* 152–53.

67. The idea is most concretely expressed in *Or.* 16.207b.

68. *Or.* 16.202c-d. Here he makes his case by emphasizing that Theodosius appointed only the best men for each job in the empire.

69. Themistius even prepares for the tension this step would cause by writing Gratian almost entirely out of the imperial decision-making process (*Or.* 16.207b). For this, see Heather and Moncur, *Politics, Philosophy, and Empire,* 256–57, 264. For a change in visual propaganda following the proclamation of Arcadius, see figure 13, *RIC* IX.15 (Cyzicus). This coin, which shows Arcadius crowned by the hand of God, was issued between Arcadius's proclamation on January 19, 383, and the death of Gratian that August. It also features a portrait type that differed significantly from the standard, nearly identical images of Gratian, Valentinian II, and Theodosius that had appeared on coins since 379.

70. This would, of course, prove controversial. For more on the controversy surrounding his appointment, see Heather and Moncur, *Politics, Philosophy, and Empire,* 287–98. If accepted, the redating of Palladas to the early fourth century by Kevin Wilkinson ("Palladas and the Age of Constantine," *JRS* 99 [2009]: 36–60) will complicate the traditional argument that Themistius's *Oration* 34 was framed as a response to a criticism voiced by Palladas in *Greek Anthology* 11.292.

71. He says as much at *Or.* 34.xiii. Further complicating matters was his earlier assertion (in *Or.* 23.292c-d) of a distinction between representing one's city and serving in an imperial office. The former was acceptable for a philosopher; the latter was not. For this, see G. Dagron, *Naissance d'une capitale* (Paris, 1974), 46–48, 52–3; Heather and Moncur, *Politics, Philosophy, and Empire,* 286–87. For more on the context of this appointment, see chapter 9.

72. He had already acknowledged, at the beginning of *Oration* 16, "I have often thought to myself that, since my body is worn out and old age advances, now is the time to lay aside my writing tablet" (*Or.* 16.199c, trans. Heather and Moncur). This is said for rhetorical effect, but the realization of one's mortality that lies behind it was quite real. It is also notable how much *Oration* 34 dwells on his previous public service (e.g., *Or.* 34.xii-xiv, xxix). Implicit in these two recitations of Themistius's curriculum vitae is the idea that the urban prefecture appropriately caps a long career of public service.

73. As *Oration* 34 shows, Themistius framed his service as that of a philosopher who worked alongside the most philosophical emperor he had ever encountered. Serving under such a sovereign did not conflict with his status as a philosopher; it proved an essential complement to it.

74. These defenses are *Orations* 17, 31, and 34.

75. For a discussion of Gregory's various professional peregrinations, see now B. Storin, "The *Letters* of Gregory of Nazianzus: Discourse and Community in Late Antique Epistolary Culture" (PhD diss., Indiana University, 2012), 12–80.

76. For the council at Antioch, see G. Bardy, "Le concile d'Antioche (379)," *Revue Benedictine* 45 (1933): 196–213; Storin, "*Letters* of Gregory," 50; N. Lenski, *Failure of Empire: Valens and the Roman State in the Fourth Century* (Berkeley, 2002), 262; R. Staats, "Die römische Tradition im Symbol von 381 (n. C.) und seine Entstehung auf der Synode von Antiochien 379," *VChr* 44 (1990): 209–22.

77. For Theodosius's efforts to co-opt Demophilus, the non-Nicene bishop of Constantinople, see Socrates, *HE* 5.7, as well as the discussion of McLynn, "Moments of Truth," 218–19; T. Urbainczyk, *Socrates of Constantinople* (Ann Arbor, MI, 1997), 150.

78. Socrates, *HE* 5.7.

79. *Or.* 33.1–5. For discussion, see McLynn, "Moments of Truth," 222–24. This was a oration primarily about Arian misdeeds not imperial policy, but its beginning and the fact that it was delivered in the context of Theodosius's pro-Nicene legislative activities in the early 380s is not coincidental. For the dating of this to the Easter season of 380, see J. McGuckin, *St. Gregory of Nazianzus* (Crestwood, NY, 2001), ix and 240 n. 44.

80. For *Oration* 37, see McLynn, "Moments of Truth," 230–31.

81. Gregory, *DVS* 1302–4. The *De vita sua* is a later work, but McLynn ("Moments of Truth," 217) is correct to see passages of it as reflections of Gregory's presentation of Theodosius during the time of his episcopacy. For more on the context of this, see chapter 9.

82. Themistius, of course, made the same point at basically the same time in *Oration* 15.

83. For the December date, see McLynn, "Moments of Truth," 220, on the basis of Marcellinus Comes, *Chron.* s. a. 380. See too B. Croke, *The Chronicle of Marcellinus: Translation and Commentary* (Sydney, 1995), 57. For violence directed against Gregory, see Gregory, *Or.* 23.5; 33.3–5; 41.5; Storin, "*Letters* of Gregory," 52–54.

84. Theodosius particularly wanted to secure the agreement of the followers of Macedonius, the former bishop of Constantinople (Socrates, *HE* 5.8; Sozomen, *HE* 7.7).

85. Gregory, *DVS* 1798. Note the discussion of McLynn, "Moments of Truth," 236.

86. For Nectarius's background, see Socrates, *HE* 5.8; Sozomen, *HE* 7.8; Rufinus 2.21.

87. Storin, "*Letters* of Gregory," 62; N. McLynn, "The Voice of Conscience: Gregory Nazianzen in Retirement," in *Vescovi e pastori in epoca Teodosiana* (Rome, 1997), 2:299–308. He agreed to take up a position as bishop of Nazianzus in 382 before resigning in 383 or 384, never to hold episcopal office again.

88. *CTh* 16.10.8.

89. *CTh* 16.10.9, trans. Pharr.

90. *CTh* 16.10.9.

91. This is made clear from a reference to a now-lost law of Gratian in *CTh* 16.10.20.1 and also from Symmachus's Third *Relatio*. For discussion, see Alan Cameron, *Last Pagans of Rome* (Oxford, 2012), 39–51.

92. The Altar of Victory had first been removed by Constantius before being replaced, presumably by Julian.

93. Symmachus, *Rel.* 3.7 and Ambrose, *Ep.* 17.3 (Altar of Victory); Symmachus, *Rel.* 3.11–12 and Ambrose, *Ep.* 18.13 and 18.18 (Vestals); Symmachus, *Rel.* 3.12–14 and Ambrose, *Ep.* 18.13–16 (public funding). Extensive modern discussion of these measures exists. See, among many others, Salzman, *Letters of Symmachus*, xxxii; Cameron, *Last Pagans*, 33–48; Sogno, *Symmachus*, 45–46; McLynn, *Ambrose of Milan*, 151–52; R. Lizzi Testa, "Christian Emperor, Vestal Virgins, and Priestly Colleges: Reconsidering the End of Roman Paganism," *Ant. Tard.* 15 (2007): 251–62.

94. For this line of interpretation, see McLynn, *Ambrose of Milan*, 151–52.

95. Cameron, *Last Pagans*, 46. On the nature of public sacrifices in Rome in this period, see M. Salzman, "The End of Public Sacrifice: Changing Definitions of Sacrifice in Post-Constantinian Rome and Italy," in *Ancient Mediterranean Sacrifice*, ed. J. Wright Knust and Z. Várhelyi (Oxford, 2011), 168–77; and chapter 1.

96. Cameron, *Last Pagans*, 45.

97. Cameron, *Last Pagans*, 37; Sogno, *Symmachus*, 46.

98. For discussion of the sources, see Alan Cameron, "Gratian's Repudiation of the Pontifical Robe," *JRS* 58 (1968): 96–102.

99. Ammianus 16.10. For discussion, see chapter 4.

100. *Rel.* 3.1.

101. Ambrose, *Ep.* 17. For discussion, see Salzman, *Letters of Symmachus*, xxxii; McLynn, *Ambrose*, 151–52.

102. An identification proposed by D. Vera, *Commento storico alle "Relationes" di Q. Aurelius Symmachus* (Pisa, 1981), 26–27, and accepted by Sogno, *Symmachus*, 47–48.

103. For the brilliant portrait of imperial dysfunction in the last years of Gratian's reign, see McLynn, *Ambrose*, 149–57.

104. *PLRE* 1: Magnus Maximus 39. For the nature of his position in Britain, see Gregory of Tours, *HF* 1.43; *Chron. Min.* 1.646.7.

105. See here the discussion of McLynn, *Ambrose*, 154; Matthews, *Western Aristocracies*, 175–76.

106. For his Illyricum position, see Zosimus 4.33; McLynn, *Ambrose*, 161.

107. For this view of Ambrose's mission to Maximus, see McLynn, *Ambrose*, 162.

108. Ambrose, *Ep.* 24; McLynn, *Ambrose*, 161–62; Matthews, *Western Aristocracies*, 177.

109. Themistius, *Or.* 18.221a. In the summer of 384, Theodosius sent an expedition of troops west to avenge the murder of Gratian, but the force never reached Maximus and may simply have been a symbolic gesture of support. For discussion of Theodosius's policy toward Maximus, note Matthews, *Western Aristocracies*, 177–79. For the eventual breaking of this freeze, see chapter 9.

110. For Bauto's career, see *PLRE* 1: Flavius Bauto. For the marriage of his daughter Eudoxia, arranged while she was still a child, see Philostorgius, *HE* 11.6.

111. On his prefecture, see Matthews, *Western Aristocracies,* 174; Lizzi Testa, *Senatori, popolo, papi,* 318 n. 418. Probus's close attachment to the regime of Valentinian II is shown by his decision to flee with the emperor to Thessaloniki in 387 when Maximus advanced into Italy (Socrates, *HE* 5.11).

112. The difficulty of the task comes through in Symmachus's various state papers written during his tenure as urban prefect. For a survey of the various frustrations that Symmachus encountered (which ranged from incompetent subordinates to concern about finding enough grain for the city of Rome), see the discussion of Sogno, *Symmachus,* 52–56.

113. Symmachus, *Rel.* 36, 44. See the discussion of Sogno, *Symmachus,* 48.

114. Symmachus, *Rel.* 21.1. Praetextatus's involvement is also suggested by the *Carmen contra paganos* 112–14. For this poem's association with Praetextatus, see Cameron, *Last Pagans,* 273–318; and chapter 10.

115. *CCP* 103–9.

116. *Rel.* 3.1–2. For discussion, see Matthews, *Western Aristocracies,* 206.

117. *Rel.* 3.10.

118. For a similar line of inquiry, see Matthews, *Western Aristocracies,* 208.

119. *Rel.* 3.8–9.

120. *Rel.* 3.4. As Peter Brown (*Through the Eye of a Needle: Wealth, the Fall of Rome, and the Making of Christianity in the West, 350–550 AD* [Princeton, NJ, 2012], 103–9) has noted, this appeal to a divine victory misses some of the thrust of later fourth-century imperial self-presentation in which Victory is the emperor's personal companion. The Altar was therefore potentially unnecessary.

121. *Rel.* 3.14.

122. This had happened to Symmachus's own father in 375 (Ammianus 27.3). For discussion of this tendency, see Sogno, *Symmachus,* 52–53; Matthews, *Western Aristocracies,* 19–20. For the particular problems Symmachus faced, see *Rel.* 18 and 35.

123. *Rel.* 3.17.

124. For Praetextatus's possible connection to the request, see Matthews, *Western Aristocracies,* 205. Symmachus's claim that a majority of senators backed his appeal can be contested, but he certainly represented a large group. For discussion of this question, see Matthews, *Western Aristocracies,* 206–7.

125. Ambrose, *Ep.* 17.8; all translations of *Ep.* 17 are adapted from the NPNF translation.

126. Ambrose, *Ep.* 17.1–3.

127. Ambrose, *Ep.* 17.4–6. Symmachus does not make this argument, but Ambrose evidently imagined that he would.

128. Ambrose, *Ep.* 17.9–11.

129. Ambrose, *Ep.* 17.14–18.

130. Ambrose, *Ep.* 17.10.

131. Ambrose, *Ep.* 17.13.

132. McLynn, *Ambrose,* 167.

133. McLynn, *Ambrose,* 167 n. 35. The letter is Ambrose, *Ep.* 18. For this letter and its irrelevance to the actual decision made by the consistory, see Ambrose, *Ep. extra coll.* 57.3.

134. It is worth emphasizing that, despite these claims, bishops still seldom actually tried to use this influence that they claimed to have.

CHAPTER 9. OLD AGE IN A YOUNG MAN'S EMPIRE

1. For an examination of this point, see T. Parkin, *Old Age in the Roman World: A Social and Cultural History* (Baltimore, 2003), chap. 9.

2. This is not to suggest that Libanius and those like him did not interact at all with such men. Libanius, for example, taught a number of men who would become bishops and corresponded with the bishop Amphilochius of Iconium (see chapter 7).

3. *Or.* 16.199c, trans. Heather and Moncur.

4. *Or.* 16.199d, quoting Euripides, *Bacchae* 204.

5. For discussion of the context of this peace treaty, see chapter 8.

6. These are *Orations* 17, 31, and 34. For discussion of them, see chapter 8.

7. Quoted by Stobaeus, *Flor.* 50.2.85 [W-H p. 1051.3–14]. The translation is that of Parkin, *Old Age,* 244. For discussion of Juncus's possible identity, see J.H. Oliver, "Xenophon of Ephesus and the Antithesis Historia-Philosophia," in *Arktouros: Hellenic Studies Presented to Bernard M.W. Knox,* ed. G. Bowersock, W. Burkert, and M.C. Putnam (New York, 1979), 401–6, at 401 n. 1.

8. Maximianus, *Eleg.* 1.281–82. See the discussion of Parkin, *Old Age,* 245.

9. Pliny, *Ep.* 4.23, trans. Firth. For this ideal expressed in other authors, see Seneca, *Ep.* 93 and *Dial.* 10, as well as the discussion of Parkin, *Old Age,* 61–74.

10. Plutarch's *On Whether an Old Man Should Engage in Public Affairs* argues for the moral obligation for continued public service. His view was, however, an outlier.

11. Parkin, *Old Age,* 126, on the basis of Cassius Dio 55.3.1; Pliny, *Ep.* 4.23; Seneca the Elder, *Controv.* 1.8.4; cf. Ps.-Quintilian, *Decl. min.* 306.16.

12. Parkin, *Old Age,* 134–53. The Constantinian reduction in the legal age is demonstrated by *P.Oxy* 889 and *PSI* 685. For discussion, see as well T.D. Barnes, *The New Empire of Diocletian and Constantine* (Cambridge, MA, 1982), 237. For another example of Constantinian concern for retirees, see the discussion of S. Connolly, "Constantine Answers the Veterans," in *From the Tetrarchs to the Theodosians,* ed. S. McGill, C. Sogno, and E. Watts (Cambridge, 2010), 93–114.

13. Parkin, *Old Age,* 150 (for deliberate early retirement); B. Frier, "Roman Life Expectancy: Ulpian's Evidence," *HSCP* 86 (1982): 226 (for age rounding).

14. These numbers are based on Parkin, *Old Age,* 104. Parkin's numbers are broadly consistent with the demographic information analyzed by Frier ("Roman Life Expectancy," table 5), which shows that 10 percent of the people who lived past age five survived into their seventies, and 2 percent lived into their eighties. Frier estimates, however, that fifty-two out of every one hundred babies failed to make it to age five, leading to a population in which the overall number of old people was far smaller than the number of young.

15. For this senatorial expansion, see chapter 8.

16. Symmachus, the urban prefect of Rome when Themistius was prefect of Constantinople, was forty-four. For a broader survey of the ages at which senators held high office, see Parkin, *Old Age,* 116–17.

17. For discussion, see chapter 4.

18. *Ep.* 21.13–15, trans. Evelyn-White.

19. Ausonius, *Ep.* 22, quoting Aristophanes, *Clouds* 1417.

20. These are letters 840–1112 in Foerster's edition. For discussion of this collection and its relationship to the other surviving Libanian correspondence, see L. Van Hoof, "(Self-) Censorship or Self Fashioning? Gaps in Libanius' Letter Collection," *Revue Belge,* forthcoming. Van Hoof does not claim that letters 840–1112 now represent a separate, distinctly organized collection, but there is reason to think that it might once have been such a thing. As will be discussed below, the thematic coherence of this group of letters and the particular personalities it features suggest strongly that the letters assembled here were deliberately selected, grouped, and organized to reflect in particular ways on Libanius's later career. None of the main manuscripts distinguish this batch of letters from the earlier groups, but it is clear that letter 840 marks a new start in the collection. For what it is worth, letter 1113, which begins the third discrete batch of Libanian letters in the Vaticanus Graecus 83 manuscript (the letters now numbered 1113–1544 and dating to the years 363–65), works essentially as a meditation on how a letter should function. It too seems like the beginning of a discrete collection. It is possible, then, that three distinct large collections of Libanian letters were once prepared, each of which functioned in its own thematically unique way. I am also intrigued by an idea that Jorit Wintjes expressed to me in a personal conversation that letters 840–1112 may have been originally intended as a teaching collection assembled for the use of either the students of Libanius or those of an immediate successor.

21. This is Libanius, *Ep.* 947. For Hilarius, see *PLRE* 1: Hilarius 7.

22. *Ep.* 947.3, trans. Norman, adapted.

23. The migraines, a persistent problem, are described in *Or.* 1.268. For his failing eyesight, see *Or.* 1.281; *Ep.* 1039.

24. *Or.* 1.256. For Libanius's interactions with governors in the later 380s and early 390s, see the discussion in J. Wintjes, *Das Leben des Libanius* (Rahden, 2005), 221–26. It is notable that Libanius speaks in *Or.* 1 about even his difficulties with governors as challenges he overcomes. One can then doubt how serious the problems really were given Libanius's tendency to overstate the significance of his triumphs in that oration. For more discussion of the rhetorical nature of *Oration* 1, see Van Hoof, "Libanius' *Life* and Life," in *The Cambridge Companion to Libanius,* ed. L. Van Hoof (Cambridge, 2014).

25. Libanius, *Or.* 1.254, trans. Norman. Note, though, *Or.* 1.267, where Libanius claims to speak before a governor again, possibly either Timocrates (the governor who is praised in *Or.* 41) or Jullus (*Epp.* 935, 1038).

26. Theophilus is at Seeck, *BLZG* 312 (v). For Libanius's relationship with Theophilus, see O. Seeck, *Die Briefe des Libanius* (Leipzig, 1906), 464, as well as the more moderate discussion of A. Norman, *Libanius: Autobiography and Selected Letters* (Cambridge, MA, 1990), 438 note a.

27. *Ep.* 1075.2, trans. Norman.

28. *Ep.* 1075.3–4.

29. This letter is *Ep.* 1106.7.

30. For his death, see *Or.* 1.213.

31. *Or.* 1.232.

32. For the death of the friend's wife, see *Ep.* 1050.2. For Calliopius, see *Epp.* 1051.4; 1063.6. For the importance of assistants like Calliopius in the operation of a fourth-century school of rhetoric, see E. Watts, *City and School in Late Antique Athens and Alexandria* (Berkeley, 2006), 49–53.

33. *Or.* 1.278.

34. Cimon is mentioned as a child of school age in *Ep.* 625, a letter from the summer of 361, suggesting that the liaison that led to his birth occurred sometime in the early or mid-350s.

35. On her death, see Wintjes, *Libanius*, 233.

36. He is called Arabius in *Or.* 28.9; *Epp.* 625, 678, 1000, 1002; Cimon when mentioned in *Or.* 1.283, 54.12–13; *Epp.* 844, 1042, 1048–50. For a discussion of the situation with Cimon in the 390s, see Wintjes, *Libanius*, 229, 232–33.

37. For his education, see *Epp.* 625, 678.

38. He mentions his efforts at *Or.* 17.37 (under Julian), *Ep.* 1221 (under Jovian), *Or.* 1.145 (under Valentinian and Valens), and *Or.* 1.195–96 (under Theodosius).

39. One such figure was Heracleius (*PLRE* 1: Heracleius 7), Cimon's colleague as an advocate in the early 380s who would become *praeses Armeniae*. For their overlap, see Libanius, *Or.* 28.9, 13; 54.7–15, 76.

40. *Or.* 1.257.

41. The stripping of Cimon's governorship is described in *Or.* 1.278 and *Ep.* 1001. For the circumstances of this, see P. Petit, "Les senateurs de Constantinople dans l'oeuvre de Libanius," *L'Antiquité Classique* 26 (1957): 347–83, at 358ff.

42. On Cimon's injury, see *Ep.* 1023. For his death, see *Or.* 1.279–80; *Epp.* 1023, 1024, 1026, 1028, 1036–39, 1042, 1045, 1048–51, 1063–64.

43. *Or.* 1.280 (all translated passages of *Or.* 1 are based on Norman's translation, with slight modifications where context requires).

44. *Or.* 1.281.

45. *Ep.* 1051.2.

46. S. Bradbury, *Selected Letters of Libanius* (Liverpool, 2004), 12; cf. Norman (*Autobiography*, 2:4), who speaks of "melancholia and depression verging on paranoia," and calls (*Selected Letters*, 2:396 note a) the period after Cimon's death "another breakdown." For a counter to this, see Wintjes, *Libanius*, 236–37.

47. For this as it relates to the *Autobiography* in particular, see Van Hoof, "Libanius' *Life*."

48. *Ep.* 1051.8.

49. *PLRE* 1: Firminus 3. The letter is *Ep.* 1048 (all translated passages are based on Norman's translation, with slight modifications).

50. *Ep.* 1048.6, trans. Norman.

51. *Ep.* 1048.7.

52. *Ep.* 1048.8–9.

53. For discussion of how correspondents negotiated their relative status through the letters they exchanged, see J. Congrove, "Friendship, Rhetoric, and Authority in the Letters of St. Augustine of Hippo" (PhD diss., Indiana University, 2011).

54. For the need for this sort of balance in any consideration of Libanius's later years, see Wintjes, *Libanius,* 236–37.

55. For letter collections more generally, see E. Watts, C. Sogno, and B. Storin, "Late Antique Epistolography," in *Late Antique Epistolography,* ed. C. Sogno, B. Storin, and E. Watts (Berkeley, forthcoming); and, on the collection of Libanius in particular, see L. Van Hoof, "The Letters of Libanius," in the same volume. On the nature of this second group of Libanian letters, see too Van Hoof, "Self-Censorship."

56. A number of letters explain Cimon's journey to Constantinople as something taken against Libanius's advice (e.g., *Epp.* 1000.3, 1001.3, 1002.4, 1023.4). These details may or may not be true, but these letters combine with *Or.* 1.279 to create a narrative that absolves Libanius of any responsibility for the fiasco.

57. *PLRE* 1: Fl. Eutolmius Tatianus 5. For Libanius's relationship with Tatianus and his son Proculus, see Wintjes, *Libanius,* 204–9, 230–31. For reasons that the discussion below makes clear, I am not convinced by Wintjes's idea that Libanius must have destroyed correspondence with Tatianus after the latter's fall.

58. For discussion of this tendency during the reign of Valens, see chapter 6.

59. For the family estate in Sidyma, see Cedrenus 603–4; Theophanes 104 (AM 5943); Nicephorus Callistus, *HE* 15.1. For his connection to Sidyma, see too *IGC* 293² = D 8844 Sidyma.

60. For Maximus's invasion of Italy, see Zosimus 4.42; Socrates, *HE* 5.11. For his usurpation, see chapter 8.

61. For Theodosius's campaign, see Zosimus 4.45–7. For the administrative necessities in the East, see J. Matthews, *Western Aristocracies and Imperial Court, A.D. 364–425* (Oxford, 1975), 224–25.

62. Zosimus 4.45.

63. Van Hoof, "(Self-) Censorship."

64. Τῶν πρώτων σου γραμμάτων εὐθὺς ἡμῖν ἐν ἀρχῇ τῆς ἀρχῆς ἡκόντων (*Ep.* 840.1).

65. *Ep.* 840.2.

66. *Ep.* 840.3.

67. *Ep.* 840.3.

68. For a list of all of the high-level officials in the later letters, see Seeck, *Die Briefe,* 442–44.

69. This letter is *Ep.* 1021. The other letters to Tatianus are *Epp.* 851, 855, 871, 872, 899, 909, 941, 959, 987, 990, and 992.

70. *Ep.* 1004 went to Symmachus. *Epp.* 847, 852, 856, 874, 885, 906, 922, 938, 940, 952, 967, 970, 991, 1022, and 1028 went to Proculus, and *Epp.* 896, 1043, 1051, 1064, 1071, 1087, 1092, and 1110 to Aristaenetus.

71. *Epp.* 865 and 1106 were addressed to Rufinus; *Epp.* 866, 972, 1007, and 1024 to Richomer; *Epp.* 868, 884, 898, and 925 to Ellebichus; and *Epp.* 845, 853, and 908 to Mardonius. For Libanius's relationships with these men, see Wintjes, *Libanius*, 211–12 (Richomer), 215–17 (Ellebichus), and 226–27 (Rufinus).

72. Pagans are, of course, well represented. I. Sandwell, *Religious Identity in Late Antiquity: Greeks, Jews, and Christians in Antioch* (Cambridge, 2007), 98–99, shows the presence of individual Christians within the letters. For the role of religion within Libanius's network, see too H.-G. Nesselrath, *Libanios: Zeuge einer schwindenden Welt* (Stuttgart, 2012), chap. 5.

73. For the tension between *curiales* and *honorati* in modern historiography, see, for example, J.H.W.G. Liebeschuetz, *Antioch: City and Imperial Administration in the Later Roman Empire* (Oxford, 1972), 174–92. Libanius's interactions with the Antiochene curia were often fraught in this period—a feature that figures more prominently in his orations than in the letter collection. For discussion, see Wintjes, *Libanius*, 229.

74. For Libanius's attitudes toward monks, see H.-G. Nesselrath, "Libanios und die Mönche," in *Von Homer bis Landion: Beiträge zur Antike und Spätantike sowie zu deren Rezeptions-und Wirkungsgeschichte,* ed. B. Suchla (Berlin, 2011), 243–67. The most notable supposed exchange between Libanius and such a dropout is the series of letters supposedly written by him to Basil. These letters are certainly a later forgery that did not originally belong in the Libanian collection. On this, see H.-G. Nesselrath, "Libanio e Basilio di Cesarea: Un dialogo interreligioso?," *Adamantius* 16 (2010): 338–52; as well as the discussion in chapter 10.

75. For Libanius teaching Chrysostom, see Palladius, *Vit. Chrysos.* 5; Socrates, *HE* 6.3. Note too the discussion of Wintjes, *Libanius*, 177–79.

76. For the possible nature of the tax, see the thorough summary of possibilities in R. Browning, "The Riot of A.D. 387 in Antioch: The Role of the Theatrical Claques in the Later Roman Empire," *JRS* 42 (1952): 13–20, at 14–15. For the riot in general, see now A. Quiroga Puertas, "Deflecting Attention and Shaping Reality with Rhetoric (The Case of the Riot of the Statues of A.D. 387 in Antioch), *Nova Tellus,* forthcoming. Libanius, *Or.* 22.4 seems to suggest this was an *aurum coronarium* assessed because of imperial anniversaries—a statement that cannot be correct. For other ancient sources, see Chrysostom, *Hom. de stat.* 3.7, 5.3, 8.4; Sozomen, *HE* 7.23; Zosimus 4.41; Theodoret, *HE* 5.20.

77. *Or.* 19.25, trans. Norman.

78. Libanius, *Or.* 19.26. For the nature of the elites represented here, see Liebeschuetz, *Antioch,* 41.

79. For reconstructions, see Browning, "Riot of A.D. 387," 15, on the basis of Libanius, *Or.* 22.6–7; G. Downey, *A History of Antioch in Syria* (Princeton, NJ, 1961), 426–33; Wintjes, *Libanius*, 213–15. Cf. Libanius, *Or.* 19.29; 20.4–5.

80. For the punishment of the individual rioters, see Libanius, *Or.* 19.36–37; John Chrysostom, *Hom. de stat.* 3.

81. A point made by P. Brown, *Power and Persuasion in Late Antiquity* (Madison, WI, 1992), 107–8. Many such acts were, in fact, unpunished in the

fourth century, including a memorable moment when the city of Edessa gave a statue of Constantius a public spanking (Libanius, *Or.* 19.48).

82. Libanius, *Or.* 19.56–59; 23; John Chrysostom, *Hom. de stat.* 11.2.

83. εἰσεκαλεῖτο μὲν οὗπερ ὁ δικαστὴς κατήγετο, τῶν τε ἀρξάντων οὐκ ὀλίγον τῆς τε βουλῆς ὁπόσον οὐκ ἐπεφεύγει (Libanius, *Or.* 22.20).

84. Libanius, *Or.* 21.10; 22.26.

85. Libanius, *Or.* 22.29–31; Chrysostom, *Hom. de stat.* 17.2.

86. Libanius, *Or.* 21.15–16 describes Caesarius's express journey to Constantinople, one that was so hurried that he even had "no dessert."

87. *Or.* 22.36.

88. This is a point he makes clearly in *Or.* 19.31, an oration finalized after the conclusion of the event. Former government officials come off less well in *Or.* 23.17–19, which was written before the situation had been resolved.

89. Libanius maintains this dichotomy between elite behavior and that of the Christian mob throughout his multiple discussions of the riot (e.g., *Or.* 20.3, 22.5). *Or.* 19.31 adds the detail that the mob first looked for Flavian and then rioted. For discussion of these passages and the particular way in which Libanius is navigating questions of religious identity in them, see Sandwell, *Religious Identity,* 173–76.

90. For this rhetorical attempt to excuse the city collectively by pinning blame for the riot on one segment of its population, see Sandwell, *Religious Identity,* 174.

91. *Or.* 1.253; 23.25. Downey (*History of Antioch,* 431) observes that this may have been a privilege that came from the honorary *praefectus praetorio* Libanius received in 383 or 384.

92. Libanius, *Or.* 23.26. The panegyric of 385 is mentioned at *Or.* 1.232 and 22.2.

93. Libanius, *Or.* 21.7. *Oration* 23 is the only Libanian speech that seems to have been delivered in a form close to what we have while the investigation was ongoing. It mainly argues against the chaotic flight of Antiochenes. *Orations* 19, 20, and 21 all relate to the investigation, though none reproduce the exact text of anything Libanius delivered at the time.

94. *Or.* 1.253.

95. *Or.* 1.252.

96. Suggested by Libanius, *Or.* 20.37.

97. *Or.* 23.17. Libanius certainly alludes to the trip to Constantinople made by the bishop Flavian following the riot.

98. *Or.* 22.36–37.

99. *Hom. de stat.* 17.3, NPNF trans.

100. *Hom. de stat.* 17.5. On this passage, see the analysis of Sandwell, *Religious Identities,* 139. The rhetorical contrast between Christians staying to help stricken people in a city and the flight of pagan elites bears strong similarities to Eusebius's description of Christian behavior during a plague in the reign of Maximinus Daia (*HE* 9.8.35). I thank an anonymous reader for pointing this parallel out to me. For the contrast of urban and rural space in the Riot of the Statues, see now C. Shepardson, *Controlling Contested Places: Late Antique Antioch and the Spatial Politics of Religious Controversy* (Berkeley, 2014), 147–54.

101. This is the thrust of Chrysostom, *Hom. de stat.* 21.

102. *Hom. de stat.* 21.1, 6, 8–18.

103. *Hom. de stat.* 21.6

104. *Hom. de stat.* 21.5.

105. *Hom. de stat.* 21.19.

106. See Sandwell, *Religious Identities,* 136–39.

107. *Hom. de stat.* 21.2, NPNF trans.

108. E.g., M. Maas, "People and Identity in Roman Antioch," in *Antioch: The Lost Ancient City,* ed. C. Kondoleon (Princeton, NJ, 2000), 13–22, at 19.

109. Portions of this section were previously published in E. Watts, "Libanius on Theodosian-Era Temple Violence: Rhetoric and Reality," in *Le vie del sapere nell'area siro-mesopotamica de 3rd al 12th century,* Orientalia Christiana Analecta 293, ed. C. Noce et al. (Rome, 2013), 105–14, though my thoughts on the significance of the oration have changed since I composed that paper.

110. For surveys of Libanius's attitudes toward traditional religious infrastructure, see, among others, Nesselrath, *Libanios,* chap. 4; Sandwell, *Religious Identity,* 154–72.

111. For discussion, see, in particular, chapters 3, 5, and 6.

112. *CTh* 16.10.8, discussed in chapter 8.

113. On Cynegius's campaigns, see Brown, *Power and Persuasion,* 107; Matthews, *Western Aristocracies,* 140–42; G. Fowden, "Bishops and Temples in the Eastern Roman Empire, AD 320–435," *JTS* 29 (1979): 53–78. N. McLynn ("*'Genere Hispanus':* Theodosius, Spain, and Nicene Orthodoxy," in *Hispania in Late Antiquity,* ed. K. Bowes and M. Kulikowski, [Leiden, 2005], 108–18) has argued against the idea that Cynegius's campaigns involved attacks on temples in Syria. This seems overly cautious in light of Zosimus's statement that Cynegius attacked temples in Syria, the similar language used to describe a prefect who sanctions temple attacks in Libanius's *Or.* 30, and phrases Libanius uses to describe Cynegius in *Or.* 49.3.

114. This is the *comes Orientis* in Libanius, *Or.* 1.255 (*PLRE* 1.1015.61). He seems to follow Deinias (*comes* in 386; dating based on *Or.* 33.6) in office. *Or.* 1.269 seems to suggest that this man, whatever his identity, has left office by the time Lucianus has been named *consularis Syriae* in 388.

115. For the Callinicum incident, see Brown, *Power and Persuasion,* 108–9; N. McLynn, *Ambrose of Milan: Church and Court in a Christian Capital* (Berkeley, 1994), 298–309; M. Gaddis, *There Is No Crime for Those Who Have Christ* (Berkeley, 2005), 194–99.

116. *HE* 5.20.

117. *HE* 5.20.

118. Prudentius, *Peristephanon* 2.473–84.

119. For Theodosius's persuasion working better than coercion, see Gregory Nazianzen, *Carm.* 2, 11.1292–1304. For superstition just collapsing on itself, see John Chrysostom, *in Babylam* 13.

120. For the ways in which Libanius's *Or.* 30 draws on established ideas about Roman imperial authority, see T. Sizgorich, "'Not Easily Were Stones Joined by the Strongest Bonds Pulled Asunder': Religious Violence and Imperial Order in the Later Roman World," *JECS* 15 (2007): 75–101.

121. All translated passages of *Or.* 30 follow Norman, *Libanius: Selected Orations*, vol. 2 (Cambridge, MA, 1977). For the historicity of this, see S. Bradbury, "Constantine and the Problem of Anti-Pagan Legislation in the Fourth Century," *CP* 89 (1994): 125–29.

122. *Or.* 30.7.

123. Libanius, *Or.* 30.7.

124. *Or.* 30.8.

125. E.g., *Or.* 30.15.

126. *Or.* 30.13–14.

127. For this rhetorical pivot, see Sizgorich, "Not Easily," 86. See as well the analysis of Sandwell, *Religious Identity,* 155–56.

128. *Or.* 30.44. On the possibility of Edessa as a site, see Norman, *Libanius,*2:141 note b.

129. *Or.* 30.46.

130. The description of the official here closely follows that of Cynegius in *Oration* 49.3, making it likely that the two orations refer to the same figure. On the identification with Cynegius, see Sizgorich, "Not Easily," 87–88, following P. Petit, "Sur la date du *Pro Templis,*" *Byzantion* 21 (1954): 295–309; K. Cooper, "Insinuations of Womanly Influence: An Aspect of the Christianization of the Roman Aristocracy," *JRS* 82 (1992): 161; and R. Van Dam, "From Paganism to Christianity in Late Antique Gaza," *Viator* 16 (1985): 15. McLynn, "*Genere Hispanus,*" 108–18, has argued against this identification, though, as explained above, his argument requires us to overlook evidence that explicitly ties Cynegius to these events.

131. Cf. Sandwell, *Religious Identity,* 156.

132. *Or.* 30.55.

133. In this it contrasts with many of Themistius's orations that explicitly previewed and advocated for imperial policy. On this, see P. Heather and D. Moncur, *Politics, Philosophy, and Empire: Select Orations of Themistius* (Liverpool, 2001), 142–49; Heather, "Liar in Winter: Themistius and Theodosius," in *From the Tetrarchs to the Theodosius,* ed. S. McGill, C. Sogno, and E. Watts (Cambridge, 2010), 185–213.

134. As P. Van Nuffelen has recently argued ("Not the Last Pagan: Libanius between Elite Rhetoric and Religion," in *The Cambridge Companion to Libanius,* ed. L. Van Hoof [Cambridge, 2014]), another goal Libanius advances in this oration is an appeal for the protection of elite property from confiscation following accusations that sacrifices had been performed on them.

135. On the ways in which local initiative and imperial support were balanced in the 390s, see J. Hahn, *Gewalt und religiöser Konflikt: Studien zu den Auseinandersetzungen zwischen Christen, Heiden, und Juden im Osten Römischen Reiches* (Berlin, 2004), 81–105.

136. For their selection as a counterpoint to Cynegius, see Matthews, *Western Aristocracies,* 224.

137. Julian is the exemplary figure introduced at *Or.* 49.3.

138. *Or.* 49.3, trans. Norman.

139. *Or.* 1.262.

140. *Or.* 1.263. Libanius never explicitly says that the grove in Daphne was saved, though we know from other sources that it remained at least somewhat intact until 526 when the trees were cut down in order to provide timber to reconstruct the Great Church following an earthquake. On this, see Downey, *History of Antioch,* 568.

141. *CTh* 16.10.10.

142. *CTh* 16.10.10.

143. *CTh* 16.10.11.

144. *CTh* 16.10.12.2.

145. *Or.* 30.51. For a fuller discussion of the festivals, temples, and other features of traditional religion that remained in Antioch even into the 390s, see Sandwell, *Religious Identity,* 41–43.

146. *Ep.* 1024.4.

147. For the larger pattern, see K. Sessa, "Christianity and the Cubiculum: Spiritual Politics and Domestic Space in Late Antique Rome," *JECS* 15 (2007): 179 n. 28. See as well D. Frankfurter, "Iconoclasm and Christianization in Late Antique Egypt: Christian Treatments of Space and Image," in *From Temple to Church: Destruction and Renewal of Local Cultic Topography in Late Antiquity,* ed. J. Hahn, S. Emmel, and U. Gotter (Leiden, 2008), 135–59, at 141. The best-documented example of this transition occurring because of Christian pressure comes from the Alexandrian suburb of Menouthis, where a healing shrine of Isis was shuttered by the bishop Cyril only to reopen in a private house. For discussion of this, see E. Watts, *Riot in Alexandria: Tradition and Group Dynamics in Late Antique Pagan and Christian Communities* (Berkeley, 2010), 237–40.

148. Watts, *City and School,* 93–96; A. Kaldellis, *The Christian Parthenon, Classicism and Pilgrimage in Byzantine Athens* (Cambridge, 2009), 11–23.

149. *CTh* 16.10.18, trans Pharr.

150. The abbot Shenoute's actions against the former governor Gesios show the danger of allowing such actions to be taken by private individuals. On this incident, see D. Brakke, *Demons and the Making of the Monk: Spiritual Combat in Early Christianity* (Cambridge, MA, 2006), 97–98; A. López, *Shenoute of Atripe and the Uses of Poverty* (Berkeley, 2013), 108–20.

151. For the bonfire,, see Zacharias, *Vit. Sev.* 33. For the Tychaion statuary, see Theophylact Simocatta 8.7–15.

152. Shenoute and Gesios argued over the significance of one such private collection in the later fourth century. On the conflict with Gesios, note the two Shenoutan works "Not Because a Fox Barks" and "Let Our Eyes," both written around the year 400. Important in understanding this conflict is S. Emmel, "From the Other Side of the Nile: Shenute and Panopolis," in *Perspectives on Panopolis: An Egyptian Town from Alexander the Great to the Arab Conquest,* ed. A. Egberts, B. Muhs, and J. van der Vilet (Leiden, 2002), 95–113; López, *Shenoute,* 113–18.

153. *Sermon* 91.2, trans. B. Ramsey.

154. On these limits, see *CTh* 2.18.19 and 2.8.22. The second law, dating to 395, removed pagan holidays from the calendar. For discussion, see M. Salzman,

"Religious *Koine* and Religious Dissent in the Fourth Century," in *Blackwell's Companion to Roman Religion,* ed. J. Rüpke (Oxford, 2007), 120–21. On the continued survival of these festivals in subsequent centuries, see Gelasius, *Adv. Androm.* (Corp. Script. Eccles. Lat. 35), 453–64.

155. Sandwell, *Religious Identity,* 42, offers a comprehensive list that includes the following: New Year's festival (Lib. *Or.* 9; John Chrysostom, *In Kalends*), the festival of Poseidon, the festival of Artemis (attested, with declining attendance, during the reign of Julian by Lib. *Or.* 5), a festival of Calliope (Libanius, *Ep.* 1175), the Maiumas in honor of Dionysius and Aphrodite in May (Malalas 285.12–21; Theodoret, *HE* 3.14; Libanius, *Or.* 41.16), festival of Adonis on July 17–19 (Ammianus 32.9.14 and 19.1.11), Dionysius festival during wine harvest (Libanius, *Epp.* 1212, 1288, 1480; Theodoret, *HE* 4.24.3). On the later resonance of the Kalends festival, see too A. Kaldellis, "The Kalends in Byzantium, 400–1200 AD: A New Interpretation," *Archiv für Religionsgeschichte* 13 (2012): 187–203.

156. Cameron, *Last Pagans of Rome* (Oxford, 2012), 784. This resembles a call passed along by African bishops in 399 (Augustine, *Sermon* 62.9). As Cameron (*Last Pagans,* 785) rightly notes, CTh 16.10.17 and 18, both sent to Apollodorus, the proconsul of Africa, seem to address this issue directly.

157. *CTh* 16.10.17.

158. *CTh* 16.10.19.3.

159. On the persistence of the Panathenaic procession, see Watts, *City and School,* 93–94.

160. E.g., Salzman, "The End of Public Sacrifice," 168–77; C. Goddard, "The Evolution of Pagan Sanctuaries in Late Antique Italy (Fourth-Sixth Centuries A.D.): A New Administrative and Legal Framework; A Paradox," in *Les cités de l'Italie tardo-antique (IVe-VIe siècle),* ed. M. Ghilardi, C. Goddard, and P. Porena (Rome, 2006), 281–306.

161. Seeck, *Die Briefe,* 457, tries to identify Hierophantes, without great success. Norman (*Selected Letters,* 2:366 note a) plausibly suggests that Hierophantes may in fact reflect the addressee's title rather than his name.

162. The request for a blessing is *Ep.* 964.1. The malady list is *Ep.* 964.2–3.

163. *Ep.* 964.4.

CHAPTER 10. A GENERATION'S LEGACY

1. For this view of Rufinus's aims, see the introduction.

2. This model, first articulated by Eusebius, is described in more detail in chapter 2.

3. Rufinus, *HE* 11.28. That this idea goes back to Theophilus, see T. Orlandi, "Un frammento copto di Teofilo di Alessandria," *RSO* 44 (1970): 23–26; Orlandi, "Uno scritto di Teofilo di Alessandria sulla distruzione del Serapeum," *PP* 23 (1968): 295–304. For discussion of this complex of narratives, see E. Watts, *Riot in Alexandria: Tradition and Group Dynamics in Late Antique Pagan and Christian Communities* (Berkeley, 2010), 190–207.

4. The image appears in A. Bauer and J. Strzygowski, *Eine alexandrinische Weltchronik* (Vienna, 1905), fig. VI verso. For the connection of this image with

others of Old Testament figures, see S. Davis, *The Early Coptic Papacy: The Egyptian Church and Its Leadership in Late Antiquity* (Cairo, 2004), 64, 206 n. 93.

5. Watts, *Riot in Alexandria*, 190–215.

6. D. Brakke, *Demons and the Making of the Monk: Spiritual Combat in Early Christianity* (Cambridge, MA, 2006), 97–98.

7. Damascius, *Vit. Is.* 42A, F-H; cf. Rufinus, *HE* 11.22. For discussion of his role and legacy, see P. Athanassiadi, "Persecution and Response in Late Paganism: The Evidence of Damascius," *JHS* 113 (1993): 1–29, at 14–16; E. Watts, *City and School in Late Antique Athens and Alexandria* (Berkeley, 2006), 190–91.

8. Rufinus, *HE* 11.22 (Christian); Damascius, *Vit. Is.* 42A (pagan).

9. Socrates, *HE* 5.16.

10. Eunapius, *VS* 472–73.

11. Jerome writes that "the whole city was moved by his death" (*Ep.* 23.3). Symmachus composed three *Relationes* on the subject (*Rel.* 10–12), one of which comments to the emperor that the people of Rome stayed home from the theater out of grief (*Rel.* 10.2). For discussion, see M. Kahlos, *Vettius Agorius Praetextatus: A Senatorial Life in Between* (Rome, 2002), 152–53. *Carmen contra paganos* 29–33 suggests that this mourning period may have been publicly decreed. On this, see Cameron, *Last Pagans of Rome* (Oxford, 2012), 293.

12. *CIL* 6.1179d.16–18. This poem now survives on a four-sided stele currently housed in the Capitoline Museum, but it seems to have circulated publicly as a stand-alone text in the 380s because Jerome (*Ep.* 23.2) engages with its language. For this, see Kahlos, *Praetextatus*, 160–62.

13. Her petition was granted despite the objections of Symmachus. The petition is known from Symmachus, *Ep.* 2.36.2–3, addressed to Nicomachus Flavianus, and the inscribed base of a statue honoring the Vestal Coelia Concordia that Praetextatus's wife Paulina erected (*CIL* 6.2145). For discussion, see Kahlos, *Praetextatus*, 155–56.

14. *Rel.* 12.2. For other contemporaries, see the list in Kahlos, *Praetextatus*, 154 n. 18; Cameron, *Last Pagans*, 9. Most senators in the period had their statues erected in the Forum of Trajan. For this tendency, see R. Chenault, "Statues of Senators in the Forum of Trajan and the Roman Forum in Late Antiquity," *JRS* 102 (2012): 103–32, and the larger contextualization of J. Weisweiler, "From Equality to Asymmetry: Honorific Statues, Imperial Power and Senatorial Identity in Late Antique Rome," *JRA* 25 (2012): 319–51.

15. *Rel.* 12.4. For interpretation of this passage, see Cameron, *Last Pagans*, 9. For similar imperial endorsements written for other senators honored by statues, see J. Weisweiler, "Inscribing Imperial Power: Letters from Emperors in Late Antique Rome," in *Historische Erinnerung im städtischen Raum: Rom in der Spätantike*, ed. R. Behrwald and C. Witschel (Stuttgart, 2012), 305–23.

16. Nearly everything about this poem is controversial. For arguments demonstrating that the subject of the poem is Praetextatus, see the thorough and persuasive discussion of Cameron, *Last Pagans*, 273–338. Kahlos, *Praetextatus*, 163 n. 50, provides a long list of others who have made this identification. Among the alternatives proposed are Nicomachus Flavianus. On this, see the bibliography assembled by L. Cracco Ruggini, "Il paganesimo romano tra

religion e politica (384–394): Per una reinterpretazione del *Carmen contra paganos*," *Rendiconti della classe di scienze morali, storiche e flilologishce dell'Academia dei Lincei* ser. 8.23 (1979): 3–141, at 29 n. 66). For other proposed identifications, see G. Manganaro, "La reazione pagana a Roma nel 408–9 d. C. e il poemetto anonimo Contra Paganos," *Giornale Italiano di Filologia* 13 (1960): 210–24 (Gabinius Barbarus Pompeianus); and S. Mazzarino, *Antico, tardoantica ed èra constantiniana* (Bari, 1974), 373–77, 398–441 (the father of Symmachus).

17. For this interpretation of the *CCP*, see Cameron, *Last Pagans*, 317–19.

18. *CCP* 24–86. For the reading of this passage (in particular lines 38–86) as referring to the mourning of Praetextatus rather than a marshaling of military resources to support Eugenius, see Cameron, *Last Pagans*, 285–95.

19. *CCP* 110, following the translation of Cameron.

20. For his role as a character here, see Kahlos, *Praetextatus*, 180–200.

21. Macrobius, *Sat.* 1.praef. 2–3.

22. For this dramatic date, see Cameron, *Last Pagans*, 243–46.

23. Macrobius, *Sat.* 1.praef. 11.

24. Kahlos, *Praetextatus*, 198–200.

25. For discussion, see J. Watt, "Themistius and Julian: Their Association in Syriac and Arabic Tradition," in *The Purpose of Rhetoric in Late Antiquity*, ed. A. J. Quiroga Puertas (Tübingen, 2013), 161–76, at 161–68.

26. Watt, "Themistius and Julian," 168.

27. For this collection, see D. Trout, *Paulinus of Nola: Life, Letters, and Poems* (Berkeley, 1999), 68–89, as well as the discussions of C. Aull, "Ausonius' Letters," and D. Trout, "Paulinus' Letters," both in *Late Antique Epistolography*, ed. C. Sogno, B. Storin, and E. Watts (Berkeley, forthcoming).

28. Eunapius, *VS* 496.

29. Eunapius, *VS* 496, LCL trans.

30. Eunapius, *VS* 496.

31. Eunapius (*VS* 496) comments that "very many of his works are in circulation and any intelligent man who reads them one by one will appreciate their charm." For Eunapius's reliance on Libanius's *Oration* 1 for much of the material in his profile, see E. Watts, "Orality and Communal Identity in Eunapius' *Lives of the Sophists and Philosophers*," *Byzantion* 75 (2005): 334–61, at 344–45.

32. Socrates, *HE* 3.2 (for Libanius's first connections to Julian); 3.17 (for his orations trying to mediate between Julian and Antioch in the summer of 363); 3.22–23 (for a description and refutation of Libanius's funeral oration for Julian).

33. Ἰωάννης Ἀντιοχεὺς μὲν ἦν τῆς Κοίλης Συρίας, υἱὸς δὲ Σεκούνδου καὶ μητρὸς Ἀνθούσης, ἐξ εὐπατριδῶν τῶν ἐκεῖ, μαθητὴς δὲ ἐγένετο Λιβανίου τοῦ σοφιστοῦ καὶ ἀκροατὴς Ἀνδραγαθίου τοῦ φιλοσόφου (Socrates, *HE* 6.3).

34. Socrates, *HE* 6.3.

35. Sozomen, *HE* 8.2, NPNF trans.

36. Theodore Anagnostes, *Epit. historiae tripartitae* 4.281; Theophanes Confessor, *Chron.* 75; George the Monk, *Chronicon breve (redaction recentior)* ΣΑ´. Βασιλεία Ἀρκαδίου; Simeon Logothetes, *Chronicon* 105.19–22.

37. Socrates, *HE* 4.26, NPNF trans.

38. Socrates, *HE* 4.26. The same story (in essentially the same words) is repeated by Sozomen, *HE* 6.17; Theodore Anagnostes, *Epit. historiae tripartitae* 3.204; and Simeon Logothetes, *Chronicon* 98.15–20.

39. Even more significant is the emergence of a later tradition that speaks about the Cappadocians managing to convert Libanius to Christianity. On this tradition, see the important discussion of H.-G. Nesselrath and L. Van Hoof, "The Reception of Libanius: From Pagan Friend of Julian to (almost) Christian Saint and Back," in *The Cambridge Companion to Libanius,* ed. L. Van Hoof (Cambridge, forthcoming).

40. Five additional letters are sometimes appended to the original collection of twenty-one. Scholars have long debated the authenticity of this collection. For a thorough demonstration that the letters are forgeries, see H.-G. Nesselrath, "Libanio e Basilio di Cesarea: Un dialogo interreligioso?," *Adamantius* 16 (2010): 338–52. My reading of this collection depends heavily on that proposed by L. Van Hoof, "Falsification as a Protreptic to Truth: The Forged Epistolary Exchange Between Basil and Libanius," in *Education and Religion in Late Antiquity: Genres and Discourses in Transition,* ed. P. Gemeinhardt, L. Van Hoof, and P. Van Nuffelen (Aldershot, 2015).

41. Van Hoof, "Falsification as a Protreptic to Truth," forthcoming.

42. This is a point made by Van Hoof, "Falsification as a Protreptic to Truth."

43. This is most clear in the sixth letter of the collection. After a long complimentary preamble speaking about how Basil's efforts to disavow the title of sophist made the letter even stronger, Libanius concedes that Basil should perhaps avoid the title of sophist, for it is better that he hold onto the "books which you say are inferior in language but superior in meaning." Basil, Libanius continues, should pursue this higher knowledge because it is plain that his rhetorical skill will never diminish even if he fails to tend to it.

44. Van Hoof, "Falsification as a Protreptic to Truth."

45. Zacharias, *Vit. Sev.* 11–13.

46. Zacharias, *Vit. Sev.* 13, trans. Ambjorn. For discussion of this passage and its significance for our interpretation of the rest of the collection, see Van Hoof, "Falsification as a Protreptic to Truth."

Bibliography

Allison, P. *The Insula of Menander at Pompeii*. Vol. 3, *The Finds: A Contextual Study*. Oxford, 2006.

Ando, C. *Imperial Ideology and Provincial Loyalty in the Roman Empire*. Berkeley, 2000.

———. *The Matter of the Gods: Religion and the Roman Empire*. Berkeley, 2010.

———. "Pagan Apologetics and Christian Intolerance in the Ages of Themistius and Augustine." *Journal of Early Christian Studies* 4 (1996): 171–207.

Arjava, A. "Paternal Power in Late Antiquity." *Journal of Roman Studies* 88 (1998): 147–65.

Athanassiadi, P. "Persecution and Response in Late Paganism: The Evidence of Damascius." *Journal of Hellenic Studies* 113 (1993): 1–29.

Athanassiadi-Fowden, P. *Julian and Hellenism*. Oxford, 1981.

Aull, C. "Ausonius' Letters." In *Late Antique Epistolography*, edited by C. Sogno, B. Storin, and E. Watts. Berkeley, forthcoming.

———. "Imperial Power in the Age of Valentinian I, 364–375 CE." PhD diss., Indiana University, 2013.

Bagnall, R. *Currency and Inflation in Fourth Century Egypt*. Bulletin of the American Society of Papyrologists Supplement, no. 5. Chico, CA, 1985.

———. "Religious Conversion and Onomastic Change in Early Byzantine Egypt." *Bulletin of the American Society of Papyrologists* 19 (1982): 105–24.

Baillet, J. *Inscriptions grecques et latines des Tombeaux des Rois Syringes à Thebes*. Cairo, 1920–26.

Banaji, J. *Agrarian Change in Late Antiquity*. Oxford, 2001.

———. "Economic Trajectories." In *Oxford Handbook of Late Antiquity*, edited by S. Johnson, 598–624. Oxford, 2012.

Banchich, T. "Julian's School Laws: *Cod. Theod.* 13.3.5 and *Ep.* 42." *Ancient World* 24 (1993): 5–14.

Bardy, G. "Le concile d'Antioche (379)." *Revue Benedictine* 45 (1933): 196–213.

Barnes, T.D. "Angel of Light or Mystic Initiate? The Problem of the *Life of Antony.*" *Journal of Theological Studies* 37 (1986): 354–68.

———. *Athanasius and Constantius.* Cambridge, MA, 1993.

———. "Christians and Pagans in the Reign of Constantius." In *L'Église et l'empire au IVe Siècle,* edited by A. Dihle, 301–43. Geneva, 1989.

———. *Constantine: Dynasty, Religion and Power in the Later Roman Empire.* London, 2011.

———. *Constantine and Eusebius.* Cambridge, MA, 1981.

———. *Early Christian Hagiography and Roman History.* Tübingen, 2010.

———. "The Editions of Eusebius' Church History." *Greek, Roman and Byzantine Studies* 21 (1980): 191–201.

———. *The New Empire of Diocletian and Constantine.* Cambridge, MA, 1982.

Barnes, T.D., and J. Vanderspoel. "Julian and Themistius." *Greek, Roman and Byzantine Studies* 22 (1981): 187–89.

Bassett, S. *The Urban Image of Late Antique Constantinople.* Cambridge, 2004.

Bauer, A., and J. Strzygowski. *Eine alexandrinische Weltchronik.* Vienna, 1905.

Bleckmann, B. "Pagane Visionen Konstantins in der Chronik der Johannes Zonaras." In *Constantino il Grande dall'antichita all'umanesimo,* vol. 1, edited by G. Bonamente and F. Fusco, 151–70. Macerata, 1992.

Bloch, H. "A New Document of the Last Pagan Revival in the West, 393–394 A.D." *Harvard Theological Review* 38 (1945): 199–244.

Bloomer, M. "Schooling in Persona: Imagination and Subordination in Roman Education." *Classical Antiquity* 16.1 (1997): 57–78.

Boak, A.E.R., and H.C. Youtie. *The Archive of Aurelius Isidorus in the Egyptian Museum, Cairo and the University of Michigan (P. Cair. Isidor.).* Ann Arbor, MI, 1960.

Boin, D. "Hellenistic 'Judaism' and the Social Origins of the 'Pagan-Christian' Debate." *Journal of Early Christian Studies* 22 (2014): 167–96.

Bowersock, G. *Julian the Apostate.* Cambridge, MA, 1978.

———. *Martyrdom and Rome.* Cambridge, 1995.

Bowes, K. *Private Worship, Public Values, and Religious Change in Late Antiquity.* Cambridge, 2008.

Bradbury, S. "Constantine and the Problem of Anti-Pagan Legislation in the Fourth Century." *Classical Philology* 89 (1994): 120–39.

———. "The Date of Julian's *Letter to Themistius.*" *Greek, Roman and Byzantine Studies* 28 (1987): 235–51.

———. "Julian's Pagan Revival and the Decline of Blood Sacrifice." *Phoenix* 49 (1995): 331–56.

———. *Selected Letters of Libanius.* Liverpool, 2004.

Bradley, K. "Wet-Nursing at Rome: A Study in Social Relations." In *The Family in Ancient Rome: New Perspectives,* edited by B. Rawson, 201–29. London, 1986.

Brakke, D. *Athanasius and Asceticism*. Baltimore, 1998.

———. *Demons and the Making of the Monk: Spiritual Combat in Early Christianity*. Cambridge, MA, 2006.

Brown, P. *Poverty and Leadership in the Later Roman Empire*. Hanover, NH, 2002.

———. *Power and Persuasion in Late Antiquity*. Madison, WI, 1992.

———. *Through the Eye of a Needle: Wealth, the Fall of Rome, and the Making of Christianity in the West, 350–550 AD*. Princeton, NJ, 2012.

Browning, R. "The Riot of A.D. 387 in Antioch: The Role of the Theatrical Claques in the Later Roman Empire." *Journal of Roman Studies* 42 (1952): 13–20.

Burgess, R.W. "The Dates and Editions of Eusebius' *Chronici Canones* and *Historia Ecclesiastica*." *Journal of Theological Studies* 48 (1997): 471–504.

———. "Eutropius V.C. 'Magister Memoriae?'" *Classical Philology* 96 (2001): 76–81.

———. "The Summer of Blood: The Great Massacre of 337 and the Promotion of the Sons of Constantine." *Dumbarton Oaks Papers* 62 (2008): 5–51.

Cameron, Alan. "Gratian's Repudiation of the Pontifical Robe." *Journal of Roman Studies* 58 (1968): 96–102.

———. *The Last Pagans of Rome*. Oxford, 2012.

Cameron, Alan, and J. Long. *Barbarians and Politics at the Court of Arcadius*. Berkeley, 1993.

Carter, R.E. "The Chronology of Saint John Chrysostom's Early Life." *Traditio* 18 (1962): 357–64.

Castelli, E. *Martyrdom and Memory: Early Christian Culture Making*. New York, 2004.

Cecconi, G. "Il rescritto di Spello: Prospettive recenti." In *Costantino prima e dopo Costantino*, edited by G. Bonamente, N. Lenski, and R. Lizzi Testa, 273–90. Bari, 2012.

Chastagnol, A. *L'album municipal de Timgad*. Habelt, 1978.

———. *Le sénat romain à l'époque impérial*. Paris, 1992.

Chenault, R. "Statues of Senators in the Forum of Trajan and the Roman Forum in Late Antiquity." *Journal of Roman Studies* 102 (2012): 103–32.

Chesnut, G. *First Christian Histories: Eusebius, Socrates, Sozomen, Theodoret, and Evagrius*. Macon, GA, 1986.

Congrove, J. "Friendship, Rhetoric, and Authority in the Letters of St. Augustine of Hippo." PhD diss., Indiana University, 2011.

Connolly, S. "Constantine Answers the Veterans." In *From the Tetrarchs to the Theodosians*, edited by S. McGill, C. Sogno, and E. Watts, 93–114. Cambridge, 2010.

Cooper, K. *The Fall of the Roman Household*. Cambridge, 2007.

———. "Insinuations of Womanly Influence: An Aspect of the Christianization of the Roman Aristocracy." *Journal of Roman Studies* 82 (1992): 150–64.

Corcoran, S. "Before Constantine." In *The Cambridge Companion to the Age of Constantine*, edited by N. Lenski, 14–58. 2nd ed. Cambridge, 2010.

———. *The Empire of the Tetrarchs*. 2nd ed. Oxford, 2000.

Coşkun, A. *Die gens Ausoniana an der Macht: Untersuchungen zu Decimius Magnus Ausonius und seiner Familie*. Oxford, 2002.

Countryman, L.W. *The Rich Christian in the Church of the Early Empire: Contradictions and Accommodations*. New York, 1980.

Courcelle, P. *Recherches sur les "Confessions" de saint Augustin*. Paris, 1950.

Cox, P. *Biography in Late Antiquity: A Quest for the Holy Man*. Berkeley, 1983.

Cracco Ruggini, L. "Il paganesimo romano tra religion e politica (384–394): Per una reinterpretazione del *Carmen contra paganos*." *Rendiconti della classe di scienze morali, storiche e flilologishce dell'Academia dei Lincei* ser. 8.23 (1979): 3–141.

Crespo Ortiz de Zarate, S. *"Nutrices" en el imperio romano*. 2 vols. Valladolid, 2005–6.

Cribiore, R. *Gymnastics of the Mind: Greek Education in Hellenistic and Roman Egypt*. Princeton, NJ, 2001.

———. *Libanius the Sophist: Rhetoric, Reality, and Religion in the Fourth Century*. Ithaca, NY, 2013.

———. *The School of Libanius in Late Antique Antioch*. Princeton, NJ, 2007.

———. "Spaces for Teaching in Late Antiquity." In *Alexandria Auditoria of Kom el-Dikka and Late Antique Education*, edited by T. Derda, T. Markiewicz, and E. Wipszycka, 143–50. Warsaw, 2007.

———. *Writing, Teachers, and Students in Graeco-Roman Antiquity*. Atlanta, 1996.

Croke, B. *The Chronicle of Marcellinus: Translation and Commentary*. Sydney, 1995.

———. "Reinventing Constantinople." In *From the Tetrarchs to the Theodosians*, edited by S. McGill, C. Sogno, and E. Watts, 241–64. Cambridge, 2010.

Curran, J. *Pagan City and Christian Capital: Rome in the Fourth Century*. Oxford, 2000.

Dagron, G. *Naissance d'une capitale*. Paris, 1974.

Davis, S. *The Early Coptic Papacy: The Egyptian Church and Its Leadership in Late Antiquity*. Cairo, 2004.

Dey, H. *The Aurelian Wall and the Refashioning of Imperial Rome, AD 271–855*. Cambridge, 2011.

Dickey, E. *The Colloquia of the Hermeneumata Pseudodositheana*. Cambridge, 2012.

Digeser, E. "Lactantius and the 'Edict of Milan': Does It Determine His Venue?" *Studia Patristica* 31 (1997): 287–95.

———. *The Making of a Christian Empire*. Ithaca, NY, 2000.

Dillon, J.N. *The Justice of Constantine: Law, Communication, and Control*. Ann Arbor, MI, 2012.

Dionisotti, A.C. "From Ausonius' School Days? A Schoolbook and Its Relatives." *Journal of Roman Studies* 72 (1982): 83–125.

Dolansky, F. "Honoring the Family Dead on the Parentalia: Ceremony, Spectacle, and Memory." *Phoenix* 65 (2011): 125–57.

———. "Ritual, Gender, and Status in the Roman Family." PhD diss., University of Chicago, 2005.

Downey, G. *A History of Antioch in Syria*. Princeton, NJ, 1961.

———. "The Olympic Games of Antioch in the Fourth Century A.D." *Transactions of the American Philological Association* 70 (1939): 428–38.

Drake, H.A. *Constantine and the Bishops: The Politics of Intolerance.* Baltimore, 2000.

———. "The Impact of Constantine on Christianity." In *The Cambridge Companion to the Age of Constantine,* edited by N. Lenski, 111–36. 2nd ed. Cambridge, 2010.

Drinkwater, J. *The Alamanni and Rome, 213–496 (Caracalla to Clovis).* Oxford, 2007.

Dumas, T. "A Woodstock Moment—40 Years Later." *Smithsonian Magazine,* August 13, 2009.

Dunand, F. "Le petit Serapieion romain de Louqsor." *Bulletin de l'Institut français d'archéologie orientale* 81 (1981): 115–48.

Duncan-Jones, R. *Money and Government in the Roman Empire.* Cambridge, 1994.

Edwards, M. "The Beginnings of Christianization." In *The Cambridge Companion to the Age of Constantine,* edited by N. Lenski, 137–58. 2nd ed. Cambridge, 2010.

Ehling, K. "Kaiser Julian, der Senat und die Stadt Rom." *Zeitschrift für Papyrologie und Epigraphik* 137 (2001): 292–96.

Elder, G. *Children of the Great Depression: Social Change in Life Experience.* Chicago, 1974.

Elm, S. *Sons of Hellenism, Fathers of the Church.* Berkeley, 2012.

———. *Virgins of God: The Making of Asceticism in Late Antiquity.* Oxford, 1994.

Emmel, S. "From the Other Side of the Nile: Shenute and Panopolis." In *Perspectives on Panopolis: An Egyptian Town from Alexander the Great to the Arab Conquest,* edited by A. Egberts, B. Muhs, and J. van der Vilet, 95–113. Leiden, 2002.

Erim, K.J. Reynolds, and M. Crawford. "Diocletian's Currency Reform: A New Inscription." *Journal of Roman Studies* 61 (1971): 171–77.

Errington, R.M. *Roman Imperial Policy from Julian to Theodosius.* Chapel Hill, NC, 2006.

———. "Theodosius and the Goths." *Chiron* 26 (1996): 1–27.

Fowden, G. "Bishops and Temples in the Eastern Roman Empire, AD 320–435." *Journal of Theological Studies* 29 (1979): 53–78.

———. "City and Mountain in Late Roman Attica." *Journal of Hellenic Studies* 108 (1988): 48–59.

———. "The Last Days of Constantine: Oppositional Versions and Their Influence." *Journal of Roman Studies* 84 (1994): 146–70.

———. "Nicagoras of Athens and the Lateran Obelisk." *Journal of Hellenic Studies* 107 (1987): 51–57.

Francis, J. "Late Antique Visuality." In *Shifting Cultural Frontiers in Late Antiquity,* edited by D. Brakke, D. Deliyannis, and E. Watts, 139–49. Aldershot, 2012.

Frankfurter, D. "Iconoclasm and Christianization in Late Antique Egypt: Christian Treatments of Space and Image." In *From Temple to Church: Destruc-*

tion and Renewal of Local Cultic Topography in Late Antiquity, edited by J. Hahn, S. Emmel, and U. Gotter, 135–59. Leiden, 2008.

———. *Religion in Roman Egypt: Assimilation and Resistance.* Princeton, NJ, 1998.

Fraser, P.M. "A Syriac Notitia Urbis Alexandrinae." *Journal of Egyptian Archeology* 37 (1951): 103–8.

Frier, B. "Roman Life Expectancy: Ulpian's Evidence." *Harvard Studies in Classical Philology* 86 (1982): 213–51.

Gaddis, M. *There Is No Crime for Those Who Have Christ.* Berkeley, 2005.

Garitte, G. *Un témoin important de la vie de S. Antoine: La version inédite latine des Archives de S. Pierre a Rome.* Rome, 1939.

Garnsey, P. "Child Rearing in Ancient Italy." In *The Family in Italy: From Antiquity to the Present,* edited by D. Kertzer and R. Saller, 51–54. New Haven, CT, 1991.

———. "Roman Patronage." In *From the Tetrarchs to the Theodosians,* edited by S. McGill, C. Sogno, and E. Watts, 33–54. Cambridge, 2010.

Gemeinhardt, P. *Antonius der erste Mönch: Leben, Lehre, Legende.* Munich, 2013.

Gibson, C. "Alexander in the Tychaion: Ps.-Libanius on the Statues." *Greek, Roman and Byzantine Studies* 47 (2007): 434–57.

Girardet, K.M. "Das Christentum im Denken und in der Politik Kaiser Konstantins d. Gr." In *Kaiser Konstantin der Grosse,* edited by K.M. Girardet, 29–53. Bonn, 2007.

Goddard, C. "The Evolution of Pagan Sanctuaries in Late Antique Italy (Fourth-Sixth Centuries A.D.): A New Administrative and Legal Framework; A Paradox." In *Les cités de'Italie tardo-antique (IVe-VIe siècle),* edited by M. Ghilardi, C. Goddard, and P. Porena, 281–306. Rome, 2006.

Green, R.H. *The Works of Ausonius.* Oxford, 1991.

Haas, C. *Alexandria in Late Antiquity: Topography and Social Conflict.* Baltimore, 1997.

Hahn, J. *Gewalt und religiöser Konflikt: Studien zu den Auseinandersetzungen zwischen Christen, Heiden, und Juden im Osten Römischen Reiches.* Berlin, 2004.

Hanson, A. "Ancient Illiteracy." In *Literacy in the Roman World,* edited by J.L. Humphrey, 159–98. Ann Arbor, MI, 1991.

Harl, K. *Coinage in the Roman Economy, 300 BC–700 AD.* Baltimore, 1996.

Harland, P. "Christ-Bearers and Fellow Initiates: Local Cultural Life and Christian Identity in Ignatius' Letters." *Journal of Early Christian Studies* 11 (2003): 481–99.

Harries, J. *Law and Empire in Late Antiquity.* Cambridge, 1999.

———. "The Roman Imperial Quaestor from Constantine to Theodosius II." *Journal of Roman Studies* 78 (1988): 148–72.

Harris, W. *Ancient Literacy.* Cambridge, MA, 1989.

Harvey, S. *Scenting Salvation: Ancient Christianity and the Olfactory Imagination.* Berkeley, 2006.

Heather, P. *Goths and Romans, 332–489.* Oxford, 1991.

———. "Liar in Winter: Themistius and Theodosius." In *From the Tetrarchs to the Theodosius,* edited by S. McGill, C. Sogno, and E. Watts, 185–214. Cambridge, 2010.

———. "New Men for New Constantines?" In *New Constantines: The Rhythm of Imperial Renewal in Byzantium, 4th–13th Centuries,* edited by P. Magdalino, 11–34. Aldershot, 1994.

Heather, P., and D. Moncur. *Politics, Philosophy, and Empire: Select Orations of Themistius.* Liverpool, 2001.

Hendy, M. *Studies in Byzantine Monetary Economy, c. 300–1450.* Cambridge, 2008.

Hevelone-Harper, J. *Disciples of the Desert: Monks, Laity, and Spiritual Authority in Sixth-Century Gaza.* Baltimore, 2005.

Hickey, T. "Aristocratic Landholding and the Economy of Byzantine Egypt." In *Egypt in the Byzantine World,* edited by R. Bagnall, 288–308. Cambridge, 2009.

Howgego, C. *Ancient History from Coins.* London, 1995.

Hunter, D. *A Comparison between a King and a Monk/Against the Opponents of the Monastic Life.* Lampeter, 1988.

Jones, A.H.M. *The Later Roman Empire, 284–602.* Norman, OK, 1964.

———. "Saint Chrysostom's Parentage and Education." *Harvard Theological Review* 46 (1953): 171–73.

Kahlos, M. *Vettius Agorius Praetextatus: A Senatorial Life in Between.* Rome, 2002.

Kaldellis, A. *The Christian Parthenon, Classicism and Pilgrimage in Byzantine Athens.* Cambridge, 2009.

———. "The Kalends in Byzantium, 400–1200 AD: A New Interpretation." *Archiv für Religionsgeschichte* 13 (2012): 187–203.

Kalleres, D. *City of Demons: Violence, Ritual, and Christian Power in Late Antiquity.* Berkeley, 2014.

Karla, G. "Die Klage über die zerstörte Stadt Nikomedeia bei Libanios im Spiegel der Mimesis." In *Theatron: Rhetorical Culture in Late Antiquity and the Middle Ages,* edited by Michael Grünbart, 141–56 Millenium Studies 13. Berlin, 2007.

Kaster, R. *Guardians of Language: The Grammarian and Society in Late Antiquity.* Berkeley, 1988.

Kaufmann-Heinimann, A. "Religion in the House." In *A Companion to Roman Religion,* edited by J. Rüpke, 188–201. Oxford, 2007.

Kelly, C. "Bureaucracy and Government." In *The Cambridge Companion to the Age of Constantine,* edited by N. Lenski, 183–204. Cambridge, 2006.

———. *Ruling the Later Roman Empire.* Cambridge, MA, 2004.

Kelly, G. *Ammianus Marcellinus: The Allusive Historian.* Cambridge, 2008.

———. "Pliny and Symmachus." *Arethusa* 46.2 (2013): 261–87.

———. "The Political Crisis of AD 375–6." *Chiron* 43 (2013): 357–406.

———. "The Roman World of Festus' Brevarium." In *Unclassical Traditions,* vol. 1, edited by C. Kelly, R. Flower, and M. Stuart Williams, 72–89. Cambridge, 2010.

Kelly, J.N.D. *Golden Mouth: The Story of John Chrysostom.* Ithaca, NY, 1995.

Kohns, H.P. *Versorgungskrisen und Hungerrevolten im spätantiken Rom*. Bonn, 1961.

Konstan, D. "How to Praise a Friend: Gregory Nazianzus's Funeral Oration for St. Basil the Great." In *Greek Biography and Panegyric in Late Antiquity*, edited by T. Hägg and P. Rousseau, 160–79. Berkeley, 2000.

Krumeich, R., and C. Witschel, eds. *Die Akropolis von Athen im Hellenismus und in der römischen Kaiserzeit*. Wiesbaden, 2010.

Kuhoff, W. "Die Schlacht an der Milvischen Brücke: Ein Ereignis von weltgeschichtlicher Tragweite." In *Konstantin der Große: Zwischen Sol und Christus*, edited by K. Ehling and G. Weber, 10–20. Darmstadt 2011.

Kulikowski, M. *Rome's Gothic Wars*. Cambridge, 2007.

Laes, C. *Children in the Roman Empire*. Cambridge, 2011.

Lamberton, R. *Homer the Theologian: Neoplatonist Allegorical Reading and the Growth of the Epic Tradition*. Berkeley, 1986.

Lamoreaux, J.C. "Episcopal Courts in Late Antiquity." *Journal of Early Christian Studies* 3 (1995): 143–67.

Lane Fox, R. *Pagans and Christians*. New York, 1986.

Leduc, F. "La thème de la vaine gloire chez Saint Jean Chrysostome." *Proche-Orient Chrétienne* 29 (1969): 3–32.

Lefort, L-T. "Athanase: Sur la virginité." *Le Muséon* 42 (1929): 297–374.

Lenski, N. *Failure of Empire: Valens and the Roman State in the Fourth Century*. Berkeley, 2002.

———. "The Reign of Constantine." In *The Cambridge Companion to the Age of Constantine*, edited by N. Lenski, 59–90. 2nd ed. Cambridge, 2010.

———. "Were Valentinian, Valens, and Jovian Confessors before Julian the Apostate?" *Zeitschrift für antikes Christentum* 6 (2002): 94–117.

Liebeschuetz, J.H.W.G. *Ambrose and John Chrysostom: Clerics between Desert and Empire*. Oxford, 2011.

———. *Antioch: City and Imperial Administration in the Later Roman Empire*. Oxford, 1972.

———. *Barbarians and Bishops: Army, Church, and State in the Age of Arcadius and Chrysostom*. Oxford, 1990.

———. "Why Did Synesius Become Bishop of Ptolemais?" *Byzantion* 56 (1986): 180–95.

Lieu, S.N.C. "Constantine in Legendary Literature." In *The Cambridge Companion to the Age of Constantine*, edited by N. Lenski, 298–321. 2nd ed. Cambridge, 2010.

Ligt, L. de. *Fairs and Markets in the Roman Empire*. Amsterdam, 1993.

Lizzi Testa, R. "Christian Emperor, Vestal Virgins, and Priestly Colleges: Reconsidering the End of Roman Paganism." *Antiquité Tardive* 15 (2007): 251–62.

———. *Senatori, popolo, papi: Il governo di Roma al tempo dei Valentiniani*. Bari, 2004.

Lo Cascio, E. "The Function of Gold Coinage in the Monetary Economy of the Roman Empire." In *The Monetary Systems of the Greeks and Romans*, edited by W.V. Harris, 160–73. Oxford, 2008.

Lofland, J., and R. Stark. "Becoming a World-Saver: A Theory of Conversion to a Deviant Perspective." *American Sociological Review* 30 (1965): 862–75.

Long, J. "How to Read a Halo: Three (or More) Versions of Constantine's Vision." In *The Power of Religion in Late Antiquity,* edited by A. Cain and N. Lenski, 227–35. Aldershot, 2009.

López, A. *Shenoute of Atripe and the Uses of Poverty.* Berkeley, 2013.

Lössl, J. "Profaning and Proscribing: Escalating Rhetorical Violence in Fourth Century Christian Apologetic." In *The Purpose of Rhetoric in Late Antiquity: From Performance to Exegesis,* edited by A.J. Quiroga Puertas, 71–90. Tübingen, 2013.

Maas, M. "People and Identity in Roman Antioch." In *Antioch: The Lost Ancient City,* edited by C. Kondoleon, 13–22. Princeton, NJ, 2000.

Machado, C. "Aristocratic Houses and the Making of Late Antique Rome and Constantinople." In *Two Romes: Rome and Constantinople in Late Antiquity,* edited by L. Grig and G. Kelly, 136–58. Oxford, 2012.

Macmullen, R. "Constantine and the Miraculous." *Greek, Roman and Byzantine Studies* 9 (1968): 81–96.

Majcherek, G. "The Late Roman Auditoria." In *Alexandria Auditoria of Kom el-Dikka and Late Antique Education,* edited by T. Derda, T. Markiewicz, and E. Wipszycka, 11–50. Warsaw, 2007.

Malaise, M. *Les conditions de pénétration et de diffusion des cultes égyptiens en Italie.* Leiden, 1972.

Malcus, B. "Notes sur la révolution du système administrative romain au IIIe siècle." *Opuscula Romana* 7 (1969): 213–37.

Malosse, P.-L. "Libanios, Discours 59: Texte, traduction et commentaire." PhD diss. Montpelier, 1998.

Manganaro, G. "La reazione pagana a Roma nel 408–9 d. C. e il poemetto anonimo Contra Paganos." *Giornale Italiano di Filologia* 13 (1960): 210–24.

Mango, C. "Antique Statuary and the Byzantine Beholder." *Dumbarton Oaks Papers* 17 (1963): 53–75.

Marlowe, E. "*Liberator urbis suae*: Constantine and the Ghost of Maxentius." In *The Emperor and Rome: Space, Representation, and Ritual,* edited by B. Ewald and C. Noreña, 199–219. New Haven, CT, 2010.

Marrou, H. *Histoire de l'éducation dans l'antiquité.* Paris 1956.

Matthews, J. *The Journey of Theophanes.* New Haven, CT, 2006.

———. *Laying Down the Law: A Study of the Theodosian Code.* New Haven, CT, 2000.

———. *The Roman Empire of Ammianus.* Ann Arbor, MI, 2007.

———. *Western Aristocracies and Imperial Court, A.D. 364–425.* Oxford, 1975.

Mattingly, H. "FEL. TEMP. REPARATIO." *Numismatic Chronicle* 93 (1933): 182–201.

Maxwell, J. *Christianization and Communication in Late Antiquity.* Cambridge, 2006.

Mazzarino, S. *Antico, tardoantica ed èra constantiniana.* Bari, 1974.

McEvoy, M. *Child Emperor Rule in the Late Roman West, 367–455.* Oxford, 2013.

McGill, S. *Virgil Recomposed: The Mythological and Secular Centos in Antiquity.* Oxford, 2005.

McGuckin, J. *St. Gregory of Nazianzus*. Crestwood, NY, 2001.

McKenzie, J.S. *The Architecture of Alexandria and Egypt, 300 BC–AD 700*. New Haven, CT, 2007.

McKenzie, J.S.S. Gibson, and A.T. Reyes. "Reconstructing the Serapeum in Alexandria from the Archeological Evidence." *Journal of Roman Studies* 94 (2004): 73–121.

McLynn, N. *Ambrose of Milan: Church and Court in a Christian Capital*. Berkeley, 1994.

———. "The Fourth Century *Taurobolium*." *Phoenix* 50 (1996): 312–30.

———. "'*Genere Hispanus*': Theodosius, Spain, and Nicene Orthodoxy." In *Hispania in Late Antiquity*, edited by K. Bowes and M. Kulikowski, 77–120. Leiden, 2005.

———. "Moments of Truth: Gregory Nazianzus and Theodosius I." In *From the Tetrarchs to the Theodosians*, edited by S. McGill, C. Sogno, and E. Watts, 215–39. Cambridge, 2010.

———. "The Voice of Conscience: Gregory Nazianzen in Retirement." In *Vescovi e pastori in epoca Teodosiana*, vol. 2:299–308. Studia Ephemeridis Augustinianum 58. Rome, 1997.

Meslin, M. *La fête des kalendes de janvier dans l'Empire Romain*. Brussels, 1970.

Millar, F. *The Emperor in the Roman World (31 BC–337 AD)*. Ithaca, NY, 1992.

———. *The Roman Near East, 31 B.C.–A.D. 337 AD*. Cambridge, MA, 1993.

Mitchell, S. "Maximinus and the Christians in A.D. 312: A New Latin Inscription." *Journal of Roman Studies* 78 (1988): 105–24.

Morgan, T. *Literate Education in the Hellenistic and Roman Worlds*. Cambridge, MA, 1998.

Morley, N. *Metropolis and Hinterland: The City of Rome and the Italian Economy, 200 B.C.–A.D. 200*. Cambridge, 1996.

Naiden, F.S. *Smoke Signals for the Gods: Ancient Greek Sacrifice from the Archaic through Roman Periods*. Oxford, 2013.

Nesselrath, H.-G. "Libanio e Basilio di Cesarea: Un dialogo interreligioso?" *Adamantius* 16 (2010): 338–52.

———. *Libanios: Zeuge einer schwindenden Welt*. Stuttgart, 2012.

———. "Libanios und die Mönche." In *Von Homer bis Landion: Beiträge zur Antike und Spätantike sowie zu deren Rezeptions-und Wirkungsgeschichte*, edited by B. Suchla, 243–67. Berlin, 2011.

Nesselrath, H.-G., and L. Van Hoof. "The Reception of Libanius: From Pagan Friend of Julian to (Almost) Christian Saint and Back." In *The Cambridge Companion to Libanius*, edited by L. Van Hoof. Cambridge, 2015.

Nicholson, O. "Constantine's Vision of the Cross." *Vigiliae Christianae* 54 (2000): 309–23.

Nisbet, R. *Collected Papers on Latin Literature*. Oxford, 1995.

Nixon, C.E.V., and B. Saylor Rogers. *In Praise of Later Roman Emperors: The Panegyrici Latini*. Berkeley, 1994.

Norman, A. *Libanius: Autobiography and Selected Letters*. 2 vols. Cambridge, MA, 1990.

———. *Libanius: Selected Orations*. 2 vols. Cambridge, MA, 1977.

Odahl, C. *Constantine and the Christian Empire.* New York, 2004.

Oliver, J. H. "Xenophon of Ephesus and the Antithesis Historia-Philosophia." In *Arktouros: Hellenic Studies Presented to Bernard M. W. Knox,* edited by G. Bowersock, W. Burkert, and M. C. Putnam, 401–6. New York, 1979.

Orlandi, T. "Un frammento copto di Teofilo di Alessandria." *Rivista degli Studi Orientali* 44 (1970): 23–26.

———. "Uno scritto di Teofilo di Alessandria sulla distruzione del Serapeum." *La Parola del Passato* 23 (1968): 295–304.

Panciera, S. "Tra epigrafia e topografia—I." *Archeologia Classica* 22 (1970): 131–63.

Parkin, T. *Old Age in the Roman World: A Social and Cultural History.* Baltimore, 2003.

Penella, R. *Man and the Word: The Orations of Himerius.* Berkeley, 2007.

———. *Private Orations of Themistius.* Berkeley, 2000.

Petit, P. *Les étudiants de Libanius.* Paris, 1957.

———. "Les senateurs de Constantinople dans l'oeuvre de Libanius." *L'Antiquité Classique* 26 (1957): 347–83.

———. *Libanius et la vie municipale à Antioche au IVe siècle après J. C.* Paris, 1955.

———. "Sur la date du *Pro Templis*." *Byzantion* 21 (1954): 295–309.

Pollmann, K. "Sex and Salvation in the Virgilian Cento of the Fourth Century." In *Romane Memento: Virgil in the Fourth Century,* edited by Roger Rees, 79–96. London, 2004.

Porena, P. "Trasformazioni istituzionali e assetti sociali: I prefetti del Pretorio tra III e IV secolo." In *Le trasformazioni delle "elites" in età tardoantica,* edited by R. Lizzi Testa, 325–56. Rome, 2006.

Potter, D. *Constantine the Emperor.* Oxford, 2013.

———. "Odor and Power in the Roman Empire." In *Constructions of the Classical Body,* edited by J. Porter, 169–89. Ann Arbor, MI, 1999.

———. "Procurators in Asia and Dacia under Marcus Aurelius: A Case Study of Imperial Initiative in Government." *Zeitschrift für Papyrologie und Epigraphik* 123 (1998): 270–74.

———. *The Roman Empire at Bay, AD 180–395.* London, 2004.

Priessnig, A. "Die biographishe Form der Plotinvita des Porphyrios und das Antoniosleben des Athanasios." *Byzantinische Zeitschrift* 64 (1971): 1–5.

———. "Die literarische Form der spätantiken Philosophenromane." *Byzantinische Zeitschrift* 30 (1929): 23–30.

Pucci, J. "Ausonius' *Ephemeris* and the *Hermeneumata* Tradition." *Classical Philology* 104 (2009): 50–68.

Quiroga Puertas, A. "Deflecting Attention and Shaping Reality with Rhetoric (The Case of the Riot of the Statues of A.D. 387 in Antioch)." *Nova Tellus,* forthcoming.

Rapp, C. *Holy Bishops in Late Antiquity: The Nature of Christian Leadership in an Age of Transition.* Berkeley, 2005.

Rathbone, D. "Monetisation, Not Price Inflation, in Third Century AD Egypt." In *Coin Finds and Coin Use in the Roman World,* edited by C. E. King and D. G. Wigg, 321–39. Berlin, 1996.

Rawson, B. *Children and Childhood in Roman Italy.* Oxford, 2003.

Rebillard, É. *Christians and Their Many Identities in Late Antiquity, North Africa, 200–450 CE.* Ithaca, NY, 2012.

Rémondon, R. "L'Église dans la société égyptienne à l'époque byzantine." *Chronique d'Égypte* 47 (1972): 254–77.

Riccobono, S., et al., eds. *Fontes iuris romani antejustiniani.* Florence, 1940–43.

Richardson, G. "The 'Barbarian/Hut' Cententionalis and Vergilian Iconography." *Vergilius* 54 (2008): 70–96.

Rives, J.B. "The Decree of Decius and the Religion of the Empire." *Journal of Roman Studies* 89 (1999): 145–47.

Roda, S. *Commento storico al libro IX dell'epistolario di Q. Aurelio Simmaco.* Pisa, 1981.

Roueché, C. "Rome, Asia and Aphrodisias." *Journal of Roman Studies* 71 (1981): 103–20.

Rousseau, P. *Basil of Caesarea.* Berkeley, 1994.

———. *Pachomius: The Making of a Community in Fourth-Century Egypt.* 2nd ed. Berkeley, 1999.

Rubenson, S. "Antony and Pythagoras: A Reappraisal of the Appropriation of Classical Biography in Athanasius' *Vita Antonii.*" In *Early Christianity in the Context of Antiquity,* edited by D. Brakke, A. Jacobsen, and J. Ulrich, 191–208. Berlin, 2006.

Rüpke, J. *Fasti sacerdotum.* Oxford, 2008.

Russell, N. *Theophilus of Alexandria.* London, 2007.

Salzman, M. "Apocalypse Then? Jerome and the Fall of Rome in 410." In *Maxima debetur magistro reverentia,* edited by P.B. Harvey, Jr., and C. Conybeare, 175–92. Biblioteca di Athenaeum 54. Como, 2009.

———. "The End of Public Sacrifice: Changing Definitions of Sacrifice in Post-Constantinian Rome and Italy." In *Ancient Mediterranean Sacrifice,* edited by J. Wright Knust and Z. Várhelyi, 167–83. Oxford, 2011.

———. *The "Falls" of Rome: The Transformations of Rome in Late Antiquity.* Forthcoming.

———, ed. and trans. *The Letters of Symmachus: Book 1.* Atlanta, 2011.

———. *The Making of a Christian Aristocracy.* Cambridge, MA, 2002.

———. *On Roman Time: The Codex Calendar of 354 and the Rhythms of Urban Life in Late Antiquity.* Berkeley, 1990.

———. "Religious *Koine* and Religious Dissent in the Fourth Century." In *Blackwell's Companion to Roman Religion,* edited by J. Rüpke, 109–24. Oxford, 2007.

———. "Symmachus and His Father: Patrimony and Patriarchy in the Roman Senatorial Elite." In *Le trasformazioni delle "élites" in età tardoantica,* edited by R. Lizzi Testa, 357–75. Rome, 2006.

Sandwell, I. *Religious Identity in Late Antiquity: Greeks, Jews, and Christians in Antioch.* Cambridge, 2007.

Scheidel, W. *Death on the Nile: Disease and the Demography of Roman Egypt.* Leiden, 2001.

———. "Demography, Disease, and Death." In *The Cambridge Companion to Ancient Rome,* edited by P. Erdkamp, 45–59. Cambridge, 2013.

———. "Emperors, Aristocrats, and the Grim Reaper: Towards a Demographic Profile of the Roman Elite." *Classical Quarterly* 49 (1999): 254–81.
———. "Finances, Figures, and Fiction." *Classical Quarterly* 46 (1996): 222–38.
———. "Germs for Rome." In *Rome the Cosmopolis,* edited by C. Edwards and G. Woolf, 158–76. Cambridge, 2003.
———. "Human Mobility in Roman Italy, I: The Free Population." *Journal of Roman Studies* 94 (2004): 1–26.
Schwartz, J. "La fin du Sérapeum d'Alexandrie." In *American Studies in Papyrology,* vol. 1, *Essays in Honor of C. Bradford Welles,* 98–111. New Haven, CT, 1966.
Schwartz, S. *Were the Jews a Mediterranean Society? Reciprocity and Solidarity in Ancient Judaism.* Princeton, NJ, 2010.
Sears, G. "The Fates of the Temples in North Africa." In *The Archeology of Late Antique Paganism,* edited by L. Lavan and M. Mulryan, 229–62. Leiden, 2011.
Seeck, O. "Das sogenannte Edikte von Mailand." *Zeitschrift für Kirchengeschichte* 10 (1891): 381–86.
———. *Die Briefe des Libanius.* Leipzig, 1906.
Sessa, K. "Christianity and the Cubiculum: Spiritual Politics and Domestic Space in Late Antique Rome." *Journal of Early Christian Studies* 15 (2007): 171–204.
Shanzer, D. "The Date and Literary Context of Ausonius' *Mosella*: Ausonius, Symmachus, and the *Mosella.*" In *The Discipline of the Art,* edited by P. Knox and C. Foss, 284–305. Stuttgart, 1997.
Shaw, B. *Sacred Violence: African Christians and Sectarian Hatred in the Age of Augustine.* Cambridge, 2011.
———. "Seasons of Death: Aspects of Mortality in Imperial Rome." *Journal of Roman Studies* 86 (1996): 100–138.
Shepardson, C. *Controlling Contested Places: Late Antique Antioch and the Spatial Politics of Religious Controversy.* Berkeley, 2014.
Sivan, H. *Ausonius of Bordeaux: Genesis of a Gallic Aristocracy.* London, 1993.
Sizgorich, T. "'Not Easily Were Stones Joined by the Strongest Bonds Pulled Asunder': Religious Violence and Imperial Order in the Later Roman World." *Journal of Early Christian Studies* 15 (2007): 75–101.
Skinner, A. "The Early Development of the Senate of Constantinople." *Byzantine and Modern Greek Studies* 32 (2008): 128–48.
Smith, R.R.R. "Late Roman Philosopher Portraits from Aphrodisias." *Journal of Roman Studies* 80 (1990): 127–55.
Sogno, C. *Q. Aurelius Symmachus: A Political Biography.* Ann Arbor, MI, 2006.
———. "Roman Matchmaking." In *From the Tetrarchs to the Theodosians,* edited by S. McGill, C. Sogno, and E. Watts, 55–71. Cambridge, 2010.
Sotinel, C. "Les évêques italiens dans la société de l'Antiquité tardive." In *Le trasformazioni delle "élites" in età tardoantica,* edited by R. Lizzi Testa, 377–406. Rome, 2006.
Staats, R. "Die römische Tradition im Symbol von 381 (n. C.) und seine Entstehung auf der Synode von Antiochien 379." *Vigiliae Christianae* 44 (1990): 209–22.

Stark, R. *The Rise of Christianity: A Sociologist Reconsiders History.* Princeton, NJ, 1996.

Stephenson, P. *Constantine: Roman Emperor, Christian Victor.* New York, 2010.

Stirling, L. *The Learned Collector: Mythological Statuettes and Classical Taste in Late Antique Gaul.* Ann Arbor, MI, 2005.

Storin, B. "The *Letters* of Gregory Nazianzus: Discourse and Community in Late Antique Epistolary Culture." PhD diss., Indiana University, 2012.

Swain, S. *Themistius, Julian and Greek Political Theory under Rome.* Cambridge, 2013.

Tarrant, H. "Socratic *Sunousia*: A Post-Platonic Myth?" *Journal of the History of Philosophy* 43.2 (2005): 131–55.

Tomlin, R. "*Seniores-Iuniores* in the Later Roman Field Army." *American Journal of Philology* 93 (1972): 253–78.

Trout, D. "Paulinus' Letters." In *Late Antique Epistolography*, edited by C. Sogno, B. Storin, and E. Watts. Berkeley, forthcoming.

———. *Paulinus of Nola: Life, Letters, and Poems.* Berkeley, 1999.

Urbainczyk, T. *Socrates of Constantinople.* Ann Arbor, MI, 1997.

van Bladel, K. *The Arabic Hermes: From Pagan Sage to Prophet of Science.* Oxford, 2009.

Van Dam, R. "From Paganism to Christianity in Late Antique Gaza." *Viator* 16 (1985): 1–20.

———. "The Many Conversions of the Emperor Constantine." In *Conversion in Late Antiquity and the Early Middle Ages*, edited by K. Mills and A. Grafton, 127–51. Rochester, NY, 2003.

———. *Remembering Constantine at Milvian Bridge.* Cambridge, 2011.

———. *The Roman Revolution of Constantine.* Cambridge, 2007.

Van Haeperen, F. *Le collège pontifical (3e s. a.C.–4e s. p.C.): Contribution à l'étude de la religion publique romaine.* Rome, 2002.

Van Hoof, L. "Falsification as a Protreptic to Truth: The Forged Epistolary Exchange between Basil and Libanius." In *Education and Religion in Late Antiquity: Genres and Discourses in Transition*, edited by P. Gemeinhardt, L. Van Hoof, and P. Van Nuffelen. Aldershot, 2015.

———. "Libanius' Letter Collection." In *Late Antique Epistolography*, edited by C. Sogno, B. Storin, and E. Watts. Berkeley, forthcoming.

———. "Libanius' *Life* and Life." In *The Cambridge Companion to Libanius*, edited by L. Van Hoof. Cambridge, 2014.

———. "(Self-) Censorship or Self Fashioning? Gaps in Libanius' Letter Collection." *Revue Belge*, forthcoming.

Van Hoof, L., and P. Van Nuffelen. "Monarchy and Mass Communication: Antioch A.D. 362/3 Revisited." *Journal of Roman Studies* 101 (2011): 166–84.

Van Nuffelen, P. "Earthquakes in A.D. 363–368 and the Date of Libanius, *Oratio* 18." *Classical Quarterly* 56.2 (2006): 657–61.

———. "Not the Last Pagan: Libanius between Elite Rhetoric and Religion." In *The Cambridge Companion to Libanius*, edited by L. Van Hoof. Cambridge, 2014.

Vanderspoel, J. "A Tale of Two Cities: Themistius on Rome and Constantinople." In *Two Romes: Rome and Constantinople in Late Antiquity*, edited by G. Kelly and L. Grig, 223–40. Oxford, 2012.

———. *Themistius and the Imperial Court*. Ann Arbor, MI, 1995.

Vera, D. *Commento storico alle "Relationes" di Q. Aurelius Symmachus*. Pisa, 1981.

von Haehling, R. *Die Religionszugehörigkeit der hohen Amtsträger des römischen Reiches seit Constantins I. Alleinherrschaft bis zum Ende der theodosianischen Dynastie*. Bonn, 1978.

Vööbus, A. *Syriac and Arabic Documents Regarding Legislation Relative to Syrian Asceticism*. Stockholm, 1960.

Watt, J. "Themistius and Julian: Their Association in Syriac and Arabic Tradition." In *The Purpose of Rhetoric in Late Antiquity: From Performance to Exegesis*, edited by A.J. Quiroga Puertas, 161–76. Tübingen, 2013.

Watts, E. "Christianization." In *Late Ancient Knowing: Explorations in Intellectual History*, edited by C. Chin and M. Vidas. Berkeley, forthcoming.

———. *City and School in Late Antique Athens and Alexandria*. Berkeley, 2006.

———. "Doctrine, Anecdote, and Action: Reconsidering the Social History of the Last Platonists (c. 430-c. 550 CE)." *Classical Philology* 106 (2011): 226–44.

———. "Freedom of Speech and Self-Censorship in the Roman Empire." *Revue Belge de Philologie et d'Histoire* 92 (2014).

———. "Himerius and the Personalization of Monody." In *Shifting Genres in Late Antiquity*, edited by G. Greatrex. Aldershot, forthcoming.

———. "Historical Context: The Rhetorical Use of Suffering in Libanius' Monodies, Letters, and Autobiography." In *The Cambridge Companion to Libanius*, edited by L. Van Hoof. Cambridge, 2014.

———. "Justinian, Malalas, and the End of Athenian Philosophical Teaching in AD 529." *Journal of Roman Studies* 94 (2004): 168–82.

———. "Libanius on Theodosian-Era Temple Violence: Rhetoric and Reality." In *Le vie del sapere nell'area siro-mesopotamica de 3rd al 12th century*, Orientalia Christiana Analecta 293, edited by C. Noce et al., 105–14. Rome, 2013.

———. "Orality and Communal Identity in Eunapius' *Lives of the Sophists and Philosophers*." *Byzantion* 75 (2005): 334–61.

———. *Riot in Alexandria: Tradition and Group Dynamics in Late Antique Pagan and Christian Communities*. Berkeley, 2010.

———. "Three Generations of Christian Philosophical Biography." In *From the Tetrarchs to the Theodosians*, edited by S. McGill, C. Sogno, and E. Watts, 117–34. Cambridge, 2010.

Watts, E., C. Sogno, and B. Storin. "Late Antique Epistolography." In *Late Antique Epistolography*, edited by C. Sogno, B. Storin, and E. Watts. Berkeley, forthcoming.

Webb, R. "The Progymnasmata as Practice." In *Education in Greek and Roman Antiquity*, edited by Y.L. Too, 289–316. Leiden, 2001.

Weiss, P. "The Vision of Constantine." Translated by A.R. Birley. *Journal of Roman Archaeology* 16 (2003): 237–59.

Weisweiler, J. "From Equality to Asymmetry: Honorific Statues, Imperial Power and Senatorial Identity in Late Antique Rome." *Journal of Roman Archaeology* 25 (2012): 319–51.

———. "Inscribing Imperial Power: Letters from Emperors in Late Antique Rome." In *Historische Erinnerung im städtischen Raum: Rom in der Spätantike*, edited by R. Behrwald and C. Witschel, 305–23. Stuttgart, 2012.

Welch, K. "Some Architectural Prototypes for the Auditoria at Kom el-Dikka and Three Late Antique (Fifth Century AD) Comparanda from Aphrodisias in Caria." In *Alexandria Auditoria of Kom el-Dikka and Late Antique Education*, edited by T. Derda, T. Markiewicz, and E. Wipszycka, 115–34. Warsaw, 2007.

Whitby, M. "John of Ephesus and the Pagans: Pagan Survivals in the Sixth-Century." In *Paganism in the Later Roman Empire and Byzantium*, edited by M. Salaman, 111–31. Krakow, 1991.

Wiebe, F. J. *Kaiser Valens und die heidnische Opposition*. Bonn, 1995.

Wiemer, H.-U. *Libanios und Julian: Studien zum Verhältnis von Rhetorik und Politik im vierten Jahrhundert n. Chr.* Munich, 1995.

Wilken, R. L. *John Chrysostom and the Jews: Rhetoric and Reality in the Late Fourth Century*. Berkeley, 1983.

Wilkinson, K. "Palladas and the Age of Constantine." *Journal of Roman Studies* 99 (2009): 26–60.

Wintjes, J. *Das Leben des Libanius*. Rahden, 2005.

Wirth, G. "Rome and Its Germanic Partners in the Fourth Century." In *Kingdoms of the Empire: The Integration of Barbarians in Late Antiquity*, edited by W. Pohl, 13–56. Leiden, 1997.

Wolfram, H. *History of the Goths*. Translated by Thomas Dunlap. Berkeley, 1988.

Index

Ablabius, 83
Achaea, 106, 128; proconsulship of, 140–42
Achilles, 107
Achilles Tatius, 24
Acilius Glabrio, 73
Aco Catullinus, 72
Adams, Eddie, 7
Adrianople: battle of, 3, 167–68, 173, 189
Aegeae, 48, 50, 89, 111, 136–37
Aelius Aristides, 137
Aemilia, 151
Aemilia Aeonia, 32
Aemilia Corinthia Maura, 32
Aemilius Magnus Arborius, 32, 56, 73, 144
Aemilia Melania, 29
Agamemnon, 107
Alamanni, 84, 115, 144
Alaric, 3
Alexander the Great, 22, 175
Alexander Severus, 59
Alexandria, 86, 157; buildings and temples
    of, 1–5, 18–19, 22, 50, 88, 208, 213;
    festival of Serapis, 23–25; schools of, 53,
    56; statues in, 23, 111
Alps, 43, 107, 184
Altar of Victory, 3, 15, 182–88
Ambrose, 168, 171, 191; and Altar of
    Victory, 183–89; episcopal career, 5, 15,
    152–53, 160, 183–89; political career
    of, 5, 15, 151–52; See also Altar of
    Victory

Amida, 107
Ammianus Marcellinus, 86
Ammonius (grammarian), 1, 215
Ammonius Hermeiou (philosopher), 113
Amphilochius, 161–62, 167
Ancyra, 75, 91, 130, 133
Andronicus, 69
Antioch, 3, 10, 67, 68, 70, 108, 111, 115,
    124, 136, 179, 180, 195, 196; city
    council of, 101, 53; festivals of, 209;
    and Julian, 115, 118–20, 138; and
    Libanius, 76–77, 94–96, 100–102, 119,
    201–3, 218, 219; Riot of the Statues,
    192, 200–203, 211; schools of, 13, 94,
    106; temples of, 207–8
Antiochus of Ascalon, 176,
Antoninus Pius, 3fig., 169
Antony, 150, 154–57, 160, 279n37. See also
    Life of Antony
Apamea, 112
Aphrodisias, 56
Aphrodite, 48, 50
Apollo, 111, 112, 120, 137, 138, 208
Apuleius, 25
Aquileia, 83
Arabia, 123
Aradius Rufinus, 171
Arborius, 170
Arcadius (emperor), 177, 178fig.
Arcadius (friend of Himerius), 53
Aristaenetus, 98–99, 197–99

Ariston of Chios, 176
Aristotle, 72, 90, 117, 140, 175
Armenia, 62, 159
Artemis, 39, 123
Asclepius, 48, 50, 89, 111, 136–37
Asia Minor, 38, 74, 77
Athanasius, 14, 150, 154–57; exile of, 84–86. See also *Life of Antony*
Athens, 77, 78, 94, 95, 108, 138, 140, 141, 161, 208, 209, 219; Acropolis of, 18, 22–23; schools of, 53, 54–56, 58, 62, 159
Augustine, 31, 54, 158
Augustus, 31, 66, 79, 182, 193
Aurelian, 132
Ausonius, 10, 59, 64, 78, 151, 156, 167, 168, 181, 210; consulship of, 170; at the court of Valentinian, 11, 14, 128–29, 144–48; education of, 38, 52–53, 56–58; *Ephemeris*, 34; family of, 63, 70, 73, 75, 82, 144, 150; and Gratian, 15, 128, 170–71, 188–189; historical legacy of, 16, 215, 217, 220; marriage to Sabina, 73–74, 82; *Mosella*, 145; *Nuptial Cento*, 145; *Parentalia*, 29, 32, 33; and Paulinus of Nola, 217; praetorian prefecture, 170–72; quaestorship of, 145, 170; retirement of, 188, 191–92, 194; and Symmachus, 146–47; teaching career of, 11, 13, 70, 80–81, 73–74, 76, 102, 106
Avitianus, 29

Barachus, 146
Basil of Caesarea, 5, 158–63, 167, 218–20; and Gregory Nazianzen, 55, 159–61; and John Chrysostom, 158–59, 162–63
Bassus, 69, 73–74
Bauto, 184
Birla Mandir, 19, 21*fig.*
bishops, 111, 157, 199; as a career, 14, 150–54, 161–62; political influence of, 15–16, 47, 84–86, 111, 164–65, 179–83, 187–88, 191, 201–5, 209, 220; and violence, 1, 142, 204–5, 213; wealth of, 46, 55 152–53
Bithynia, 79
Bordeaux, 11, 57, 58; schools of, 53, 57, 58, 73–74, 106, 144
Bostra, 123
The Box Tops, 8
Bradbury, Scott, 49
Brennus, 185
Britain, 40, 62, 129, 184

Brown, Peter, 13, 62
Byzantium, 38, 76

Caesarea, 159
Caesarea, 134, 200–203
Callinicum, 204
Calliopius, 196
Canaan, 47
Canopus, 19
Capitoline temple, 18
Cappadocia, 159, 179, 181
Caristia, 33
Carmen contra paganos: See *Poem against the Pagans*
Carthage, 171, 209
Chalcedon, 109–10, 117, 133
Christianization, 4–6, 12–16, 28, 34–36, 57, 82, 149–50, 153–57, 161–65, 167, 171, 179, 183, 188, 202, 208, 210, 213, 217, 219, 220; and Constantine, 38–51; 86; and Constantius, 86–88, 101, 115; and Gratian, 182, 185; and Jovian, 115–16; and Julian, 105, 109–15; and Theodosius I, 204–6
Chromatius, 69
Chrysopolis, 38
Cilicia, 119, 123, 215
Cimon, 151, 196–98, 211
Claudius (emperor), 193
Claudius Antonius, 170
Claudius Gothicus, 42
Clement of Alexandria, 28
Coelia Concordia, 215
comes Orientis, 68, 163, 204
comes rei privatae, 101, 257n133
Constans, 62, 83–87, 92, 94
Constantine, 4, 6, 14, 41*fig.*, 56, 58, 73, 101, 112, 115, 127, 133, 144; administrative reforms of, 60, 62, 65, 70, 79, 140, 193; conversion of, 14, 42, 109–10; death of, 59, 83; financial policies of, 61–63; relation to Claudius Gothicus, 42; as *pontifex maximus*, 50; religious policies of, 12–13, 43–51, 82, 86–87, 111, 123, 131, 136–37, 152, 204–5; war with Licinius, 38, 44, 46, 59; war with Maxentius, 40, 42–43, 107–8; war with Maximinus Daia, 43–44. See also *Life of Constantine*
Constantine II, 83
Constantinople, 10, 67, 70, 71, 74–79, 106, 108, 109, 115, 118, 119, 141, 179, 181, 192, 209; and Constantius II, 92–98; Council of, 180–82; and Procopius, 133,

135; senate of, 10, 67, 90, 90–93, 102, 106, 116–19, 173, 174, 176, 179, 192–94, 196, 201, 203; temples and statues in, 48–49; and Theodosius, 173–75, 178, 198

Constantius I, 40

Constantius II, 12, 81, 105, 115, 122, 127, 129, 133, 134, 174; and Athanasius, 84–86; and Julian, 106–12 religious policies of, 14, 49, 86–89, 101–3, 105, 110–12, 114, 116 123, 126, 131, 136, 141, 183, 205; and Themistius, 75, 90–96, 106, 116–18, 120, 125; visit to Rome, 91–93; war against Magnentius, 65, 81, 83–85

consul, 11, 72, 91, 93, 118, 120, 170, 176, 178, 184, 192, 199

Corinth, 54, 108

corrector, 70, 71, 140, 271n86

Corsica, 135

Cynegius, 204–7, 210

Cyprus, 196

Dalmatia, 3

Dalmatius, 73, 83

Damasus, 142, 183

Danube, 3, 108, 145, 172

Daphne, 3, 111–12, 120, 137, 204, 207

Datianus, 138

Decius, 39

Delos, 23

Delphi, 141

Deuteronomy, 47

Digest, 31

Diocletian, 13, 40, 59, 74, 115, 188, 241n6; reforms of, 60–62, 65, 70, 79, 83

Domitian, 30

donatives, 132

Doryphorianus, 169

duces, 60

Edessa, 206

Edict of Milan, 44

Egypt, 4, 84, 85, 154–57, 163, 180, 204

Elder, Glen, 7

Eleusis, 51, 141

Ellebichus, 199–203

Eminem, 64

Etruria, 143

Eubulus, 100

Eudaemon, 136

Eugenius, 74, 96–97

Eunapius, 5, 55, 215, 217–18

Eunus, 64

Eusebius (historian), 6, 42–44, 46–50, 101, 122, 136, 204. See also Life of Constantine

Eusebius (bishop of Caesarea), 160

Eutropius, 132

Evagrius, 157

Fabia Aconia Paulina, 72

festivals, 6, 8, 12, 17, 24–25, 33–36, 57, 64, 76, 112–13, 122–22, 125, 185; persistence of, 51, 88, 209; skipping of, 39

Firmicus Maternus, 86–87, 101–2

Firminus, 197–98

Flavian of Antioch, 201–3

Flavius Dionysius, 78

Flavius Eutolmius Tatianus, 134, 198

Flavius Simplicius, 169

Florentius, 67, 68, 110

Frigidus: battle of, 3

Fronto, 188

Furius Maecius Gracchus, 171

Galerius, 40, 42–44,

Gallus, 81, 84, 89, 94, 95, 110, 111

Gaul, 11, 40, 73, 84, 107, 110, 130, 135, 144, 151, 170, 172, 184, 188

George, 111

Goths, 2–3, 139, 167, 172–8, 185, 189, 192

Gratian (emperor), 11, 15, 146, 167–79, 177fig.; appointment by Valentinian I, 144, 168; and Ausonius, 128, 170–71, 189; religious policies of, 173, 182–86; and Theodosius I, 172–79

Gratian (father of Valentinian I and Valens), 62, 64–66, 85, 129

Greece, 3, 141, 159, 195; temples in, 136

Greek, 30, 56, 64, 77, 140, 157

Gregory Nazianzen, 5, 15, 118, 157, 167–68, 189, 204, 218–19; and Basil of Caesarea, 55, 159–61; and Theodosius I, 179–81

Hannibal, 185

Hanuman, 19, 21fig.

Helladius, 1, 215

Helpidius, 100

Hendrix, Jimi, 8

Hephaestion, 55

Heraclea, 77, 78

hermeneumata, 34

Hermione, 162, 163

Hesiod, 114

Hesperius, 150, 170, 171

Hierophantes, 209–210
Hilarius, 195
Himerius, 53–54, 57–58, 138, 140, 219
Hispellum, 50–51
Homer, 114
Honorius, 208
House of Menander, 23
House of the Vettii, 23

Iconium, 161
Illyricum, 84, 92, 130, 170, 173, 176, 180, 184, 185
India, 19–23
Ingalls Wilder, Laura, 9, 224n25
Isis, 24–26
Italy, 11, 40, 42–3, 70, 83–84, 108, 170, 184–85, 188, 198; traditional cults of, 3

Jaipur, 19
Jai Gurudev, 19
Jefferson Airplane, 8
Jerome, 157,
John Chrysostom, 5, 15, 16, 158, 162, 202, 204, 218–19
Joplin, Janis, 8
Jovian, 14, 115–19, 127–30, 132–33, 147–48, 152
Julian (emperor), 5, 14, 66, 84, 88, 91, 127–29, 133, 134, 140, 145, 174, 182, 195, 217; financial policies of, 34, 128, 130–132, 147, 152; and Libanius, 119–25, 138–139, 146, 148, 196, 218; religious policies of, 109, 110–16, 119, 122, 136, 182, 203, 205; and Themistius, 116–119; war against Constantius II, 81, 106–109, 130; war in Persia, 115, 120, 130–31
Julian (rhetorician), 147
Julius Hymetius, 171
Juncus, 193, 195, 198, 210
Justinian, 31

Kom el-Dikka, 56

lararia, 23
Lares Compitales, 23
Latin, 30, 140, 157, 220
Libanius, 10–16, 31, 73, 111, 145, 151, 167, 181, 191, 192; in Antioch, 95, 100; in Athens, 78; Autobiography, 78, 196–97; in Constantinople, 77–79, 94; and death of Cimon, 196–97; declining influence of under Valentinian and Valens, 128–9, 138–39, 148; and earthquake at

Nicomedia, 98–100; education of, 38, 52–59; on episcopal careers, 161–62; family of, 70, 76, 82, 96–98, 100; historical legacy of, 215, 217–20; and Julian, 106, 119–121, 138–39, 146; lawsuits, 100–101; letters of, 67–70, 76, 93–94, 98, 99, 100, 118, 121–124, 136–137, 195, 197–200, 219–11, 219; in Nicomedia, 94, 95, 119; on old age, 195, 198; Oration 30, 49, 205–7; oration on Gallus, 89; political influence of in the 380s and 390s, 195–207; teaching career of, 39, 51, 55–56, 77–81, 94–102, 156, 195–96; and Themistius, 93–94, 98. See also Riot of the Statues
Licinius, 38, 42–46, 59
Life of Antony, 14, 150, 154, 156–158. See also Athanasius
Life of Constantine, 46, 48–49, 50. See also Eusebius
Life of Severus, 219
Liguria, 151
Luciolus, 73
Lusitania, 70, 71, 102
Lycia, 198
Lycurgus, 176

Macedonia, 92, 170, 173
Macedonius, 183, 185
Macrobius, 35, 216–17
magister officiorum, 47, 183,
Magnentius, 13, 59, 65, 81, 83–85, 92, 108
Magnus Maximus, 168, 184, 187, 189, 191, 198–200, 206
Mancini, Henry, 8
Marcellus, 73
Marcus Aurelius, 169
Mardonius, 199
marriage, 29, 43, 64, 68; between pagans and Christians, 28; political and social aspects of, 72, 74–75, 77, 80–81, 97–98, 102, 124, 184
Mathura, 19, 21fig.
Maxentius, 40–43, 107
Maximian, 40
Maximianus, 193
Maximinus Daia, 43, 44
Maximus of Ephesus, 110, 138
Maximinus of Sopianae, 135, 169–171
Maximus of Turin, 208
McLynn, Neil, 152
Melania, 63
Meletius of Antioch, 180

Mesopotamia, 4, 115, 129, 204
Miccalus, 67–69, 73
Milan, 151–52, 183
Mithras, 140
Modestus, 68, 134, 163
The Monkees, 8
Moore, Charles, 7

Narbonne, 73
Nectarius, 181
Neocaesarea, 74
Nepotianus, 250n5
Nero, 30, 31
Nerva, 169
Nicaea, 10, 78; council of, 173, 179
Nicagoras, 51, 249n118
Nicocles of Sparta, 78
Nicomedia, 10, 74, 75, 78, 94, 95, 106, 119; earthquake at, 98–100, 121, 256n110
North Africa, 44, 108, 129, 136, 209
Numa, 33
Numidia, 65
nummus, 61

Olybrius, 140, 270n87
Olympiodorus, 63
Olympius, 67, 68, 100
Olympus (philosopher), 1, 4, 215
Oribasius, 138
Orion, 123, 124
Osiris, 26
otium, 128, 140, 143, 181
Ovid, 33

Pachomius, 154, 163
pagan, 5–7, 221n2
Panathenaic procession, 209
Pannonia, 62, 84, 127, 128, 134, 135, 142, 144, 147, 148, 169, 184, 188
Paphlagonia, 74, 97
Palestine, 69
Palladius, 146
Panolbius, 76
Paris, 107
Paul the Chain, 107, 110
Paulinus (friend of Ausonius), 145
Paulinus of Pella, 63, 217, 220
pedagogue, 30–34, 37, 53, 64
Persia, 67, 118, 200, 206; and Constantius, 107; and Julian, 115, 120, 130–31
Peter of Alexandria, 180
Petronius, 132, 134
Petronius Probus, 140, 147, 170, 184–5

Phasganius, 76, 94, 100, 101
Philagrius, 121–2
Phoenicia, 23, 69, 100, 124, 207
pietas, 33
Plato, 90, 92, 117, 175
Pliny the Younger, 30
Plutarch, 193
Poem against the Pagans, 11, 216
Pompeii, 23
Pomponius Bassus, 193
pontifex maximus, 50, 91
Pontus, 74, 159, 160
Praetextatus, Vettius Agorius, 10, 16, 59, 77, 78, 129, 151, 152, 153, 167, 168, 184; career of, 14, 15, 58, 80, 81, 147; childhood of, 70; corrector, 71; death of, 192, 215; education of, 38, 52, 56; family background of, 11, 70–72, 76; governor of Lusitania, 13, 71, 102; historical legacy of, 215–17; interest in philosophy, 72; in Macrobius' *Saturnalia,* 35, 216; marriage of, 72, 74, 75; and *otium,* 128, 140, 143–44; and the *Poem against the Pagans,* 11, 216; praetorian prefecture of, 185–87; praetorship, 71; priesthoods of, 140; proconsul of Achaea, 71, 106, 128, 140–42; quaestorship, 71; translations of, 72, 140; urban prefecture of, 13, 128, 142; and Valentinian, 140–44, 148, 186
praetorian prefect, 11, 99–100, 124, 135, 138, 151, 198, 204; and proconsul of Achaea, 140; role in imperial administration, 47, 60, 83, 85, 206, 242n9
praetura, 71–73
Praxagoras, 51
Presley, Elvis, 8
Priscus, 120, 138, 195
Procopius, 128, 129, 133–34, 134*fig.,* 138
Proculus, 196, 198–99, 206
progymnasmata, 10, 52
Prohaeresius, 55, 62–66, 122, 219
Ptolemy Soter, 22

quaestor, 47, 70–71, 145, 170
quaestura, 71–72

Ramses VI, 51
Rebillar, Éric, 39
Rheims, 129
Rhine, 84, 106, 107, 109, 128, 129, 176
Richomer, 199, 207
Riot of the Statues, 200–203, 211

Rome, 11, 15, 40, 43, 53, 63, 71, 76, 84,
    135, 142, 143, 146, 151, 169, 171, 174,
    215; festivals of, 24, 209; Genius of,
    108; Gothic sack of, 2–3; temples and
    shrines of, 23, 89, 102; senate of, 3, 15,
    67, 91–93, 108, 169–170, 182–38,
    185–87, 193, 194; visit of Constantius
    II, 91–93
Rufinus (historian), 4, 9, 19, 23, 213, 215
Rufinus (prefect of the East), 199

Sabina, 74
sacrifice, 1, 6, 19, 26, 27fig. 32–34, 36, 39,
    47, 102, 109, 111–12, 119–25, 220;
    laws against, 14, 46, 48–51, 82, 86–89,
    101, 110, 113, 116, 136, 141, 182, 203,
    205, 207–8, 213
Saint Babylas, 111
Salustius, 134, 138
Salvius, 121
Salzman, Michelle, 146
Sardinia, 135
Saturninus, 176–78, 192
Satyrus, 151
Scipio Africanus, 175
Scylacius, 121–22
Sebon, 101
Sedatus, 73
Segusio, 43
Seleucus, 138
Seneca, 188
Serapeum, 2fig., 18–19, 23, 50 destruction
    of, 1–5, 9, 16, 213–15
Serapis: festivals of, 24–25 statues of, 2,
    3fig., 23, 111, 213, 214fig.
Sicininus, 142
Sidyma, 198
Silenus, 23
Silvanus, 84, 110
Sirmium, 173
Slick, Grace, 8
Socrates Scholasticus, 215, 218
Sol Invictus, 44, 45fig.
solidus, 61–64, 79
Spain, 70
Spectatus, 67–68, 100–102
Strasbourg, 106
Strategius, 99–100
Symmachus, Quintus Aurelius, 11, 35, 66,
    72, 169–70, 194, 199; and Altar of
    Victory, 183–188; and Ausonius,
    145–147; and Praetextatus, 142–43,
    216; Pro Patre, 170
and Ausonius, 146–147;

Synesius, 55
Syria, 4, 76, 78, 112, 119, 122, 154, 192,
    196, 200, 202, 204, 205, 219
syriarch, 76

taxes, 59–61, 65, 117, 128, 132–33, 135,
    162, 193, 200, 201
temples, 4, 6, 12, 14, 16, 17–26, 20fig.,
    47–51, 55, 63, 125, 137, 208, 220;
    closing of, 88–89, 101–102, 109–111,
    116, 182, 207; destruction of, 50,
    86–87, 123–24, 204, 208, 213, 215,
    220; Hindu, 19, 21fig., 22fig.; and
    Libanius, 205–6, 210–11; rehabilitation
    of, 136, 142, 203
Terracius Basus, 171
Tertullian, 28, 32,-33, 36, 57
tetrarchy, 5, 40, 42, 164
Thalassius, 124, 170
Thamugadi, 65
Themistius, 11, 58, 59, 70, 89, 110, 151,
    156, 167, 168; and Constantius, 89–96,
    102, 110, 116, 125; education of, 38,
    52, 56, 57, 74, 97; estate in Paphlagonia,
    97; family of, 13, 70, 74–76, 82, 96–97;
    historical legacy of, 16, 215, 217, 220;
    and Julian, 106, 116–20, 125, 138; and
    Libanius, 67, 118, 138; marriage of, 75,
    97–98; philosophical interests of, 72, 90,
    97, 106, 140; political career of, 10, 13,
    14, 15, 73, 77, 79–81, 83, 89–98, 106,
    116–20, 128, 138, 147–48, 174–81,
    189, 192–94; teaching career of, 73–75,
    78, 80–81, 90, 106; and Theodosius I,
    174–81, 189, 192; urban prefecture of,
    178–79, 193–94
Theodore, 158, 162, 163
Theodoret, 136, 204
Theodorus, 137
Theodosian Code, 49, 86, 87, 111, 141, 182
Theodosius I, 3, 12, 15, 168, 170, 173 184,
    177fig., 189, 192, 194, 196, 199; and
    Constantinople, 173–75, 178, 198; and
    Gratian, 172–79; and Gregory
    Nazianzen, 179–81; religious policies of,
    168, 173, 179–82, 204–11; Riot of the
    Statues, 200–203, 211
Theodulus, 123–24
Theophanes of Hermopolis, 23
Theophilus (bishop of Alexandria), 1, 213,
    214fig.
Theophilus (friend of Libanius), 195, 197
Thessaloniki, 172, 174, 198
Thrace, 68, 108, 109, 173, 176

Tiber, 43
Tigris, 176
Titus, 176
Toulouse, 73
Trajan, 169
Trier, 40, 107, 144, 158, 163, 164, 183, 184, 187
Turin, 43
Tuscany, 70, 135, 140
Tychaion, 22, 208

Umbria, 70, 140
Urbanus, 162–63
Ursinus, 142
Uttar Pradesh, 19
Uzzle, Burk, 7–9, 250n5

Valens, 14, 131fig., 167, 180, 182; administration of, 134–35, 137, 147, 198; appointment as co-emperor of Valentinian I, 127, 130; fiscal policies of, 131–33, 135; career of, 129–30; family of, 85, 129; Gothic wars of, 139, 172–77, 185, 189; and the Procopius Revolt, 133, 138; religious policies of, 136–37, 140–42, 205; treatment of Julian's supporters, 138–41, 148

Valentinian I, 14, 131fig., 150, 158, 181; administration of, 135, 148, 169–71; appointment of Gratian, 144, 168; appointment of Valens, 127, 130; and Ausonius, 11, 128, 145–48, 168; career of, 127, 129–30; death of, 147, 149, 167–69; family of, 62, 85, 129; fiscal policies of, 131–33, 135; and Praetextatus, 128, 139–44, 186; religious policies of, 136–37, 140–42, 186–89, 205; and the Roman senate, 143, 169, 171
Valentinian II, 15, 167–70, 184–89, 198
Valley of the Kings, 51
Valli, Frankie, 8
Vergil, 145
Verona, 43
Vestal Virgins, 33, 182, 186, 215
Vetranio, 92, 230n5
vicarius, 60, 62, 135, 170
Viventius, 142

Woodstock, 7–9

York, 40

Zacharias Scholasticus, 219
Zosimus, 140–41